THE COURAGE TO STAY

JOURNAL

An Affair Recovery Workbook
for the Hurt Partner

Kathy Nickerson, Ph.D.

Copyright © 2024
Kathy Nickerson, Ph.D.
The Courage To Stay Journal
An Affair Recovery Workbook
For The Hurt Partner
All rights reserved.

No part of this publication may be reproduced, distributed, or transmitted in any form or by any means, including photocopying, recording, or other electronic or mechanical methods, without the prior written permission of the author, except in the case of brief quotations embodied in critical reviews and certain other non-commercial uses permitted by copyright law.

Kathy Nickerson, Ph.D.

Printed Worldwide
First Printing 2024
First Edition 2024

10 9 8 7 6 5 4 3 2 1

ISBN 979-8-9869404-0-3 (paperback)
ISBN 979-8-9869404-1-0 (epub)

The Library of Congress Cataloging-in-Publication data
is available upon request.

In the discussions of Dr. Nickerson's clients, all names and many identifying details have been changed, and some discussions include a conflation of clinical situations.

For information, address
Kathleen Nickerson, Ph.D.
350 Forest Avenue, #418
Laguna Beach, CA 92652.

www.drkathynickerson.com

Cover design by Bianca Miranda

Interior Book Design by Walt's Book Design
www.waltsbookdesign.com

THE COURAGE TO STAY JOURNAL

For my sister, Joanna -

You are the North Star by which I navigate life's shifting tides. Your boundless wisdom, profound insight, creative spirit, and unwavering compassion inspire and sustain me. Thank you for your unfailing strength, for all that you give, and for all that you are to me and to our family. I love you.

For the members of the affair recovery community -

You show me—and the world—what true love really is. In the darkest moments, you find compassion; in the grip of grief, you choose kindness. You move forward with fierce determination, undeterred by doubt or the voices of naysayers. Brave, resilient, and tireless, you reveal the best in all of us every single day. You deserve all the love and joy life has to offer.

Advance Praise for
The Courage to Stay Journal

"As a therapist who has worked on relationship issues with clients for decades, I found this workbook for couples dealing with affairs, to be the best I have ever read. Whether you are working on repairing a relationship after an affair, or simply trying to understand the complexity of affairs, this workbook gives compassion, hope, and inspiration from Dr. Nickerson's expertise, as well as couples who have gone through these challenges. Whether you are working with a therapist, or on your own, you will find this workbook a clear blueprint to guide you to a better understanding and potentially a better, stronger relationship than before the affair. I will immediately start using this with my clients going through these complexities dealing with affairs."

-Shirley Furman, MFT, PMHNP, Psychiatric Mental Health Nurse Practitioner

"Having counseled couples for over 30 years, I have witnessed firsthand the profound pain and turmoil that an affair can bring. Dr. Kathy has crafted an extraordinary, one-of-a-kind resource for betrayed partners seeking to navigate this devastation with courage and resilience. Her workbook is a masterful blend of compassionate guidance and practical tools, offering a lifeline to those committed to rebuilding their relationships after betrayal. Perhaps her most powerful gift to readers is the message of hope—the hope that, with effort and determination, a stronger, more authentic, and deeply loving relationship can emerge from the ashes of infidelity. I will wholeheartedly recommend this journal to my clients who are ready to embark on the courageous journey up what Dr. Kathy so aptly calls "Affair Mountain." This is an invaluable resource for anyone choosing the path of healing and renewal."

-Cindy M. Fazendin, LMFT, Licensed Marriage and Family Therapist

"Dr. Kathy Nickerson has created an exceptional guide for anyone reeling from the pain of infidelity. This workbook gently supports betrayed partners in processing the trauma of betrayal, offering both solace and strength along the way. Dr. Kathy's approach is deeply empathetic, informed not only by her clinical experience but also by her personal journey. Her methods create a healing environment that empowers individuals to navigate their pain with resilience and compassion. "

— Jessica Rayburn, LCSW, Trauma Therapist

"Dr. Kathy Nickerson's *The Courage to Stay Journal* is a powerful and healing guide for anyone seeking to transcend the pain of betrayal. As a clinician who understands the devastation of infidelity, I am moved by the depth of empathy and wisdom woven into every page. Dr. Kathy's experience as a clinician and her own personal journey make this book an extraordinary resource for finding healing beyond heartbreak. This workbook gently guides readers through the hurt, inspiring them to rise above and reclaim a sense of wholeness. I will be recommending it to anyone searching for a meaningful, transformative way forward after betrayal."

— *Laura Bennett, Ph.D., Clinical Psychologist*

"As a neuropsychologist specializing in PTSD, I have seen firsthand the deep and lasting impact infidelity can have on mental health. *The Courage to Stay Journal* by Dr. Kathy Nickerson offers a practical, accessible, and truly transformative approach for individuals suffering from Post-Infidelity Stress Disorder. Dr. Nickerson's blend of trauma-informed techniques and compassionate guidance creates a supportive environment where readers can process their pain and begin to heal."

— *David S. Carlson, Ph.D.*

"Dr. Kathy has truly outdone herself with this masterpiece! From the very first page, her warmth, empathy, and compassion shine through, creating an inviting and deeply personal connection. Her authenticity, paired with a touch of light humor, makes the journey not only inspiring but also remarkably relatable. Kathy has an extraordinary gift for blending scientific rigor with heartfelt wisdom, crafting a resource that is as engaging as it is transformative. Drawing insights from research and renowned thinkers, Kathy distills their teachings into practical, actionable guidance. Her unique ability to speak to both the mind and the heart ensures that readers feel genuinely seen, heard, and understood. Kathy masterfully explores the transformative nature of forgiveness, offering alternative pathways to access its power without forcing the act itself. This book is a treasure I will enthusiastically recommend to my clients. Thank you, Kathy, for this extraordinary contribution to the field. It is truly a gift to all who embark on the journey of healing."

– Dustan Drake, Certified Neurolinguistic Programming Practitioner, NLP Trainer, and Hypnotherapist

Table of Contents

Introduction 1

Chapter One 3
    Overcoming Overwhelm & Hopelessness

Chapter Two 31
    Riding the Emotional Rollercoaster

Chapter Three 59
    Cultivating Confidence & Defeating Doubt

Chapter Four 87
    Challenging Your Core Beliefs

Chapter Five 115
    Exploring Your Anger

Chapter Six 143
    Taming Your Triggers & Fears

Chapter Seven 173
    Overcoming Obsessive & Intrusive Thoughts

Chapter Eight 203
    Defeating Depression & Sadness

Chapter Nine 233
    Growing Through Grief

Chapter Ten 263
    Accepting What You Can't Forgive

Acknowledgments 289

50 Ways to Soothe Your Nervous System 291

Further Reading 295

Finding A Therapist 299

References 301

About the Author 305

Introduction

Hello, and thank you for choosing this journal to support you on your healing journey. I'm honored to walk beside you as you work through the pain of infidelity.

First, let me say how sorry I am that you are going through this. Betrayal is one of the most painful experiences anyone can face, and I wish you didn't have to go through it. My hope is that this journal will offer you comfort, guidance, and the tools you need to find your way forward.

Each chapter begins with a short essay that introduces the topic, offers encouragement, and gives you tools to manage the emotions and thoughts you may be facing. After each essay, you'll find ten multi-part journal prompts. You can answer as many or as few as you like—whatever feels right to you. These questions are designed to help you process your feelings, have meaningful conversations with your partner, and explore new ideas with your therapist or support group.

This journal is meant to support you, not pressure you. There are no rules here. You can skip around, revisit sections, or take breaks whenever you need. Use it in a way that feels helpful to you—there is no right or wrong way.

Throughout the journal, you'll also find inspiring quotes and stories from other members of the affair recovery community. These voices are here to remind you that you are not alone. On the hard days, know that we are all standing with you, cheering you on, and believing in your strength.

This journal was designed to complement my book, *The Courage to Stay: How to Heal from an Affair and Save Your Marriage*. While the book isn't required to use the journal, working through both together may enhance your experience. You are also welcome to use this journal alongside other affair recovery books and resources.

If the topic of a chapter speaks to you and you'd like to learn more, I've included a list of my favorite self-help books at the end of the journal. Feel free to explore them when you're ready.

Thank you for trusting this journal to be part of your healing. I hope it brings you peace and clarity as you move forward. I believe in you, and I know that healing is possible.

Let's begin.

Chapter One

Overcoming Overwhelm & Hopelessness

As you begin your affair recovery journey, healing may seem impossible. It's as if you are standing at the base of a gigantic mountain, looking up and thinking, "How am I ever going to get over this? It's just not possible!". If you are feeling hopeless and overwhelmed as you think about how you're going to get over this, or if it's even possible to get over it, please know that this is completely understandable. You are having a normal reaction to an extraordinary trauma.

Many hurt partners have told me that the journey ahead seems too hard and too intense, most feeling too broken to even begin. Some see so many obstacles that it feels completely overwhelming, while others are consumed by a complex mix of hurt and confusion about whether they should even try… or if it would be better to just give up. These feelings are completely reasonable: your world has been turned upside down by the person you trusted the most. It would be surprising if you were not feeling this way!

This is the way almost everyone who has hiked over affair mountain feels, and you may find yourself feeling hopeless at several points on your journey. What I want you to know is: you absolutely can do it. You can do it even if it feels impossible right now, you can succeed even if you do not know how you're going to take the next step.

The first secret to success is that you have to believe you can do it, and tell yourself that you can do it, because your brain is going to work against you.

The human brain has evolved to prioritize survival and safety, so when you are trying to do something difficult or dangerous, it will always guide you towards a less perilous path. When faced with a potentially dangerous or physically difficult task, the brain evaluates the risks and sends signals that caution against proceeding if it seems too risky. This is an evolutionary adaptation meant to protect you from harm. The brain is also wired to respond to threats with fear and anxiety. When contemplating a challenging activity, these emotions can surface to discourage you from taking risks that could result in injury. Your self-perception and confidence levels also play a significant role in influencing your brain. If you perceive a task is beyond your abilities, the brain can generate negative thoughts to prevent you from engaging in what it perceives as futile or a waste of time. To conquer affair mountain, you have to actively work against these protection mechanisms and tell your brain that you can do this, that people have done this before and succeeded. That you can also do this!

The second secret to success is that you need to focus on navigating just one step at a time, don't worry about hiking the whole mountain.

When you're at the base of the mountain, you look up and see a million steps in front of you. You're already feeling awful, so then you start to think about how hard all of those steps will be and you become completely overwhelmed. As you just discovered, your brain's defense mechanisms kick in and tell you this is going to be too difficult, so you might as well just surrender the fantasy! You can override this defense mechanism by focusing on today, this step, and what you need to do in just this moment. The harder life seems, the narrower or smaller your focus should be. You do not need to see the whole path in order to walk up the path. Focus on the section you're on, take a breath, and when you're ready, go on to the next section. You will succeed if you keep your focus on one step at a time, one day at a time. If focusing on a whole day seems overwhelming, focus on just part of the day. If that seems too much, focus on the next hour.

So how do we know that you really can heal from infidelity and get back to having a healthy, happy relationship again?

Research finds that most people do reconcile after an affair and go on to have a better relationship.

Four different clinical studies found that 60-75% of couples stay together after discovering an affair (Gordon, Baucom, & Snyder, 2004; Solomon & Teagno, 2006;

Nickerson et al., 2023; AAMFT, 2012). The 2012 survey by the American Association for Marriage and Family Therapy (AAMFT) reported that 74% of couples who sought therapy following infidelity were able to recover and rebuild their relationship. Not only is reconciliation likely, many people feel their relationship is better after the affair and have stronger feelings of commitment after the affair. A study published in the Journal of Couple and Relationship Therapy found that 70% of couples who sought therapy after infidelity were able to recover and reported greater relationship satisfaction (Gordon, Baucom, & Snyder, 2004).

In our survey of 2,115 straying partners and 3,668 betrayed partners, we found that 75% of straying partners reconciled with their original partner after the affair. Interestingly, men who strayed ended up reconciling at higher rates than women who strayed. 85% of men who strayed reported that they reconciled with their original partner after the affair, compared to 68% of women. We also found that 58% of straying partners felt their relationship was better after the affair than it was before. 57% of men reported that their marriage or relationship was better after the affair, compared to 39% of women who strayed. 73% of men who strayed also reported being more committed to their relationships after their affair (Nickerson et al., 2023).

Most couples who stay together after an affair do not talk about the affair publicly. Millions of people around you have healed from an affair and you just don't know about it! A study by Afifi and colleagues (2001) found that people are more likely to disclose infidelity to friends, rather than family members, due to fear of judgment and the need for unbiased support. A study done by Cramer and Jowett (2010) published in the Journal of Family Psychology found that many couples who work through infidelity do so with minimal disclosure beyond their immediate support network and therapists because they fear judgment and discouragement.

Please know that you are not alone, what has happened to you has also happened to many people around you and they never talk about it. I have found that the people who do not heal from infidelity are the ones telling everyone that it is impossible to heal. While it may not be their fault that they did not recover (there are so many factors that could be at play), they often do not realize how biased their perspective is. They believe because they did not do it, it is impossible. My heart goes out them, but I want you to know this is absolutely NOT true. The research tells us it is possible to heal, my professional experience with thousands of couples tells me it is possible, and those who have healed will tell you it is possible. You are part of a large invisible club of emotionally strong superheroes. And while this is not a club you probably never wanted to join, many of the members are around you, cheering you on in silence. You will see their voices represented on nearly every page of this journal and you can find them online in our affair recovery community.

If you are feeling overwhelmed on your affair recovery hike, there are a few things you can do to feel better. You can and should rest as much as you want to. This hike is strenuous and it will take a lot out of you. Take more naps, reduce your workload where you can, ask for more help at home and with the kids. Also do things to soothe yourself and your nervous system, such as taking walks in nature, getting a massage, deep breathing, meditation, or dance to your favorite music in your bedroom. At the end of this book, you'll find a list of 50 different things you can do to soothe your nervous system when you're upset. I encourage you to try as many as you can and find the right combination for yourself. If you're really struggling, I recommend box breathing for 5 minutes while you hold an ice pack on the back of your neck. This is my go-to recommendation for clients who are struggling and almost everyone has said it really helps when they're overwhelmed. I hope it will help you too.

If you are feeling hopeless, I'd like you to try a couple of different things. The first thing is to sit down with something delicious to eat or drink and focus on your "why." Why do you want to do this? Why do you want to keep hiking this mountain? What do you hope you will be able to do or have in the future? Thinking about why you want to keep going will help you keep going. It's ok to struggle, it's ok to want to give up, just tell yourself that you know why you're doing this and you'll see if you feel like you can keep going tomorrow. If you have a couple days in a row where you feel like you can't keep going, please reach out to a therapist to discuss your next steps. And if you're ever feeling really down, like you'd rather just get off this planet and get out of this pain, please reach out for emergency care, there's so much we can do to help you. In the United States, you can call 988 for emergency mental health care and someone will help connect you with resources.

Gratitude and joy are antidotes to hopelessness and overwhelm. So when you're struggling, take a moment to go through all of the things that you feel grateful for, even silly things. As I sit here right now, I am grateful for my stretchy yoga pants, my cozy slippers, my coffee, my family, my reading glasses, and my new favorite Netflix series. As you are reading this, what are some silly things that you are grateful for? Then when you have a moment later today, start thinking about how you can infuse a bit more joy into every day. You are experiencing joy when you do something that makes you lose track of time, or that you feel you could do all day long and never get tired. Think about some of the things that bring you joy, or used to bring you joy, and start scheduling time for those things. You might not feel like doing these things right now because you're not feeling great, but doing them will really make you feel better. If it's been a long time since you did something that brought you joy, think back to your school days, what did you once love doing? Maybe it was an art class, singing in a choir, or skateboarding? Let's find a way to do something like that soon.

Please know that you absolutely will heal from this if you both want to, if you believe that you can recover, and if you focus on climbing one step of the mountain at a time. I believe in you and I am here to support you every step of the way.

Now, let's spend some time exploring your thoughts and feelings. You can write as little or as much as you want in response to each prompt. Once you've finished all the questions, I encourage you to look over what you wrote and share a couple of your thoughts with your partner during your next discussion appointment. Ask your partner to listen to your feelings, validate what they heard that makes sense, and reassure you that they understand and care. Reassurance soothes a broken heart like nothing else!

Journal Prompt 1:

What emotions and fears come up when you think about your healing journey? What deeper thoughts, feelings, and fears do these emotions connect to? How do these deeper feelings affect your actions and sense of hope?

THE COURAGE TO STAY JOURNAL

"Hope, for me, is love. I see how much he's trying, how much he's changed for the best, and doing the work to heal us because he loves me. He's still the love of my life and I am his." -SF

Journal Prompt 2:

Take a moment to visualize your healing journey as a mountain. What are the obstacles you see? What do you think the major sections or steps will be? How do you feel about the climb? Write about the emotions and thoughts that arise when you picture this journey.

___

___

___

___

___

___

___

___

___

___

___

___

___

___

___

___

___

"The love I feel between us is stronger than ever. 18 months strong." – IW

Journal Prompt 3:

Think about the protective mechanisms your brain has been using. What negative or fearful thoughts have you been struggling with? How can you talk back to your brain when it gives you a negative thought? How can you reframe these thoughts to be less negative and more hopeful? Which statistic mentioned in the introduction encourages you?

_____
_____
_____
_____
_____
_____
_____
_____
_____
_____
_____
_____
_____
_____

THE COURAGE TO STAY JOURNAL

"This unfortunate event might actually save our marriage. It's made us look at what was lacking before, it's made my husband face things about himself that I've been asking him to. Knowing I'm not alone gives me hope." -Anonymous

Journal Prompt 4:

What small step can you take today toward healing? How can you focus on this without becoming overwhelmed by the whole process? Who are the people in your life that you can trust and lean on for support during this time? What can they do to support you? How can you ask for this?

"I'm encouraged by seeing him consistently working hard in therapy, support groups, practicing empathy, apologizing and making amends over and over." - JG

Journal Prompt 5:

How can you take good care of yourself during this time? What can you do to comfort and relax yourself? What can you do to soothe yourself when you are feeling upset? How can you talk nicely to yourself when you're feeling sad or overwhelmed? How can you bring more positive feelings into each day?

THE COURAGE TO STAY JOURNAL

"What gives me hope is the work my husband has put into it all. He told me he wanted to change and then he followed through... and continues to prove by actions, not just words." - Brandi

Sara and Carlo's Story

I never thought I'd be here—two years after Carlo's affair, looking back at how far we've come. If you told me then that we'd survive, let alone be stronger, I wouldn't have believed you. Back then, I felt like my world shattered in a second.

Carlo and I always said we were made for each other. We came from the same place—we grew up in poverty, experienced racism and abuse, which left us with scars most people couldn't understand. Both of us had been through divorces, and we swore we'd never get married again. Until we met each other. It was like all the broken pieces in both of us fit together perfectly. I thought we had something unbreakable.

That's why, when I found out Carlo had been having an affair, it hit me like a freight train. I was at work when I got the email—from her, of all people. There were texts, photos, the whole ugly truth, laid out in black and white. I felt sick, like my chest had caved in. I flew home that night and confronted him. At first, he denied it—said it wasn't what it looked like, that nothing really happened. But when I showed him the proof, bit by bit, the truth started coming out over the next few days. That slow drip of trickle truth was almost worse than the affair itself. I asked him to leave.

Those first few days without him were a blur. I cried until I had nothing left, sat in silence for hours, and thought about calling a lawyer more times than I could count. But somewhere in that silence, I found clarity. I realized that, despite everything, I still loved him. I missed the sound of his laugh, the way he knew exactly how to comfort me without saying a word. There was so much good between us, so much worth fighting for. It hit me that we had spent years holding back parts of ourselves—hiding pain instead of sharing it, trying to be strong instead of vulnerable. If we were going to heal, we'd have to be honest about everything.

The road back was rough. We cried more tears than I thought humanly possible. There were so many times I wanted to walk away and never look back. I said things I wish I could take back, and so did Carlo. Some days we made progress, and other days we fought so hard it felt like we were right back where we started. But slowly, with a lot of talking and therapy, we began to understand why we ended up in this place.

I learned that my anxious attachment made me lash out when I was scared—especially when Carlo withdrew. His avoidant attachment meant that when things got tough, he shut down. He didn't let me see his pain, and I took that as a sign that he didn't care. The truth was, he cared deeply—he just didn't know how to show it. He kept it all bottled up because he was afraid of being a burden. He thought I was happy in my dream job, so he stayed quiet about his loneliness, even though it was eating him alive.

We spent so many years hurting in silence, both afraid to ask for what we really needed. But now, we know better. We've learned that we can't let those old patterns control us. We have to be intentional—every single day—about how we show up for each other. We check in, even when things seem fine, because we know how easy it is to drift apart. And we make sure that both of us feel safe, heard, and loved.

It hasn't been easy, but two years later, I can honestly say we're closer than we've ever been. The affair forced us to look at the cracks we were too scared to face before, and now we've filled them with understanding, trust, and a deeper kind of love. Carlo and I made it through because we finally let each other see the messy, vulnerable parts we used to hide. And that's what saved us.

We're not perfect. We still have our moments, but we've built something real—something stronger than before. And now I know that no matter what life throws at us, we'll get through it together—because if we survived the affair, we can handle anything.

Journal Prompt 6:

Reconciliation can look different for everyone. What would it take for you to feel comfortable staying in the relationship? Write about the actions, changes, and reassurances you need from your partner—and from yourself—to feel secure?

"My husband has gone above and beyond to fix what was broken. Just celebrated our 45th wedding anniversary. Thank you for the best gift." -BL

Journal Prompt 7:

Think about a past challenge you overcame. What strategies did you use to get through it? How can these strategies be applied to your current situation? How can you keep yourself going when you want to give up?

"What gives me hope? Seeing him validate and reassure me, making real plans for the future again, the stats and research, and seeing my husband not neglect individual therapy." - CB

Journal Prompt 8:

Even though this is a very difficult time, what is still good in your life? What positive things have happened in the last few days? What has your partner been getting right? What things are you grateful for? What is something that brings you joy?

"The amount of love I have for him is still the same. And all the work he's doing gives me hope." - SF

Journal Prompt 9:

Take a moment to reflect on this quote by Paulo Coelho: "When you feel like giving up, remember why you held on for so long in the first place." What makes you feel like giving up sometimes? What reasons have kept you holding on until now? How does thinking about why you're staying make you feel? What matters most to you now?

"In the beginning, it was really hard not to think about the affair every second of every day. It's been 3 years and I do not think about it daily or even weekly. I am sleeping without nightmares. It does get better!" - TAS

Journal Prompt 10:

Reflecting on everything you've read, thought about, and written during this chapter, how have your thoughts and feelings shifted? Write about any new insights or realizations you've had. What stands out as the most important lesson or understanding that you've gained? What will you take with you as you continue to heal?

_____
_____
_____
_____
_____
_____
_____
_____
_____
_____
_____
_____
_____
_____
_____

THE COURAGE TO STAY JOURNAL

"The empathy my husband has for the hurt he caused, and his actions aligning with his words, gives me hope. He's in therapy to work on himself, not just for our family, but because he wants to be better for himself. More in love now than before." – HG

Chapter Two

Riding the Emotional Rollercoaster

As people, we crave predictability, stability, and a sense of control over what's coming next. We expect healing from an affair to be linear, as if each week we'll get a little better until the pain disappears. But unfortunately, recovery isn't a straight path. Instead, it feels more like a wild rollercoaster ride—full of unexpected drops, twists, and turns. One moment, you might feel hopeful, as if you're finally making progress. The next, you're plummeting into sadness or despair, questioning whether you'll ever feel okay again.

The reason this ride is so intense is that you're not just healing from a wound—you're healing from trauma. And trauma has a way of stirring up a wide range of conflicting emotions. It's normal to feel emotionally raw, overwhelmed, and unsteady. As awful as it feels to be on this ride, please know that it's not a sign that something is wrong with you. It's an expected part of the healing process. Whoever decided to put a rollercoaster on Affair Mountain wasn't thinking clearly—but here we are, holding on tight.

Many people describe being emotionally overloaded, cycling through feelings of depression, anxiety, shame, irritability, rage, and hopelessness. You may feel numb, on edge, or constantly on guard, waiting for the next shoe to drop. It's also common to experience physical symptoms—trouble sleeping, nightmares, intrusive thoughts, flashbacks, a loss of appetite or emotional eating, and even struggles with substance use. You may feel like you've lost your sense of self, with no interest in things you once enjoyed. Some people describe these moments as feeling "not like myself" or disconnected from reality.

Please know that these feelings are not only normal—they are common. They are evidence that you are profoundly hurt and struggling to feel safe again. Try not to judge yourself for what you feel, even if your emotions feel overwhelming or messy. There is no "right" or "wrong" way to respond to betrayal. However you feel right now is valid.

As wild as it sounds, one of the best things you can do is embrace the rollercoaster. Understand that the ups and downs are part of the healing process. Some days will be easier; others will be unbearably hard. But one bad day doesn't erase the progress you've made. Just because healing isn't linear doesn't mean you aren't moving forward. Every dip in the ride brings new insights and opportunities for growth. Be patient with yourself during the hard moments, and trust that with time, things will get better.

There may be times when the most dominant emotion you feel is anger. And if you're feeling angry right now, let me reassure you: your anger is completely valid. Anger is a natural response when someone you trusted deeply has hurt you. It's a protective emotion, often covering up more vulnerable feelings—like fear, sadness, rejection, or powerlessness. These emotions might seem buried beneath the rage, but they're just as important to acknowledge.

Sadness is another common companion on this journey. It's natural to grieve the loss of trust, safety, and certainty that once defined your relationship. You may find yourself asking painful questions: "What was real? Can I trust anything? Who is my partner, really?" You may even feel as if your entire relationship was a lie, leaving you questioning everything. These feelings are painful, but they are also normal reactions to betrayal.

You might also feel embarrassment or shame, especially when others judge your decision to stay and try to work things out. If that's the case, please remember that your relationship is unique, and no one else can fully understand your experience. There is no shame in choosing to stay and rebuild—just as there is no shame in deciding to leave. What matters most is that you make the choice that feels right for you. Surround yourself with people who support your journey and avoid those who make you feel worse.

While you're on this emotional rollercoaster, it can be tempting to close your eyes, hold your breath, and pretend the lows aren't happening. I get it. Every hurt partner has felt the urge to numb out or shut down at some point. But as difficult as it is, try to stay present with your feelings. The only way to heal is to feel—allowing the painful emotions to surface so they can be understood and processed.

When a difficult emotion rises, take a deep breath and lean in. Instead of fighting it, let it come. Ask yourself, "What is really hurting me about this?" Breathe deeply, and let the feeling unfold without judgment. If it helps, wrap your arms around yourself in a comforting hug as you ride the wave of emotion. Feelings are like waves—they build, crest, crash, and eventually recede. This feeling will pass, just like the others have. Once the emotion fades, jot down a few thoughts in your journal so you can explore it later. Then, take time to do something soothing—call a friend, take a bath, go for a walk, or organize a small space at home. Whatever brings you comfort, lean into that, too.

You may be wondering, "How long will this rollercoaster ride last?" That's a common concern, and the truth is, there's no set timeline for healing. For some, the process may take a few months; for others, it may take years. Research suggests that recovery from infidelity typically takes 18 months to two years, though the exact timeline varies based on several factors, including the depth of the betrayal, the length of the affair, and the emotional state of the relationship before the affair (Gottman & Gottman, 2017). Many hurt partners begin to feel some relief around the six-month mark, notice significant improvement at twelve months, and feel closer to "normal" by two years after D-Day (Nickerson et al., 2023). But remember, your healing journey is unique. Instead of focusing on how fast you're moving, focus on taking one step at a time—doing what you can each day to rebuild your sense of safety, peace, and connection.

You are not alone in this experience. Infidelity is far more common than most people realize. Large studies show that about 21% of men and 13% of women have engaged in infidelity during a committed relationship (Labrecque & Whisman, 2017). Many of them have ridden the same emotional rollercoaster and emerged stronger, more resilient, and more connected to themselves than ever before. You can, too.

Take it one day at a time and be gentle with yourself along the way. The ups and downs of this ride may be exhausting, but each turn brings you closer to healing. Trust in your strength and your ability to rebuild your life, whether that means staying in your relationship or choosing a different path. You are resilient, and you have the power to find peace and happiness again—no matter what lies ahead.

Now, let's explore some of the emotions you've experienced on this rollercoaster and reflect on what they mean for your healing. Please take your time with the following journal prompts—write as little or as much as you'd like. At the end of the week, review your answers and consider sharing a few thoughts with your partner. I lovingly encourage you to ask for the changes you need to feel better. Big hugs to you.

Journal Prompt 1:

What are you feeling right now? How strong is this feeling? Where are you feeling it in your body? What is this feeling telling you? What do you need or crave right now? What small step can you take to get or ask for what you need?

"What we had before wasn't even as good as what it is now." -Victoria

Journal Prompt 2:

Think about the emotional ups and downs you've experienced so far. What moments have felt particularly overwhelming? What moments have brought you a sense of peace or hope? How have these shifts in emotion affected the way you view your healing process?

"We are 3 years post D-Day. I will never ever forget, but our relationship now has never been better. It's been a hard journey, it's not for the weak." -Anonymous

Journal Prompt 3:

Write about the specific things that make you feel angry right now. When you allow the anger to surface, what else comes up for you? What deeper feelings or needs might be beneath this anger? In what ways might your anger be protecting you?

_____
_____
_____
_____
_____
_____
_____
_____
_____
_____
_____
_____
_____
_____
_____
_____
_____

"I have found that it's true, you have a better and stronger relationship on the other side IF you can both put 1000% into fixing what was broken to begin with." - Jodi

Journal Prompt 4:

How do you wish you could express yourself in this moment? If you knew there would be no consequences and you could say anything you'd want to, what would you say to your partner? To the affair partner?

"I will definitely never forget and it will change u forever, but I feel like u can grow and also make something positive out of something negative and life can be so much better than it ever was." -
Leela

Journal Prompt 5:

Reflect on your sense of safety and security. How have these been affected by the affair? What steps can you take to begin rebuilding a sense of security for yourself? What else do you crave to feel safer? How can you ask your partner for this?

"Consistency is the key. He never deviates from our newfound marriage. I can only take one day at a time and pray he never does it again." - CB

Danielle's Story

There are two things I know for sure. First, healing from an affair requires both partners to be fully committed. My husband's willingness to do the deep work, uncover the root causes of his own pain, and take responsibility for healing was essential. Healing can't be one-sided. Just as the betrayed can't force the betrayer to heal, the betrayer can't force the betrayed to heal. Both have to engage in their own processes. Second, without therapy, we wouldn't have had the communication tools necessary to work through this. Though my husband had always been skeptical of therapy—likely due to his past (his mother had an affair with her marriage counselor)—he quickly changed his stance after the affair was revealed. We began online therapy within a week of discovery.

Our story began in 2007, when we started dating in our early twenties. We married in 2010, and in 2013, we welcomed our daughter. In February 2020, I was diagnosed with breast cancer at age 34. I mention the cancer because I believe it played a significant role in what followed. I went through 21 rounds of chemotherapy, multiple breast surgeries, 31 rounds of radiation, and a total hysterectomy. Naturally, during this time, physical intimacy was not a priority for me. Losing my hormones only added to my lack of interest in sex. While my sex drive faded, my husband's didn't, and this became a point of contention between us.

At the time, I had a friend who supported me through my cancer treatment. She lived a rather unconventional life—she was in an open marriage with her trans husband—but I never saw that as an issue. I confided in her about my struggles with intimacy, my lack of sex drive, and the negative impact it was having on my marriage. I also shared my feelings of disgust with my body. After the surgeries and treatments, I had one nipple, was covered in scars, and had been completely bald. I felt stripped of my femininity. Little did I know, my friend was using everything I told her to manipulate her way into my husband's life.

My husband later admitted that she had been flirting with him for about a year before anything physical happened. Although he initially resisted her advances, he didn't tell me about it because he was also attracted to her. Eventually, the affair began and lasted for about two months. Days before I found out, I noticed my husband was acting strangely, and we got into a huge argument. My gut told me something was wrong. When I discovered the truth, he said all the usual things: he loved her, she understood him, she matched his sexual needs. I was convinced our marriage was over.

The next morning, after my mother came to check on me (she had taken our daughter for the night), she confronted my husband and somehow managed to pull him out of what I now know was an "affair fog." He went from being ready to leave me to ending things with the other woman. He blocked her everywhere and committed to working on our relationship. However, I made it clear to him that while I wasn't walking away immediately, I wasn't staying unconditionally either. I told him he would have to show me what he wanted through his actions, not just his words.

We started therapy and did the necessary work. Eventually, our therapist suggested that my husband also begin individual therapy to address his own issues. It became clear that our marriage as we knew it was over, but we had the opportunity to create a new, healthier relationship. As Esther Perel says, we mourned the loss of our first marriage but chose to step into a second one. This experience, while painful, exposed cracks that already existed in our relationship and forced both of us to engage in deep self-reflection. It also showed us how much we wanted to fight for each other.

If I could offer any advice, it would be this: There can be a beautiful rainbow at the end of this storm. You have to endure the storm to make it to the rainbow, but it's there, full of beauty. Embrace your second marriage and make the changes you wish you had made before.

As for my cancer journey, I celebrated three years cancer-free on August 14, and I'm finally starting to feel like myself again. When people see me now, they don't see a cancer patient—they see a healthy, happy person who has made herself a priority. Healing from both cancer and betrayal has given me a new perspective on life, and I'm grateful for the strength that has come from these challenges.

Journal Prompt 6:

Sometimes, other people's opinions can make the healing process even harder. Have you experienced judgment from friends or family about your choices? How has that made you feel? What did you think about their opinions? What steps can you take to stay true to your own path, regardless of what others think?

THE COURAGE TO STAY JOURNAL

"It gives me hope hearing that others are going through the same thing. Knowing I'm not alone helps me feel less stupid about this going on right under my nose." - PJ

Journal Prompt 7:

Describe your thoughts on your healing process so far. What small signs of progress have you noticed recently? When have you felt strong and resilient during this process? What has helped you cope so far? How can you tap into your inner strength more consistently?

"Patience and reassurance from my partner give me hope." - Mandy

Journal Prompt 8:

When uncomfortable feelings arise, what is your typical response? Do you lean into them or try to avoid them? Describe a time when you allowed yourself to fully experience a painful emotion. What happened? How did you feel afterward? What fears or beliefs make it hard to face certain feelings? How might avoiding them affect your healing journey?

THE COURAGE TO STAY JOURNAL

"I get hope from the immense love we share, our history as a couple, increasing my understanding of affairs, seeing the work and effort we're both putting in, and from supportive and experienced peers." - Lindz

Journal Prompt 9:

How do you feel about the idea that healing can take two years or longer, depending on personal circumstances? Does this timeline give you comfort or make you feel anxious? What expectations do you have for your own healing process? Are there ways in which these expectations help or hinder you?

"He's been so much more attentive, and I see him taking accountability and acknowledging my pain. I see his love for me every day now instead of just hearing it. I see and feel the difference." - Courtney

Journal Prompt 10:

Reflecting on everything you've read, thought about, and written during this chapter, how have your thoughts and feelings shifted? Write about any new insights or realizations you've had. What stands out as the most important lesson or understanding that you've gained? What will you take with you as you continue to heal?

"Hope is knowing and seeing the changes he has made in himself. After 35 years, I am seeing a whole new side of my husband. He has started communicating, sharing emotions and he is giving me hope." – *Anonymous*

Chapter Three

Cultivating Confidence & Defeating Doubt

How is your self-confidence after discovering the affair? If you're like most injured partners hiking up Affair Mountain, your self-esteem has probably taken a big hit. I'm so sorry you're feeling this way, and it's completely understandable. In times like these, it's easy to find yourself asking: *Was this my fault? Did I do something to cause this? Maybe I wasn't doing enough. Maybe I'm not good enough at parenting, cleaning, conversation, or intimacy? Maybe I'm not attractive enough? Maybe I'm just boring?* We are all so good at finding a million reasons to blame ourselves for the affair.

This tendency to blame ourselves stems from a deep human need to understand and make sense of traumatic experiences. Self-blame is essentially a coping mechanism that gives us a sense of control over the situation. When something bad happens, especially something that feels out of our control, we want to believe that we played a role in causing it, because if we caused it, then maybe we can prevent it from happening again. While self-blame helps us cope in the short-term, it ultimately hurts us more than helps us. It can trap us in feelings of guilt, shame, and unworthiness, eroding our self-esteem more and more.

Research supports this. A study by Miller and Maner (2009) found that when trust is broken by an affair, it often leads to deep insecurity and self-doubt in the betrayed partner. Jealousy and comparisons with the affair partner can worsen these feelings, making us believe we aren't "good enough" or as attractive, further lowering our self-esteem. Another study by Finkel and colleagues (2002) found that trust violations don't just damage self-esteem, they also harm the betrayed partner's ability to trust their own judgment. We start questioning our own value and even our judgment in trusting others, leading to a profound sense of inadequacy and insecurity.

Let me reassure you: *no matter what you did or didn't do, the affair was NOT your fault.* There is no perfect person out there, and your partner made the choice to stray because of their unhealed trauma or unresolved feelings, not because of something you did. Your partner made that choice, you were not part of that decision. And if you were not part of the decision, how could you be responsible for it? Please keep reminding yourself that this was not your choice and absolutely not your fault.

You might still be thinking, *"Okay, I hear you, but what if the AP (affair partner) really was better than me? Maybe she was the right person for my partner, and he's just stuck with me."* To this, I would tell you—hugs, I'm sorry you're thinking that. I know how painful those thoughts can be. But it's so unlikely to be true! We are all more than the sum of our parts. You might not be the world's greatest cook, but you're probably kind, funny, warm, a fantastic friend, and a wonderful parent. It's possible that the AP had a different set of attributes than you do, but that doesn't make them better, it makes them different. And different was what your partner was really craving—someone they could pretend to be different with because they wanted an escape from reality.

As Esther Perel wisely said: *"We have affairs to become a different person, not to be with a different person."* Time and again, I've found this to be true. Your partner was looking for someone they could act out a fantasy with because they were in too much pain being themselves. The affair partner wasn't magical, special, or better. They were simply available and willing to play a part in your partner's fantasy. In reality, your partner was just a typical person, struggling with their own feelings of inadequacy, insecurity, and emotional pain. With the AP, they could pretend to be someone else— someone more confident, more successful, richer, or more influential. The AP didn't know these things weren't true, so they accepted the fantasy version, which made your partner feel better. Your partner kept returning to that fantasy because it was easier than facing reality or doing the work to improve themselves. Instead of sitting down with you, being vulnerable, and asking for help, they opted for the temporary relief the AP provided. I wish they had chosen differently—I know you do too.

Sometimes, the AP was a person you'd never imagine your partner being attracted to, which can unlock some new fears. You may wonder if your partner finds you unattractive or undesirable because the affair partner seemed less appealing or somehow 'less than' in your eyes. You might also feel more vulnerable, thinking that someone you wouldn't have considered a threat could, in fact, pose one – and this can make it feel like anyone could be a potential threat. I completely understand why you would feel this way and I want to reassure you: most people who stray aren't selective about their choice of affair partner. They often choose someone who's simply available and willing. It's typically more about convenience than anything else.

If you're struggling with thoughts that the affair partner might be "better" than you, remember this: odds are that no matter who your partner was with, they still would have strayed. Betrayal was their way of coping with complicated feelings, and even if they'd been with someone as remarkable as Beyoncé, Taylor Swift, Shakira, Cardi B, Gwen Stefani, Halle Berry, Sandra Bullock, Maria Shriver, Sylvia Plath, Frida Kahlo, Jackie Kennedy, or Eleanor Roosevelt, the outcome would likely have been the same. No one can be the perfect partner who takes away another person's pain or fills a void they haven't worked to heal. That journey is their own to take. (And in case you didn't know, all of these remarkable people were betrayed in their relationships.)

You might be wondering why you weren't "special" enough for your partner to stay faithful, or why they would risk losing someone as loving and good as you. You may even think that if they really loved you, the affair wouldn't have happened. I completely understand why you'd be asking these questions, and I know how painful they are. But the hard truth is that during the affair, they weren't thinking about you—they were mostly thinking about themselves. Straying partners often get caught up in a selfish narrative that allows them to justify their actions. They may even tell themselves things like, *"I didn't want to bother her, and what she doesn't know won't hurt her."* It's magical thinking and completely disconnected from reality. Of course, it would hurt you! But they created these stories to give themselves permission to continue seeking relief from their pain. They weren't thinking clearly or logically, and they were being selfish and hurtful in ways they likely couldn't even grasp at the time.

So, let me reassure you: *you are enough, just as you are right now.* None of us are perfect, and none of us behave perfectly all the time. We are all flawed, imperfect creatures, but that doesn't mean we deserve to be betrayed. If you weren't enough, your partner would not have chosen you to build a long-term relationship with in the first place. You were enough then, you are enough now. You will always be enough and no one deserves to be betrayed, ever.

When you feel your self-esteem dropping, there are a few things you can do to help yourself feel better:

Do a Gratitude Exercise: Practicing gratitude helps shift your focus from what you feel is missing to the abundance that's already present in your life. Each day, take a few moments to jot down three things you're grateful for—big or small. It could be supportive friends, a cozy home, a favorite hobby, or a quiet moment of peace. Over time, this practice can reframe your outlook, making it easier to notice the positives even when life feels difficult. Reflecting on what you have can build a sense of abundance, helping you feel grounded and supported. (And remember you can be grateful for silly things, like pumpkin spice lattes and really good cheese!)

Create a Success Inventory: Reflect on what you've accomplished recently and over the years, no matter how small. Maybe you achieved a personal goal, handled a tough conversation gracefully, or completed a task you've been putting off. Focusing on these successes reinforces a positive self-image and reminds you of your resilience and capability. Keep this list where you can see it—revisiting it during challenging times can reassure you of all you're capable of.

Focus on Your Strengths: Spend some time identifying what naturally comes to you. Are you a great listener, a creative thinker, or an empathetic friend? Write down these strengths and keep the list somewhere visible as a reminder of your unique gifts.

Recognizing what you do well helps you reconnect with your value, building confidence and self-worth. Whenever self-doubt creeps in, return to this list to remember what makes you uniquely strong and resilient.

Create a Smile File: Gather meaningful notes, cards, photos, emails, ticket stubs, and other mementos that remind you that you are loved and appreciated. Include things like your children's drawings, a valentine from your partner, or even recent notes of encouragement from friends. Think of it as a collection of love and support that you can look through anytime you need a lift.

Practice Affirmations: Choose affirmations that resonate with you—statements like "I am resilient," "I deserve love and respect," or "I am enough just as I am." Repeat these daily to reinforce a positive self-image and shift your inner dialogue to something supportive and empowering. You can find some great ideas on Pinterest.

Take Care of Your Body: Physical self-care is closely tied to emotional well-being. Nourish yourself with healthy food, get plenty of rest, and move in ways that feel good to you. Prioritizing your physical health can uplift your mind and emotions, reinforcing a sense of strength and self-worth.

Learn Something New: Engage in something that sparks your curiosity—a class, book, or hobby that inspires you. Learning new things boosts confidence, reminding you that you're capable and growing beyond your current circumstances. Personal growth is empowering and connects you to your potential.

Volunteer Your Time: Helping others can be profoundly fulfilling and a powerful boost to your self-esteem. Find a cause close to your heart—whether it's volunteering at an animal shelter, helping at a food bank, or tutoring. Volunteering reinforces your sense of purpose and reminds you of the positive impact you have in the world.

Now, let's explore some ideas about self-esteem a little further. Please take your time in responding to each journal prompt. At the end of the week, review your answers and choose a few key thoughts to share with your partner. Then, ask for the changes you need to feel better. You're doing incredible work, and I'm so proud of you!

Journal Prompt 1:

How has the affair changed your thinking about yourself? What self-doubt has been triggered? What fears and worries about yourself have been brought up? What fears about what your partner thinks about you have surfaced?

THE COURAGE TO STAY JOURNAL

"It's so true, we always want to run away and think leaving is the answer… but the friendship created, kids, etcetera…it's a lot to consider and hence, I'm staying." -Chipo

Journal Prompt 2:

What are some of the ways you've blamed yourself for the affair? How has this self-blame affected your sense of worth and confidence? In what areas of your life do you tend to feel like you are "not enough"? How have these feelings been influenced by the affair?

"It's going to take some time. It helps when the betrayed partner puts in the work. I'm 6 months from D-Day, it's still very hard, but it's getting better because he's putting in the work." -Sarah

Journal Prompt 3:

Reflecting on your responses to prompts 1 and 2, what evidence can you find that contradicts your worries and fears? Even if part of you believes these fears could be somewhat true, what other, more compassionate possibilities could also be true? Take a moment to challenge your negative thoughts—does someone really have to look or be perfect to be lovable? What else might be true about your worth and your ability to be loved just as you are?

THE COURAGE TO STAY JOURNAL

"A successful recovery is highly dependent on the actions of the cheater. They have to do the work to change and become a safe partner." -Smitty

Journal Prompt 4:

Write about a time when you felt confident and valued. What were the circumstances, and what made you feel that way? As you think back on this time, what do you know for sure to be true about yourself, regardless of any challenges you're facing now?

"My husband told his AP he loved her. They'd only known each other for about a month when she told him she loved him. He claims he said it back because he didn't want to hurt her feelings. We've been together almost 20 years and have two young children. My situation is complicated, but I will say he was a hurt person who acted selfishly. He's still my person." -Lindsay

Journal Prompt 5:

What are your strengths? List five of your personal strengths and provide examples of how you have demonstrated each one in your life. Why are these strengths valuable? What positive things can you tell yourself about these strengths? How are these strengths connected to you being lovable and special?

"Cheating is mostly a poor coping strategy and wanting a distraction from yourself and life. I was the cheater. It was not about love for me at all. I just told my AP whatever she wanted to hear." - Jason

Bruce's Story

I want to share my experience as an unfaithful spouse to offer some encouragement for anyone walking through this painful chapter in their lives. To give you some background, I struggled with alcohol and porn addiction for over 16 years. These addictions became crutches, a way for me to self-soothe and avoid facing the trauma I didn't want to deal with. These habits created a double life that I carried into my marriage.

I often found myself trapped in what I now call my "Bermuda Triangle"—the pressure to succeed at work and in life, the grief from losing my father, and constant financial stress. When the affair happened and was exposed by someone else, my entire life was laid bare. There was no hiding anymore.

At that moment, I knew I had a choice: I could continue running from my problems, or I could face the wreckage I'd caused. I was tired of running. Hitting rock bottom forced me to confront the damage I had done—not just to myself but to the person who had always been there for me. I realized I would be facing this journey alone because of the betrayal I had inflicted, but even so, I was determined to change.

Now, we are a year and a half past D-Day. I never imagined we could rebuild our relationship; much less be given another chance at it. Before the affair, there was always love between us, but my refusal to face my issues and seek help robbed us of true connection. Since then, I've given up the destructive habits that led me astray, and I've become a completely different person. My focus shifted toward healing, self-awareness, and personal growth. I knew I had to change for myself. I couldn't stand the person I had become, and I faced the reality that if my wife chose to leave, I would be left with nothing but myself—and I needed to be someone I could live with.

I sought out self-led therapy through affair recovery and mindset videos. I dove into studies about pornography and alcohol addiction to fully grasp the extent of the harm they cause. I had to understand just how toxic these habits were, not just to my relationship but to my own well-being. Most importantly, I wanted to change for myself. I hated who I had been, and I knew I needed to transform into the man she had always deserved. I wanted to be someone who could offer her safety and help her heal, regardless of whether we stayed together.

Over the past year and a half, we have experienced countless highs and lows. We've faced triggers, overwhelming emotions, and the painful aftermath of my choices. We both understand that this will always be a part of our story, but we've chosen to see it as a restart. The personal growth we've each undergone has made us stronger as individuals and as a couple. We connect now in ways I never thought possible before the affair.

To anyone going through this and wanting to fight for their relationship, I encourage you to embrace the discomfort and uncertainty. Accept the consequences of your actions and take full responsibility for the pain you've caused. Honesty will be the key to healing, and it will propel you toward the opportunity to mend the broken parts of yourself that need healing.

Journal Prompt 6:

Let's do a gratitude exercise and success inventory. List three things you are grateful for today and explain why they are meaningful to you. Then, write about three recent accomplishments, no matter how small, and why they make you proud. Feel free to do more if you like.

"I realized my husband did not love his AP ...and it took a long time...but he rewrote our history to write this false narrative with the AP...and it was all just liiieessss. He realized he couldn't find real happiness or true comfort in that space. He said he still gets horribly ashamed over it." -CB

Journal Prompt 7:

Please make a list of all the compliments, praise, and nice things people have said to you over the last several years. Look at old emails, birthday cards, or anything you like to jog your memory. Write those things down here, then reflecting on what you have written, please come up with 5 affirmations you can say to yourself when you are struggling.

"Even if he loved her, he still loves you. You get to decide if it's worth staying. Cheating is rarely about love." - Anna

Journal Prompt 8:

Your partner has hurt you very deeply. Even though they have hurt you and lied to you, not everything they have ever told you has been a lie. Thinking back on some of the happier times, what are some of the loving things your partner told you? What if we believed these ideas were still true? Is your partner saying any loving things to you now? What if we believed them?

THE COURAGE TO STAY JOURNAL

"It's been 5.5 years for me and we are stronger and healthier than ever before. I always hesitate saying that because I get a lot of negative comments (you're lying to yourself, you'll never trust again) but I just want others to know that if both of you are committed to healing, it is possible! My husband has honored my boundaries and his efforts have not let up at all. I have never felt more loved and wanted." -Mimi

Journal Prompt 9:

What would it feel like to truly believe that you are enough, just as you are? How would believing this change how you treat yourself? How could this change the way you approach your relationships?

THE COURAGE TO STAY JOURNAL

_____

_____

_____

_____

_____

_____

_____

_____

_____

_____

_____

_____

_____

_____

_____

_____

_____

_____

_____

"Sometimes you have to get to rock bottom! The light you see as you are looking up is the hand of the person you devastated. You realize you will put in the work because 18 years together is worth more than a few bad months." -Melanie

Journal Prompt 10:

Reflecting on everything you've read, thought about, and written during this chapter, how have your thoughts and feelings shifted? Write about any new insights or realizations you've had. What stands out as the most important lesson or understanding that you've gained? What will you take with you as you continue to heal?

"I stayed and decided that I wasn't a victim but a hero. I saved my family and my cheating partner. His AP was never going to marry him and he would be lost by himself. I also made a list of all the good things about me (we tend to concentrate on our failings) and decided that I was a pretty neat person and he was lucky to have me." - Gail

Chapter Four
Challenging Your Core Beliefs

One of the most distressing and insidious aspects of infidelity is how it activates your core wounds and causes you to question your core beliefs. A core belief is a deeply held conclusion about yourself, others, and the world, typically formed in childhood when your parents, family members, and caregivers helped you interpret and navigate your life's experiences. These beliefs shape how you view and understand future experiences, essentially becoming the lens through which you make sense of reality.

As you grew up, your ideas about your value, abilities, strengths, and identity were influenced by your experiences and the feedback you received from those around you. If you received positive, consistent attention and loving feedback from your caregivers, you likely developed strong self-worth and confidence. However, if you experienced neglect, abuse, bullying, or frequent criticism, you may have developed a core wound—a painful belief about yourself, such as believing that you are unworthy, incapable, or unlovable.

You also developed core beliefs about what to expect from others and how the world works. These beliefs were shaped by how your caregivers helped you interpret interactions with others. You concluded whether people were trustworthy, kind, reliable, or safe based on the feedback you received. Similarly, you formed beliefs about the safety of the world, the availability of resources, and what was within your control.

Positive messages would have led you to believe that most people are reliable and kind, while negative messages fostered beliefs that others are dangerous and untrustworthy. Likewise, positive feedback about the world might have led you to believe it was safe and abundant, while negative or inconsistent messages may have caused you to see the world as dangerous or scarce in resources.

Few people emerge from childhood without some core wounds or painful core beliefs. These wounds are typical and expected. However, an affair can challenge these core beliefs and activate old wounds, leaving you questioning your ability to trust yourself, others, and your understanding of how the world works. When I ask hurt partners about their core beliefs, they often say: "I am not lovable," "I am not special," "I am undesirable," "I am defective," "I am broken," "I am too much," or "It's all my fault." If any of these thoughts resonate with you, please know that your feelings make sense and many of us who have conquered Affair Mountain felt exactly the same way.

A core wound is also known as an attachment injury. You may have heard about attachment before and may be familiar with the idea of attachment styles. These terms all come from attachment theory. Attachment theory helps us understand how early relationships with our caregivers shape the way we connect with others throughout our lives.

Developed by psychologist John Bowlby, attachment theory explains that we all form attachment styles, which are patterns of relating to others, that influence our sense of safety, trust, and emotional security in relationships. These attachment styles shape how we approach intimacy, handle conflict, and respond to relationship challenges. Our attachment styles also affect our emotional responses and coping mechanisms in significant ways. There are three main attachment styles:

Anxious Attachment: People with an anxious attachment style tend to fear abandonment and crave reassurance from their partners. For those with anxious attachment, infidelity can confirm their deepest fears of inadequacy and rejection. They may find themselves overthinking or clinging tightly to their partner, desperate for signs of commitment and love. An affair can make them question their worth and reinforce the core wound that they're "not enough" or unlovable. The majority of hurt partners have an anxious style, but sometimes, anxious types are the ones who stray. Healing often involves learning to self-soothe and recognize that their value is not determined by someone else's actions.

Avoidant Attachment: Those with an avoidant attachment style often distance themselves in relationships to protect against vulnerability and perceived dependency. Close relationships can threaten their sense of independence and emotional safety, prompting them to withdraw further. The majority of straying partners have an avoidant attachment style. Avoidantly attached individuals might feel trapped or fear losing control, reinforcing beliefs that relying on others is unsafe. For them, healing requires working through the discomfort of vulnerability and learning to open up emotionally without fearing dependency.

Disorganized Attachment: This attachment style is a mix of both anxious and avoidant tendencies, often stemming from traumatic or inconsistent caregiving in childhood. People with disorganized attachment may have conflicting desires—wanting closeness but fearing it at the same time. An affair can feel like a betrayal of the fragile trust they've worked to build, leaving them caught between wanting to connect with their partner and pushing them away. They may feel deeply unsafe and unable to trust their own judgment. Healing for this attachment style involves understanding these conflicting needs and developing a more stable sense of security within themselves and in their relationships.

Attachment research tells us that the emotional shock and distress caused by infidelity can leave you feeling disconnected from yourself, your partner, and even your surroundings (Johnson et al., 2001). This sense of helplessness can become ingrained in your thinking, shaping how you view yourself and future relationships (Macintosh et al., 2007). Another study found that many hurt partners experience a profound disruption in their core beliefs about themselves, their partners, and the relationship, making it hard to regain emotional security (Snyder et al., 2007).

These studies demonstrate that the impact of infidelity goes far beyond the initial emotional pain—it challenges your core beliefs about the fairness and predictability of life. You may have believed that love and effort would protect your relationship, only to find that certain factors were beyond your control. This realization can lead to feelings of helplessness and a loss of trust in life's fairness. Ironically, attachment injuries play a role in creating affairs and affairs then create more attachment injuries.

Despite the pain and confusion you are experiencing right now, please know that healing your attachment injuries is possible. You can re-evaluate and redefine your core beliefs, incorporating new insights and a different perspective. In time, you may develop beliefs that allow you to hold both the good and painful aspects of your experiences, such as "the world is generally safe, but bad things can happen," at the same time.

Healing involves rebuilding your sense of self-worth, trust in others, and your perception of safety. You may even redefine what safety means in relationships. Though the process may seem daunting, each step brings you closer to becoming a stronger, more resilient version of yourself—one who understands the depths of pain and who is capable of rebuilding trust and hope.

As you reflect on your core beliefs, please keep a couple of things in mind. Two seemingly contradictory things can be true at the same time. For example, your partner may have lied to you, but that doesn't mean everything they've ever said is a lie. So instead of seeing your partner as a liar, I encourage you to see them as someone who lies and someone who tells the truth. Similarly, you can love your partner and hate their behavior at the same time. Try to view things in shades of gray, rather than seeing everything in black and white. Look for ways to accept that two truths can coexist at the same time.

Most of us enter relationships with core wounds and have complex coping mechanisms to manage them. For instance, a child who was frequently left alone might develop a core wound of abandonment and, as an adult, form codependent relationships as a way to cope with the fear of being abandoned. Problematic behaviors often come from a way we learned to protect ourselves. Through the years, I have come to believe that behind every problematic behavior is pain and some complicated way to protect ourselves. If you can see your partner's transgressions as a misguided way to help themselves (even though it was absolutely the wrong choice), this may help you have a bit more compassion for them. The first step toward healing problematic behaviors is to recognize how they're connected to core wounds and how they've served to keep us emotionally safe in the past. Our goal is to find healthy, positive ways to cope with our emotional pain and develop secure attachment to our partner.

To learn more about attachment styles and how to become more securely attached, I highly recommend the book Secure Love by Julie Menanno, LMFT. It is the best book I've ever read on attachment and it will give you tremendous insight into your and your partner's behavior.

Now, let's explore your core beliefs and wounds in more detail. Please respond to each journal prompt as fully as you can and consider inviting your partner to reflect on them as well. At the end of the week, review your answers and share any key insights with your partner. Remember, you deserve the reassurance and support you need to heal. Big hugs.

Journal Prompt 1:

Reflect on your childhood experiences and the feedback you received from your parents or caregivers. What core beliefs about yourself, others, and the world did you develop from these experiences? What core wounds did you develop?

_____
_____
_____
_____
_____
_____
_____
_____
_____
_____
_____
_____
_____
_____
_____
_____
_____

"A year since finding out about the affair. The worst pain I've ever felt. But our relationship now is stronger than ever. I almost want to thank the AP." -IW

Journal Prompt 2:

Reflect on how the betrayal has impacted your core beliefs. In what ways did it challenge the beliefs you held about yourself, your partner, and the world? Were there any beliefs that the betrayal reinforced? What core wounds were activated by this experience? Describe the emotions and thoughts that have surfaced for you.

_____
_____
_____
_____
_____
_____
_____
_____
_____
_____
_____
_____
_____
_____
_____
_____

THE COURAGE TO STAY JOURNAL

"While my trust is pretty much gone after his affair, I can say it brought to light how toxic we were to each other. It's still really painful, but we are actually better than we ever were." -Shannan

Journal Prompt 3:

Reflect on your core beliefs about trust and safety. How have these beliefs been affected by the betrayal? What are you craving from your partner to feel safer or be able to trust more? What steps can you take to rebuild a sense of trust and safety in your life?

"His affair actually helped us too. We finally talk openly with each other about our needs, fears and worries. Before, he just didn't understand that I was just as unhappy as he was." -Elsie

Journal Prompt 4:

What are your core beliefs about your value? How have these beliefs been impacted by the betrayal? Where did these beliefs come from originally? What evidence can you find to support the belief that you are valuable and worthy of love? (Extra credit: Go online and find a mantra or inspirational quote that you can recite when you're struggling with how lovable and valuable you are.)

_____
_____
_____
_____
_____
_____
_____
_____
_____
_____
_____
_____
_____
_____

THE COURAGE TO STAY JOURNAL

"I felt like our relationship wasn't very deep prior. Just surface level. Now we have all the hard talks and so much more connection." -OM

Journal Prompt 5:

Reflect on any cognitive dissonance you've experienced since the betrayal. Cognitive dissonance is the discomfort that arises when you hold two conflicting beliefs, ideas, or values at the same time. How have you tried to reconcile the conflict between your past beliefs and your new reality? What insights have you gained from this process? Finally, what do you need from your partner to help resolve any remaining dissonance and support your healing?

"After my partner's affair, we took a long/hard/painful look at what was happening before and have both made the effort to start over and learn to love again and heal from the betrayal. We have both said multiple times that we hate what happened but are grateful for how it opened our eyes." -Jodi

Tammy's Story

Our story began quietly, with my husband sexting women from his past. At the time, I didn't even realize this was cheating. He'd always apologize, say he'd stop, and for a while, he would. But I started to notice a pattern: it always happened during major milestones in our lives—when he moved in, before our wedding, when we began IVF. I also found him on dating and porn sites. We sought therapy, and I mentioned the pattern, suspecting it might stem from his childhood trauma, having grown up in foster care. The therapist agreed, but my husband didn't believe his past affected him.

In 2018, he crossed a line I never thought he would. He met two women from a dating site, leading to two one-night stands. One of those women blackmailed him into a strange, toxic relationship where she demanded he text, call, and even visit her, threatening to reveal everything if he didn't comply. This dragged on for four long years.

In July 2020, we moved into what I thought was our dream home. A month later, I discovered he had been sexting a woman he met at a hotel where he stayed for work. He promised to stop, and I trusted him—still naive, thinking it was only texting, never suspecting it could be more. But it was. For two years, instead of staying at the hotel, he went to her house.

In July 2022, everything unraveled. I picked up his phone to turn off the music, and the first thing I saw were messages—"I love you," "I miss you." They weren't meant for me. My heart shattered. At first, he said he would leave me, claiming she was his soulmate, his perfect match. That lasted all of a few hours. He came back, and we tried to rebuild. We made a recovery plan, and for a while, things seemed to improve. Then he reached out to her again in August. And again in September.

It was gut-wrenching. But we both committed to the work. We went through counseling, coaching, read countless books, and watched endless videos, all in an attempt to understand what had gone wrong and how we could fix it. Slowly, we began to heal—not just individually, but as a couple.

Today, I describe us as a work in progress. We talk, we connect, and we've learned to be intimate in ways that go beyond the bedroom. We handle our conflicts with communication instead of shutting down. We've built boundaries and learned to be authentic with each other and those around us. My husband has taken full responsibility for his actions, and while I don't blame myself for his choices, I have reflected on how I can contribute to a healthier relationship. He now talks openly about what bothers him—something he never used to do.

People who know what we've been through often tell us they admire our relationship. I know most people wouldn't stay after what happened. I've lost count of how many "D-days" we've had. But as painful as the journey has been, I wouldn't trade the relationship we have now for anything. We've grown, not just as a couple but as individuals, and I believe our bond is stronger than ever.

Journal Prompt 6:

How have you learned to cope with your core wounds? In what ways have these coping mechanisms protected you? Are there any unhealthy coping strategies you'd like to change? What healthier alternatives can you try to adopt?

"I was so embarrassed about the affair in the beginning, then shifted to embarrassed for him. Now, because of our growth in our marriage, I'm proud of us both." -BKS

Journal Prompt 7:

What new information or insights you have gained since the betrayal? How have these insights influenced your core beliefs? What new beliefs are you forming that blend your old beliefs and incorporate your new understanding? (Remember to resist black and white thinking.)

"A year out, we are soooo much better as a couple. It's still hard but my husband (avoidant) has learned a lot, and we are closer than ever!" -Stacy

Journal Prompt 8:

Let's focus on your strengths and resilience. Reflect on difficult times you've overcome in the past. What helped you get through them? How can you draw on those same strengths to navigate the betrayal and its aftermath? What can you do to further build on these strengths as you continue your healing journey?

"His actions are proving he is willing to do ANYTHING to fix us. It's hard and some days are brutal, but several months later we're having more good days than bad." -Britt

Journal Prompt 9:

Write a letter to yourself, offering the same kindness and compassion you would give to a close friend facing the same struggles you've expressed in prompts 1-8. What words of encouragement and support would you offer to help them keep going?

THE COURAGE TO STAY JOURNAL

"It took me way longer than 6 weeks to feel stable. The change came from his and my behavior. We now tell each other that the floor is open for to say whatever you feel without the other getting mad." -MPP

Journal Prompt 10:

Reflecting on everything you've read, thought about, and written during this chapter, how have your thoughts and feelings shifted? Write about any new insights or realizations you've had. What stands out as the most important lesson or understanding that you've gained? What will you take with you as you continue to heal?

"I have tried the scorched earth method to no avail. I wanted him to know my pain but alas, the affair was about his pain. That's on him to fix. I hope he will." -Jewels

Chapter Five

Exploring Your Anger

You have every right to feel angry about being betrayed. Anger is a natural, valid response to feeling hurt, disrespected, and let down by someone you trusted deeply. It's a sign that your boundaries and values have been violated, reflecting the depth of your pain and disappointment. This anger isn't just justified—it's a crucial part of your healing process. It allows you to recognize the full impact of the betrayal and encourages you to stand up for what you truly deserve in relationships.

Acknowledging your anger, rather than suppressing it or feeling guilty about it, allows you to process your emotions in a healthy, constructive way. By honoring this response, you're respecting your feelings and taking the first step toward making sense of what happened. Research by Gordon, Baucom, & Snyder (2004) shows that anger is a nearly universal reaction among hurt partners. This anger arises because trust has been broken and emotional safety in the relationship has been badly damaged. Their research confirms that your anger is not only normal but also directly tied to the loss of security in your relationship.

Anger helps you protect yourself. It acts as a powerful emotional buffer and a clear signal that your boundaries have been crossed. At its core, anger is often a response to feeling wronged or violated, helping you identify what's unacceptable or hurtful. This anger can provide necessary distance from the pain and confusion of betrayal, giving you the energy to establish and enforce boundaries, resist mistreatment, and restore your sense of self-respect. Anger serves as a kind of internal warning system, highlighting unmet needs and suppressed emotions and urging you to address underlying issues rather than ignore them. This kind of anger is constructive, guiding you to articulate what you need to feel safe again, whether that's transparency, honesty, or a commitment to rebuilding trust.

Anger can also be a powerful tool for open, honest communication. It often brings clarity to your true feelings, helping you express what's genuinely hurting you, rather than holding it in or minimizing it. This clarity gives you the courage to speak up, clearly communicating your needs, boundaries, and expectations. Instead of relying on passive or indirect communication, anger empowers you to be assertive, ensuring that your partner fully understands the depth of your hurt and what you need to heal. In this way, anger becomes a tool for authenticity, allowing you to communicate in a way that feels real, complete, and true to yourself.

In your journey to heal, anger can be an invaluable ally. It gives you the strength and motivation to confront what's painful and unfair about hiking Affair Mountain. Rather than allowing hurt and sadness to overwhelm you, anger fuels your resilience, helping you stand up for yourself. Anger offers an emotional release, allowing you to express and let go of intense feelings that might otherwise build up inside. When you approach anger with intention, it brings clarity to your needs and limits, guiding you toward decisions that align with your values. Embracing anger as part of your healing journey enables you to process your feelings fully, transforming pain into growth, self-respect, and a renewed sense of strength.

Beneath anger, there are often deeper, more vulnerable emotions—like sadness, hurt, fear, or disappointment. While anger may feel safer or easier to express, it can act as a protective layer, shielding you from these raw, often painful emotions. These deeper feelings tell a fuller story of your needs and fears. By taking time to explore what's beneath the anger, you can discover what you truly need for healing, whether it's reassurance, understanding, or validation. When we allow ourselves to acknowledge these underlying emotions, we can prevent anger from turning into resentment or bitterness and turn towards true healing instead.

Just as anger can help us, it can hurt us. Unchecked anger can turn into rage. Rage is an intense, uncontrolled form of anger that can easily lead to harmful behaviors. In moments of rage, you may find yourself discharging pain and discomfort in ways that hurt your partner—through name-calling, belittling, or shaming. This reaction can feel like a release, but often it's a way of avoiding your own deeper vulnerabilities and fears. Rage can serve as a defense mechanism, a way to protect yourself when you feel exposed or threatened. While it may provide a temporary sense of power or control, rage ultimately undermines genuine connection and understanding. By recognizing and processing your anger constructively, it can remain a positive force in your life, allowing you to grow and to connect with others.

With this thought in mind, I encourage you to be mindful about how you express your anger to your partner. I often tell hurt partners: "You are allowed to be angry, but you are not allowed to be mean." Sometimes, they will push back, saying, "Dr. Kathy, you expect me to be kind and compassionate to my cheating partner and never show my anger? That's wacky! My partner deserves to see my full fury!" I understand why you might feel that way, so let's talk about it a little further…

I absolutely want you to feel your anger and work through it—just not entirely with your partner. As we discussed in *The Courage to Stay*, your partner is also struggling. I picture you both underwater, each fighting to reach the surface. If you unleash your full fury on them, as justified as it may feel, it could push them further down, and they may "drown" in their own distress. In turn, they won't have enough emotional energy to offer you the comfort and reassurance you need to recover from the affair. So, I encourage you to process some of your anger on your own and talk through some with your partner. I know that it is not fair, I am sorry, I wish it was fairer. Unfortunately, this is one of those times in life where we have to tolerate a bit of unfairness to get the results we want. And when you do talk to your partner about your anger, focus on sharing your feelings and how their behavior has affected you, rather than engaging in name-calling or character attacks.

You may have been taught that you should just push your anger down and ignore your feelings of anger. I encourage you *not* to do this. Instead of burying your anger or pretending it doesn't exist, it's important to express it in healthy, productive ways. Research shows that learning how to manage anger is a crucial part of recovering from an affair. When left unchecked, anger can lead to destructive communication and slow down the affair recovery process (Snyder, Baucom, & Gordon, 2007). To help you do this, let's discuss four healthy ways to express and process your anger now.

The Empty Chair Exercise – Go into an unoccupied room in your home where there is an empty chair. Close the door behind you, ensure that you have privacy and that no one can hear you (we don't want to scare any kids or cats). Pretend that the person you are angry with – your partner, the AP, the friend who did not tell you about the AP – is sitting in the chair. Then allow yourself to yell, scream, curse, and say anything and everything you'd like to the chair. Throw a pillow at the chair if you'd like, shake the chair if you want (try not to destroy the chair). Completely and totally vent all of your anger out onto the chair!

Write A Mean Letter – Sit down with a pad of paper and a pen and write the meanest, nastiest note you can to the person who hurt you. It can be directed to your partner, your neighbor, the AP, your boss, or anyone you are angry with. Say exactly what you want, however you want to say it, and just pour all of that anger out onto the page. When you're done, destroy the letter or store it in a secure location. Do NOT give the letter to anyone, this is just an exercise to express your feelings.

Physical Task and Venting – Choose a hard physical task to do. It can be push-ups, lifting weights, running, chopping wood, scrubbing a bathtub, carrying heavy boxes, a cycling class, or anything that is physically challenging. While you are doing this physical work, start venting out your feelings. Say what you want, how you want, really let yourself rant and get it all out! Completely expressing yourself will help you feel better.

Talking to Your Partner – Schedule a time to have a chat with your partner about your anger. Tell your partner that you would like them to listen to your feelings, validate the feelings they hear you expressing, and then reassure you about those feelings. Then share more about what you are angry about and why. Please focus on your feelings and how your partner's behavior contributed to those feelings, avoid demonizing your partner, degrading them, or criticizing their character.

After you are done with one of these techniques, I'd like you to do something very soothing to help your body calm down. You can take a nap, go for a slow walk in nature, take a bath, listen to soothing music, get a massage, give yourself a facial, rock in a rocking chair, do a breathing exercise, put an ice pack on the back of your neck, or anything that soothes you.

I also would like you to validate your own feelings. Sometimes we criticize ourselves and beat ourselves up for struggling and not doing as well as we think we should be doing. If you're having a bad day, you might be tempted to tell yourself, "This is ridiculous, D-Day was 6 months ago, I should be doing better by now, I'm really overreacting." Instead of talking to yourself like this, please validate your feelings the way a very compassionate, loving parent would. Say to yourself, "Of course you feel this way, you have been through a big trauma, it completely makes sense that you are struggling and having a hard time, everything you're feeling makes so much sense." You will find yourself managing your anger (and all other feelings) so much better if you validate yourself instead of fighting with yourself.

Now, with these things in mind, let's explore some of your anger a little more deeply. Take as many breaks as you need as you work through these prompts and if you find yourself getting overwhelmed, stop and go do something relaxing. Remember that there is a list of 50 ways to soothe your nervous system at the back of this book. You do not need to force yourself to speed through this, there is no speed prize for answering these prompts. Take your time and when you're ready, pick out a few things to share with your partner. Please ask for what you need to feel better. I'm proud of you!

Journal Prompt 1:

Write in detail about a recent moment when you felt intense anger at your partner. What triggered it? How did your body react? What thoughts were running through your mind? If you knew you could say anything to your partner – and there would be no consequences – what do you wish you could say?

"It has almost destroyed me, my heart, my spirit. It's a brutal journey and lesson. 8 months post D Day. Still often angry, in disbelief, disgusted, shocked, sick. But making progress and staying curious about how I can improve, grow, and forgive." -Jeremy

Journal Prompt 2:

Which emotions do you think might be hiding beneath your anger at your partner? Are you feeling sadness, fear, hurt, or something else? To explore this, ask yourself: "So what? What does this mean to me?" How do these emotions show up in your daily life?

"It gives me hope hearing others that are going through the same thing. Knowing I'm not alone helps me feel less stupid about this going on right under my nose." -PJ

Journal Prompt 3:

Write in detail about a recent moment when you felt intense anger at the affair partner. What triggered it? How did your body react? What thoughts were running through your mind? If you could say anything to the AP – and knew that there would be no consequences – what would you say? (If there was no one specific AP, please write about your anger about the situation and circumstances.)

"My hope is that he will continue to do the work on himself and us. Consistency is the key. He never deviates from our newfound marriage. I can only take one day at a time and pray he never does it again." -CB

Journal Prompt 4:

Write about any anger you feel towards yourself. Are you angry that you did not trust your instincts before? That you believed your partner when they were lying to you? That you didn't figure things out sooner and dismissed some red flags? That you're considering staying? Say more about your feelings. *(Please be compassionate to yourself. Most of the time, red flags only look red in the rearview mirror, when we were going through them, they looked yellow! You gave your partner the benefit of the doubt, which was a completely appropriate thing to do.)*

"At some point I realized the affair was not much different than drinking or any other coping mechanism. Just a distraction and a symptom of not facing life." -Dazy

Journal Prompt 5:

Many betrayed partners feel like something precious has been stolen from them. They once had a clear picture of their relationship and dreams for the future, which were destroyed by the betrayal. Write about the anger you feel from losing these pictures and dreams. How has this loss affected you emotionally, physically, and in your daily life? *(Imagine that I'm sitting next to you, giving you a big hug, as you write this.)*

THE COURAGE TO STAY JOURNAL

"There's a lot to what unfolded, but we're making sense of it together. Love is an action, not a feeling. My husband's two-month affair with a stranger doesn't erase the almost two decades of loyalty, love, joy, and partnership." -Lindsay

KATHY NICKERSON, Ph.D.

Teena's Story

In September 2021, I found deleted messages on my husband's phone that confirmed my suspicions. He had an affair with someone we knew back in 2015-2016, and now he was trying to reconnect with her. After seeing her at a party, he became obsessed, like an addict craving a fix. While I was away visiting our daughter, he spent four days trying to meet her again, and they finally connected one night at her house. But when he arrived, she stopped him, saying, "You have a beautiful wife and family—why are you here?" He says that was his wake-up call, and he left, overwhelmed by shame. Two weeks later, I discovered everything, and our world was shattered.

The anger I felt was unlike anything I'd ever experienced. It wasn't just about the betrayal; it felt like every old hurt and unresolved trauma surfaced all at once. I was furious—with him, with her, and with myself for not seeing things more clearly. I slipped into a state of rage and despair, constantly replaying the details he shared with me. It was torture. I fought with him while he was in the fog of the affair, and I heard things that I should never have had to hear. It felt like my anger was burning me alive.

At first, therapy didn't help. I was too angry to make progress, and the more I dug, the more pain I found. But eventually, I connected with a therapist who specialized in betrayal trauma. She made me realize that my anger wasn't just about the affair—it was tied to deeper wounds, unresolved traumas from my past. The affair was the trigger that brought everything to the surface. The anger wasn't just about him; it was about my own pain that I had buried for years.

As I began to understand my husband's actions, the anger shifted. I saw that his affair had more to do with his unresolved childhood trauma and his constant need for validation. He had spent our marriage seeking external approval, and the affair fed that need. I was angry at the years he spent in this limerence, while I suffered in silence. He was addicted to the attention she gave him, and I could see how she manipulated him. She knew exactly what she was doing, and that only made my anger toward her even stronger.

Over time, though, I started to let go of some of that anger. I realized that I didn't have to carry the weight of his affair—it was his burden to bear. I began focusing on my own healing and self-care. It wasn't easy, but I knew that managing my anger was key to moving forward. I had to let go of the idea that this was something I could control or fix for him.

Today, we are both in different places. He has worked hard to heal, and I can see that he no longer seeks external validation. He communicates more openly and is vulnerable in ways he never was before. I can talk to him about anything now, and he listens. As for me, I've learned to manage my anger and not let it define me. I've handed the pain of his actions back to him, and I'm focusing on my own recovery.

There are still moments when I feel triggered or angry, but those episodes are shorter and less intense now. I've come to understand that healing is a long journey, and anger is part of that process. I'm still in therapy, and my husband attends men's groups that have been incredibly helpful for him. We've both learned so much, and while I don't know what the future holds for our marriage, I do know that I've come a long way in healing the anger that once consumed me.

Journal Prompt 6:

What did you learn from your family and your parents about anger? How did they handle conflict? How did you learn to behave in order to keep yourself safe during conflict? How did you respond to your parents' anger? How did each of these things connect to how you are feeling and coping now?

"We're 4 months from D-Day. We can now talk about it more openly and he is genuinely putting in the work, day in and out, without being asked! I had to get past all of my emotions to understand any of it. We both had changes to make for it to work." -Lorena

Journal Prompt 7:

Think back to a time when you felt similarly betrayed or deeply hurt. How did you react in that moment? What emotions surfaced, and how did you respond to them? Reflect on how that experience impacted you—did it change the way you view yourself, others, or relationships? Now consider how you coped with that pain. What strategies, healthy or unhealthy, did you use to get through it?

"For me personally, it's about trying to always show up as the person I want to be, even if it's not the person my inner anger wants me to be. It's extremely difficult. -MM

Journal Prompt 8:

Earlier in the chapter, I presented four healthy ways to express and process your anger. Choose one of the following ways and give it a try: The empty chair exercise, writing a mean letter, doing a physical task and venting, or talking to your partner. Before starting, take a moment to notice how you're feeling. As you go through the exercise, what emotions surface for you? Afterward, reflect on how your feelings have shifted. What did this experience teach you about expressing your anger in a healthy way? How might this exercise be useful for you in the future?

"Bottom line is I'm hurt and want her to understand how hurt I am. I felt that being harsh, degrading, and constantly bringing it up somehow would provide me relief and it didn't. It made it 10x worse. Trying to be kind and understanding has really helped her to be truthful and remorseful." -JM

Journal Prompt 9:

During my own affair recovery journey, a quote that deeply resonated with me was: *"I sat with my anger long enough until she told me her real name was grief."* Take a moment to reflect on this idea. What comes up for you when you think about this? How might your own anger be a way of shielding or expressing deeper feelings of sadness, loss, or disappointment? What might you be grieving?

"Eight years later and he's still open to talking about it. We talked today!! I laid down some serious boundaries and he has not crossed a single one. Healing can happen!!" -Anonymous

Journal Prompt 10:

Reflecting on everything you've read, thought about, and written during this chapter, how have your thoughts and feelings changed? What stands out as the most important lesson or understanding that you've gained? What are a few specific things you can do when you feel angry again? What is something that your partner can do to help you manage your anger?

_____
_____
_____
_____
_____
_____
_____
_____
_____
_____
_____
_____
_____
_____
_____

"I completely agree that affairs can create healthier relationships. This was exactly what my husband and I went through. We are so much better now 2 yrs after his affair." -Geno

Chapter Six

Taming Your Triggers & Fears

After you have been through something traumatic, it's completely understandable that you would be afraid and few things are more traumatic than discovering that your partner has strayed. I imagine that you're afraid that it will happen again, afraid that it's not really over, afraid that your partner does not love you, afraid that you'll never be able to get back to how things used to be, and maybe afraid that you'll never recover. All of these fears make sense and are thoughts that most of us confront on our journey over Affair Mountain.

One of the most common fears hurt partners struggle with is the fear of being hurt again. You might find yourself doubting your partner's intentions, questioning whether the relationship is truly safe, and wondering if you should allow yourself to be vulnerable again. The fear of another affair occurring is well-documented by research (Gordon, Baucom, & Snyder, 2004), and it makes sense that you would struggle with whether you can trust your partner or not. Many betrayed partners also struggle with the thought of being replaceable and doubting the sincerity of their partner's words and actions. Questions like, "Is my partner staying because they truly love me, or just because it's easier?" are common, making it difficult to rebuild the connection you once had. Please know that all of these fears are reasonable and normal.

As scary as all of these thoughts are, fear is an essential survival tool, helping us detect and avoid potential danger. Fear is your mind's way of signaling that something significant has happened, danger is still present, and that caution is needed. When we feel fear, our bodies enter a state of heightened awareness—commonly known as the "fight-or-flight" response—so that we can either confront the threat or escape from it. This response increases our chances of survival, as it readies us to act quickly in the face of real or perceived danger. After an affair, fear tells us that something has gone terribly wrong and that there is a need for caution and self-protection.

Fear is also a way of trying to prevent future pain. By anticipating threats—such as the affair partner attempting to communicate with your partner or your spouse straying again—we are subconsciously working to shield ourselves from further pain. While this heightened alertness can feel like self-protection, it can also become exhausting and lead to defensive behaviors that hinder our ability to connect with our partners.

Fear can also trap you in a cycle of self-protection that prevents healing. Fear doesn't just disappear; it often transforms into anxiety, which is more constant and long-lasting. Anxiety leaves you feeling constantly on guard, as if you must protect yourself from being blindsided again. Research has shown that anxiety after infidelity is often linked to hypervigilance, where betrayed partners remain on high alert, scanning for signs of further betrayal (McNulty, 2012). You might find yourself wondering how you didn't see the signs of the affair earlier, or whether you'll see them if it happens again. This can lead to resisting reconnection, as you attempt to rebuild the relationship while also staying "on guard."

Many betrayed partners report struggling with fear, anxiety, intrusive thoughts, nightmares, flashbacks, rumination, and compulsive behaviors after discovering their partner's affair. Research has shown that betrayal by a spouse or partner can lead to trauma responses similar to those seen in post-traumatic stress disorder (PTSD). Jennifer Freyd was the first to recognize betrayal trauma and identify these symptoms (Freyd, 1996). She found that betrayal trauma arises when there is a conflict between acknowledging the betrayal and the need to stay connected to the betrayer. Her work found that this type of trauma can lead to a range of PTSD-like symptoms, including intrusive thoughts, hypervigilance, emotional numbness, and avoidance of triggers that bring up the betrayal. When a trusted partner has broken that trust, the emotional aftermath can feel destabilizing and even surreal, as if your body and mind are on constant alert.

Several studies have expanded on Freyd's work, confirming the intensity of betrayal-related trauma. Research by Gordon, Baucom, & Snyder (2004) found that betrayed partners often face flashbacks, hypervigilance, and a need to avoid reminders of the betrayal, all of which contribute to ongoing emotional distress. Ortman (2009) was the first to use the term post infidelity stress disorder when he reported that many betrayed partners had trauma symptoms that disrupted daily life, including sleep disturbances and nightmares. Recent research by Roos and colleagues (2021) further confirmed that betrayal deeply impacts core beliefs, evoking sadness, anger, and avoidance.

I share all of this so that you will know that if you are struggling with these thoughts and feelings, and things do not feel like they are getting better, that you are not broken, you are injured. It is not your fault that you are struggling with these feelings, nearly all betrayed partners do. In fact, our research found that 93% of hurt partners felt they had post infidelity stress disorder (Nickerson et al., 2023). So while we focus on fear and triggers in this chapter, please reach out for further care to help you if you feel you could be struggling from PISD. At the end of this book, you will find a list of excellent trauma recovery books, along with some sites to connect with a trauma informed therapist, to help you continue to heal.

Now, let's discuss a few ways to cope with fear and anxiety…

1. Slow down and soothe yourself. When you are very upset, the first thing to do is notice this, then intentionally do something to slow down and soothe yourself. I recommend you stop whatever you are doing, find a cozy place to sit down, give yourself a hug, and rock back and forth for a couple of minutes. It sounds a little goofy, but doing this will allow you to catch your breath and come back to yourself. You can do anything you like that helps you slow down and soothe, including a walk outside, a bath, a nap, or even a good cry.

2. Try the 5-4-3-2-1 Method. When we are spinning, it helps to slow our thoughts down and focus on the here and now. You can anchor yourself in the present moment by identifying five things you can see, four things you can feel, three things you can hear, two things you can smell, and one thing you can taste. Whenever you feel overwhelmed, try to slow down and think of these things to bring you back to the current moment you're in.

3. Progressive Muscle Relaxation. When you're triggered, your body often responds with a fight, flight, or freeze reaction, which heightens anxiety and fear. To cope with anxiety and fear more effectively, you need to help your body release the tension. Progressive muscle relaxation (PMR) is a great way to do this. To do PMR, tense a muscle group for a few seconds and then release it, moving from your toes up to your head. Start by crinkling up all of the muscles in your feet and holding the tension for 10 seconds, then release and relax. As you release the tension, focus on the sensation of relaxation spreading through your feet. Continue to your calves, knees, thighs and each part of your body. You can find lots of sample videos of this technique online.

4. Ask the Magic 4 Questions. To work through a distressing thought, try asking and answering these four questions: (1) Is this scary thought true? (2) Is it absolutely, 100%, beyond a shadow of a doubt true? (3) Could anything else be true instead? (4) What can I choose to believe right now that will help me feel better? These questions can help you challenge your anxious thoughts and find some relief.

5. Box Breathing and Ice. If you're really struggling and starting to feel out of control, please try this technique. Grab a bag of ice, wrap it in a tea towel and place it at the back of your neck. Hold it there with one hand and relax your body. Then focus on breathing in for 4 seconds, holding your breath for 4 seconds, breathing out for 4 seconds, and holding for 4 seconds. Imagine yourself going around the edges of a box (or walking the bases of a baseball diamond) as you're doing this. If it feels too hard do this, modify it by doing 3 seconds for each step, or just focus on breathing in and out slowly.

6. Cognitive Shuffling. This technique is especially helpful if you're struggling to fall asleep or want to quickly distract your mind. Essentially, it's a simple word game you play with yourself to redirect your thoughts. Start by thinking of a word—any word. Let's say you choose "chocolate." Now, think of another word that starts with the last letter of "chocolate." The last letter is E, so we might think of "elephant." Next, take the last letter of that word—T—and think of another random word, e.g., "tomatoes." And on you go, creating a chain of random words. This process works by blocking distressing thoughts and gently guiding your mind away from worries. Cognitive shuffling relaxes the brain and helps you calm your racing thoughts, making it easier to drift into a peaceful state.

As you are struggling with fear and anxiety, you are probably also struggling with triggers. A trigger is anything—such as a specific place, situation, word, image, sound, or memory—that evokes a strong emotional response. Triggers after betrayal are extremely common, with many partners reporting being triggered by their partner's phone, the sound of a text message, or specific locations associated with the affair. External triggers might include anniversaries, photos, or songs that remind you of the affair partner. If you are triggered by any of these things, know that you are not "crazy"—these feelings are completely understandable. Triggers remind you of the betrayal in ways that feel sudden and painful, and they can derail your mood (and your day) in an instant.

While triggers are upsetting and disruptive they also serve a purpose. They show you where healing is still needed. You might feel like you should just shut your eyes, shake your head, and pretend the trigger isn't happening. I get that, and sometimes, if you need to, you should do that. Other times, I'd like you to lean into the trigger and try to process it and what it means.

To process a trigger, I'd like you to get into a safe place, take a moment to calm and soothe yourself, then ask yourself these questions:

- What about this trigger is really bothering me?
- What does this mean to me?
- What is the significance of this?

- Why does this matter so much to me?
- What else could this be connected to?

We are essentially trying to find the root of the trigger. When you understand the root of a trigger, it becomes easier to work through. When you find the root, allow yourself to feel your emotions, rather than suppressing them. Self-compassion is key here, be kind to yourself as you navigate these difficult feelings. Acknowledge that these emotions, while intense, are temporary and part of your healing process.

After you've identified the root of a trigger, try to find a way to reframe or "spin" the story into something that feels more positive and is also true. For example, you might be very triggered when you drive by the AP's house. When you've seen the house in the past, you've had a strong reaction and thought, something like, "That's where my husband threw away our marriage vows." Take some time to work through that thought and see if you can get to the root fear, which might be, "I am afraid our vows are meaningless, and he will do this again." Now try to reframe that thought into something that is more positive and still seems true to you. For example: "He did forsake our vows for a while at that house, but that house does not have power. It only has the power I give it, and I am not giving it any more power or value. I am going to value my husband's efforts to change way more than that darn house." Please use any positive reframe that works for you.

Remember that you don't have to face your triggers alone—ask your partner for reassurance when needed, join a support group where you can talk about your triggers, and reach out to a trusted friend for encouragement when you're struggling.

Please also keep reminding yourself that healing from infidelity is not a linear journey, and it's normal to have setbacks. It's ok for you to struggle, just keep trying. With patience, self-compassion, and by actively challenging your negative thoughts, you will find that fear, anxiety, and triggers lose their intensity over time. Your partner's behavior also plays a crucial role—when they demonstrate consistent empathy, genuine remorse, and ongoing change, your ability to heal and rebuild trust will grow. In the meantime, remember that every step you take toward understanding and processing these emotions brings you closer to peace. You really will get there—keep going.

Now, let's take some time to explore your specific fears, triggers, and anxious thoughts. As you respond to each journal prompt, allow yourself to reflect deeply and take as much time as you need to work through each question. At the end of the week, review your insights and consider sharing some of your thoughts with your partner. Ask for the reassurance you need and deserve to continue healing.

Journal Prompt 1:

How does fear affect you? What are your earliest signs of anxiety, and how do you typically respond? What are some techniques that help you soothe yourself when you feel anxious or triggered? What plan can you make for the next time you experience a big wave of fear, anxiety, or a strong trigger?

_____
_____
_____
_____
_____
_____
_____
_____
_____
_____
_____
_____
_____
_____
_____

THE COURAGE TO STAY JOURNAL

"Having my partner willingly talk whenever I need to talk has been the biggest part of healing our relationship and rebuilding trust. Because of this, my need to talk about the affair keeps lessening." -Jodi

Journal Prompt 2:

Reflect on your fears of being replaced or not being enough. What are the underlying thoughts and beliefs that fuel this fear? What evidence is there to support or refute these thoughts? Please ask your partner for reassurance about these thoughts.

"My trust was shattered by the affair. When I saw a picture of Japanese kintsugi pottery, I got inspired and thought, we could be like that… a broken bowl that is glued back together with gold. I posted a kintsugi picture on my Instagram on our anniversary. I feel we will be stronger and better." -Lara

Journal Prompt 3:

Reflect on the fear of another affair happening or the possibility of continued contact with the affair partner. What thoughts and feelings come up for you when you think about this? How has this fear impacted your ability to trust and feel safe in the relationship? What evidence do you have that supports or challenges this fear? What reassurance or actions from your partner would help you feel more secure?

"It's been 9 or 10 months since D-day and we are healing. Not 100% yet but getting there. Although there isn't a day I don't think about his affair, we are on the path." -Coreen

Journal Prompt 4:

Write about any doubts you have regarding your partner's honesty and intentions. How do these doubts influence your interactions? In what ways have you noticed yourself becoming guarded in communication with your partner? How does this impact your connection? How can you talk to your partner about this?

"I thought I would be stuck forever. I'm 1 year from D-day and we've come a long way. Wasn't easy, but we've been pushing through." -Victoria

Journal Prompt 5:

What are some common triggers you've noticed? How do these triggers make you feel? What memories or emotions do they bring up? What did you do in response? How can your partner help you with these triggers?

___
___
___
___
___
___
___
___
___
___
___
___
___
___
___
___
___
___

"I felt less than for a while. It's been almost a year. We are both better than the poor choices she made. It can be overcome if both want it. I actually feel bad for her, not for myself. A lot of people, even myself, get stuck being a victim instead of a survivor. We are both more resilient and closer than ever. Don't let it define who you are." -Jake

KATHY NICKERSON, Ph.D.

Samantha's Story

My husband and I have been married for 19 years and have two children. Our marriage was steady until last December, when everything changed. He began texting and calling a coworker daily, and over time, they became close friends—what I later discovered were thousands of messages and hours on the phone.

At first, I tried to rationalize it, knowing he was still deeply grieving his mother's passing from cancer in her 50s. Our eldest had just left for college, and he was about to turn 40. It seemed like a perfect storm of emotional vulnerability, and he turned to his coworker for comfort. She was also married, with two small children, and 10 years younger, which only compounded my feelings of insecurity and hurt. I had met her before, even knew her husband—it felt like a double betrayal.

Initially, it was just emotional—texting, talking, supporting each other. They kissed a few times after work and swore to stop, but they couldn't let go of the outlet they had created for themselves. When I went to pick up our daughter from college in May, they took things further. They met for breakfast before a work function, went out for drinks with coworkers, and stayed behind after everyone left. That's when it happened—they had sex in the car, in a parking lot. The next week, they decided to end the relationship. He confessed to me just one week later. It was the most excruciating day of my life. The pain hit me like a tidal wave; it was so overwhelming that I couldn't see straight.

Fear and anxiety became my constant companions after that. I thought I knew my limits—cheating had always been my line in the sand. But when faced with the reality, I found myself in a state of disbelief, as if everything I had believed about us, about him, had suddenly crumbled. I asked him to leave that day, but hours later, I called him back. Somehow, even through the immense pain, I felt that we could find a way through this. That decision to stay was just the beginning of a long and difficult journey.

The fear didn't leave me, though. In fact, it only grew. I was terrified that it might happen again. Every time his phone rang or he was late coming home, my heart would race, and I'd find myself checking the call logs, wondering if he was still in contact with her. I felt constantly on edge, always alert, scanning for signs of another betrayal. This anxiety felt all-consuming—my mind kept replaying the images of them together, wondering what I missed, what red flags I didn't see. I was terrified of being blindsided again.

A month after the confession, I looked up the call records and discovered that he hadn't told me the full truth. He had been withholding details to "protect my feelings." That revelation sent me spiraling. The fear I had been trying to suppress exploded, confirming my worst suspicions that there were more lies. He had still been in contact with her, even after they'd agreed to end the affair. The feeling of betrayal resurfaced in full force, and I wasn't sure if I could trust him ever again.

Triggers were everywhere—simple things like his phone lighting up or seeing a car that resembled hers would send me into a panic. I couldn't predict when these emotional flashbacks would hit, and they left me feeling powerless and overwhelmed. I would find myself reliving the betrayal, going over every detail in my mind, searching for answers that never came. It felt like my world had been turned upside down, and I was constantly bracing for more pain.

In that moment, though, something changed. He left his job immediately and committed to therapy, not just for himself but for us. He started seeing a counselor, went back to school to finish the degree he had always wanted, and took a job with better hours so he could be home with me more. We began to take steps toward healing, slowly at first—trips together, long conversations, rebuilding the connection we had once lost.

But it wasn't easy. There were days when the fear and anxiety still felt insurmountable, when the triggers would pull me back into the depths of pain. However, I've come to understand that fear and anxiety are natural responses to trauma. They serve as reminders of what has happened, yes, but they also guide us toward the places where we need to heal. With time, and through both of our efforts, I'm beginning to see that fear doesn't have to define the future of our relationship. The trust isn't fully rebuilt, and some days are harder than others, but there is a light now—faint, but it's there. I can see a future for us, one that includes the hard work we've put in, the pain we've faced, and, hopefully, the strength we'll find on the other side.

Journal Prompt 6:

Recall a recent time when you were triggered. Describe the situation that triggered you. With this situation in mind, ask yourself the four questions mentioned in the introduction to this chapter:

1. Is this scary thought true?

2. Is it absolutely, 100% beyond a shadow of a doubt true?

3. Could anything else be true instead?

4. What do you choose to believe instead?

(Please come back to this page and repeat this exercise whenever you want to journal about a trigger.)

_____

_____

_____

_____

_____

_____

_____

_____

_____

_____

"I am focusing on all of the good things that have come out of this nightmare, for both of us. It's truly a new beginning." -Valerie

Journal Prompt 7:

Think about your most painful trigger (sorry to ask you to do this, I know it hurts). Please write about it below, say as much as you can about it. Then ask yourself the magic 4 questions. How do these questions shift your perspective? What can you choose to believe instead?

_____
_____
_____
_____
_____
_____
_____
_____
_____
_____
_____
_____
_____
_____

"I stayed, we have grown children, and I make my own money. We have 31 years together and I know we love one another. We did the work and our marriage is better than ever. And I do not fear him cheating again." -Anonymous

Journal Prompt 8:

How can you show yourself kindness and compassion as you navigate fear, anxiety, and triggers that come up? What would you say to a friend who was going through the same struggle? What kind of reassurance do you need from your partner when you feel triggered? How can you ask for this?

(Please take a moment to find a quote or a mantra that comforts you when you're struggling. Write this on a sticky note and keep it nearby.)

_____

_____

_____

_____

_____

_____

_____

_____

_____

_____

_____

_____

_____

"When we got to the roots of his "reasons" for the affair, it broke my heart all over again and helped me understand logically. Emotionally I'm still a wreck, but we are working through it. Understanding why he did it made a big difference for me." -Britt

Journal Prompt 9:

Think about your most painful trigger (sorry to ask you to do this, I know it hurts). Please write about it below, say as much as you can about it. Then ask yourself: What about this trigger is really bothering me? What does this mean to me? What is the significance of this? Why does this matter so much to me? What else could this be connected to? Is there some reassurance that your partner can offer you that will help?

"I stayed. 18 months later we are stronger than ever, but it's been a long hard road" -Sandi

Journal Prompt 10:

Reflecting on everything you've read, thought about, and written during this chapter, how have your thoughts and feelings shifted? Write about any new insights or realizations you've had. What stands out as the most important lesson or understanding that you've gained? What will you take with you as you continue to heal?

"If you're worried about your anniversary date of D-Day, you can take control of how you choose to mark the day. I take the day off work and I give a gift card for brand new walking shoes for my previous marriage counselor to give anonymously to another betrayed spouse with a note to "keep moving forward" and "feel all other betrayed spouses in the world cheering for you as you do." Then I spend the day doing something that brings me joy. I don't fear the day. I look forward to it and have done this for 7 years now." -Ann

Chapter Seven

Overcoming Obsessive & Intrusive Thoughts

As you continue hiking Affair Mountain, you probably find yourself plagued by upsetting intrusive thoughts, obsessive thinking, and rumination. If you're dealing with these thoughts, please know you're not going "crazy"—you are injured. In fact, when we asked thousands of betrayed partners about their experience, 97% reported struggling with intrusive thoughts. As overwhelming and distressing as they are, these thoughts are a normal part of the healing process. Understanding the differences between them, why they happen, and how to manage them is essential for your recovery.

Intrusive thoughts are spontaneous, unwelcome thoughts or images that suddenly pop into your mind, often provoking discomfort or anxiety. Intrusive thoughts are typically random, fleeting, and might not recur unless a specific trigger brings them back. They're usually distressing because they feel out of place or contrary to what you want to think about. Sometimes you will be able to shake off or dismiss an intrusive thought, sometimes these thoughts will send you on a downward spiral. Left unchecked, they can prolong your suffering and significantly hinder your and your relationship's healing process.

You may be struck by a range of intrusive thoughts that surface suddenly and often feel overwhelming. Vivid, unwanted images of your partner with the other person might flash through your mind, each one hitting you with a surge of pain. Self-doubt may creep in, making you question your worthiness and your role in the relationship's past, as you wonder, "Did they ever truly love me?" or "Am I somehow responsible for this?" These thoughts can trigger waves of blame and erode your self-confidence. You might also experience sudden fears that chip away at your ability to trust, thinking, "Am I the only one who didn't know?" or "How long would this have continued if I hadn't found out?"

Such thoughts can make even ordinary moments feel unsafe. Flashbacks of conversations or clues from before D-day may replay, leaving you wondering if everything in the past was a lie. You might also find yourself worrying about how others view your situation, fearing thoughts like, "Do they think I deserved this?" or "Is everyone judging me for staying?" You may be consumed by sudden, paralyzing doubts about your future, ability to rebuild or feel whole again. Each of these thoughts can feel like reopening a wound, making it challenging to imagine a path forward.

The reason you are having intrusive thoughts is that your brain is trying to process the trauma you've experienced. After something as deeply painful as infidelity, your brain keeps circling back to the details, trying to make sense of the situation. Research by Horowitz (1976) supports this idea, suggesting that when we experience a traumatic event, our brain tends to process it through repetitive, unwanted thoughts. These thoughts are your brain's attempt to resolve the emotional and cognitive disconnect caused by the betrayal. Unfortunately, this process can become stuck, where the thoughts keep repeating, leaving you feeling trapped in a painful loop that makes you feel worse and worse!

Obsessive thoughts, on the other hand, are repetitive, persistent, and often feel unshakable. Obsessive thoughts are fear-based and often provoke intense anxiety and distress, leading to compulsive behaviors, like repeatedly checking your partner's phone or social media. However, this only creates a cycle where each intrusive thought triggers more anxiety, and actions meant to neutralize the anxiety offer only temporary relief. This cycle is mentally exhausting and can significantly interfere with daily life, as the obsessive thinking continues to fuel anxiety rather than resolve it.

As a betrayed partner, you might find yourself caught in obsessive cycles of comparison, analysis, and self-doubt. Thoughts about the affair partner may fill your mind, with questions like, "Am I as attractive, fun, or interesting as they are?" or "What did my partner see in them?" spiraling into repeated cycles of self-comparison and diminished self-worth. You may also find yourself closely scrutinizing your partner's every word and action, wondering, "Are they acting differently now?" or "Was that compliment genuine?" as you try to detect any signs of dishonesty. Repetitive questions may arise as you search for reasons, asking, "Why did they choose to hurt me?" or "How could they risk everything we built?"—but the answers often feel elusive. Fears of recurrence might fill your mind, like "Will they cheat again?" or "Are they still in contact with the other person?" driving a constant need for reassurance and perhaps even an urge to control where your partner goes and what they do. You might also replay moments, repeatedly wondering, "What signs did I miss?" or "How could I have not seen this?" as you search for clues you may have overlooked. And then, there are the rehearsed confrontations, past or imagined, where you find yourself going over conversations or confrontations with your partner or the affair partner, thinking about what you "should have" said or will say. These thoughts can feel relentless!

With obsessive thinking, your brain fixates on specific details—who, what, when, where, and why—and you might replay conversations or picture imaginary scenarios with the affair partner repeatedly. There's a constant need to know more, investigate more, and check more, as if gathering all the information could somehow give you control or make you feel safe again. However, this relentless pursuit of details often deepens the emotional pain rather than bringing answers. According to Glass and Wright (1997), repetitive questioning and searching for details is a way people try to make sense of betrayal, but it can feed the cycle of intrusive thoughts, making it even harder to move forward and recover.

Many betrayed partners also struggle with rumination. Rumination is like obsessive thinking, but different in a couple of important ways. Rumination tends to focus on the past and is linked to depression and self-blame, while obsessive thinking is more future- or fear-focused and connected to anxiety. Rumination is the act of continuously thinking about the same negative thoughts or events, often focusing on painful or unresolved experiences from the past. It involves going over and over a situation, trying to make sense of it or figure out what went wrong, yet never reaching a satisfying conclusion.

Common in those dealing with depression, trauma, and betrayal, rumination tends to focus on blame, feelings of inadequacy, and the haunting "what ifs" that make it hard to move forward. It's like being stuck in a mental loop, endlessly replaying past scenarios, searching for answers to questions like, "Why did this happen?" or "What happened on that day and what was he thinking?" This cycle of negative emotions, driven by sadness, regret, and helplessness, can deepen your emotional pain and worsen depressive feelings. The distress caused by rumination can disrupt your daily life, interfere with sleep, and make it difficult to concentrate on even the simplest tasks. According to Miller (2005), betrayed partners who experience frequent intrusive thoughts and rumination often struggle more in their emotional recovery from an affair.

Both obsessive thinking and rumination are understandable and expected responses to betrayal. Your brain is doing what it can to make sense of the hurt and protect you from further pain. It's trying to find some kind of control in the chaos, hoping that by focusing on the details or the emotional meaning, you might be able to protect yourself from being hurt again. But here's the thing: while these thought patterns are understandable and expected, they often end up backfiring. Obsessive thinking rarely brings clarity, and rumination seldom leads to healing. Instead, they keep you stuck in the pain, preventing you from processing and letting go.

It's important to recognize these thoughts for what they are—your brain's way of coping with something that feels impossible to understand. Healing doesn't come from staying stuck in these loops but from gradually letting go of the need to know every detail or resolve every emotion. While these thought patterns have a purpose, the benefit they provide is often not worth the cost. Intrusive thoughts, obsessive thinking, and rumination are very emotionally expensive – they drain your energy, mood, and confidence, all while offering very little benefit in return.

So, how do we stop these painful cycles? Let's talk about seven ways to break free from these thought traps now...

1. Reframing: Reframing means to consciously change the way you interpret or think about a situation, event, or belief, so you can see it from a more positive or balanced perspective. Reframing doesn't deny the reality of what happened but shifts the focus away from negative emotions and towards seeing things from a more neutral perspective. For example, if an intrusive thought centers around the fear that "I wasn't enough, and that's why they cheated," we could reframe it to something more neutral and fact-based, like "Their choice to cheat was made by them, I did not have a vote in it, and the choice is not necessarily a reflection on me."

2. Thought Stopping: In this technique, you literally tell yourself "stop" when an intrusive thought begins. This interrupts the cycle of negative thinking and can help you reduce the frequency of these thoughts. I imagine my brain as a committee of people and every once in a while, a very disruptive member of the committee likes to stand up and start yelling unhelpful things at me. So I practice thought stopping by saying to my brain "Hey, that is not helpful right now, please sit down!" This makes me laugh and quiets the thought.

3. Body Scan with Breathing: The body scan technique begins by taking deep breaths to center yourself. You start with your feet, noticing any feelings or sensations, and releasing tension as you exhale. Then, you gradually shift your focus upward, moving through your legs, torso, and arms, relaxing each area as you go. Continue to your neck, shoulders, and face, breathing out any tension you feel. Finally, take one last deep breath to relax your entire body and finish feeling grounded and calm.

4. Distraction: When obsessive thoughts become overwhelming, it is absolutely ok to distract yourself and do something pleasurable. Engaging in an activity you enjoy can break the obsessive cycle. Taking a walk, calling a friend, doing a craft, watching a movie, reading a book, playing a game, or cooking something delicious, can give your brain a break from the relentless cycle of obsessive thinking. Do whatever brings you joy or creates a feeling of calm and peace.

5. Safe Place Visualization: Creating a mental "safe place" where you can go when intrusive thoughts arise can help soothe your mind. Visualizing a calm, peaceful environment can shift your mental focus away from distress. Picture your favorite vacation spot, imagine yourself walking to that spot, savoring a moment in that place, and truly, deeply relaxing.

6. Cold Water Splash: If you're having a particularly hard time breaking out of a destructive thought pattern, try a cold water splash. Splashing cold water on your face, or submerging your face into a bowl of ice water, activates the "diving reflex," which slows your heart rate and promotes relaxation. This can reduce panic symptoms and bring a sense of immediate relief.

7. Humming: One of my favorite ways to rapidly shift my thoughts and get out of rumination or obsession is to hum. I particularly benefit from humming Christmas music because that music reminds me of happy memories and it tends to be upbeat. You can hum anything you like and I encourage you to do this for about 5 minutes. Humming a specific song makes it much harder to think obsessively because it occupies both your auditory and cognitive processing systems. When you hum a melody, your brain is focused on recalling the rhythm and tune, making it nearly impossible to hum and obsess at the same time. I bet you'll be surprised by how well humming works!

When we asked betrayed partners what helped them recover from intrusive thoughts, obsessive thinking, and rumination, they said these activities (listed in order) were the most helpful to them: talking to friends and family, individual therapy, watching social media videos to gain understanding, talking to their partner, self-help books, exercise, being in nature, prayer, journaling, hobbies, reading, breathing exercises, meditation, and support groups. Please challenge yourself to experiment with several of these strategies so you can find the right combination for yourself.

If you've tried a variety of things to make these thoughts better and you're still struggling with intrusive thoughts, obsessive thoughts, or rumination, it's important to remember that you've gone through a significant trauma. Some of us become so injured by the trauma, through no fault of our own, that we struggle to recover. If this is happening to you, you are not to blame! Please seek support from a therapist who specializes in trauma to learn about additional methods for healing yourself. Trauma therapists can teach you about EMDR (eye movement desensitization and reprocessing), somatic healing, neurolinguistic programming, and a variety of other techniques that should help. Many people also get significant relief by trying anti-anxiety and anti-depression medications.

Above all, please be gentle with yourself. Healing from infidelity is an individual process, and it's different for everyone. Don't pressure yourself to heal faster or be like everyone else. This is your journey, it's okay to do it your way! Just take it one step at a time. Remind yourself that your thoughts, while upsetting, do not define you or your ability to recover. With time, patience, and support, you can move through this pain and recover. I am in your corner, cheering you on every step of the way!

Journal Prompt 1:

Which intrusive thoughts have you been struggling with lately? When do these thoughts pop up for you? What specific situations seem to trigger intrusive thoughts? How can you reframe one of the intrusive thoughts into something less negative?

THE COURAGE TO STAY JOURNAL

"I love the facts you give us, sometimes my brain can understand, but it just takes time for my heart to heal." -Jennifer

Journal Prompt 2:

What affair related details or thoughts do you find yourself obsessing over? What underlying emotions or fears might be driving these thoughts? How can you reassure yourself about these fears? What can your partner do to help you feel better?

"I feel like I've mostly healed. I've moved on, but man, I still get triggered at times. Eight years later." -Sue

Journal Prompt 3:

What specific scenarios do you find yourself ruminating on the most? How does this make you feel in the moment? What purpose do you think rumination serves—seeking understanding, protection, or something else? How do you think it's hindering or helping your healing process? Please try humming your favorite song now and make a note about how it affects you.

"We traveled for spring break and I was forced to lay off the betrayal talk. I didn't think I could. But it ended up being very much what I needed to pull me up from the deep, deep acute shock." -
LAH

Journal Prompt 4:

Nearly all betrayed partners have unwanted, intrusive thoughts that overwhelm them. Think of a recent moment when an intrusive thought overwhelmed you. What was the thought? What was that thought trying to prevent, protect you from or help you avoid? Were you asking yourself an unanswerable question? How did you cope in the moment? Which one of the coping strategies mentioned in the introduction could you try next time you're overwhelmed?

_____
_____
_____
_____
_____
_____
_____
_____
_____
_____
_____
_____
_____
_____
_____

"It's been 4 months since d-day. I was feeling that it would be impossible, but things are getting better. I decided to start exercising and we decided to do it together. It's helping a lot and we are feeling closer and hopeful." -Lara

Journal Prompt 5:

How do your obsessive thoughts affect your relationships with your partner? How do they affect your communication? What patterns or behaviors have you noticed? Thinking about it now, what's one coping thought you can use next time you are struggling with one of these thought spirals?

"I decided that what has been done isn't going to change me or keep me in the rut of depression. I pictured a red stop sign to help." -DanZ

DD's Story

A little over a year ago, I found the proof I needed to confront my wife. I had suspected for months that she was hiding something, and finally I had the undeniable evidence. The moment she confessed to having an affair, my world collapsed. Rage, sadness, and disbelief surged through me all at once. It felt like everything I knew, everything we had built, shattered in an instant. My heart was broken, my mind spinning out of control.

In the days that followed, I made the decision to stay. We had four children, a home, and what I thought was a great marriage. But as I began replaying the past few years over and over in my mind, I realized that there had been cracks all along. I hadn't been the husband I should have been. I had been distant, distracted, and stopped making her a priority. And while none of that justified her affair, it became painfully clear that I had played a role in the breakdown of our relationship.

But knowing that didn't stop the obsessive thoughts. The details of her affair gnawed at me, day and night. I became fixated on the "whys" and "hows" of it all—what did she see in him? Where did they go? What did they talk about? Every question was a dagger to my heart, yet I couldn't stop myself from digging deeper, trying to find answers that might bring me some sense of control. But the more I obsessed, the worse I felt. It was like being trapped in a loop I couldn't escape.

Even on the days when things seemed better between us, the thoughts would sneak back in. I could be sitting at the dinner table with my kids, but in my mind, I was back in that dark place, replaying the affair. My mind would drift to images of them together, moments I hadn't witnessed but had imagined so vividly they felt real. The worst part was, no matter how much reassurance she gave me, the thoughts never fully went away. They were always lurking in the background, ready to strike when I least expected it.

I realized then that my obsession with the details was holding me back from healing. I couldn't undo what had happened and replaying it in my mind wasn't giving me the control I craved—it was robbing me of my peace. I had to find a way to let go, to focus on rebuilding what we had instead of obsessing over what we had lost.

I started by making small but significant changes in my daily life. I began leaving work on time every day, committing to spending more focused time with her when I got home, even if it was just 15 minutes before the chaos of kids took over. I stopped talking only about my job and started listening—really listening—to her. I realized how much that had mattered to her, how much she had needed to feel heard. These small shifts, combined with all of her efforts, began to reshape our marriage.

Still, it wasn't easy. Even though she was doing everything she could to reassure me and make amends, there were days when the intrusive thoughts came back with a vengeance, pulling me back into that dark place. But each time, I tried to remind myself of the bigger picture—that I was working toward a future worth fighting for. I couldn't erase the past, but I could control how I responded to it. Slowly, those valleys of despair became fewer, and the peaks of hope higher.

Now, we're happier than we've ever been. We both did a lot of work to improve ourselves and the relationship. We talk more, we listen to each other, and we approach our marriage with intention. I'd be lying if I said I don't still have bad days. There are times when the thoughts resurface, and I find myself revisiting old wounds. But I've learned how to recognize when I'm spiraling, how to ask my wife for what I need to feel better, and how to bring myself back to the present. It's a constant battle, but one worth fighting.

To anyone walking this path, I want you to know this: the obsessive thoughts and the intrusive memories will feel overwhelming at times, but they don't have to define your future. Healing takes time, and it takes effort. But step by step, you can find your way out of the darkness.

You have to fight for the life you want, and that means making small, intentional choices every day. Because in the end, I know that when I'm sitting in that rocking chair 40 years from now, I won't be holding onto the pain or the betrayal—I'll be holding my wife's hand, and that's worth fighting for.

Journal Prompt 6:

Reflect on a recurring intrusive thought and consider how it might connect to a core wound you experienced in childhood. Was there a moment in your early life when you felt abandoned, rejected, or unworthy? How does this past hurt still affect your thoughts and emotions today? What steps can you take to nurture the part of you that was hurt as a child? (Sending you a really big hug.)

"What healed my intrusive thoughts was curiosity about their meaning (often related to my childhood), emotions and the need underneath. I used somatic experiencing a lot to get to the subconscious root." -ILC

Journal Prompt 7:

Betrayal can leave us feeling powerless. How has the affair affected your sense of control in various aspects of your life? What emotions surface when you feel out of control? What small, practical steps can you take to rebuild a sense of stability and make you feel more in control? Please remember that while you cannot control others, you can control yourself and make decisions about what you'll do if you're ever hurt again.

> "I heard someone say that they gave intrusive thoughts a name so they could say "that's not helpful right now Ruth. Thank you. Go away." I do this now and it helps me cope." -Manda

Journal Prompt 8:

Reflect on the role of self-forgiveness and self-compassion in your healing journey. How can you be kinder to yourself when intrusive or obsessive thoughts arise? What can you forgive yourself for not knowing or not doing? What might help you maintain a more compassionate perspective towards yourself?

"I stay busy. Intrusive thoughts come when I am sad. I journal and exercise ALOT." -Lynn

Journal Prompt 9:

How does this quote affect you: "It all begins and ends in your mind. What you give power to, has power over you, if you allow it." What does this make you think about? How can you give your obsessive thoughts less power? What can you tell yourself next time an intrusive thought comes up?

"The way I have coped with intrusive thoughts is letting the thought take its course. I let it feel, then come back to how it is now. He is more attentive, affectionate, and reassures me he loves me." -GXO

Journal Prompt 10:

Reflecting on everything you've read, thought about, and written during this chapter, how have your thoughts and feelings shifted? Write about any new insights or realizations you've had. What stands out as the most important lesson or understanding that you've gained? What will you take with you as you continue to heal?

___
___
___
___
___
___
___
___
___
___
___
___
___
___
___

"It was 13 long, painful, confusing and exhausting months after D-day before the guilt and shame lifted enough to allow us to really begin to rebuild and heal together. We did finally get there, and it really is a better relationship than before." -AB&TB

Chapter Eight

Defeating Depression & Sadness

As you continue your journey over Affair Mountain, your feelings begin to settle and the roller coaster gets less intense. When this happens, many betrayed partners start to struggle with deep hurt and sadness. Every aspect of an affair is profoundly painful. It's not just the betrayal itself, but the ripple effect it has on your entire life—your sense of self, your relationship, your future, and your family. You grieve the loss of what was, the shattering of what could have been, and the uncertainty of what will be. This sadness can feel like it touches every corner of your life, seeping into everything. For many, this sadness evolves into depression.

When you experience trauma, your risk of depression increases significantly. Trauma disrupts your brain's natural ability to process emotions and manage stress, often leaving you feeling helpless and disconnected from activities that once brought you joy. The emotional shock can overwhelm your capacity to cope, creating a vulnerability to depression. In response, your body's stress system may stay activated for an extended period, leaving you emotionally and physically depleted. This prolonged state of stress can lead to deep exhaustion and numbness, making it even more challenging to engage with life and replenish your emotional energy bank.

Depression doesn't just impact your emotions—it also alters the structure and function of your brain. It can shrink the hippocampus, a region essential for forming new memories and regulating emotions, which can make it harder to recover and process experiences. The amygdala, responsible for fear and emotional responses, may become overactive, heightening anxiety, irritability, and intrusive thoughts. Depression also reduces activity in the prefrontal cortex, impairing your ability to focus, make decisions, and manage your emotions effectively. Additionally, trauma can disrupt the balance of mood-regulating chemicals like serotonin and dopamine, leading to persistent sadness, low motivation, and difficulty finding pleasure in activities that once brought joy.

You're probably asking yourself some very tough questions these days: Will I ever see or think about my partner the way I did before the betrayal? Will we ever have what we had? Will we ever be happy again? Can I ever feel truly safe and loved in this relationship again? Will I always view my partner as someone who strayed? Will I ever be the same again? Will I ever actually get over this?

These questions can feel daunting and impossible to answer. Grappling with them is quite painful, and the process of working through them can seem like an insurmountable task. Please know we all go through this same valley of despair on our journey and struggle in this low spot. While the path looks different for each of us, the journey is very similar. Let me reassure you - we have climbed out of this spot, you can too.

It is so important to be patient and compassionate with yourself now. You may find yourself stuck in what feels like a deep, dark valley of sadness, and it may take longer to climb out than you'd like. But if you keep working at recovering, one small step at a time, you will make it through. Healing is not an orderly, predictable process; it's a hot mess! And it is okay to have setbacks along the way. What matters most is your commitment to keep moving forward, no matter how slowly.

One of the most powerful things you can do for yourself is to challenge your negative thoughts. It's easy to let sadness and depression overshadow everything, but by actively challenging those thoughts, you can begin to reclaim your life. Look for positive changes, no matter how small. Find things to be grateful for, even if they seem insignificant—stretchy shoelaces, chai lattes, a new true crime podcast, anything. Challenge yourself to find five good things for every negative thought. Gratitude is a powerful antidote to despair.

It's also important to resist letting the pain rewrite your memories and your story. Yes, you've been hurt, and yes, things have changed. But that doesn't mean your entire relationship is ruined or that your future is lost. Your story has a chapter in it that you did not choose, and that you do not like, but you can choose to see this as a chapter, not the whole book! Challenge the pain and the hurt. Don't let the pain steal your future from you. Your story is not over, and you have the power to write the next chapter.

Hopelessness and isolation also keep you stuck in depression. It's tempting to withdraw from the world, to retreat into yourself and away from others. When we are hurting, we often feel safer when we hide alone in our caves. But connection is a fundamental human need. Please reach out to the people you love, even when it feels difficult. Join a support group of any kind to connect with others who are also struggling. Reconnect with the things that bring you joy, no matter how small. Do something every day that reminds you of the goodness in life, whether it's taking a walk, reading a book, or simply enjoying a beautiful sunset.

We heal when we feel more powerful and purposeful. I encourage you to look for opportunities to make a difference, even in small ways. Turn your pain into purpose, whether it's offering a kind word to someone else who is struggling or finding a way to contribute to something meaningful. Volunteer with a group that does something meaningful that matters to you; it could be dog rescue, building homes for the homeless, knitting hats for people with cancer, anything that means something to you. Helping others is a powerful way to help yourself heal.

Healing from post-infidelity depression also involves challenging the intense feelings of shame that often accompany betrayal. Research shows that feelings of rejection, shame, and self-blame increase risk for depression after an affair, particularly when you see the betrayal as a reflection of your self-worth or value in the relationship (Gordon, Baucom, & Snyder, 2004; Allen & Atkins, 2012). It's easy to feel like you're not enough, like you're unworthy of love and connection, especially if you start to believe the affair happened because of your own inadequacies. But please hear me when I tell you: none of this is your fault, and you are worthy – you really are - just as you are right now.

You deserve to be loved, not just by others, but also by yourself. It's natural to question your value when you've been betrayed, but like all of us, you are perfectly imperfect. There's only one you in this world, and there will never be another like you. The affair does not define your worth. Your heart, your soul, and your character define your worth, not something you did not choose! Please treat yourself with the same kindness and understanding that you would offer to a dear friend. Be gentle with yourself, especially in moments of struggle. Talk to yourself with the same compassion and kindness that someone who loves you would.

As you are healing and rebuilding your relationship, consider creating new plans and shared dreams with your partner. Making future plans with your partner, whether it is to go on a trip, start a new business, or build a garden shed, can help your recovery. We need things to look forward to, we thrive when we have a purpose and plans to look forward to. Please make some plans with your partner and start talking about them more regularly.

Remember that what you believe is going to happen is more likely to happen. So keep reminding yourself that even though this is hard right now, you *will* succeed, you *will* recover, and you *will* get to the other side of this. Your mind is powerful, and the beliefs you hold about your ability to heal will shape your journey. Trust in your capacity to overcome this and rediscover peace and joy. You are not defined by this betrayal—it's something that happened to you, but it's not who you are. You are an amazing person *who has experienced betrayal*, you are not simply a betrayed person. This is not your identity, you are so much more.

When I went through my breast cancer journey, I refused to let it define me. On the day of my diagnosis, I decided I would focus on writing *The Courage to Stay*. I chose to be an author working on her book, who happened to be dealing with cancer, rather than being a "breast cancer patient." I believed with my whole heart that I would beat it. My days were organized around writing, and I fit cancer treatments into my life—rather than organizing my life around cancer. What I believed then, and what I know to be true, is that how you see the journey profoundly affects how your journey unfolds. Don't let betrayal be the main character in your story. You are the main character, the betrayal is just a small part of your story, it's definitely not your identity.

I know that this is hard to do and if you have not been feeling good, it can be hard to shift your thoughts in this direction. Please try. Practicing new ways of thinking consistently over a 21-day period can start to create new neural pathways in your brain. This concept is rooted in neuroplasticity—the brain's ability to reorganize itself by forming new neural connections throughout life. Repeating positive or constructive thought patterns, such as gratitude or self-compassion exercises, can help "rewire" the brain to make these positive thoughts more automatic (Seligman, 2005). Pushing yourself to think positively, even when you don't feel like it, will improve your mood, perspective, and resilience, as the brain gradually starts to favor these more positive thought patterns.

If you've been struggling for a while and find that your mood is dangerously low or that you're just not getting better, please reach out for additional help. There's no shame in asking for help; in fact, it's one of the bravest things you can do. You may benefit from some specialized trauma therapy or medication to help you continue healing. In the U.S., you can dial 988 for immediate mental health assistance. If you need help finding a therapist or would like a recommendation for a self-help book, please see the back of this book for listings of both.

No matter how hard or dark the path seems, please know that you are not alone. Our affair recovery community is here for you. There are people who care about you and want to help you heal. The world is a much better place with you in it, and your story is far from over. Keep going, one day at a time, and know that brighter days are ahead. Sending you the biggest hug!

Journal Prompt 1:

What is hurting you most these days? What other feelings does that bring up for you? What do these hurtful thoughts mean to you? Do these thoughts and feelings connect to anything else or any other unhealed pain for you?

"It will take time, but opening up your feelings with your partner will definitely help. Talking and reassurance from her helped me with my healing in a big way." -Anonymous

Journal Prompt 2:

What negative thoughts that have been weighing you down recently? What evidence is there that these thoughts are true? What evidence is there that they are NOT true? How can you reframe them in a more neutral or positive way? Now, challenge yourself to think of 5 things you're grateful for. Notice how this shift in focus feels.

"We're 10 months post d-day and I can definitely say we're both healing beautifully. I see his effort, plus willingness to save our marriage. My person is back, but as a better person." -Kathleen

Journal Prompt 3:

When you think about how you view your partner now, and whether you'll ever think about them the way you did before the betrayal, what comes up for you? How do these thoughts affect you? What do these thoughts cause you to feel? What comforts you when you think or feel these things?

THE COURAGE TO STAY JOURNAL

"10 years later and we're stronger for sure. I haven't forgotten, but have forgiven." -Fangro

Journal Prompt 4:

When you think about how you view your relationship now, and whether you'll ever have the safety, love, peace, and connection you did before the affair, what comes up for you? How do these thoughts affect you? What do these thoughts cause you to feel? What comforts you when you think or feel these things?

"I stayed. I made sure we changed our situation and our surroundings for a fresh start. We worked together to come to a resolution and figure out what we both needed. Life has been the best yet!" -Jayme

Journal Prompt 5:

When you think about how you view yourself, and whether you'll ever be the same again or feel "normal" again, what comes up for you? How do these thoughts affect you? What deeper feelings do these thoughts bring up? What comforts you when you think or feel these things?

"It IS possible to heal and rebuild trust with hard work from both parties in the relationship. Setting boundaries, being transparent, having open communication and creating emotional safety helped us heal together." -JH

Kerry's Story

The rain tapped gently against the windowpane as I sat alone in our dimly lit kitchen, the hum of the refrigerator the only sound accompanying my thoughts. My husband, Grant, had been coming home later than usual—first by minutes, then by hours. The once warm and familiar atmosphere of our home felt increasingly cold and distant, mirroring the growing distance between us.

It all began innocently enough. Grant mentioned he'd stopped by a hardware store after work to pick up supplies for a project. He seemed distracted, his eyes avoiding mine as he recounted his day. Soon, his late returns became a pattern. "Just a big project at work," he'd say with a tired smile, but his excuses felt rehearsed, hollow.

Our children still lived with us—our eldest son and his partner, along with their one-year-old twins, and our daughter. The house was full, yet I'd never felt more alone. Grant started withdrawing cash on Fridays, a departure from his usual habit of using his bank card. "It's always good to have some cash on hand," he'd shrug off my inquiries, but it never sat right with me.

One evening, he announced abruptly, "I want to move to the countryside." His eyes searched mine, perhaps hoping for agreement. "The city's wearing me down." I was taken aback. "But our lives are here—our children, our grandchildren." "I'm going, with or without you," he replied, a hint of anger in his tone. His words hung in the air, heavy and final.

That night, confusion and dread overwhelmed me. I retreated to our daughter's room, tears spilling over as I confided in her. "Something's not right," I whispered. "I think your father's having an affair." She insisted we stay at her brother's place that night. The drive over was silent, each of us lost in our own thoughts. When we arrived, I laid out my suspicions to my sons. They decided to confront Grant.

The confrontation was tense. My son looked his father in the eyes. "Dad, are you seeing someone else?" Grant's gaze faltered. "No," he said, but his voice lacked conviction. "Look me in the eyes and tell me," his son pressed. Grant's handshake was weak, his eyes evasive. The seed of doubt he'd planted began to sprout, its roots digging deep into my heart.

In the days that followed, I felt myself slipping into a fog. Simple tasks became monumental challenges. I visited the doctor for a routine check-up, only to receive unsettling news. "You have an infection," she said gently. "Is everything okay at home?"

I knew then. The pieces fit too neatly together to ignore. Confronting Grant seemed both necessary and unbearable. When I told him about the diagnosis, he deflected with a hollow laugh. "Who have you been seeing?" he joked, but the words stung. He did not tell me the truth, but I knew.

For my birthday in May, our son gifted us a voucher for a weekend getaway. Desperate to salvage any remnants of our marriage, I suggested we use it. Surprisingly, Grant agreed. For a brief moment, it felt like old times. We soaked in hot springs, walked among treetops, and I dared to hope. I took photos of us smiling—evidence of happiness I desperately wanted to reclaim.

But shadows lurked even in daylight. "Don't post any photos on Facebook," he insisted. "You know I hate that." I ignored his request, needing to share this slice of joy. The repercussions were swift. The following Monday, he was agitated. "Did you post those photos?" he demanded. "My boss's wife saw them." I knew his explanation was a lie, but I was too weary to argue.

Then came the message that shattered everything. A stranger reached out on social media: "You don't know me, but we need to talk about your husband."

My hands trembled as I showed our daughter. She made the call on my behalf, and the truth unraveled like a frayed thread. Grant had been having an affair with a woman named Amy, whom he'd met at the hardware store. The lies he'd spun were intricate—stories of a failed marriage, of separate lives under one roof, all to justify his betrayal.

Confronting him was a storm of denial and anger. He concocted stories, each more implausible than the last. When cornered, he lashed out, drove to confront Amy and, in a fit of rage, smashed her phone. That night, he was arrested and I told him never to come home again. The man I thought I knew was unrecognizable—a stranger wearing my husband's face.

I was devastated. Heartbroken. Empty. My whole world was gone just like that. This was the man I'd loved for 30 years, my husband of 27. And in a heartbeat, he was gone. The life we'd built, the future I'd imagined, it all vanished like smoke. There were no issues between us, nothing to prepare me for this. I still don't understand why. To this day, I'm trying to find out why.

In the weeks that followed, I was engulfed by darkness. Depression wrapped itself around me, a suffocating blanket I couldn't shake off. Mornings were the hardest; the weight of reality pressed down before I even opened my eyes. The house felt emptier, each room echoing with memories tainted by deceit. I felt myself spiraling, sinking deeper each day, until finally, I sought help. The doctor prescribed medication to help lift the weight of despair, and it became my lifeline.

Then, after about three months of silence and distance, Grant reached out. Tentatively at first. We started to talk again, little by little. Finally, I poured my heart into a letter, capturing the sorrow, the rage, and the emptiness his actions had left. One evening, I read it aloud to him, each word heavy with pain. He sat there, remorse evident in his eyes, and when I finished, he whispered, "I'm so sorry. I want to make this better. I want our marriage back. I'll do anything."

I was skeptical, my wounds too deep, but a part of me remembered the man he'd once been. We started meeting, initially in public places where the weight of our shared history felt less oppressive. He listened as I poured out my hurt, his eyes reflecting his own pain and remorse. "I don't know why I did it," he confessed. "But I want to fix this. I want us back."

Rebuilding wasn't easy. Trust, once shattered, isn't easily mended. But for the sake of our family and the life we'd built together, I decided to try. Grant moved back home, and though we occupied separate rooms, the proximity allowed us to confront our issues head-on. He made tangible efforts to regain my trust—leaving his phone out in the open, sharing his location without prompting, and checking in regularly. Small gestures, but they began to chip away at the wall between us.

Grant took full responsibility for what he had done. Time and again, he would say, "Never blame yourself for any of this. None of this was your fault." His words, though sometimes painful to hear, began to soothe the gaping wound he'd left. I saw how deeply he regretted the hurt he'd caused, not just to me but to our children as well. The damage he'd done had spread to everyone we loved, and watching our kids struggle to forgive was almost as painful as his betrayal. He knew he'd have to live with the consequences of his actions, not just with me but with them, for the rest of his life.

Our children, initially distant, started to thaw as well. Family dinners became a platform for open dialogue, and slowly, the fractures in our relationships began to heal.

There are days when the shadows creep back in, when doubt and sadness threaten to overwhelm me. But there are also days filled with laughter and genuine smiles. We're not where we once were, but we're moving forward, one step at a time.

Depression still lingers at the edges, but its grip has loosened. Through therapy, support, and a renewed commitment to our marriage, the weight has become more manageable. Grant's unwavering efforts to make amends have been a beacon during the darkest times.

As I reflect on the past year and a half since that fateful day, I recognize the strength it took to confront the pain, both his and mine. We're about 80% of the way there, rebuilding not just our marriage but ourselves. Together, we're stepping out of the darkness and into the light, embracing the possibility of a future that's better and brighter than our past.

Journal Prompt 6:

In the aftermath of a trauma, there are often small moments of growth or positive change. What are some small positive changes you've noticed lately? What things are you grateful for? How have you've grown stronger through this experience? How can you focus a little more on these positive aspects every day?

THE COURAGE TO STAY JOURNAL

"My therapist had me get a bunch of cheap plates and write all of my hurt and frustrations on them with a marker. Then one night, when I was ready, I smashed them. Felt so good!." -Sarah

Journal Prompt 7:

How has the affair influenced the way you see your past and your memories? How has the affair rewritten parts of your life story? What's a different way to incorporate this event as part of your story and not let it define your entire story or future?

"After d-day, we started taking 2-3 beach vacations a year to focus on us. It was about 4 yrs before we had an entire vacation without me crying at some point. It definitely takes time to let go and have fun, but you can get there." -Mimi

Journal Prompt 8:

How can you turn your pain into purpose? Are there ways you can use what you've learned from this experience to help others? What steps can you take to begin this process? Has your pain sculpted you into a better, more empathetic version of yourself? Please say more about that.

"Yes, we are different people post affair. My husband has changed for the better. We have been married for more than 20 years." -CLB

Journal Prompt 9:

In what ways are you being hard on yourself? How can you practice more self-compassion, treating yourself with the kindness and understanding you would offer a close friend who is going through something similar? What activities or connections have you found comforting or joyful during this time? How can you incorporate more of these into your daily life?

THE COURAGE TO STAY JOURNAL

"It's only been 6 months for me. I've NEVER suspected infidelity in the past, he's been an amazingly supportive, accepting, caring, and selfless partner. I don't fully trust him yet, I know that will take time to build back." -Lindsay

Journal Prompt 10:

If you feel like you're struggling to recover, what kind of additional support might be helpful for you? What concrete steps can you take to get that support? Are you open to seeking therapy, talking to a trusted friend, reading a self-help book, or joining a support group that resonates with you? Which one of these steps can you take tomorrow? (Please remember, if you need urgent help, call 988 in the U.S.)

"We've been reading the book Secure Love by Julie Menanno you posted about. He's avoidant, I'm disorganized. Understanding our triggers has been game changing. Also a very humbling experience to realize I'm disorganized. I can already see the healing in our attachment styles. He's no longer defensive when I bring up a concern." -OM

Chapter Nine

Growing Through Grief

You've been on this journey for some time now, navigating the rough and steep terrain of Affair Mountain. As the days turn into weeks and weeks into months, you have likely paused for a moment, taken a breath, and realized, *"I'm changing, I'm not the same person I was before."* This realization can hit like a ton of bricks. You might feel that you've lost so much of yourself along the way, and the grief that comes with that awareness is immense.

You've been through something incredibly painful, and the sadness that follows is understandable and profound. You might find yourself thinking, *"I didn't choose this. I didn't sign up for this. How could this happen? This is so unfair!"* And you're right—it's deeply unfair. You did not ask for the loss of the relationship you had, the loss of the person you thought you knew, the loss of your feeling of safety. These losses are real, and it's perfectly okay to grieve the changes brought about by these losses.

Research shows that betrayed partners who have experienced a relational trauma go through a period of profound grief over the loss of their original relationship (Ortman, 2005). Infidelity causes grief not only for the individual but also for the couple and even their children, underscoring its ripple effect on the entire family (Rokach & Chan, 2023). So please know that your feelings of grief and sadness are very normal.

Grief is messy and unpredictable. Some days, you might feel like you're starting to heal, only to be blindsided by a wave of sadness or anger the next day. This is all part of the journey. It's normal to have good days and bad days, and it's important to be patient with yourself as you navigate these ups and downs.

You might wonder, "Grief? Really? No one died." But grief isn't just about losing a person; it's about losing pieces of yourself, your life, your future. The old you, the person who believed in your relationship without question, has been lost. And that loss hurts more than words can express. Your old relationship has been lost, some friendships have likely been lost, and some precious memories have been lost. These losses are devastating, and they deserve to be mourned.

When you're grieving, your body often stores that pain as physical tension, discomfort, and changes in how you handle stress. Losing someone or something important activates your body's stress response, releasing hormones like cortisol and adrenaline that impact your physical health. This emotional pain frequently manifests as muscle tension (especially in the neck, shoulders, and back), digestive issues, and sensations like chest tightness or "heartache." The overlap between emotional and physical pain circuits in the brain can make these sensations feel very real. You might also experience fatigue, sleep disturbances, or a weakened immune system, leaving you feeling physically depleted. If you don't fully process your grief, trauma and somatic experts believe it can get "trapped" in your body, which may cause you to feel more physically drained or tense over time.

Grief isn't just an emotion or feeling; it's a process that causes a profound transformation. It changes you, not because you've moved on from your losses, but because you're learning to live with them. You're slowly becoming someone new, someone who carries the weight of what's been lost while continuing to walk forward. This process is both horrible and valuable. It's horrible because the pain is immense, and many of us suffer deeply while grieving. It's valuable because it carves out a deep hole in your heart, and over time, that space will fill with many beautiful things, like compassion, understanding, and a deeper wisdom about yourself and others.

Grief teaches us about the fragility of our experiences and the incredible strength we possess, even when we feel weakest. Gordon and Mitchell (2020) describe infidelity as a wrenching and devastating event, that is challenging even under the best of circumstances. Their research also found that couples can be astonishingly resilient, sometimes transforming the pain of betrayal into immense growth.

Grief and pain, as difficult as they are to endure, have a way of sculpting us into stronger, wiser versions of ourselves. While it's nearly impossible to see this transformation when you're in the depths of your suffering, with time, you may look back and realize how far you've come. A few years from now, the growth and resilience you have developed from this experience will likely become more visible, like a remarkable sculpture slowly emerging from raw stone.

As I write this, I can hear you saying "I don't want to become a beautiful statue, Dr. Kathy. I don't want any of this, I just want my old life back. I want this all to go away." I know, I hear you, I wish we could do that. If I had a magic wand, I would absolutely do that for you. Unfortunately, we can't go back. We must go forward, we must go through it.

To fully heal and transform, it's important to pause, reflect, and acknowledge how things have changed, both within you and around you. Feeling your feelings is essential. Grieving is essential. It's not something you can bypass or rush through. The way out of grief is through it. You must let yourself feel the pain, the sadness, and the anger, to move forward. I know it's scary and hard, but you can do it.

One way to begin this process is through journaling (and we will do this in just a minute). Write down your thoughts, your feelings, your grief. Pour your heart onto the pages. Let the ink capture your pain, your sorrow, your anger, and your confusion. Don't censor yourself—your journal is your safe space.

Incorporating grief rituals into your life can also help you process these feelings. A grief ritual is a symbolic act or ceremony that helps you let go of some of the pain associated with your loss. It's a way to honor your grief and begin to heal.

One ritual you might try is writing a letter to the universe. Pour out all your thoughts and feelings about what you've lost. Then, take the letter outside and safely burn it, releasing those emotions into the air, letting them go. You can say a prayer or make a wish as you burn the letter, do what feels right to you.

Another option is to create a small altar with a meaningful photo and a candle. Light the candle, and as the flame flickers, speak your thoughts and feelings aloud. Let yourself vent, cry, or yell if you need to. Then, give yourself a comforting hug, blow out the candle, and imagine some of the pain floating away into the air.

Creating something beautiful is a powerful act of rebellion against pain. Whether it's taking a photograph, planting a tree, painting a sunset, or writing a poem, let your grief fuel your creativity. As you create, remind yourself, "I won't let this pain transform me into someone I'm not."

Another idea is to gather a handful of small rocks and go to a lake, ocean, forest, or other vast open area. Holding each rock, speak some of your grief onto it, then throw it as far as you can. With each throw, imagine releasing a bit of the pain that's been weighing you down. Repeat this with several rocks, gather more as needed.

You might also find comfort in trying an AI-assisted version of the letter and response exercise. Traditionally, this exercise involves writing a letter to your partner expressing how you feel, followed by writing the response you wish you would receive from them. The goal is to engage in a back-and-forth conversation, creating a simulated discussion that offers emotional support and comfort.

In the AI version, you can use a tool like ChatGPT to help with the response. Instead of writing both parts yourself, you express your pain through the computer, and the AI responds as a compassionate and empathetic partner might. This approach isn't meant to replace real communication with your partner but to provide emotional relief and simulate the healing exchange you crave. If you find the AI's response particularly meaningful, you could even share it with your partner as a way to open a conversation about your feelings and needs.

To start this exercise, go to your computer or tablet and navigate to OpenAI / ChatGPT – or any AI service you like. Once there, post this prompt, followed by a short letter about your feelings: "I've been deeply hurt by my partner's infidelity. Below is a letter expressing my pain. Can you respond as if you were my partner, with the kind of compassion, apology, and empathy I need to hear? Please help me feel seen and validated."

Here's another prompt you could use: "I feel broken by what my partner did to me, and I need to express everything that's weighing on my heart. Below is my letter. Could you respond as if you were my partner, apologizing and offering empathy in a way that comforts me?"

This exercise provides an interactive way to explore your emotions. It can also help you clarify your feelings and needs, making it easier to communicate them in real life.

Remember, healing is a journey, not an event. It unfolds gradually, often in ways that are hard to see in the moment. Some days, you may feel like you're taking steps forward, only to be met with setbacks the next day. Even when it doesn't feel like it, each day can bring small moments of healing.

Be gentle with yourself—there's no rush to reach the other side. Grief isn't something to "get over"; it's something to move through. It's important to move at your own pace, allowing yourself to grieve in a way that feels right for you. There's no perfect process, no expected timeline, and healing looks different for everyone. On hard days, practice self-compassion—remind yourself that you're doing the best you can. Growth doesn't come all at once, but it can bloom quietly in moments of gratitude, conversation with your partner, or finding meaning in your pain. Even the smallest acts —like getting out of bed or reaching out to a friend—are steps toward healing.

Caring for yourself while you grieve means giving yourself permission to embrace the process fully, with patience and compassion. Honor your emotions, no matter how messy or inconvenient they feel. Healing is about learning to live with your losses and gradually finding a way to feel whole again. Surround yourself with supportive people—friends, family, or support groups—who provide comfort and remind you that you are not alone. Activities that connect your body and mind, such as walking, yoga, or simply sitting in nature, can bring moments of peace while releasing emotional tension.

When in doubt, know that you are exactly where you need to be, even if it doesn't feel that way. Keep going, step by step, and trust that healing is happening, little by little. There's no "right" way to grieve—your path is unique, and so is your process. You are slowly rebuilding and that in itself is an incredible act of resilience!

Now, let's take some time to explore your grief a little further. Write from your heart, knowing that this space is for you to honor your feelings and the journey you're on. I am so proud of you and so honored to walk this path with you.

Journal Prompt 1:

What are some ways you feel you have changed since this journey began? List specific qualities or parts of yourself you feel have shifted, both positively and negatively. How do you feel about these changes?

"I don't think I would have been capable of the growth I achieved in the last year if d-day had never happened. Your choice is either to crumble and let it destroy you, or grow and transcend it."
-Anonymous

Journal Prompt 2:

What are the things you feel you have lost as a result of this betrayal—trust, a sense of safety, certain dreams for the future? Describe each one and what it meant to you.

"Darn it, Dr. Kathy… you make me keep going! I believe in your message and even though I can't see the finish line yet, I believe it's true." -PJ

Journal Prompt 3:

Reflect on a time when you felt an unexpected wave of grief. What triggered it? How did you feel? What did it make you think about? How did you cope with the emotions that surfaced?

"I'm just a few months from D-Day and I am leaning into my faith. It's a daily battle, but I am a warrior!" -Cyndi

Journal Prompt 4:

Where there is deep grief, there once was great love. What thoughts and feelings does this sentiment bring up for you? What sensations does it cause in your body? What do you crave from your partner to reconnect with those feelings of love?

"17 months post discovery, what a wild journey. I bought your book the day I found out, wrote the letter and all. Not only saved the relationship of 17 years, but saved me." -SP

Journal Prompt 5:

When you committed to your partner, you probably had a dream about how your lives would play out together. The affair likely changed that dream. What about that do you find yourself grieving the most? What about this particular loss means so much to you? Is there any way to rewrite the story or make it into a new dream?

"3 years post d-day, 30 years married, 5 year affair. It shattered my soul. Seeing both sides showed me a whole new perspective. Staying is not for the weak, but life has never been better." - *Anonymous*

Jo's Story

We are a married lesbian couple, together for 18 years and married for 15. We have two children, ages 7 and 13. My wife's affair lasted 18 months physically, though it began emotionally before that. It was an incredibly painful experience, but we are committed to healing and rebuilding our life together—one day at a time.

Our story began in 2005 while we were both serving in the military. We married in 2008, moving frequently for deployments, but when our eldest child's anxiety became overwhelming, we decided to put down roots. I left the military after 22 years, and we relocated to the UK to be near my wife's family. She had three years left in the military and spent much of that time working away—five days at home, five days away. It was during those absences that her emotional connection with a colleague grew into something more.

Grief has been a constant undercurrent in both of our lives, and the affair was not the first emotional challenge we faced. We've experienced the losses of family members—my brother, my father, her grandmother—and navigated complicated relationships with our mothers. Unresolved grief and emotional burdens shaped us in ways we didn't fully understand until now. We carried these unhealed wounds into our relationship, and while we didn't know it at the time, they planted the seeds for emotional distance and unmet needs. Therapy came too late to prevent the affair, but it is now helping us understand the deeper layers of pain we both carried.

When I discovered the affair on a family holiday in Spain, it felt like the ground had been pulled from beneath me. I'd suspected something was wrong for over a year but couldn't believe it—how could this happen to us? We had a great relationship, or so I thought. In that moment of discovery, I was flooded with grief—not only for the betrayal but for the life I believed we had and the dreams we shared. But instead of unraveling completely, we chose to stay in Spain for the children, giving them a happy memory even as our world shifted beneath us. It wasn't easy, but that decision became a small but significant step toward rebuilding.

Over the past 15 months, we have both done deep, difficult work. Therapy has been a lifeline, helping us peel back the layers of unresolved trauma that had silently shaped our lives. My wife continues to confront her childhood wounds, guilt, and shame, working to become the partner she always wanted to be. I've come to understand that the affair, while devastating, was not the only source of my pain—it was the final layer on a foundation of past trauma, loss, and emotional struggle. Acknowledging this has allowed me to extend compassion to myself and my wife as we move through the messy, unpredictable process of healing.

There are still hard days. Triggers appear unexpectedly, especially with my children, but I've learned to manage them as they come. Some days, the grief feels heavy, and I miss the ease and simplicity of our old life. But we've also found moments of hope and connection. We are learning to check in with each other, take accountability, and communicate in ways we never did before. With each conversation, we rebuild trust. With each small act of kindness, we reclaim the love that was always there.

We made the difficult decision to keep the affair private, choosing not to tell anyone out of fear of judgment. It has been lonely at times, but I find comfort in knowing that we are moving forward, side by side. Even though no one else knows what we are going through, we see each other. We acknowledge the mistakes and the pain, but we also see the growth, the resilience, and the love that has carried us through.

I have never stopped loving my wife, and I believe she will never hurt me like this again. Her remorse is real, and so is her commitment to becoming a better person—not just for me, but for herself. She is working through her guilt and shame, but I remind her that healing is a journey, and we are both allowed to grow. We carry the grief of what we lost, but we are also building something new—something deeper, more intentional, and more honest.

This experience has been transformative. I've discovered strength I didn't know I had, and I've learned that love isn't about never falling—it's about standing up and trying again, even when it feels impossible. We take it one day at a time, celebrating small victories and forgiving setbacks. We've found inspiration in books like yours, and we know we are far from the end of this journey, but we also know we are walking it together.

Writing this has been cathartic, reminding me of how far we've come. My wife has read this story, and while her perspective may be different, this is my truth. We've carried a lot of pain—miscarriages, difficult births, family conflict—but we've also found a way through. This journey hasn't been easy, but it has been meaningful. We are not the same people we were before, and perhaps that's a good thing. We've grown, we've changed, and we are still here, choosing each other every day.

This is not the end of our story—it's just a new beginning. And while the road ahead may still be uncertain, we are walking it with hope, knowing that grief has shaped us, but love will sustain us.

Journal Prompt 6:

Write a farewell letter to the part of yourself or your life that you feel you have lost. Express what you loved about it, what you'll miss, and what you hope to carry forward in memory or spirit.

_____
_____
_____
_____
_____
_____
_____
_____
_____
_____
_____
_____
_____
_____
_____
_____
_____

"I wish it could have happened any other way…but his affair was the catalyst for a marriage that grew so beautiful I couldn't have dreamed it. I gained far more than I lost." -Adriane

Journal Prompt 7:

Which grief ritual idea resonated with you the most? Please go ahead and try that ritual, or a variation of it, now (it's ok, I'll wait). How did that ritual affect you? What did it make you feel? What thoughts came up for you? How can you see yourself incorporating grief rituals into your healing journey?

THE COURAGE TO STAY JOURNAL

"Navigating the grieving process has been really challenging for me. I'm learning to let go of my expectations about our marriage and who I believed my partner to be. It's a journey of discovering the reality of our relationship and understanding who he truly is." -Anonymous

Journal Prompt 8:

Reflect on the idea of transformation through grief. How do you think this experience is reshaping you? How is it shifting your identity, values, or outlook on life? How is grief sculpting your relationship? Are some of these changes positive?

___
___
___
___
___
___
___
___
___
___
___
___
___
___
___
___

"I was a zombie, going through the motions of the day and then coming home to lay in bed at night. It's a year later and while the grief isn't overwhelming anymore, it's still there." -OTF

Journal Prompt 9:

Brené Brown wrote, "Owning our story can be hard, but not nearly as difficult as spending our lives running from it. Embracing our vulnerabilities is risky but not nearly as dangerous as giving up on love and belonging and joy." What does this passage mean to you? When you think about owning your story, even the painful parts, what thoughts and feelings come up? How do you feel about opening yourself up to love and possibly being hurt again?

THE COURAGE TO STAY JOURNAL

"Grief comes almost daily. I grieve the loss of the thought that we were something special, that no one could ever come between. I hope with work I will feel that way again someday." -TB

Journal Prompt 10:

Reflecting on everything you've read, thought about, and written during this chapter, how have your thoughts and feelings changed? Write about any new insights or realizations you've had. What stands out as the most important lesson or understanding that you've gained? What will you take with you as you continue to heal?

THE COURAGE TO STAY JOURNAL

"I grieved the marriage that I thought I had, the safety I thought I had. We chose to stay together and for me, it's a constant learning process of how to trust him again and let go of the past." -Mrs A

Chapter Ten

Accepting What You Can't Forgive

Forgiveness comes easily to some, but not to me. After my partner's betrayal, I really struggled with forgiveness. The idea of forgiving felt like a betrayal of myself - a way of saying that what happened didn't really matter, that it was no big deal, or that it was okay somehow. But that couldn't have been further from the truth! The pain was real, it mattered, and it was definitely not okay.

I vividly recall the moment when my therapist, Gloria, first brought up the idea of forgiveness. I immediately pushed back, saying, "No, no, I will never forget, and I will never forgive. This is unforgivable!" She listened empathetically, we talked for a while longer, and then she said: "You're going to have a very hard time moving forward with him if you can't find some way to make peace with this."

Her words surprised me. I replied, "But if I forgive, it means I'm saying it was okay, that it didn't really hurt me, that it didn't really matter." That was my belief—that forgiveness equaled approval or dismissal of the wrong that was done. Gloria responded with something that radically shifted my perspective. "Who said that's the definition of forgiveness? Forgiveness can mean acceptance. It can mean understanding and compassion. It doesn't mean endorsement." That simple redefinition of forgiveness made all the difference for me.

What I didn't know then, but do know now, is that forgiveness is essential—not just for your personal healing but also for the survival of your relationship. Research shows that forgiveness plays a crucial role in both individual recovery and relationship repair after a deep betrayal (Fenell, 1993; Gordon & Baucom, 1999). Couples who can ask for and give forgiveness often report higher levels of marital satisfaction and stability (Fenell, 1993). When it comes to infidelity, true healing and reconciliation simply aren't possible without forgiveness (Fife et al., 2013). While a relationship might survive without it, it can't fully thrive or return to a place of genuine connection (Fife et al., 2013). That's why, even though it's hard, we have to move towards forgiveness—it's the key to healing.

What happened to you will never be okay, it will never be "no big deal," and it will never not matter. It was a huge, life-altering trauma. But we can find a way to make peace with it. So, let's talk about how to make peace with something and accept some horrible behavior that feels unforgivable.

Begin by giving yourself permission to feel whatever you actually feel at this moment in your ascent up Affair Mountain. However you feel today, whether it's angry, sad, hurt, confused, or a mixture of these feelings, know that it's ok and it's normal. All of these emotions are expected responses to betrayal. You don't have to rush to forgiveness or acceptance; it's okay to sit with your feelings for a while and honor them.

Forgiveness isn't something you *have* to do. It's a deeply personal decision that should be made on your own terms, not because someone else expects it of you. Forgiveness is something I encourage you to move towards because the research, and my clinical experience, shows that it's a critical step in recovery. Despite this, please know that forgiveness is a choice, and if you're not ready—or if you decide it's not right for you—that's perfectly okay.

Take a step back and assess the relationship. Has your partner shown genuine remorse? Are they making efforts to rebuild trust? Do they understand the impact of their actions? Do they understand why they chose the affair? Are they willing to do the work to change? Sometimes, unforgivable actions reveal deeper issues that need to be addressed before forgiveness can even be considered. It's ok for you to ask your partner to do this work and make progress on their own healing before you move closer to forgiveness.

Instead of thinking of forgiveness as wiping the slate clean or erasing the past, think about it as accepting a fault or failure in your partner. All of us are flawed, messy, imperfect creatures. Some of us have unhealed past trauma that has greatly injured us and changed how our brains function. Some of us have mental health issues (ADHD, autism, bipolar depression) that cause us to struggle with impulsivity and regulation of our behavior. I encourage you to find a way to hold your partner accountable while having compassion for their individual struggles.

Consider acceptance over forgiveness. Start by writing an acceptance statement for yourself. Here's an example: *"I accept that _____ happened. I accept that you chose to do _____. I am deeply hurt by your actions, and I am choosing to have compassion for you because _____. I believe that you can and will do better. I believe that you can and will work to understand why you strayed. I believe that you can and will make different choices in the future. I will accept your bad behavior and put this issue down, as long as I continue to see positive changes and choices, like _____. I am not forgetting, I am not forgiving; I am accepting that it happened, and you are more than your mistakes and poor choices."*

Rewrite this statement however you like so that it resonates with you. If you feel good about saying that you forgive, then please do and say so. But if you're like me and have a complicated relationship with the word forgiveness, think about forgiveness as understanding and acceptance. When I say, "I forgive you" these days, I'm really thinking, "I understand, I have compassion for you, I get it, and we can move on together." I hope this definition might help you too.

Start with acceptance and realize that forgiveness, if it comes, takes time. Don't rush the process. Healing from infidelity is a journey that unfolds at your own pace, and it's important to be patient with yourself. If you choose to forgive or accept now, it doesn't mean you have to hold that position forever. If your partner hurts you again or stops acting in ways that make you feel safe, you can always change your mind. You are not locked into this decision now or ever.

Whether or not you choose to forgive, communicating clear consequences is essential. This could involve establishing which behaviors are unacceptable, what your expectations are, and deciding how you want to move forward. An important step in protecting yourself might be communicating that a consequence for future transgressions will be you taking a break from the relationship, or even ending the relationship.

Sometimes, the hurt is too deep, and forgiveness may not be attainable. If that's the case, it's okay to accept that and focus on moving forward in a way that honors your feelings and needs. You deserve peace, whether that comes through forgiveness, acceptance, or deciding that you do not want to do this anymore. It is your life, your choice.

The work of Viktor Frankl might inspire you as you grapple with forgiveness. Frankl, an Austrian neurologist, psychiatrist, and Holocaust survivor, explored the concept of forgiveness through his writing on suffering, meaning, and personal responsibility. I read Frankl's book when I was struggling with forgiveness and thought, "If he can forgive his captors after leaving a concentration camp, maybe I can move towards forgiving."

Frankl wrote that even in the most harrowing circumstances, we have the ability to find meaning. Finding meaning in suffering can involve letting go of resentment and choosing to forgive or accept as a way to transcend the pain. By forgiving, we might find a deeper purpose or understanding of our experiences, transforming them into something that contributes to our personal growth.

If we can find meaning in the process of affair recovery, if our relationship becomes stronger as a result of going through a horrible betrayal, maybe the pain happened for a valuable reason. This perspective doesn't make the betrayal okay, but it can help you move forward with a sense of purpose and direction.

Let's explore some of these ideas a little further as we journal about forgiveness and acceptance.

Journal Prompt 1:

What thoughts come up for you when you consider forgiving your partner? What emotions come up as you think about forgiveness? What beliefs do you hold about forgiveness? How do those beliefs influence you?

"After the affair, we started to connect again in ways we hadn't for a long time. I still believe that there is love between us." -Trent

Journal Prompt 2:

How do you personally define forgiveness? Consider whether forgiveness, for you, means absolution, acceptance, or something else entirely. How does this definition impact your ability or willingness to forgive?

"I don't think you need to forgive. I think you can move forward and at the same time say I can't forgive that behaviour but I'm willing to love you still." -SBH

Journal Prompt 3:

What does acceptance mean to you in the context of infidelity? How might accepting what happened, rather than forgiving, offer you a path to healing? What does acceptance allow you to do or feel?

"I can have compassion, but I don't think I can forgive the fact that he chose to hurt me. He's doing everything to change and I see that and I think I can move forward." -Genevieve

Journal Prompt 4:

Write about the ways in which your partner has shown remorse and tried to rebuild trust. How do these efforts influence your feelings about forgiveness or acceptance? What do you still need from them to move forward?

"During my journey of healing, I've come to understand that forgiveness is not for her. It's for me. It's when I have stopped the hate and the anger and am more at peace. When I forgive her, it's for me." -Anonymous

Journal Prompt 5:

Explore the balance between holding your partner accountable for their actions and having compassion for their struggles. How have you held your partner accountable? What challenges has your partner had that allow you to have compassion? How do you balance these two ideas? What challenges arise when trying to balance compassion and accountability?

"Forgiveness just means accepting that this happens and holding compassion for the person who did it. It does not mean you let your boundaries slide or that you never talk about it again. In truth, forgiveness is for YOU to make peace in your heart for the situation, it's not a free pass." - ENV

Angi's Story

I grew up in chaos. My parents fought constantly, and the emotional abuse in my home left me feeling unsafe, unseen, and unworthy. I spent my whole life learning how to survive. I told myself that when I got older, I'd find someone different—someone who wouldn't hurt me, who would keep me safe. And I thought I'd found that person in my husband. When we married, I was certain I'd chosen wisely. I trusted him completely. I believed, with every fiber of my being, that he would never hurt me.

Then he betrayed me. And it wasn't just with anyone—it was with my best friend. The moment I found out, my world shattered. It felt like the only thing keeping me grounded—the one safe place I had—was gone. I could barely breathe. I kept thinking, How could he do this to me? How could she? It wasn't just a betrayal of our marriage; it was a betrayal of my sense of reality. I had carefully built a life that I thought would keep me safe, and it crumbled to dust.

At first, all I could feel was rage and pain. I was furious with him, with her, with myself. But underneath the anger was something even harder to face: fear. If I couldn't trust him, who could I trust? If he could hurt me like this, after everything we promised each other, was anyone really safe? I wanted to run, but something in me said, Stay. See if there's a way to make sense of this. He begged me to give him a chance to make things right, and after a lot of soul-searching, I decided to try.

It wasn't easy. I demanded the truth from him—every ugly, painful truth. And what came out was a story I had never fully heard. My husband grew up with a single mom who was always working, never there when he needed her. His father had abandoned him when he was just three years old, and no one ever taught him how to handle the pain that came with that loss. He fell in with the wrong crowd, numbing his feelings with sex and porn because it was easier than dealing with his emotions. He didn't know how to talk about what was going on inside him, so he shoved everything down, hoping it would just go away. But it didn't. It stayed with him, and eventually, it found a way out.

Hearing his story didn't excuse what he did, but it gave me a deeper understanding of the man I married. I saw that he wasn't the perfect person I had imagined. He was flawed, just like me, with wounds that ran as deep as my own. I realized that both of us had brought the pain of our pasts into our marriage. I had chosen him, hoping he would make me feel completely safe, but that was never his sole responsibility. And he had leaned on me to fill the emptiness inside him, which was something I could never do.

We both had a lot of work to do—not just to heal from the betrayal, but to heal from the wounds we carried from childhood. He had to face the shame he felt about his past and learn how to forgive himself and his parents. And I had to forgive myself for trusting someone who hurt me. I had to forgive my family for not giving me the safety I needed growing up. And eventually, I had to forgive him—not because what he did was okay, but because holding on to the anger was hurting me more than it was helping me.

Forgiveness was not a straight path. It took time, and I fought with it every step of the way. Some days, I felt like I could do it. Other days, it felt impossible. But we kept showing up for each other, and little by little, things began to shift. We learned how to talk about our feelings without fear. He stopped shutting down, and I stopped chasing him for reassurance. We found new ways to connect—ways that felt honest and safe. And most importantly, we agreed that we would not pass down the pain of our pasts to our children. We are working hard every day to create a family built on secure attachment, where emotions are welcomed, not buried, and where safety comes from connection, not perfection.

Looking back, I see that forgiveness isn't about erasing the past. It's about understanding that we are all carrying things that shape who we are, and sometimes, those things make us hurt the people we love. I've come to accept that forgiveness doesn't have to be perfect. You don't have to forgive completely. You just have to get close enough. Close enough to let go of the anger. Close enough to find peace. Close enough to move forward. And that, I've learned, is more than enough.

Journal Prompt 6:

While we are thinking about forgiveness, let's consider forgiving ourselves. When you look back, what do you wish you could forgive yourself for? How can you think about your choices with compassion? Do you believe that you did the best you could with what you knew then? How have you grown and changed since that time?

_____
_____
_____
_____
_____
_____
_____
_____
_____
_____
_____
_____
_____
_____

"The level of vulnerability that is required to heal after infidelity is a level I didn't know existed. And I am choosing to believe that the fact that my wife is willing to get that vulnerable with me now is a good thing and a hopeful thing." -Marc

Journal Prompt 7:

Draft your own acceptance statement, similar to the sample one provided in the beginning of this chapter. How does this statement feel to you? Does it resonate with your experience? What would you add or change to make it more personal? How can you share this statement with your partner?

"His actions make me feel hopeful about healing. He is changing into a better man. He had to lose his entire life know it." -DJ

Journal Prompt 8:

Consider the idea that forgiveness or acceptance is not a permanent decision. How might your feelings about forgiveness change in the future? What factors could influence this change? If your partner is acting in ways that make you feel unsafe or question whether you can stay, how could you talk to them about this?

"The affair definitely changed who I was, and still is changing me. It is easier now as I get to know who this new person is. And it is so sad and yet so solidifying to know there are so many people who can relate." -Cass

Journal Prompt 9:

Reflect on the idea that the betrayal, while deeply painful, might have led to something valuable, such as personal growth or a stronger relationship. How do you feel about this concept? Can you find any value or meaning in the situation? How does thinking about this influence your thoughts on forgiveness or acceptance?

_____
_____
_____
_____
_____
_____
_____
_____
_____
_____
_____
_____
_____

"For me, forgiveness means I understand why it happened and I have compassion for his struggles. I am also still able to love and like him and move forward to heal. I'll never forget. It will never be ok." -Kelly

Journal Prompt 10:

Given all that you've reflected on regarding forgiveness, compassion, accountability, and acceptance, what steps will you take moving forward? How will you apply what you've learned to your healing journey? What will you tell yourself as you continue to navigate these complex emotions? Write about the actions you intend to take, the mindset you wish to cultivate, and any affirmations or self-reminders that will support you in this process.

_____
_____
_____
_____
_____
_____
_____
_____
_____
_____
_____
_____
_____

"I was the emotionally stronger one and I forgave my wife. She did her absolute best to make our relationship stronger for it and I chose to forgive her because we deserve to move on." -BRL

Acknowledgments

Dr. Kathy would like to deeply thank the following individuals who reviewed this book and offered guidance prior to publication:

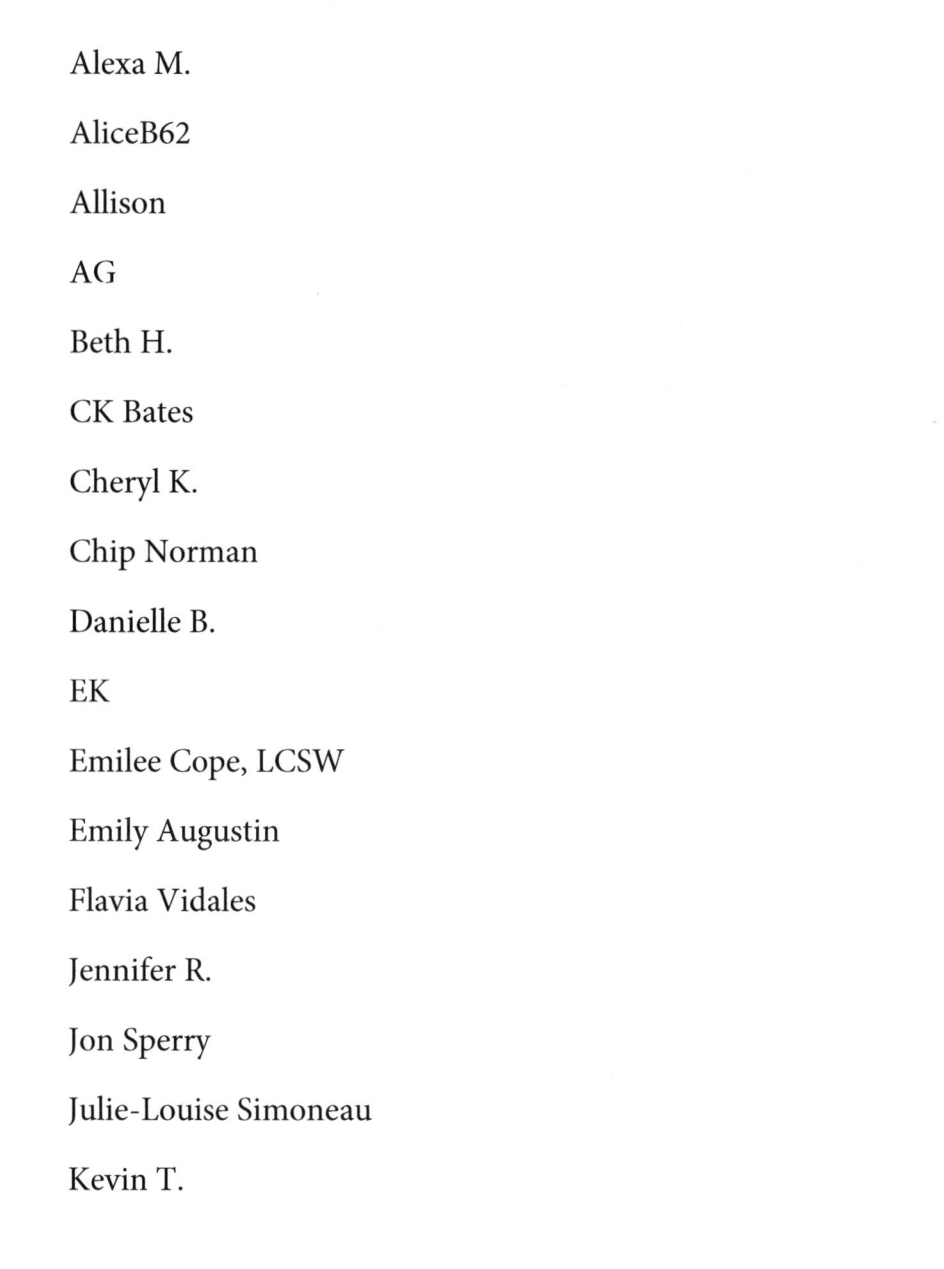

Alexa M.

AliceB62

Allison

AG

Beth H.

CK Bates

Cheryl K.

Chip Norman

Danielle B.

EK

Emilee Cope, LCSW

Emily Augustin

Flavia Vidales

Jennifer R.

Jon Sperry

Julie-Louise Simoneau

Kevin T.

Laura M.

Lori L. Goelz

Dr. Maria Bautista

MLS

MP

Natalie Giorno

Nicki Jay

Paige G.

Rebeca A

Sara Muftic

Sarah Carmona, LCSW

AR

Tina Ilene Hayes

Vicki L. Znavor

50 Ways to Soothe Your Nervous System

1. Go into quiet mode (Stop all noise, technology, anything agitating)
2. Hum your favorite song
3. Box breathing (in for 4s, hold for 4s, out for 4s, hold for 4s)
4. Dance to your favorite song
5. Stretch for 5 minutes
6. Walk (especially in nature)
7. Sit and rock back and forth in sunlight (wear sunblock)
8. Jump on a rebounder or trampoline
9. Do a yoga pose (or a class)
10. Let yourself cry
11. Take a warm bath
12. Wall push-ups
13. Tap alternate sides of your body
14. Progressive Muscle Relaxation
15. 5-7-8 Breathing
16. Hug yourself (while rocking or rubbing upper arms)
17. Massage your hands or feet
18. Apply a face mask
19. Sing your favorite song (or holiday music!)

20. Yawn

21. Splash cold water on face

22. Suck on ice cubes or sour candy

23. Put hands or feet in cold water

24. Take a cold shower

25. Do a cold plunge (only for the brave!)

26. Wrap yourself in a weighted blanket

27. Take a nap (I love this idea!)

28. Listen to music (especially Weightless by Marconi Union)

29. Watch some silly animal videos

30. Remember a funny story and have a laugh

31. Savor something delicious

32. Journal (sit and write about whatever is bothering you)

33. Do a guided meditation (tons of great ones on YouTube)

34. Practice mindfulness

35. Do a grounding exercise (5 things you can see, 4 things you can hear, etc.)

36. Do a gratitude exercise

37. Vividly remember a pleasant memory or experience

38. Chat with a loved one

39. Pet your cat/dog/bird/llama

40. Think about something you're looking forward to

41. Do something creative - paint, knit, doodle

42. Write a letter to a friend

43. Organize 1 drawer in your home

44. Organize 1 box in your closet or garage

45. Work in your garden (something repetitive, like raking, picking up leaves)

46. Engage in aromatherapy (use essential oils or scented candle)

47. Use a stress ball or squeeze a soft object

48. Play with a fidget spinner or fidget toy

49. Practice self-compassion by speaking kindly to yourself

50. Read a loving card that your partner gave you

…..and here are 30 more bonus ideas!

51. Play with some watercolor paints

52. Write down affirmations and read them aloud

53. Make a cup of herbal tea and drink it slowly

54. Give yourself a scalp massage

55. Try acupressure by pressing between your thumb and index finger

56. Do guided visualization of a safe place

57. Listen to nature sounds, like ocean waves or rain

58. Take slow, intentional sips of water

59. Do a simple body scan to notice tension

60. Try a biofeedback app to practice calming exercises

61. Do gentle neck rolls to release tension
62. Focus on relaxing your jaw, neck, and shoulders
63. Practice gratitude by writing down three things you're thankful for
64. Practice self-massage on your shoulders or neck
65. Engage in grounding exercises, like naming things you see, hear, and feel
66. Listen to a podcast that makes you feel calm or inspired
67. Try progressive counting, like counting backward from 100 by fives
68. Practice sensory relaxation by focusing on smells, textures, and sounds around you
69. Lie down with legs up against a wall for 10-15 minutes
70. Try facial tapping or massage with gentle pressure
71. Create a vision board of peaceful, calming images
72. Look at pictures or a photo album of a happy time
73. Take a leisurely bath with Epsom salts
74. Play with clay or putty to release tension
75. Light a candle and watch the flame, focusing on its movement
76. Fold clothes or towels mindfully
77. Imagine yourself in a calming place, like a beach or forest
78. Do a small act of kindness, like texting a compliment to someone
79. Listen to a soothing audiobook or calming story
80. Color in an adult coloring book (particularly the Swearing Cats Coloring Book)

Further Reading

Affair Recovery Books:

- *The Courage to Stay: How to Heal from an Affair and Save Your Marriage* by Kathy Nickerson, Ph.D.

- *Not "Just Friends": Rebuilding Trust and Recovering Your Sanity After Infidelity* by Shirley P. Glass, Ph.D.

- *The State of Affairs: Rethinking Infidelity* by Esther Perel

- *After the Affair, Third Edition: Healing the Pain and Rebuilding Trust When a Partner Has Been Unfaithful* by Janis A. Spring, Ph.D.

- *The Betrayal Bind: How to Heal When the Person You Love the Most Hurts You the Worst* by Michelle Mays, LPC, CSAT

- *Transcending Post-infidelity Stress Disorder (PISD): The Six Stages of Healing* by Dennis C. Ortman

Attachment Books:

- *Secure Love: Create a Relationship That Lasts a Lifetime* by Julie Menanno

- *Attached: The New Science of Adult Attachment and How It Can Help You Find—and Keep—Love* by Amir Levine, MD

- *Securely Attached: Transform Your Attachment Patterns into Loving, Lasting Romantic Relationships* by Eli Harwood

- *Anxiously Attached: Becoming More Secure in Life and Love* by Jessica Baum, LMHC

- *Loving an Avoidant Partner: Understand Dismissive Attachment Style to Bridge Emotional Distance and Create a Secure Relationship* by Krista Cantell

Trauma Books:

- *Complex PTSD: From Surviving to Thriving: A Guide and Map for Recovering from Childhood Trauma* by Pete Walker
- *Getting Past Your Past: Take Control of Your Life with Self-Help Techniques from EMDR Therapy Paperback* by Francine Shapiro, Ph.D.
- *What Happened to You? Conversations on Trauma, Resilience, and Healing* by Oprah Winfrey and Bruce D. Perry, M.D,, Ph.D.
- *The Deepest Well: Healing the Long-Term Effects of Childhood Trauma and Adversity* by Nadine Burke Harris
- *How To Do the Work: Recognize Your Patterns, Heal from Your Past, and Create Your Self* by Dr. Nicole LePera
- *In an Unspoken Voice: How the Body Releases Trauma and Restores Goodness* by Peter A. Levine
- *The Myth of Normal: Trauma, Illness, and Healing in a Toxic Culture* by Gabor Maté, MD

Relationship Books:

- *The Seven Principles for Making Marriage Work* by John Gottman, Ph.D. and Nan Silver
- *What Makes Love Last? : How to Build Trust and Avoid Betrayal* by John Gottman, Ph.D. and Nan Silver
- *Hold Me Tight: Seven Conversations for a Lifetime of Love* by Dr. Sue Johnson

- *How to Be an Adult in Relationships: The Five Keys to Mindful Loving* by David Richo
- *Fight Right: How Successful Couples Turn Conflict Into Connection* by Julie Schwartz Gottman, Ph.D. and John Gottman, Ph.D.
- *Feeling Good Together: The Secret to Making Troubled Relationships* Work by David D. Burns M.D.

Depression, Anxiety, and Grief Books:

- *The Upward Spiral: Using Neuroscience to Reverse the Course of Depression, One Small Change at a Time* by Alex Korb, Ph.D.
- *Mind Over Mood: Change How You Feel by Changing the Way You Think* by Dennis Greenberger, Ph.D. and Christine A. Padesky, Ph.D.
- *Retrain Your Brain: Cognitive Behavioral Therapy in 7 Weeks: A Workbook for Managing Depression and Anxiety* by Seth J. Gillihan, Ph.D.
- *Stop Overthinking: 23 Techniques to Relieve Stress, Stop Negative Spirals, Declutter Your Mind, and Focus on the Present* by Nick Trenton
- *Unwinding Anxiety: New Science Shows How to Break the Cycles of Worry and Fear to Heal Your Mind* by Judson Brewer M.D., Ph.D.
- *It's OK That You're Not OK* by Megan Devine
- *Bearing the Unbearable: Love, Loss, and the Heartbreaking Path of Grief* by Joanne Cacciatore, Ph.D.

Finding A Therapist

How To Find a Therapist:

- I believe the best therapist to help you heal from infidelity is knowledgeable about general couples therapy, affair recovery, attachment theory, trauma, and addiction. Look for someone experienced in Gottman Couples Therapy, Emotionally Focused Couples Therapy (EFCT), and trained in trauma and addiction.

- If you have the opportunity to interview a therapist before your first session (this is not always possible), ask about their approach to couples work, their experience with Gottman/EFCT, and their training in trauma and addiction. It's rare to find someone with all these credentials, but if they have some, that's great!

- The most important question to ask a potential couples therapist before you start working with them is: *What's your perspective on healing from infidelity? Do you think it's possible or is it pretty rare?* If someone tells you it's rare or the relationship will never be the same, then look for someone else.

- If you are looking for an individual therapist for yourself to heal from infidelity, I'd recommend a trauma specialist for the betrayed partner and either a trauma or addiction specialist for the straying partner.

- PsychologyToday.com has a therapist finder tool where you can search for a therapist in your area and filter by insurance type, cost, area of specialization, and more.

- TherapyDen.com offers a therapist directory where you can search for therapists to meet with in person or virtually, filtering by specialties, services, and location.

- Gottman.com has the Gottman Referral Network, where you can easily find a Gottman-trained couples therapist near you.

- EMDRIA.org offers a Trauma Specialist Directory. EMDR International Association is a professional organization for EMDR practitioners and researchers, and you can search their database of licensed therapists specializing in EMDR and trauma.

- AffairRecovery.com offers courses, retreats, and groups that past clients have found beneficial. They have a Christian orientation but welcome clients of any faith. Their programs support anyone seeking recovery from betrayal, regardless of religious beliefs.

- Visit my website, DrKathyNickerson.com, and search for therapy referrals to find a list of individual therapists I personally know, work with regularly, and recommend.

References

Afifi, W. S., Falato, W. L., & Weiner, J. L. (2001). Identity concerns following a severe relational transgression: The role of discovery method for the relational outcomes of infidelity. *Journal of Social and Personal Relationships, 18*(2), 291–308. https://doi.org/10.1177/0265407501182003

Allen, E. S., & Atkins, D. C. (2012). The association of divorce and extramarital sex in a representative U.S. sample. *Journal of Family Issues, 33*(11), 1477–1493. https://doi.org/10.1177/0192513X12446058

American Association for Marriage and Family Therapy. (2012). *Infidelity: Causes, consequences, and treatment strategies.* American Association for Marriage and Family Therapy. Retrieved from https://www.aamft.org

Cramer, D., & Jowett, S. (2010). Perceived empathy, accurate empathy, and relationship satisfaction in romantic relationships. *Journal of Social and Personal Relationships, 27*(3), 327–349. https://doi.org/10.1177/0265407510371323

Fenell, D. L. (1993). Characteristics of long-term first marriages. *Journal of Mental Health Counseling, 15*(4), 446–460.

Fife, S. T., Weeks, G. R., & Stellberg-Filbert, J. (2013). Facilitating forgiveness in the treatment of infidelity: An interpersonal model. *Journal of Family Therapy, 35*(4), 343–367. https://doi.org/10.1111/j.1467-6427.2013.00578.x

Finkel, E. J., Rusbult, C. E., Kumashiro, M., & Hannon, P. A. (2002). Dealing with betrayal in close relationships: Does commitment promote forgiveness? *Journal of Personality and Social Psychology, 82*(6), 956–974. https://doi.org/10.1037/0022-3514.82.6.956

Freyd, J. J. (1996). *Betrayal trauma: The logic of forgetting childhood abuse.* Harvard University Press.

Glass, S. P., & Wright, T. L. (1997). Reconstructing marriages after the trauma of infidelity. In W. K. Halford & H. J. Markman (Eds.), *Clinical handbook of marriage and couples interventions* (pp. 471-507). Wiley.

Gordon, K. C., & Baucom, D. H. (1999). Understanding betrayals in marriage: A synthesized model of forgiveness. *Family Process, 38*(4), 425–449. https://doi.org/10.1111/j.1545-5300.1999.00425.x

Gordon, K. C., Baucom, D. H., & Snyder, D. K. (2004). An integrative intervention for promoting recovery from extramarital affairs. *Journal of Marital and Family Therapy, 30*(2), 213–231. https://doi.org/10.1111/j.1752-0606.2004.tb01264.x

Gordon, K. C., & Mitchell, E. A. (2020). Infidelity in the time of COVID-19. *Family Process, 59*(3), 956–966. https://doi.org/10.1111/famp.12605

Gottman, J., & Gottman, J. (2017). *Treating affairs and trauma* (Unpublished manuscript). Gottman Institute, Seattle, USA.

Horowitz, M. J. (1976). Stress response syndromes. *Archives of General Psychiatry, 33*(11), 1457–1463. https://doi.org/10.1001/archpsyc.1976.01770240029002

Johnson, S. M., Makinen, J. A., & Millikin, J. W. (2001). Attachment injuries in couple relationships: A new perspective on impasses in couples therapy. *Journal of Marital and Family Therapy, 27*(2), 145–155. https://doi.org/10.1111/j.1752-0606.2001.tb01119.x

Labrecque, L. T., & Whisman, M. A. (2017). Attitudes toward and prevalence of extramarital sex and descriptions of extramarital partners in the 21st century. *Journal of Family Psychology, 31*(7), 952–957. https://doi.org/10.1037/fam0000313

MacIntosh, H. B., Reissing, E. D., & Andruff, H. L. (2007). Attachment and the experience of betrayal. *Journal of Social and Personal Relationships, 24*(5), 739–757. https://doi.org/10.1177/0265407507079273

McNulty, J. K., Finkel, E. J., DeWall, C. N., Slotter, E. B., & Oaten, M. (2012). Using I^3 theory to clarify when dispositional aggressiveness predicts intimate partner violence perpetration. *Journal of Personality and Social Psychology, 102*(3), 533–549. https://doi.org/10.1037/a0026007

Miller, S. L., & Maner, J. K. (2009). Coping with romantic betrayal: Gender differences in how emotions are linked to infidelity. *Evolutionary Psychology, 7*(3), 342–363.

Miller, W. R. (2005). What predicts recovery from the emotional impact of infidelity? A longitudinal study of betrayed partners. *Journal of Marital and Family Therapy, 31*(3), 291–306. https://doi.org/10.1111/j.1752-0606.2005.tb01548.x

Nickerson, K., Stone, R., & Davies, R. (2023). Affair attitudes survey. In *Cheating statistics - How men and women compare based on 5,783 reports*. Retrieved from https://drkathynickerson.com/blogs/relationship/cheating-statistics-how-men-and-women-compare-based-on-5-783-reports

Ortman, D. C. (2005). Post-infidelity stress disorder. *Journal of Psychosocial Nursing and Mental Health Services, 43*(10), 46–54. https://doi.org/10.3928/02793695-20051001-04

Ortman, D. (2009). *Transcending post-infidelity stress disorder: The six stages of healing.* Celestial Arts.

Roos, L. E., Hodson, A., & Fergus, T. A. (2021). The association between social support and posttraumatic stress symptoms among survivors of betrayal trauma. *European Journal of Psychotraumatology, 12*(1), 1883925. https://doi.org/10.1080/20008198.2021.1883925

Rokach, A., & Chan, S. H. (2023). Love and infidelity: Causes and consequences. *International Journal of Environmental Research and Public Health, 20*(5), 3904. https://doi.org/10.3390/ijerph20053904

Seligman, M. E. P., Steen, T. A., Park, N., & Peterson, C. (2005). Positive psychology progress: Empirical validation of interventions. *American Psychologist, 60*(5), 410–421. https://doi.org/10.1037/0003-066X.60.5.410

Shrout, M. R., & Weigel, D. J. (2020). Coping with infidelity: The moderating role of self-esteem. *Personality and Individual Differences, 154,* 109631. https://doi.org/10.1016/j.paid.2019.109631

Snyder, D. K., Baucom, D. H., & Gordon, K. C. (2007). *Getting past the affair: A program to help you cope, heal, and move on — together or apart.* The Guilford Press.

Snyder, D. K., & Mitchell, A. E. (2008). Affective reconstructive couple therapy. In A. S. Gurman (Ed.), *Clinical handbook of couple therapy* (4th ed., pp. 353–382). The Guilford Press.

Solomon, S. D., & Teagno, L. J. (2006). *Intimacy after infidelity: How to rebuild and affair-proof your marriage.* New Harbinger Publications.

About the Author

Kathy Nickerson, Ph.D., is a highly respected clinical psychologist, acclaimed author, and foremost authority in relationships. Over her 24-year career, Dr. Kathy has emerged as a trusted expert in guiding couples through the complexities of love, betrayal, and infidelity. Her latest book, "The Courage to Stay: How to Heal from an Affair and Save Your Marriage," released in October 2022, has received six independent book awards for its groundbreaking insights into affair recovery.

Dr. Kathy's commitment to understanding betrayal trauma led her to conduct one of the largest studies of betrayed and unfaithful partners ever undertaken, advancing the field's understanding of affair dynamics and recovery. Her research, combined with her clinical expertise, has driven the development of innovative therapeutic approaches that integrate trauma therapy with proven relationship-healing methodologies, bringing new hope to couples navigating the aftermath of infidelity.

Throughout her remarkable career, Dr. Kathy has shared her insights at over 70 conferences, captivating audiences with her compassionate approach and practical advice. She has authored more than 85 professional articles and books, solidifying her as a leading figure in relationship psychology. Her expert perspectives are regularly featured in national publications like *CNBC, Reader's Digest, The Independent, Yahoo News, MSN, Good Housekeeping, Thrive Global, Psychology Today, Newsweek,* and *Forbes.*

Driven by her deep commitment to saving marriages and healing relationships, Dr. Kathy has devoted her private practice in Southern California to affair recovery, a subject she holds close to her heart. In addition to her clinical work, Dr. Kathy has an active presence on social media platforms like TikTok, where she shares valuable advice on infidelity, affair recovery, and relationship repair. Through her website (www.DrKathyNickerson.com) and insightful blog, she provides a wealth of resources, including tips, guidance, and engaging Q&A sessions, all designed to empower couples with the tools they need to navigate the complexities of love and commitment.

Dr. Kathy earned her Ph.D. and M.S. in psychology, following her undergraduate work at UC Irvine in Chemistry. Kathy began her career teaching and counseling at-risk youth with the Orange County Health Care Agency. Kathy then led a distinguished program for the United States Department of Justice, where she and her team trained people how to recognize and respond to domestic violence and child abuse. During these years, Kathy discovered the critical connection between healthy relationships and healthy families.

Happily married for 25 years, Dr. Kathy brings both clinical expertise and real-life experience to her work. Outside the office, she enjoys her roles as a wife, sister, auntie, and friend. She and her husband love traveling, digging for fossils, and volunteering with Southern California Bulldog Rescue. When unwinding, Dr. Kathy is often found reading, gardening, experimenting in the kitchen, making handmade gifts, or relaxing with her dogs and a glass of wine while watching true crime shows.

Made in the USA
Monee, IL
22 May 2025

"Our sympathy is cold to the RELATION of distant misery." — Edward Gibbon

HOW TRADITIONS LIVE AND DIE

FOUNDATIONS OF HUMAN INTERACTION

General Editor

N.J. Enfield, Max Planck Institute for Psycholinguistics, Radboud University, Nijmegen, and the University of Sydney

This series promotes new interdisciplinary research on the elements of human sociality, in particular as they relate to the activity and experience of communicative interaction and human relationships. Books in this series explore the foundations of human interaction from a wide range of perspectives, using multiple theoretical and methodological tools. A premise of the series is that a proper understanding of human sociality is only possible if we take a truly interdisciplinary approach.

Series Editorial Board

Michael Tomasello (Max Planck Institute Leipzig)
Dan Sperber (Jean Nicod Institute)
Elizabeth Couper-Kuhlen (University of Helsinki)
Paul Kockelman (University of Texas, Austin)
Sotaro Kita (University of Warwick)
Tanya Stivers (University of California, Los Angeles)
Jack Sidnell (University of Toronto)

Recently Published in the Series

Agent, Person, Subject, Self
Paul Kockelman

Exploring the Interactional Instinct
Edited by Anna Dina L. Joaquin and John H. Schumann

Relationship Thinking
N.J. Enfield

Talking About Troubles in Conversation
Gail Jefferson
Edited by Paul Drew, John Heritage, Gene Lerner, and Anita Pomerantz

The Instruction of Imagination
Daniel Dor

How Traditions Live and Die
Olivier Morin

*I act w/ complete certainty.
But this certainty is my own.
— Ludwig —*

HOW TRADITIONS LIVE AND DIE

see Whybrow Brain Well Tuned Instrument

Olivier Morin

*CREATIVITY IS ALLOWING YOURSELF TO MAKE MISTAKES.
ART IS KNOWING WHICH ONES TO KEEP.
— Scott Adams —*

They (Traditions) have to thrive to survive

OXFORD UNIVERSITY PRESS

OXFORD
UNIVERSITY PRESS

Oxford University Press is a department of the University of Oxford.
It furthers the University's objective of excellence in research, scholarship,
and education by publishing worldwide.

Oxford New York
Auckland Cape Town Dar es Salaam Hong Kong Karachi
Kuala Lumpur Madrid Melbourne Mexico City Nairobi
New Delhi Shanghai Taipei Toronto

With offices in
Argentina Austria Brazil Chile Czech Republic France Greece
Guatemala Hungary Italy Japan Poland Portugal Singapore
South Korea Switzerland Thailand Turkey Ukraine Vietnam

Oxford is a registered trade mark of Oxford University Press in the UK and certain other countries.

Published in the United States of America by
Oxford University Press
198 Madison Avenue, New York, NY 10016

Originally published in French as *Comment les traditions naissent et meurent*
© ODILE JACOB, 2011. Translated and Revised by the author, Olivier Morin.

First published in English in 2016 by Oxford University Press.

All rights reserved. No part of this publication may be reproduced, stored in a retrieval system,
or transmitted, in any form or by any means, without the prior permission in writing
of Oxford University Press, or as expressly permitted by law, by license, or under terms agreed
with the appropriate reproduction rights organization. Inquiries concerning reproduction outside
the scope of the above should be sent to the Rights Department, Oxford University Press,
at the address above.

You must not circulate this work in any other form
and you must impose this same condition on any acquirer.

Library of Congress Cataloging-in-Publication Data
Morin, Olivier.
 [Comment les traditions naissent et meurent. English]
 How traditions live and die / Olivier Morin.
  p. cm. — (Foundations of human interaction)
 Includes bibliographical references and index.
 ISBN 978-0-19-021050-2 (pbk. : alk. paper) — ISBN 978-0-19-021049-6
(hardcover : alk. paper) 1. Tradition (Philosophy) 2. Knowledge, Sociology of. 3. Social change—
Sociological aspects. 4. Social values. 5. Socialization. 6. Culture diffusion. 7. Interpersonal
communication and culture. I. Title.
 B105.T7M6713 2015
 306—dc23
                    2015013931

9 8 7 6 5 4 3 2 1

Printed in the United States of America on acid-free paper

CONTENTS

Foreword   xi
Series Editor Preface   xiii
Acknowledgments   xv

Introduction. The Flop Problem and the Wear-and-Tear Problem   1

1. The Transmission and Diffusion of Traditions   12

    Culture as Distributed   13
        Cultural Homogeneity Is Overrated . . .   14
        . . . Yet Homogeneity Remains a Heavily Influential Hypothesis   20
        A Quantitative and Abstract View of Culture   21
    What Is Cultural Transmission?   23
        Distinguishing Diffusion and Transmission   23
        Transmission and Invention Are Not Opposites   26
        Not All Differences between Societies Are Traditional   31
        Our Cultural Repertoires Could Not Exist without
            Transmission   35
        Culture: A Set of Traditions Rather than a Set of Differences   36
    Do Traditions Exist?   37
        Some Traditions Are as Durable as They Seem   37
        Culture Is Not an Undecomposable Whole   41
        Why Anthropologists Are No Longer Interested in Traditions   43
        Traditions Do Not Exist Solely as Ideas   47
    Two Questions   50
        Why Are There Traditions Rather than Nothing?   50
        Why Does One Species Monopolize Traditions?   51

2. Communication and Imitation   53

   Imitating and Understanding Others 54
      Looking for "True Imitation" 56
      Imitation Is neither a Human Privilege nor the Source of Our Cultures 58
   Human Ostensive Communication 60
      Involuntary Transmission: When Behaviors Leak Information 62
      Non-Ostensive Voluntary Transmission 63
      Voluntary and Overt Transmission: a Human Phenomenon 65
      Culture Did Not Build Our Communicative Skills from the Ground Up 66
      Ostensive Communication Is Not Particularly Faithful 69
   Communicating to Imitate, Imitating to Communicate 70
      Communication for Imitation: Demonstrations and "Rational" Imitation 70
      Ostensive Communication Goes Beyond Teaching 74
      It Takes Place at Any Time, from Anyone, and for Any Reason 75
      It Requires an Active Reconstruction of the Transmitted Material 77
      It Can Bypass Language 79
      It Does Not Need Adults 83
   "A Light, Insubstantial, Fugitive Web" 84

3. The Myth of Compulsive Imitation   87

   How Far Do We Follow Conformity and Deference? 88
      An Ambiguity of Dual Inheritance Theory 88
   "Simple Heuristics that Make Us Smart"—Really? 91
      Docility: Does Compulsive Imitation Breed Altruism? 93
   The Case for Flexible Imitation 99
   Imitation: the Key that Unlocks Every Door? 104
      Conformity and Deference: Psychological Mechanisms or Social Facts? 104
      Cultural Diffusion in a Population of Flexible Imitators 106
      Negative Informational Cascades Are Short or Rare 108
      Waves of Compulsive Imitation: Often Evoked, Seldom Documented 110

The Influence of Influentials: Tautology or
  Misunderstanding?   115
Closing the Case against the Imitation Hypothesis   119

4. A Theory of Diffusion Chains   121

Transmission Is Easy, Diffusion Is Hard   122
  There Is No Inertia for Transmission   122
  Why a Few Transmission Episodes Do Not Make a Diffusion
    Chain   124
  Transmission Fidelity Is Not the Problem   128
For Transmission, Quantity Matters More than Quality   130
  Cultural Transmission Is No Chinese Whispers Game   130
  A Tradition Must Be Carried by Many Robust
    Diffusion Chains   131
  Redundancy and Repetition Make Diffusion Chains
    Less Fragile   132
  Traditions Must Proliferate in Order to Survive   133
  Stability and Success Go Together   134
Why Do Traditions Proliferate?   136
  Accessibility: Certain Populations Make Contacts Easier   136
  Many Ways to Proliferate, Several Types of Diffusion Chains   138
Cultural Selection—Many Are Called, Few Are Chosen   140
  Traditions Survive Cultural Selection by Being Attractive   144
  Attraction Can Be Linked to a Restricted Context,
    or More General   146
  Traditions Are Appealing in Many Ways, Not All of Them
    Cognitive   148
  Transmission Is Not Memorization, Culture Is Not
    Collective Memory   152
When Does Psychology Drive Culture?   155
  Politeness Norms Last Longer if They Tap into Our Sense
    of Disgust   156
  Among the Kwaio, Beliefs about Spirits Survived
    by Being Intuitive   157
  Generally Attractive Traditions Do Not Always Prevail   158
  How the Vagaries of Diffusion Dilute General Attraction   160
  Local Attraction Can Override General Attraction, Locally   160

General Attraction Prevails in Long and Narrow Diffusion
   Chains   162
For Instance, Widely Diffused Languages Tend to Be Easier
   on the Mind   164
The Benefit of Moving across Scales When Looking
   at Culture   167

5. The Passing of Generations   169

"That Constant Stream of Recruits to Mankind"   170
   Demographic Generations Are Not Social Generations   170
   How to Link Humans Scattered across Time   174
   How Generational Overlap Makes Diffusion Easier   175
   Demographic and Social Obstacles to Transmission   177
   Everything Your Parents Did Not Teach You about Culture   180
Why Do Children Have Traditions?   185
   The *Lost World* of Children's Peer Culture   187
   Children's Traditions Are Not Vestigial Adult Practices   190
   They Are Mostly Transmitted from Child to Child   192
   They Are Children's Games, and They Look Like It   194
   They Are at Least as Durable as Cross-Generational
      Traditions   196
   They Are Homogenic and Share a Common Fate   199
What Makes Children's Peer Culture Last?   201
   Traditionalism Is Not What Took Children's Culture
      across Time   201
   Neither Does Memorability Preserve Children's Rhymes   204
   Children's Traditions Were Selected to Proliferate   207
   Generational Turnover Need Not Impair Cultural Survival   210

6. An Ever More Cultural Animal   213

Three Clues for One Puzzle   215
What Is Cultural Accumulation?   219
   "Cumulative Culture" Is an Avatar of Evolutionary
      Gradualism   220
   Faithfully Replicated Small Changes Cannot Explain
      Everything   222
   Traditions Often Endure without Improving . . .   223

...and Cultural Progress May Do without Conservation 224
The Growing Number of Traditions Is What Matters 226
The Opening Up of the Human Public Domain 228
   Human Populations Became Increasingly Hospitable
      to Culture... 228
   ...But Hospitable Populations Are No Guarantee
      of Cultural Progress 232
   The Extreme Accumulation Hypothesis 233
What Kind of Cultural Animal Are We? 237
   We Need Not Believe that We Are Wired for Culture... 238
   ...or that Communication Is Designed for Cultural
      Transmission 243
   A Species Taken in a Cultural Avalanche 246
   The Growing Weight of Traditions Does Not Erase
      Human Nature 248
   A Cultural Animal by Accident 251

Appendix 253
Bibliography 267
Index 291

FOREWORD

In a way, this book is the third incarnation of my PhD thesis, defended in 2010 and published in French in 2011, as *Comment les traditions naissent et meurent—la transmission culturelle*. While translating that book, I felt it necessary to revise various parts, and the book that you have opened substantially departs from the French version. Chapters 1, 2, and 4 were translated almost as they were, but chapters 3, 5, and 6 have been thoroughly rewritten. A technical appendix now supplements the essay on children's traditions that forms the core of chapter 5. I have made available the relevant data in a database that can be consulted online (http://sites.google.com/site/sitedoliviermorin/morin-rabelais-online-material.pdf).

This book, however, is not quite a second edition of the 2011 version. There is no change in the overall claims and arguments worth signaling, and no attempt has been made to update the references with the post-2011 literature on the many topics this book touches on. The literature on cultural evolution is growing at such a pace that an altogether new book would be needed to deal with these developments. On the other hand, I also felt that the present argument could still stand on its own today.

In fact, there are only so many books and articles that I think would have made a huge difference to this book, had it been written now. One of them is Thom Scott-Phillips's *Speaking Our Minds* (2014). Chapters 2 and 6 of the present work dwell on the evolution of ostensive communication on more than one occasion. They echo the view that ostensive communication could have evolved in rather straightforward ways described by the theory of natural selection, and that its cultural exploitation by languages was secondary to its biological evolution. In 2010 arguments to back this claim existed but were scattered among dozens of papers. Now a book exists that makes the case quite elegantly.

Two sections of chapter 2 have been adapted, with many modifications, in a 2014 *Biological Theory* paper: "Is cooperation a maladaptive by-product of cultural transmission? Simon's Docility Hypothesis reconsidered" (Morin 2014). The part of chapter 5 that dwells on children's peer culture was published (in an early version much amended since) in 2010 under the title "Pourquoi les enfants ont-ils des traditions ?" in *Terrain : revue d'ethnologie de l'Europe* (Morin 2010).

Durkheim is quoted in G. Simpson's translation, Johannes Herder in T. O. Churchill's translation. The version of Marcel Proust's *Remembrance of Things Past* used here was due to C. K. S. Moncrieff. Gabriel Tarde's *Laws of Imitation* is quoted in E. C. Parsons's translation. Additional quotes from these and other francophone authors are translated by me.

SERIES EDITOR PREFACE

Human interaction is the engine room of social reality. It is where minds meet, and thus where minds go public. When we encounter other people, we learn what they do and how they do it, what they have and why. And as Olivier Morin richly explores here, we may find others' actions, ideas, inventions and possessions more or less attractive. If there is enough attraction, we will copy, adopt, or transform the bits of culture that appeal to us, and in this way we drive the spread and possible transformation of traditions. This is how traditions become distributed across minds, places, times, and worlds. They are not just the products of interacting agents; they become contexts for interacting agents. So just as human interaction is a foundation of culture, culture becomes a foundation of human interaction.

N. J. Enfield
Sydney, July 2015

ACKNOWLEDGMENTS

The dissertation that became this book was completed in 2010 at the Institut Jean Nicod in Paris and the Central European University in Budapest, under the supervision of Dan Sperber. In Paris, I received help and advice from Pierre Jacob, Élisabeth Pacherie, Jérôme Dokic, Gloria Origgi, Steven Davis, Frédérique de Vignemont, Delphine Blitman, Florian Cova, Valeria Giardini and Marie Guillot. Not at Nicod, but still in Paris, I learnt a lot from Maurice Bloch, Julie Grèzes, and Swann Pichon. Christophe Heintz kindly greeted me at the CEU Budapest, where I also benefited from conversations with György Gergely and Gergely Csibra. The "Nash" group (standing for "Naturalisme et sciences humaines") has been, then and now, a decisive intellectual influence: Nicolas Baumard, Pierrick Bourrat, Nicolas Claidière, Coralie Chevallier, Olivier Mascaro, Hugo Mercier, Hugo Viciana, Ophélia Deroy, Anikó Sebestény, Guillaume Dezecache, Christophe Heintz, Thom Scott-Phillips. Part of the work that went into chapter 5's theory of intra-generational diffusion was produced with Jean-Baptiste André, who influenced this whole work in many different ways, always with acumen. I was lucky in being able to present this work to a wide range of audiences from different disciplines. For this I am grateful to David Berliner, Odile Jacob Jean-Baptiste van der Hernst, Michael Stewart—and, especially, to Christine Langlois and the whole team of the journal *Terrain*. My very special thanks, and more, go to Olivier Mascaro.

The dissertation's jury, composed of Daniel Andler, Pascal Boyer, Jean Gayon, Bruno Karsenti, and Bernard Thierry, examined my text with tireless, generous thoroughness, and this version owes them a lot. My debt to my supervisor, Dan Sperber, will be apparent to any one who reads this book and his work. It is through Dan that I first came across most of the people cited here, and most of the ideas in this work.

The English version was written while I was a post-doctoral fellow at the KLI Institute in Klosterneuburg. Thanks to Daniel Dennett's generous invitation, I was fortunate enough to discuss preliminary drafts of this version in

Santa Fe with Susan Blackmore, Robert Boyd, Nicolas Claidière, Peter Godfrey-Smith, Joseph Henrich, Peter Richerson, Dan Sperber, and Kim Sterelny. Their feedback was extremely precious. So were the advice and comments given by Jay Fogelman, Thom Scott-Phillips, Dan Sperber, and Radu Umbres. I also wish to thank two anonymous reviewers for their efforts. This edition benefitted from the technical help of the SOMICS grant (*Constructing Social Minds: Coordination, Communication, and Cultural Transmission*) of the ERC.

HOW TRADITIONS LIVE AND DIE

INTRODUCTION

THE FLOP PROBLEM AND THE WEAR-AND-TEAR PROBLEM

> ... or again, if any of her friends were to reproach her, in terms which she felt to be undeserved [Albertine said]: "That really is magnificent!" an expression dictated in such cases by a sort of middle-class tradition almost as old as the Magnificat itself, and one which a girl slightly out of temper and confident that she is in the right employs, as the saying is, "quite naturally," that is to say because she has heard the words from her mother, just as she has learned to say her prayers or to greet a friend. All these expressions Mme. Bontemps had imparted to her at the same time as her hatred of the Jews and her feeling for black, which was always suitable and becoming, indeed without any formal instruction, but as the piping of the parent goldfinches serves as a model for that of the young ones, recently hatched, so that they in turn grow into true goldfinches also.
>
> *(Proust 1921/1982, 369–370)*

This depiction of cultural transmission reflects a view that guides many researches in this field. Cultural transmission goes from one generation to the other. It can be so unconscious and automatic as to seem natural: Albertine faithfully absorbed the customs of her society, which she reproduces without even thinking about it. Culture, in this view, is acquired in bulk. Prayers, antisemitism, greeting conventions, the elegance of the bourgeoisie: one smooth socialization process got all these things from Mrs. Bontemps's head into her niece's.

Are traditions always passed on in that way—faithfully, vertically, and en bloc? This book would like to convince you that they are not—that transmission inside a generation matters as much as transmission between generations; that we do not spontaneously copy everything that is done around us; that culture is made of relatively discrete, relatively independent traditions. If true, these ideas can shed light on the life of traditions—what makes some of them last, thrive, or go extinct, and why they are more numerous among modern humans than anywhere else.

Johann Herder may have been the first philosopher clearly to make the claim (to make it clearly and to substantiate it with evidence) that human populations are not influenced solely by their heredity, their milieu, their laws. In his *Ideas for the Philosophy of History of Humanity*, he argued that another force should be added to the mix: the traditions that are passed on inside each human group. Our species being everywhere the same, he argued, environmental factors do not suffice to explain the differences between human groups: these differences are *cultural*.

This idea raises many questions: why does culture play such a role in human life? What is so special about us that makes us cultural animals?

God, Herder replied, endowed us with special "receptive powers" (Herder, 1791/2010: 313). Because of those, we inevitably absorb our culture from the moment we are born, "like a wet sponge that has long been soaking on a wet floor" (Herder, 2010, 315). Thus, a young girl soaked in a bourgeois education cannot fail to catch good manners and antisemitism, as one picks up germs from a swimming pool.

Where would this capacity come from? Herder cited imitation, language, a spontaneous sympathy for others' feelings, the plasticity of the human brain. The psychology of his time did not allow him to develop those hypotheses.

Why would God choose to turn us, and us alone, into cultural animals? How does imitation work? How does language? Two centuries later, these questions have changed. Divine intervention does not seem quite such a satisfactory explanation of how we became cultural. We seek an answer that would be compatible with what we know of the past of our species—hence with the theory of evolution by natural selection. In other words, we seek a biologically and psychologically plausible theory of culture. This objective seems more accessible today than it was even thirty years ago. Interdisciplinary approaches have thrived. Anthropologists, psychologists, biologists, ethologists, and philosophers each bring their piece of the puzzle. The way we look at culture has been transformed.

Ethologists, for instance, have discovered what rapidly became known as animal traditions: behaviors that are specific to certain groups, whose existence seems best explained by transmission from one individual to another. While trying to account for this discovery, comparative psychologists have investigated behavior transmission in a variety of species, from fishes and rats to great apes and humans. These explorations may help us learn how humans became cultural animals.

The same question can also be explored by studying cultural transmission as it functions among humans today. That second way of approaching the problem is older. Its beginnings can be dated to the writings of Gabriel Tarde. It is now being revived, with models borrowed from epidemiology and population biology. The successes of these methods raises a certain number of questions. Is cultural transmission comparable to the spread of genes and viruses? Is it comparably faithful? Is it primarily vertical, from parent to child, or does it take other paths?

These new approaches to culture differ on many such issues. How much similarity is there between the history of traditions and the biological evolution of species? For some, the analogy is all but perfect, for others it is so vague as to be confusing. Do traditions tend to travel along generational lines, or could they survive without ever taking that path? Both options have defenders. How faithful is cultural transmission? Some claim that we copy them faithfully, almost automatically. Others think we pick and choose what suits us among the traditions that surround us, refashioning and customizing culture as we acquire it.

Still, the new approaches agree on at least two counts. First, a taste for quantitative methods (mostly mathematical models and controlled experiments) and quantitative questions. How long do traditions live? What makes them (more or less) successful? How do they accumulate through time? Why are they so much more numerous among humans? How homogeneous can human cultures get? The answers to all these questions cannot be yes or no: they ask for quantitative estimates, albeit often very rough ones.

The new approaches have another thing in common: they see culture as a set of ideas and practices, each of which could spread independently from the others. This idea is at odds with the view that prevails in many contemporary anthropological circles, where cultures are readily described as coherent structures, well-integrated blocks of signification, where everything hangs together with everything else. The reverse, I will argue, is equally plausible. Religious rites, dressing etiquette, political opinions, can be acquired separately. They do not necessarily hang together in a block. Their association in certain heads, at certain times, is in large part a product of the vagaries of cultural histories. Cultures could be made of elements that need not stick together. These elements have received various names, depending on the author or the century: *items, culturgenes, memes, representations*, and so on. Herder simply called them *traditions*, and that is the name they will be given in this book.

Cultures made of independent traditions—this idea was common currency in anthropology, not such a long time ago. It will be defended in the first chapter of this book. I will review the motivations (most of them excellent) that drove anthropologists to abandon this view, and I will try to rehabilitate it. Some issues of definition will be addressed along the way. An idea or a behavior is traditional on two conditions. It has to be transmitted from one individual to another (instead of being the fruit of independent inventions) and to be widely distributed in space and time. This definition is fuzzy. It defines no sharp qualitative boundary between what is traditional and what is not. That is quite deliberate. Traditions are fuzzy objects. They are never completely copied without a share of reinvention. They are traditional only to the extent that they manage to spread to remote times and places. All this is a matter of degree. Hence, this book offers no strict definition of traditions. On the contrary, it tries to turn a philosophical question into an empirical matter. What does or does not make a practice traditional will not concern us much; what makes traditions travel far will.

In the next chapters, I will try to address two big questions: *Why is there culture rather than nothing? Why among humans rather than elsewhere?* These are philosophical questions in that, at first glance, they seem too broad to be solved. The philosopher's job is to try to make them specific enough that they can be solved, without losing their generality.

So let us specify the first question. Some practices and some ideas diffuse very far in space and time. Traditionalists have been known to overestimate their longevity, but on the whole, we can prove that their stability is quite real—and surprising! After all, most of our actions and ideas are not transmitted more than once or twice. Why, then, are things different for a few lucky ideas? Why are there traditions?

This question cannot be raised without running into a second issue: Why are all the cultural riches of this world (with few exceptions) in the hands of a single species? Humans, after all, are not the only cultural species on earth. Traditions exist in other species, too: some animal practices are learnt under the influence of conspecifics, and some of these animal practices travel far and wide, both in space and time. But why are they so rare?

That question will be kept for the last chapter. In the meantime, I shall try to explain how traditions get propagated in spite of the dangers of travel, and the passing of time. Doing so requires two problems to be solved: the Wear-and-Tear Problem and the Flop Problem.

The best known and best explored of the two is the Wear-and-Tear Problem. We all know it from playing Chinese Whispers (known in the United States as the game of Telephone): when a message goes through a transmission chain, it takes no more than a small number of links for mistakes to accumulate. The message suffers corruption and is eventually lost in little time, unless transmission is absolutely perfect (a condition that in reality never obtains).

The Flop Problem is different. It has nothing to do with the quality of transmission. We can reproduce a gesture quite faithfully and never see it again. We can retain a sentence with near-perfect exactitude, without transmitting it to others. In those cases, the transmission chain just peters out for lack of success. The message does not even have the time to suffer wear and tear: it is a flop.

How are these two problems solved? The answer will depend on which problem is considered to be the more serious. Many authors seem to think that triumphing over the Wear-and-Tear Problem is the hard part. After that, the Flop Problem takes care of itself. Others, myself included, consider that if a tradition manages not to flop, its success all but cancels the damage of frequent transmission. Solving the Flop Problem, then, is the hard part: master it, and the Wear-and-Tear Problem will take care of itself.

The first view (putting the Wear-and-Tear Problem first) characterizes the numerous scholars who have sought the root of culture in imitation. The Flop Problem seldom arises in their writing. After all, they assume that humans have a natural tendency to reproduce the ideas and behavior they are exposed to, as if driven by a compulsion to imitate. Social influence pushes us spontaneously to copy traditions. Its strength may vary, depending on the models around us: are they numerous? Are they prestigious? Most of the time, however, we end up spontaneously replicating many traditions, without necessarily knowing why. The Flop Problem thus solved, one has to explain how ideas and behaviors manage to survive deformation, as they undergo one transmission episode after the other. As a solution to the Wear-and-Tear Problem, these theories usually propose high-fidelity transmission mechanisms. Those mechanisms permit efficient communication, faithful imitation, and accurate memorization. Thanks to them, traditions survive.

In brief, the received view sees the life of traditions as being driven by faithful and compulsive transmission. They are born from imitation. Humans create long-lived traditions because they possess a capacity to imitate, with unique fidelity, what is done around them. This answer, which we will call the *imitation hypothesis*, is quite old. Herder theorized it. It is that of many contemporary authors. Though they would grant that our closest cousins possess some mimetic capacity, most hasten to add that cultural transmission outside our species is not faithful enough to permit more than the transmission of a handful of simple techniques. Only human imitation can take us further. Humans owe their many traditions to the cognitive capacities that allow us to imitate, to communicate, and to retain cultural information. Herder would have said that God endowed us with special "receptive powers."

That theory will be the target of chapters 2 and 3. I will argue that the transmission of traditions is neither particularly faithful nor especially compulsive. We lack both the desire and the capacity to imitate everything that circulates around us. Instead we transform, we customize, we reinvent, we forget, we select.

Chapter 2, *Communication and Imitation*, explains why I do not think that cultural transmission usually takes the form of teaching, or imitation. It seems that in our species—and, I will contend, nowhere else—transmission passes mostly through ostensive communication, a soft and flexible form of transmission that always includes a reconstruction of what is transmitted. Unlike imitation, communication does not require behaviors to be faithfully replicated. Unlike what happens in teaching, communicators do not necessarily have close control over those who learn from them. Unlike many forms of teaching and imitation, communication is voluntary and ostensive.

The transmission of behaviors, or pieces of information, can be voluntary or involuntary. Outside our species, it is often involuntary. For instance, upon seeing that other birds have gathered around a source of food, a bird may be driven to imitate them. The models need not know they are serving as models.

Voluntary transmission, in contrast, entails that the model deliberately seek to be imitated by, or to instruct, her target. Adult meerkats, for instance, provide their young with small, weakened, stinger-free scorpions to play with. The only plausible function of this behavior is to transmit a know-how. Such cases of voluntary transmission are rare outside of our species. Furthermore, these instances of animal "teaching" are always (with only one or two possible exceptions) *non-ostensive*. Non-ostensive transmission is what we do when we attach small wheels to a child's bicycle. The extra wheels certainly help the child learn how to ride a bike; but knowing this is not what helps her the most. Non-ostensive transmission need not be manifest in order to succeed. Ostensive transmission is different. It cannot work unless the intention of the model is shown and recognized. Pointing at something with your index finger, waving a hand—these signs mean something because they rely on the recognition of an intention. The target understands the source's communicative intention, and the source uses this recognition to get her message across. In spite of its apparent simplicity, this mode of transmission seems rare or inexistent outside our species.

We shall see that ostensive communication has yet another special property. To understand what is communicated to us, we must reconstruct the communicator's message, selecting what we need to learn from the signals she sends us. Communication is not achieved by copying information. It is not particularly faithful, or designed for cultural transmission. As a result, most of the ideas and practices conveyed through communication will never become traditional. Communication, as Herder remarked, is a poor tool for faithful cultural transmission.

The critique of imitation goes on in chapter 3, where *The Myth of Compulsive Imitation* is described. That chapter has a simple message: we are not as docile as most of the literature on cultural transmission would have us think. We are not so easily influenced that we would copy anything from the majority or the prestigious, without good reasons to do so. Making this point will require a brief review of an enormous literature that seems to demonstrate exactly the opposite. One often hears, for instance, that suicides are readily imitated, especially prestigious suicides. Taking one's life is an extremely costly behavior; if people were joining massive waves of suicide out of sheer imitative docility, it would be hard to call them discerning. Yet such stories are much less plausible than they seem. The studies supporting the assumption of compulsive imitation, be they coming from social psychology or from sociology, suffer from several problems and biases. The data that are used to show that prestige and conformity drive the diffusion of innovations, technological or linguistic, often happen to show the contrary. On the whole, we acquire our culture in a selective, cost-sensitive, and discerning way.

If true, all this implies that the imitation hypothesis cannot explain the existence of traditions. Absent a compulsion to imitate prevailing customs, the Flop Problem remains unresolved. If human cultural transmission is not a high-fidelity device, the Wear-and-Tear Problem still stands.

The *Theory of Diffusion Chains* described in chapter 4 suggests another solution. It begins with a reversal of priorities. The imitation hypothesis tackles the Wear-and-Tear Problem first of all. The Flop Problem is almost an afterthought (compulsive imitation is supposed to take care of it). In my view, the opposite is true. When the Flop Problem is solved—and only when it is solved—the Wear-and-Tear Problem stops being a problem. At any rate, no high-fidelity transmission mechanisms are needed to solve it. On the other hand, the Wear-and-Tear Problem is unlikely to be solved if the Flop Problem is not. Traditions do not last without a modicum of success; they have to thrive if they are to survive. Being well transmitted, faithfully imitated, or committed to a reliable memory is useless if this process happens only once and concerns only a handful of individuals. The quantity of transmission episodes matters more to the survival of traditions than the quality of the transmission itself.

Experiments that simulate cultural transmission in laboratories illustrate this principle. They are quite similar to the game of Chinese Whispers: in almost all of them, a few transmission episodes are enough to distort the message until it is barely recognizable. This effect is often blamed on a lack of fidelity in transmission mechanisms: what is Wear-and-Tear, after all, but an accumulation of copying errors? Yet I do not think this problem could be solved by making transmission more faithful. A very small error rate (and such rates are never zero) is enough for errors to accumulate inexorably. Furthermore, outside the laboratory, traditions very often get distorted with no dire consequence for their survival. Thus the Wear-and-Tear Problem, as observed in the lab, does not seem to result from a lack of fidelity.

Then whence comes wear and tear? In these experiments, I think, it comes from the fact that participants cannot transmit one thing several times to several persons, or learn from several sources. Just as in the game of Chinese Whispers, the rules of these experiments block the repetition, redundancy, and proliferation of transmission episodes. In the real world, cultural diffusion chains never take a Chinese Whispers form—and that is precisely why real-world transmission chains are stable. Repetition, redundancy, and proliferation constitute the cultural success of a tradition. Without them, even the most faithful transmission cannot stave off extinction. With success on its side, though, transmission does not even need to be particularly faithful.

The rest of chapter 4 explores the causes of cultural success. It depends on two things: accessible individuals and attractive traditions. The accessibility of individuals is built by technologies, by institutions, and by contacts between generations. These things make it possible for traditions to circulate, but they do not give us reasons to diffuse them around. "Attractivity" does. Traditions are attractive when they are catchy, interesting, or useful—and, of course, many things can make them so. Some of these "factors of attraction" will be described. But the theory does not merely list attraction factors. It can predict what kind of factors of attraction will favor the success of a tradition in a population, depending on the accessibility of individuals.

The argument starts from the idea, made popular by cognitive anthropologists, that some cultural items tap into psychological mechanisms that are found in the wide majority of humans. They are "generally attractive." They should, therefore, be more successful than others. Yet, according to the theory, those items do not outcompete others in every case. They do so, mostly, when accessibility is low—in other words, in dispersed populations, where information-storage technologies are poorly developed, and where generations rotate too rapidly for the oldest to instruct the youngest. In such cases, general "attractivity" is predicted to drive cultural diffusion. This could explain why certain traditions manage to last in populations where contacts are difficult—how they can thrive in sparse populations, without the help of powerful institutions, and without the help of information-storage technologies.

These are the kind of traditions our cultures must have begun with. The only way they can cover wide distances in space and time is by being transmitted on a great number of occasions. Each individual who passes them is a small link in the diffusion chain. When accessibility is low, however, many small links are required to build a long chain. As a result, traditions have to engage a great number of distinct individuals, in a great number of different contexts. In other words, they have to be generally attractive. This constraint, I shall argue, is weaker for other traditions.

Chapter 5 applies the theory of diffusion chains to an ancient problem in the philosophy of history: *The Passing of Generations*. How can a population's culture remain the same, when that population is continuously restocked by the cycle of deaths and births? One path is generally admitted to afford the passing of generations: vertical transmission, through which older individuals pass something on to much younger individuals. This, it is often suggested, is the only way to obtain cultural transmission through time—at any rate, the only way that we understand well enough. The chapter will focus on other forms of transmission, which may also ensure cultural diffusion through time, on their own or as a complement to vertical transmission.

The second half of chapter 5 studies children's peer culture. Folklorists have good reasons to think that some traditions (mostly games and rhymes) are passed down inside groups of children, with minimal adult intervention. This raises a problem. Children do not stay children for very long. Thus, groups of children are very frequently renewed, as the individuals that compose them get older. As a result, accessibility is low inside children's populations, and cultural transmission is almost completely horizontal (or quasi-horizontal, from slightly older to slightly younger). The traditions whose transmission is confined to these groups need to be transmitted to newcomers again and again, with all the risks of distortion and failure that attach to frequent transmission. We should expect them to have shorter life spans than comparable adult traditions. Yet it seems that the reverse holds true! Their life span is at least comparable, and arguably greater than, the life span of analogous adult traditions.

How do they achieve this? Well, most of them do not achieve anything. Cultural selection is tough to children's traditions. It only retains a few. These traditions, my hypothesis goes, tend to be generally attractive: they are sufficiently appealing to a sufficiently large number of children. They are more likely to be abundantly transmitted, to last, and to be recorded by folklorists. The sample we observe is heavily biased toward survival.

What about the Wear-and-Tear Problem? Children's traditions, if they last, have to confront it—even more so than adult traditions, since they are more frequently transmitted. The theory of diffusion chains predicts that this deformation problem should all but vanish for the successful traditions (and only for them). The repetition, redundancy, and proliferation of children's traditions (not their memorability, nor the alleged traditionalism of children) ensures their survival through time.

Only in chapter 6 will I use the theory of diffusion chains to answer my second question: Why is the cultural wealth of the world into our human hands? How did Homo sapiens become *An Ever More Cultural Animal*?

The first thing to do is dismiss the answer suggested by the imitation hypothesis: Humans would be particularly gifted to copy traditions faithfully. That is not a necessary condition. Indeed, it might not even be useful. Sure enough, we have unique and extraordinary abilities for communication. Yet this is merely one of the things that make us uniquely fitted to learn from and cooperate with our conspecifics. If the flow of information is considerably more important in human societies than it is elsewhere, we have more than our cognitive capacities to thank for this. Our peculiar demography and sociability also play a part. Their conjunction forms what might be called the "human public domain."

Sharing information, however, is not enough. Ideas that are put in common are not made traditional by this very fact. They need (this book claims) to fulfill at least one of two conditions: they need to be attractive, or to be carried by accessible individuals. These two conditions have one thing in common: they are not immutable traits of human nature. In human populations of the past, individuals were not always as accessible to one another as they are now.

Consequently, the conditions that make traditions more likely to appear and thrive probably underwent important variations. The presence of attractive traditions is not wired in our genes, either. Our ability to exchange information does not enable us to control the destiny of traditions over time, or to ensure that they will thrive and survive.

In the end I will offer a conjecture. The accumulation of traditions in human populations—not the progressive amelioration of some traditions, but the quantitative increase of our cultural repertoires—was a slow, gradual process. At some point in their evolution, humans were gifted with unprecedented capacities for information transmission. Yet this capacity did not give birth, all at once, to human cultures as we know them. Traditions accumulated one by one, as attractive items appeared, as circumstances became fit for them to become stable.

Why would this take a long time? Because (quantitative data gathered in diverse fields show) the life spans of traditions follow an extremely unequal distribution, most being quite unstable, while a few live long. The traditions popular enough to survive the passing of generations are a minority, their apparition a rare event. Hence, they were probably not born all at the same time. Once born, however, they would last long enough to see the birth of more stubborn traditions just like them. Together these "extreme" traditions would drive a slow (but hard to reverse) process of accumulation.

If this bit of speculation is accurate, it lends some plausibility to a strange vision: there could have been human populations, societies just like we know them, with humans communicating and cooperating like we do, but whose cultural repertoire would resemble those of modern chimpanzees. Only by going through a long history would they have reached the level of cultural wealth common to all humans today. We could imagine humankind without culture.

1 THE TRANSMISSION AND DIFFUSION OF TRADITIONS

This chapter explains in what respects the new approaches to culture differ from the methods usually employed in the study of traditions. Their originality can be summed up in two words: they are quantitative and abstract. Thanks to this, they can explore a wide array of scales in space and time; compare not only different cultures, but also different species; and try to explain why certain traditions live much longer than others. What I really value about them, though, is something different. They reveal traditions in their most characteristic shape: the shape that survives the passing of generations, that proves resilient to changing social contexts. In this way we can observe culture on its own scale—a scale beyond the short time frame of human lives, beyond shifting social arrangements. Culture, as defined here, consists in stable traditions that travel far, thanks to cultural transmission.

A tradition's transmission may refer to two things related but distinct. The transmission of Thales's theorem or that of hula hooping may be seen as a diffusion chain that extends through space and time: the trajectory of Thales's work from its origins to our times, or the spread of hula hooping in playgrounds. The word *transmission*, however, may also point to the process by which someone learns to reproduce an idea or a behavior from someone else: we would, then, be talking about the activity of teaching Thales's theorem, or demonstrating hula hooping. What one points at, in the former case, is the *diffusion* of hula hooping (or Thales's theorem): its spread through space and time. In the latter case, we point to the passing of the game (or the theorem) from one individual to the other. For this process I shall keep the word *transmission*. Diffusion is a distribution of ideas and practices in time or space; transmission is an interaction among individuals.

This chapter characterizes these three notions—transmission, diffusion, and traditions—with an eye on their recent past. Common though the words may be, the notions that they cover are not today as central to social science as they used to be; yet new tools promise to revive a mindset that such authors as Tylor or Tarde might share with contemporary biologists, psychologists, or linguists. I will try to explain why this mindset slowly fell from grace with the main stream of the social sciences (which had good reasons to reject it)—and why the time seems ripe for granting it a second chance.

Culture as Distributed

How can urban legends or Icelandic sagas be preserved by many successive generations? Why do certain words decay faster than others? What makes a principle of etiquette, or a rule of politeness, stick? These are the kinds of questions that will be raised in this book. To address them, one needs to look at traditions from a historical and statistical point of view. Such an approach is nothing original in social science, but when talking about culture, it cannot be taken for granted. Distributive views of culture are opposed by two strong (though antithetic) prejudices.

First is the view that a group's culture is a mindset shared by all its members, and almost no one else. Time does little to change it. The question of its diffusion is not worth asking, for we know in advance that the common mindset is perfectly shared within the boundaries of the associated social group, and spreads not an inch further. The reverse prejudice is what brought many authors to disregard the issue of cultural continuity (when they were not busy denying said continuity). For decades, traditions have mostly been a myth to be debunked by social anthropologists. The only legitimate way of using the word is to refer it to fragmented, precarious, hybrid constructions. There are no enduring cultures, only fragile, constantly renegotiated social constructs. Beware those who preach the continuity or homogeneity of cultures! Their essentialist, reified stereotypes must be deconstructed in earnest. Such misgivings have gone far enough that many anthropologists would not mind giving up on the whole idea of culture (Abu-Lughod 1991, *contra* Brumann 1999). Outside anthropology, though, these warnings have not caught on (to say the least). Essentialized stereotypes are as popular as ever; the habit of viewing cultures as stable and homogeneous wholes has inspired many research programs outside anthropology or at its margins—in biology, psychology, or economics. Are anthropological warnings worth heeding?

Cultural Homogeneity Is Overrated . . .

Cultural homogeneity once was a well-established hypothesis in social science. It supposedly characterized those societies that were still called primitive: their members were deemed to share the same knowledge, the same aspirations, the same beliefs. So well shared were these elements, they could rightly be called a *collective conscience*. We owe the clearest expression of this thesis to Durkheim. In his *Division of Labor in Society* (1893/1963), he stated that, in those societies that are held together by the "mechanical" form of solidarity (a Durkheimian term meaning that theirs is a minimal division of labor), everyone must abide by the group's norms and make others abide by them; must master the technologies required for collective survival; must bear in their mind the beliefs that ensure its cohesion; and so on. All these things must consequently be transmitted to any and every member of the group.

> The totality of beliefs and sentiments common to average citizens of the same society forms a determinate system which has its own life; one may call it the *collective* or *common conscience*. No doubt, it has not a specific organ as a substratum; it is, by definition, diffuse in every reach of society. Nevertheless, it has specific characteristics which make it a distinct reality. It is, in effect, independent of the particular conditions in which individuals are placed. It is the same in the North and in the South, in great cities and in smalls, in different professions. Moreover, it does not change with each generation, but on the contrary, it connects successive generations with one another. It is, thus, an entirely different thing from particular consciences, although it can be realized only through them.
> (Durkheim 1893, 79–80.)[1]

Let us not be deceived by Durkheim's apparent statistical prudence when he mentions "beliefs and sentiments common to average citizens." It soon turns

---

1. Here and in the rest of this book, emphases are in the original.

out that collective conscience is not merely possessed by an average sample of society, or even by most of its members. From other parts of the book, it is clear that it concerns each and every one of its members—past, present, and future. Durkheim also speaks of "their universality, their permanence" (1893/1963, 100) with the exception of a few criminals, lost to "pathological perversion" (p. 74). There is, then, little doubt that the only limits to the diffusion of social norms or moral sentiments lie at the boundaries of societies. Inside these boundaries, almost no one fails to share in the collective conscience; but how can it be transmitted in such a perfect way?

It took some time for Durkheim's anthropological heirs to start doubting that cultural transmission could be effective enough to guarantee such homogeneity of belief. Researchers of the Culture and Personality movement, for instance, who mixed psychology and anthropology to understand how culture gets a hold on our mind, started with the axiom that all cultures are wholly and perfectly transmitted to all the children that grow up within them (Shweder 1979). They assumed, in Margaret Mead's words, "the inevitability and complete effectiveness of the transmission of culture" (1940, 92). In this view (Mead was describing the prevalent opinion in her field, not offering a view of her own), a Pueblo child raised by Pueblo parents cannot fail to become an adequate representative of Pueblo culture. Pueblo culture might cease to be transmitted, but that would simply mean that there are no more Pueblos. Meanwhile, any Pueblo is as Pueblo as a Pueblo can be. The many ways of bringing up children, of passing one's culture on to them, are various and sundry, but there is one thing that they share: they always work.

> ... any educational technique would work—in the sense that a group of adults sharing a homogeneous culture would always succeed in imparting it to their children.
>
> (Mead 1940, 93)

The same axiom can be found in many different schools of social science. Marcel Mauss himself was not shy of cutting a long story short: "the transmission of things, practices and collective representations happens by itself" (Mauss 1931). His view endured. In the 1990s Pascal Boyer was not being too unfair when he described the claim that cultural transmission is perfect and exhaustive as forming part of the majority outlook in social science (Boyer 1994). It is, in a way, an astounding view: of all the communicative actions that we attempt, and often fail to carry out, the transmission of culture is the one that cannot fail—the social equivalent of cooking a hard-boiled egg. Have a child simmer in a society for enough time and you will obtain a perfectly competent cultural agent. How so? Through a slightly mysterious process of osmosis between the child and her society—a process that Herder likened to the impregnation of a sponge. This image of culture being invisibly infused into our minds is a *leitmotiv* in popular descriptions of transmission, from Proust's portrayal of Albertine's education to this testimony collected from a potter:

> Mehmet Gürsoy, a leading potter in Kütahya, a city in western Turkey where forty thousand people work in the ceramic trade, employed Sufi metaphor to put it like this. In youth, while learning, you breathe in the air of experience. The air circulates within, mingling with the breath of your own soul. Then in creation you exhale and your works emit a certain *hava*, an air that they inevitably share with works created by others who inhale and exhale within the same atmosphere.
> (Glassie 1995, 408)

The same idea of passive impregnation is less graphically but as forcefully expressed in this description of the southern "culture of honor" in the United States:

> How do southerners learn that violence is acceptable in some circumstances, but not others? This aspect of culture, I suggest, is simply taken in like others. Like the words to *Blessed Assurance*, the technique of the yo-yo, or the conviction that okra is edible, it is absorbed, pretty much without reflection, in childhood ... [as a schoolboy,] if you were called out for some offense, you fought. I guess you could have appealed to the teacher, but that just—wasn't done. And that phrase speaks volumes.
> (J. Reed, *Below the Smith and Wesson Line*, cited by Nisbett and Cohen 1996, 124)

However vague this outlook may be, it warrants one clear prediction. If we inevitably absorb any and all practices that float about in our social environment, cultural transmission should not be selective, and it should produce very homogenic societies. Yet in this regard, the earliest fieldwork ethnographers had warned that the cultural heterogeneity found in many societies jarred with the Maussian assumption of infallible cultural transmission.

One of the first articles to question the degree of cultural consensus and the coherence of traditions in societies then called "primitive" was written by Arthur Hocart (1927), an ethnographer who found himself, to his surprise, to be much more knowledgeable than most of his informants about the customs of the Fiji islands. Even the oldest children, he claimed, knew next to nothing about them, and even elders got elementary things wrong—like the correct formula that one must use to accept a gift during ritual exchanges. Make a jump through time and we find the thesis that small-scale societies are culturally heterogeneous to be much better accepted. Anthropologist Ron Brunton, who documented that thesis thoroughly (1980, 1989), thought he knew why testimonies like Hocart's were relatively rare. Such reports were, he argued, so incredible that they could appear to taint the ethnographer's professionalism. After all, if cultures are coherent sets of beliefs, a failure to bring back such a coherent set from one's field could carry with it a suspicion of incompetence. This would explain why, in the words of a famous opponent of the culture concept, "cultural theories (...) tend to overemphasize coherence" (Abu-Lughod, 1991, 146).

Brunton cites a number of cues that suggest how culturally heterogeneous even small-scale societies can be. Ethnographer Brian Morris, for instance, reports important variations in the way people in his field conceive of important topics like incest-related norms, rituals linked to the life cycle, or the knowledge and techniques used to exploit the forest. These last items are quite sophisticated, and presumably very useful; yet the range of variation between informants on their account is such that one may doubt whether their acquisition owed anything at all to cultural transmission. Informants are not simply lacking in specificity and consistency when displaying their cultural knowledge; they disagree on many topics—judgments regarding incest, for instance:

> Their responses even to such a matter as incestuous relationships were very contradictory: some Hill Pandarams expressed their disapproval in no uncertain terms, others seemed rather vague as to what their sentiments ought to be, but many could see nothing to censure and, although they did not explicitly approve of the arrangement, certainly did not regard it as something to be deprecated.
> (Brunton citing Morris, 1989, 675)

Christoph Brumann, while reviewing the numerous critiques made toward the notion of cultural homogeneity (Brumann 1999), tells how a fundamental myth can be known by only a fraction of a village's inhabitants, each informer giving a different version of it. "Cultural" knowledge is, in fact, idiosyncratic. It varies a great deal from one informant to the next.

According to Brunton, this heterogeneity is specific to small and egalitarian societies. Other cultures are more coherent. This point, though, is very much one that he asks readers to take his word for. Besides, the kind of contradiction that he finds among the Pandarams is easily met in quite different societies. Reactions to consensual brother-sister incest, for instance, seem as inconsistent among southern Americans as in Pandarams (as documented in Haidt, Bjorklund, and Murphy 2000). Religious beliefs, too, appear as heterogeneous in American Christians, in spite of their having a written dogma sustained by powerful institutions. Members of a Bible study group investigated by Scott Atran give stunningly variable glosses on basic tenets of their faith—for instance, the meaning of "Thou shalt not kill" and other such consensual and durable bases of Protestant culture (Atran 2001).

Since Brunton's contribution, other authors have added to the stock of reports showing how culturally heterogeneous societies could be. This includes authors that Brunton criticized, like Barth, who revisited his own work on the Ok of the mounts of Indonesia to showcase the variability of their rituals (Barth 1987). To compare two Ok initiation rituals is (I borrow his own comparison) to be like a Christian who, having left his village for the one beyond the next hill, would find out that people, over there, use wine mass for Baptism and put Satan on the cross.

This reevaluation of cultural heterogeneity rests on more systematic and quantitative grounds as well. The statistical tools developed by "cultural consensus theory" (rather ill-named, since it is just as much a theory of cultural dissensus) have permitted to measure in a fine-grained way how inconsistent and poorly shared things like botanical knowledge or magical beliefs could be. More recent measures, using a cultural analogue of genetic F_{ST} (the portion of variance that is accounted for by membership in a group) estimate the current portion of cultural variation accounted for by national boundaries, rather than variations among individuals, at less than one tenth of the total (Bell, Richerson, and McElreath 2009). Thus, Roy D'Andrade had reasons to worry when he wrote, in 1987:

> For a long time there has been a minor scandal at the heart of the study of culture. . . . Culture is shared knowledge and belief; but when we study human groups, we find that there is considerable disagreement concerning most items.
>
> (D'Andrade, cited by Aunger 1999, 94)

There were two ways out of this minor scandal: either give up altogether on the notion of culture, or go back to ways of studying traditions that would take their unequal distribution into account. In both cases, one had to renounce viewing cultural transmission as something as simple as cooking hard-boiled eggs. Renounce this and renounce the hope of finding shared, coherent, and meaningful structures wherever one looked. In other words, the only way to save the culture concept appeared to consist in studying the distribution of cultural things, without making hazardous predictions about its extent, its shape, or its causes. Fredrik Barth (1987) or Dan Sperber (1996) have conceived such research programs. In these approaches, nothing about the coherence or sharedness of traditions is taken for granted—nor, of course, are they assumed to form a collective conscience. What stable and homogeneous elements as can be found in cultures should not be assumed to exist as a matter of course: their existence demands to be explained. The diffusion of cultural items is thus taken as seriously as the items themselves:

> Culture is "distributive" (...). The distribution of the items of knowledge and ideas on the interacting parties of a population is a major feature of the organization of that body of knowledge and ideas; it is not only a matter of social structure but simultaneously a matter of cultural structure.
> (Barth 1987, 77)

> Widely distributed, long-lasting representations are what we are primarily referring to when we talk about culture. (...) So, to explain culture is to answer the following question: why are some representations more successful in a human population, more "catching" than others? In order to answer this question, the distribution of representations in general has to be considered.
> (Sperber 1996, 57–58)

This was not the first time anthropologists took an interest in cultural diffusion. Languages, technologies, or tales were already being mapped, their survival measured. Historical, statistical, piecemeal approaches to culture were common currency, from Kroeber's quantitative analysis of fashion to the German school of the *Kulturkreise* (Lyman and O'Brien 2003). Barth or Sperber added little to this already existing toolkit—indeed, they made little use of it in the first place. So what difference did their distributive view of culture make?

One might say that they tried to import into the field of social anthropology a piecemeal approach to culture that is more common in linguistics, archeology, or prehistory. Even in these fields, though, a distributive view of traditions need not dominate: individual items are often taken as standing for a deeper, coherent whole. The point of distributive views of culture is to be wary of the hope that such a whole exists. It is not to deny cultural coherence altogether, but to get rid of the burden of proof: there is nothing wrong in assuming that traditions do not travel in packs. In addition, these approaches endeavored to take the study of cultural distribution where it had not been taken before: down to the scale of communication and cognition. Studies of cultural diffusion usually keep to large scales, where we see groups adopting or exporting practices from and to other groups. The distributive approaches I have in mind try to be more fine-grained; to push to the individual level and beyond, inside our brains. These different scales are seldom seen together. The bet is that a new picture of culture will emerge from their reunion.

. . . Yet Homogeneity Remains a Heavily Influential Hypothesis

To what extent are a group's traditions shared inside that group? How enduring are they? How widespread? These questions are central to the anthropologist's craft, but their implications range far beyond the borders of that discipline. As we saw, the dominant mood in social anthropology has been one of increasing skepticism toward the stability and reality of cultures. In the meanwhile, though, other disciplines have been going in the opposite direction. Theories that take it for granted that cultures are stable and homogeneous objects set apart by sharp boundaries have been enjoying an unexpected popularity in biology (Laland, Odling-Smee, and Myles 2010), psychology (Nisbett 2003), or economics (Harrison and Huntington 2000, see Jones 2004 for a critique). That assumption, given the arguments we just reviewed, is a risky one to build theories upon.

Cross-cultural psychology is one field where assumptions of cultural coherence dominate by default. Students of cross-cultural differences in cognition are keen to stress how different the American students enrolled in most experiments are from most people on the planet. They differ in many other respects, however, not least in their economic conditions or in the environments they inhabit. In spite of this, the default interpretation of geographical differences is a cultural one: differences are thought to originate from national or regional traditions, which fashioned different ways of thinking—Chinese collectivism, Scandinavian egalitarianism, and so on.

Such assumptions are likely to raise eyebrows outside psychology: aren't we overstating differences whose real causes are multiple, tangled, and mostly unknown? Sadly, without a minimal consensus on what cultural homogeneity could be and on the ways it could be measured, these debates cannot but turn sterile. Hence the importance of studying cultural transmission from a quantitative and abstract point of view.

A Quantitative and Abstract View of Culture

The words used to describe these new approaches of culture by mainstream social science are not always kind: they are said to offer a simplistic, decontextualized picture of cultural life—as though traditions had been uprooted from their natural soil and put to dry up in a botanist's collection. The charge, I think, is accurate but irrelevant. For our purposes abstraction is a virtue, not a vice.

A quantitative view of culture demands that we study the traditions themselves, instead of their bearers. This means abstracting away a great many social ties, and retaining only the links that make up long transmission chains. Such chains may bring together people who are connected in no other way: generations or societies that never come into contact but through cultural transmission. The chains might run along family lines; might respect hierarchical boundaries; economic constraints might stretch them one way or the other; revolutions or politics might shuffle them; yet none of these dimensions suffices to predict the way they will travel. The most important kind of cultural diffusion occurs at scales so vast, encompasses chains that go through so many people that a bird's eye view of their social life would fail to reveal anything but a big mess. We will often have to renounce seeing tradition-bearers as anything more precise than points on a map. Their ideals, their economic life, their feelings, their struggles, the persons they loved, the groups they identified with, will remain unknown to us. For many researchers, renouncing all this means renouncing what makes social science interesting. Not to put too fine a point on it, the vision of culture that this book advocates is a context-free, "reified" one; but it is worth defending.

The best defense came, I think, from Tarde, in the pages of *The Laws of Imitation* where he explains why social science should model itself on archeology, statistics, and philology (as they existed in his time). Tarde (as we shall see) wanted to reduce social life to one single dimension: that of cultural diffusion. The reason why he took archeology and statistics to be best equipped to handle diffusion, was because they had learnt to deal with incomplete and partial data. Human lives are run through by the currents of imitation. In the kind of material that linguists or archeologists study, individual lives have vanished, leaving only the currents themselves.

> In short, these scholars are forced, perhaps unconsciously, into surveying the social life of the past from a point of view which is continually approximating that which I claim should be adopted knowingly and willingly by the sociologist. (. . .) In distinction to historians who see nothing else in history than the conflicts and competitions of individuals, that is, of the arms and legs as well as the minds of individuals, and who, in regard to the latter, do not differentiate between ideas and desires of the most diverse origins, confusing those few that are new and personal with a mass of those that are mere copies; (. . .) archeologists stand out as makers of pure sociology, because, as the personality of those they unearth is impenetrable, and only the work of the dead, the vestiges of their wants and ideas, are open to their scrutiny, they hear, like the Wagnerian ideal, the music without seeing the orchestra of the past. In their own eyes, I know, it is a cruel deprivation; but time, in destroying the corpses and blotting out the memories of the painters and writers and modelers whose inscriptions and palimpsests they decipher and whose frescoes and torsos and postherds they so laboriously interpret, has, nevertheless, rendered them the service of setting free everything that is properly social in human events by eliminating everything that is vital and by casting aside as an impurity the carnal and fragile content of the glorious form which is truly worthy of resurrection. To archæologists, then, history becomes both simplified and transfigured. In their eyes it consists merely of the advent and development, of the competition and conflict, of original wants and ideas, or, to use a single term, of inventions. Inventions thus become great historic figures and the real agents of human progress.
>
> (Tarde 1895/1903, 101–102)

Had Tarde known of today's motion pictures, he might have devised another analogy. Think of those sequences where the same single view—on a street, an apartment, a square, or a railway station—is filmed continuously for days or months, and then shown in fast-forward mode. Passersby, if we see them at all, appear only as shadows, as blurred traces. Only the background stands still and neat: buildings, tree trunks, lamplights, those few cars that for some reason never seem to move. These things that the movie brings into focus are often those that matter least to the people on the street. The immobile car is never touched (surely its owner has been away for some time). The buildings are so permanent as fixtures of the landscapes, that no one notices them after a while. Such movies remove human activity from its scenery, to reveal the stable background of our lives.

Watching traditions through the prism of their diffusion is, likewise, to abstract away most of their bearers, along with the specifics of their individual lives. It means focusing on elements of social life whose importance may not be obvious to the people who encounter them every day. What is fascinating about traditions is not the part they play in our lives. It is not even the meanings we read into them, however deep. It is their presence in so many different times and places, the permanent shape that stays neat when the film is accelerated a thousand times. To a reader used to ethnographic descriptions—their wealth of detail, their celebrated thickness—such a way of seeing will seem hopelessly ungrounded; but there is beauty in this abstraction.

What Is Cultural Transmission?

Distinguishing Diffusion and Transmission

A practice's *distribution* is the set of points in space and time where it can be found. A wide range of factors determine its extension. Cultural transmission, one of these factors, is not necessarily the most potent. Some distributions owe nothing at all to transmission—like the various inventions of agriculture, or Newton and Leibniz's two discoveries of differential calculus. These are cases of distribution without transmission. We shall only use the word *diffusion* to point at distributions that, in contrast, owe something to transmission.

Even when we know that transmission is somewhat involved, it can be hard to judge the extent of its contribution. Take the contagion of suicide, an example made famous by the history of sociology. The epidemiology of suicides is affected by many factors that have nothing to do with transmission—like unemployment rates or weather conditions; but part of it is thought to result from some sort of imitation. How can we measure the extent of its influence, simply from knowing a given distribution of suicides?

This ancient issue has been raised again by recent statistical work (Aral, Muchnik, and Sundarajan 2009; Steglich, Snijders, and Pearson 2009). It has benefited from a method that consists in looking for clustered suicides, that is, abnormally concentrated cases (the same method applies to the epidemiology of smoking or obesity). When a cluster resists a series of controls (other risk factors having been removed—the season, for instance, or the share of males in the population), this could be a sign that some transmission has been at work. The proportion of suicides that enter these clusters (only a small minority of suicides usually does) is then taken as a rough indication of the impact of transmission on suicide. This, at any rate, is the basis on which today's researchers try to evaluate the influence of imitation in the diffusion of such practices. (These researches will be examined in greater detail in chapter 3.)

In a famous controversy that saw Durkheim facing Tarde on that precise topic, Durkheim was already using the clusters argument:

> In short, all the maps show us that suicide, far from being grouped more or less concentrically around certain centers from which it radiates more and more weakly, occurs in great roughly (but only roughly) homogeneous masses and with no central nucleus. Such a configuration in no way indicates the influence of imitation.
> (Durkheim 1897/1952 137.)[2]

If suicide did spread by imitation, Durkheim argues, one should observe that it is abnormally concentrated around certain foci; he saw, however, that suicide's distribution, though heterogeneous, is not organized into salient clusters. His argument had its flaws. People travel: suicide could spread contagiously from a handful of carriers dispatched throughout the land (in that case, France). A lack of clusters does not signify a lack of contagion. It did, however, deprive Tarde of one possible argument: focal points with abnormal concentrations of suicides, not explainable by any factor besides imitation.

Durkheim, however, lacked modern means of testing the presence of such clusters statistically. When two researchers applied the clusters method to Durkheim's actual data, they found that the results (ironically) went the other way (Baller and Richardson 2002). When controlling for the suicide-influencing variables that Durkheim had identified (religion, divorce rates, trade-unionism, etc.), a range of unexplained and clustered geographic variation remains—revealing, these authors argue, an imitative contagion of suicide.

Is this argument satisfactory? The answer, as we shall see in chapter 3, is: Not quite. Identifying clusters of unexplained suicides does not suffice to

---

2. I amended the last sentence's original translation.

establish transmission. It could always be the case that clustered suicides reflect the clustering of unknown risk factors. But suppose risk factors were all perfectly known. Even then, clusters need not indicate transmission. Something else may cause them: the tendency for similar people to live together. It is a widespread and well-attested statistical tendency (although, like all tendencies, it admits of exceptions): for all sorts of reasons, depressed people are likely to live among other depressed people, and big eaters tend not to be found at the table of small eaters. This *homophily* is just as powerful a cluster-builder as imitation is. Thus, one may find suicidal waves, or tides, to be more likely inside such and such social networks—not because misery loves company, but simply because people choose their friends, in part, on the basis of shared features that happen to stack the odds in favor of suicide.

Can we disentangle the respective contribution of these three dynamics (shared risk factors, homophily, and transmission) to the distribution of behaviors such as suicide? That is a delicate job, though not an impossible one. The complexity of the task adds to the fog that hovers over the debates on the role of imitation in social life. As we shall see, imitation plays only a trivial role in the propagation of suicide or obesity (prevailing opinions notwithstanding): these are not traditional behaviors. Their distribution does not, for the most part, result from transmission. Calling it diffusion would be misleading.

This problem will occupy us in chapter 3. In the meanwhile, let us be reassured: it is not always so difficult to show that a practice owes its distribution to transmission, as opposed to a series of spontaneous elicitations. It is sometimes possible to get direct proofs of cultural transmission, by observing transmission or by looking at some traces that it left behind. One such trace (as noted by Kroeber and by other anthropologists before him—Kroeber 1931; Tylor 1871) is the presence of arbitrary elements. Many artifacts, for instance, present features that could easily be altered or removed without damage to the artifact's function, and typically differ from culture to culture, being useful as a tracker of cultural descent. Such cues can mislead, of course, and have been badly interpreted by some anthropologists, most notoriously by Victorians; yet statistical methods exist that allow a controlled usage of them (Tehrani and Collard 2002).

In most cases of traditions studied in this book, there is little doubt about the role played by transmission. Thus the schoolyard rhymes we will study in chapter 5 are too complex and arbitrary to have been reproduced independently from any social influence. That would be like the independent writing of *Don Quixote* by someone other than Cervantes: a topic for a Borgesian short story.

Transmission and Invention Are Not Opposites

Thus, transmission is easy enough to establish for folktales, for religious creeds, for many techniques, although it is much harder to detect in the distribution of stereotyped behaviors like suicide. To say that transmission is involved is not to say that blind copying is at work, nor to deny that diffusion involves a dose of independent reconstruction by every learner. Transmission and reinvention need not exclude each other.

Before it was defended by Sperber (1996), Boyer (1994), or Atran (2001), the view that transmission implies a hefty dose of active reconstruction was already widespread. Kroeber spoke of *stimulus diffusion* for inventions that were adopted on such a slim basis that its adopters had to reinvent them almost from scratch. The history of technology provides the most telling examples, with the development of ersatz products and the emulation of inaccessible or secret techniques. When the late-eighteenth-century French economy (blockaded as a consequence of war) sought to produce its own graphite-tipped pencils, they knew how to make them, but, for lack of available graphite, they had to make do with an entirely different process (Petroski 1989). When Europeans sought to emulate porcelain, it took them some time to find kaolin; when they did, they lacked the information to use it, and had to reinvent the whole thing (Kroeber 1940). Graphite pencils and porcelain were models that offered only a meager input to their imitators. The product only told the imitators that a given problem could be solved, leaving them with the task of reinventing the solution.

Kroeber saw such stimulus diffusion as a special form of cultural transmission—and a rather deficient one. For cultural epidemiologists, on the contrary, reconstruction is always at the core of cultural transmission. It is not a degraded form of the normal process. One might trace back this idea to Chomsky's poverty of the stimulus argument (Chomsky 1980), which could be thus summarized (in one of its weakest forms): syntactic rules, as adults use them, need to be reconstructed by children from an input that is but a partial and imperfect reflection of grammatical norms. Since these rules manage to pass across generations most of the time, children's reconstruction is necessarily guided by a set of expectations that is quite precise, and as substantial as the input itself is scanty. As is well known, Chomsky had these expectations derive from an innate mental grammar. One does not have to buy this theory to admit that language transmission involves an impressive amount of inferential work (the specifics of which may be quite different from what Chomsky imagined).

This way of seeing language acquisition can be enlarged to describe cultural transmission. This is what cultural epidemiologists do. Pascal Boyer takes as an example the beliefs and intuitions that the Fang of Cameroon entertain concerning ancestral spirits. These prove to be quite rich and systematic, when probed in a thorough fashion (Boyer 2001). Spirits turn out to have quite an ordinary mental life. Like us, they trust their eyes and remember what they saw; they have friends and enemies; they occasionally hold grudges. All this is quite commonplace, but, with spirits, the most banal expectations derive from rich and complex conceptualizations. Consider what these spirits are: living dead relatives coming back to haunt this earth; beings that may materialize anywhere out of nowhere. It boggles the mind to imagine how the pedestrian intuitions just described can coexist with such outlandish properties. How can the Fang think these things together without losing their minds?

When probed, the Fang spontaneously express rich, coherent, and solid intuitions regarding the spirits. Yet, according to Boyer, everyday Fang conversation offers nothing like a rich, coherent, and self-assured dogma on this matter. On the contrary, the narratives or testimonies one hears about ghosts are rife with confusion. Most importantly, they are rare. Rich and coherent beliefs are nevertheless transmitted, because every Fang treats the scarce cues that she gets with very strong expectations in her mind. These expectations have to do with the nature of thinking beings. They are activated as soon as ghosts are understood to have some kind of mental life. Hearing a testimony suggesting that a ghost *saw* something is enough to put in motion an inconspicuous machinery of expectations that continuously generates a set of taken-for-granted predictions: any being with a mental life has memories, has beliefs, and so on. Thus a small set of cues can trigger the formation of a much more elaborate representation.

This way of approaching cultural transmission, which sees it as a reconstruction based on incomplete cues, is not just useful to explain the permanence of certain traditions, like Fang beliefs in ancestral spirits. It may also allow us to account for some changes in the distribution of cultural practices. This is what David Lightfoot does in his account of the changes that affected the use of modal verbs in the history of the English language. That theory nicely illustrates the interplay of transmission and reconstruction, and I will come back to it on occasion. Hence it will be summarized in some detail.

> In Old English, modal verbs like *may, should, will,* or *can,* could be used in the same way as normal verbs are—in the way French modal verbs like *vouloir* or *pouvoir* are used today. Such sentences as

"Il voulait pouvoir lire le chapitre"

"Un lecteur pouvant lire le chapitre,"

or

"Il le peut"

are grammatical in French. So were their Old English equivalents; but this usage has disappeared from modern English. One cannot say:

*"He will can understand the chapter"

*"A reader canning to read the chapter"

or

*"He can it"

Lightfoot notes that this practice disappeared in a rather abrupt fashion. Furthermore, when it disappeared, it disappeared completely. (Today, only a few modals, like *need* and *dare*, may sometimes be used in the old-fashioned way.) Among sixteenth-century writers, those who use forms that today we would consider ungrammatical show all varieties of ungrammatical uses. Those who respect the new usage show no violation at all. This, according to Lightfoot, is a reason to think that we are dealing with a systematic change: a change driven by rules. How could this change spread in such a rapid fashion? One thing is sure: the new rules haven't been explicitly formulated by anyone. Today's speakers are unaware of them, unless they are linguists. No academy, no lobby of sticklers imposed the new usage. On the contrary, the old forms are attested quite late in reputed writers (like Thomas More) and there is no sign of an organized effort to make them go away. Since the change manifested itself only by the absence of forbidden constructions—sentences that were not produced anymore—speakers could not pick up the new form by imitation.

This is where it becomes useful to think of transmission as involving a reconstruction based on cues. In Lightfoot's hypothesis, modal verbs ceased being used as normal verbs because they had stopped sounding like them. In Old English, all verbs were endowed with a rich system of inflections: they changed forms for nearly all persons and all times. Among these inflexions, the third-person singular *-s* (of *says*, *eats*, or *mews*) is one of the few survivors. The verbs that were to become today's modal verbs also had a system of inflexions, but a very different one. Like today, their third-person singular form took no -*s*, but that difference between future modals and other verbs was not as salient as it is in today's English, where that -*s* is the only regular, present-tense conjugation. The contrast was drowned, so to speak, in the abundance and variety of inflectional systems; but things were about to change.

Between the eleventh and fifteenth centuries, the inflectional morphology of English underwent a drastic simplification, losing its declensions and most of its verbal inflections. For regular verbs, only third-person singular -*s*'s remain today. Modal verbs lost some inflexions. They also lost many neighbors—verbs that belonged to the same groups but disappeared or were assimilated into other groups. As a result of these changes, the contrast between modal verbs and other verbs became much more salient for speakers. Another consequence of this simplification, with similar effects, was that the past tense of modal verbs became increasingly opaque: forms like *might*, *could*, or *should* were increasingly hard to relate to the present forms of *may*, *can*, or *shall*. This also contributed to their growing distinctiveness.

At first, the speakers whose language had undergone this drastic morphological simplification simply went on using modal verbs as they used other, normal verbs. The children who grew up among them, however, could hear that modals came in a specific and salient form—a distinction so evident that it was easier to handle them by creating a new category, modals, rather than treating them as special cases of normal verbs. For that generation of speakers, it became impossible to use modals like one uses ordinary verbs. For the new usage to appear, in the sixteenth century, the morphological revolution that simplified English inflections had to be completed. Once the final stages of the change had been reached, it was (the theory goes) only a matter of one or two generations before the use of modals shifted. All the new speakers had to do was to follow the cues present in the conversation around them. These cues strongly nudged them to treat modals as a sui generis category. A few years in a child's life is enough to learn to categorize verbs in this way. Having no reason to produce sentences where modals functioned as normal verbs, the new speakers eventually ceased producing the cues that could have kept the old usage alive.

If Lightfoot's hypothesis is correct (and also, arguably, in many cases where it is not), neither imitation nor teaching (explicit or otherwise) are responsible for the spread of the new usage. Imitation would entail that the new usage was directly perceived and reproduced without any further inferential steps. Teaching would imply that learning was somehow organized or rewarded. The new speakers spontaneously innovated new ways of categorizing and using modals, in reaction to cues that were present in the language, yet had not been deliberately planted there. Some, like third-person plural -s's, were present long before the process started. Only very late in their existence did they become salient enough to trigger a change. The emergence of a set of such cues, like the resulting spontaneous syntactic change, was a complex historical accident: English speakers did not wish it so.

Transmission and independent reinvention usually go hand in hand. They hinder each other much less than the other way around. The reason why simple geometric figures (like stars or hexagons) are easier to copy than random doodles is because geometric figures are easier to reproduce from a small set of simple cues—while a doodle demands that every trait be laboriously copied (Sperber 1999). Reinvention from cues is not a degraded, imprecise, or deficient form of transmission. It is an aspect of transmission that we cannot afford to ignore.

This point was among those that Tarde failed to get across to Durkheim, in his debate with the author of *Suicide*. Durkheim entertained very narrow views on transmission. For him, one could talk of suicide transmission if and only if learning of a suicide attempt was in itself a sufficient cause of committing one.

> (...) Imitative propagation exists only where the fact imitated, and it alone, determines the acts that reproduce it, automatically and without assistance from other factors.
> (Durkheim 1897/1952, 132)

Tarde had a much more flexible view of things, as attested by his drafted rejoinder to Durkheim's critiques:

> D. [Durkheim] failed to comprehend what I meant here by the action of imitation. I never said, or thought, that a man in full health, happy, content with his fate, could see instances of suicide around him or in the next big city, and be compelled thereby to imitate them. If, however, he fell into disease or despair—if, in other words he were *in the circumstances required to feel the influence of those examples* when he comes to learn that such or such a person killed themselves in such or such a way, he would decide to do the same, and most often in the same way. Imitation's role would be that of the additional but necessary weight.
> (Tarde 1897/2000, 21)

This flexible definition of transmission (the next two chapters will return on the topic of imitation) is, of course, the most convenient for me, and it will be adopted here. Cultural transmission (chapter 4, in particular, will insist on this) should not be reduced to the punctual influence of a single model, and it never goes without a modicum of reconstruction.

Not All Differences between Societies Are Traditional

If transmission is but one aspect of cultural learning (and not always the most important or efficient aspect), why should we bother studying it at all? This question has stirred many a debate in the new approaches to culture. What triggered those debates was the distinction made by John Tooby and Leda Cosmides between "transmitted culture," which referred to all the differences between populations that could be traced back to the influence of cultural transmission, and "evoked culture," designating all those differences that can be explained by the fact that different groups react to the different environments they live in (Tooby and Cosmides 1992). If Inuit societies have fat-rich diets, that is arguably because of the availability of fatty meats in their environment (relative to other foodstuffs), as well as their nutritional benefits in a cold climate: evoked, but not transmitted culture. On the other hand, the reason why your Hare Krishna neighbor (who shares your own environment to a large degree) abstains from onions, mushrooms, and garlic, is a transmitted taboo.

This distinction has been criticized on many grounds. It rests on two hypotheses that cannot be completely true. It implies, first, that the only practices deserving of being called "cultural" are those that differ from one society to the next. Second, it establishes an excessively sharp distinction between practices that spontaneously arise in interactions with one's environment, and those that are transmitted. For cultural epidemiologists, on the contrary, cultural practices are always partly reconstructed and partly transmitted. To put it another way, they are reconstructed in ways that can be more or less constrained by more or less specific and direct cues. There are extreme cases, of course. Some unrelated but similar innovations spontaneously arise when conditions favor them. Other practices, on the contrary, would be quite inaccessible to anyone not in contact with a rich body of traditions. Between those extremes lies a wide range of intermediate cases—a gray area where we find things that we did not owe to our own initiative or intellect, but that we might have figured out by ourselves, given enough cues: Thales's theorem, multiplication tables, the recipe for pound cakes. Call it the continuum of transmission.

The distinction between evoked and transmitted culture, though not absolute, has its uses. The kind of culture that this book studies lies, on the continuum of transmission, close to transmission, and far from reconstruction. We will require a certain modicum of transmission to speak of culture. I find it useful to reserve the term culture for culture that is transmitted (to a substantial degree), and to be wary of any use of the c-word that bypasses the question of transmission. Thus the evoked/transmitted distinction, exaggerated as it might be, is worth bearing in mind: it protects us against intemperate uses of the culture concept.

The interpretation of cross-cultural experiments in psychology shows how perilous such intemperate uses can be. A habit has taken root of calling "cultural" any difference observed among samples of subjects drawn from different parts of the world, even though many such differences owe very little to cultural transmission. Let us consider two examples, one in psychology, one in experimental economics.

The psychologist Richard Nisbett has defended an ambitious and much debated thesis: culturally "Asian" persons have been passing along, for many generations, a set of habits of thought that drastically differ from "Western" cognition, in a wide range of domains (Nisbett 2003). They have a different way of solving problems, of looking at the world, of considering philosophical issues. In all these domains the Asian cognitive style is, the theory goes, marked by a greater attention to the whole as opposed to its parts, and a greater tolerance of contradiction. This work has drawn much attention in philosophy, where Nisbett has followers (Machery et al. 2004; Doris and Plakias 2007).

In one of Nisbett's most famous experiments, a group of Asian subjects and a group of American ones are asked to observe an image (of an aquarium) and to describe it. As predicted, Asian subjects pay more attention to background elements and to the general arrangement of the image, while Americans focus on the fishes in the foreground. In a second experiment (from a different group), the moral intuitions of Chinese and American students are compared. Given their holistic, contradiction-friendly cognitive style, the Chinese should be more willing to disregard a moral command in one particular case, if doing so would benefit society as a whole. Both groups of subjects are thus presented with a dilemma—one of moral philosophy's classical conundrums: In a city where the ethnic majority lives side by side with a substantial minority, a murder has been committed. The suspected killer belongs to the minority. You, the judge, have become absolutely certain of the man's innocence. You are no less certain, however, that if you acquit him, this will infuriate the majority. Riots will ensue. Killings will occur. Is it possible for you to condemn one innocent, and save the city from bloody unrest? Compared to the American group, Chinese students are slightly more likely to answer in the affirmative (Doris and Plakias 2007).

My last example comes from experimental economics. It plays a key role in contemporary discussions on cultural differences. Theoreticians of cultural group selection (a theory to be examined in greater detail in chapter 3) claim that the norms of cooperation that are transmitted inside societies, along with the rest of their culture, influence natural selection in human populations. To back this idea, one of their favorite arguments consists in a series of experiments showing that people from different societies behave very differently in economic "games" designed to test their propensity to cooperate, to be generous, or to punish others. These games are experiments where participants are given a sum of money (or, occasionally, some other goods), which, they are told, they are free to share with some anonymous participant, or keep for themselves. Experimenters observe that, for example, Lamalera subjects (a society of Indonesian whale-hunters) are much more generous than Machiguenga subjects (hunter-gatherers from Peru) (Henrich et al. 2005). Although the original paper does not claim that such differences are culturally transmitted, that is how it has been interpreted most often (including by authors of the 2005 paper: see, for instance, Gintis, Bowles, Boyd & Fehr 2003). This allows them to claim that altruism and cooperation depend on norms passed on from generation to generation.

Do we have to embrace the standard interpretation of these three examples of "cultural" differences? No. Many of these effects are easily accounted for without resorting to cultural transmission. They are quite likely to have been "evoked" by a variety of environmental differences.

Nisbett's team was not quite satisfied with their own explanation of the aquarium experiment—the one in which American subjects focused on the fishes, while Asian subjects took a broader view. They remarked that their Chinese subjects did not merely differ from the American group by their cultural heritage, but also by their day-to-day environment. Japanese or Chinese streets, for instance, are not like American streets: they are organized in such a way that makes it vital to pay attention to one's visual field as a whole. Perhaps this could explain their Asian subjects' focus on the background? This conjecture was confirmed by repeating the experiment with American subjects, after showing them pictures of Japanese streets. This simple manipulation was enough to bring these subjects substantially closer to the Asian mean—a small effect, but we must consider that their exposure to the photograph was very short, compared to a Japanese's lifelong experience of Japanese streets (Miyamoto, Nisbett, and Matsuda 2006). If their new interpretation is on the right track, we would probably find an "Asian" way of seeing in American expatriates in Japan or China, but an "American" pattern in US residents of Chinese descent.

My explanation for Doris and Plakias's experiment ("The Judge and The Innocent") has not been tested, but it is at least as plausible as the authors' interpretation. Riots against the Chinese diaspora are rather frequent in Southeast Asia. While the Chinese media cover them, they tend to go unnoticed by US news outlets. In 1998 Jakarta saw one of the worst outbursts of violence in the city's history. The Indonesian majority persecuted Chinese merchants. Thousands of deaths and rapes were counted. Chinese media on the continent and elsewhere covered the rioting in great detail. It would be quite surprising if the Chinese subjects in Doris and Plakias's experiment (Chinese students on an exchange program) had not heard about one such riot. The actions of the judge who sacrifices an innocent to avoid bringing a bloody riot upon an ethnic minority is likely to appear more acceptable with such events in mind.

Consider now the economic games. In the Lamalera economy, based on whale-hunting, the benefits of solidarity are obvious, but the selfish strategies that are excluded there can be quite rewarding and unproblematic in an economy based on such individual activities as gathering. This could explain a large part of Machiguenga "selfishness" and Lamalera "altruism" (as the authors themselves remarked).

All the experiments reviewed here can thus be analyzed without appealing to traditions transmitted from one generation to the next; but what does it matter if there is no such chain? Lamalera altruism is no less interesting for being an adaptation to a whale-hunting economy. The peculiar arrangement of Chinese streets, or the existence of a long-established Chinese diaspora, are as central to Chinese culture as Confucianism or rice paddies. After all, these things are among those factors that are neither simply biological nor simply environmental, but nevertheless influence the way the Chinese live and think. What difference would it make if long chains of cultural diffusion supported all these things?

The difference that it would make would be one of causality. If Lamalera altruism is elicited, first of all, by whale-hunting, then we will see it fade away if the Lamalera shift to a completely different mode of subsistence (a reversion to gathering, for instance, improbable as it may be). We do not expect it to go, on the other hand, if an epidemic or a wave of migration were to disrupt the composition of Lamalera populations. We also expect very similar attitudes toward cooperation in unrelated groups of whale-hunters. If Lamalera altruism were, on the contrary, an ongoing tradition that whale-hunting did not elicit, it could survive long after the Lamalera stop hunting whales, but it would probably fail to persist after a massive renewal of the population. There would be no reason to expect similar phenomena in unrelated whale-hunters, but we should see them in non-whale hunters with cultural ties to the Lamalera. The reason, in short, that one should pay attention to cultural transmission when looking at differences among populations, is that many differences are not due to transmission. Their persistence might be weaker than that of genuine cultural differences—or they may persist for very different reasons.

Our Cultural Repertoires Could Not Exist without Transmission

There is yet another reason to focus on transmission. Anthropologists rightly stress that most of the technologies that allow us to survive are tricks we could never come up with on our own. Not all traditions are like that. Some practices owe most of their diffusion to cultural transmission, but acquiring them did not teach anything new to those who adopted them—nothing, at any rate, that they could not have figured out by themselves. Many animal traditions are like this: without transmission, they would have been less successful, but their invention seems within reach of any intelligent animal if they want to make an effort. The standard example (famous for being one of the first documented cases of a non-human tradition) is the transmission of potato-washing among macaques on Koshima island. A female named Imo is thought to have played a crucial role in diffusing that practice. In other words, she made it much more likely that other macaques would use it; but we also know that potato-washing was and remains a spontaneous practice on Koshima, before and after Imo. All she did was make more salient a possibility that most macaques could see and exploit by themselves (Tomasello and Call 1997, 276–277).

What a contrast with many human traditions! Our species' cultures teem with practices that it would be beyond anyone's ingenuity to reinvent—either because they solve very thorny problems, like survival in arctic climates, or because they are too idiosyncratic to be devised twice independently. The notion of "cumulative culture" is often used in this connection. A culture is said to be cumulative if it carries traditions that most of its users could never have invented on their own (Boyd and Richerson 1995; Tomasello 1999). A whole theory lies behind the phrase *cumulative culture*. What makes human cultures interesting, the theory goes, is the accumulation, the preservation of good tricks that other species have let slip into oblivion, because the kind of transmission they practice is not faithful, or not efficient enough. Alternatives to this theory exist: another way of seeing cultural accumulation will be outlined in chapter 6. Meanwhile, let us retain that, in human cultures, cultural transmission has effects that invention could not produce on its own. This is one more reason to give transmission center place in our definition of culture.

Culture: A Set of Traditions Rather than a Set of Differences

What is culture? This short section will not, of course, disclose the definitive formula that could put an end to disagreements surrounding the uses of that word. Its aim is simply to spell out this book's definition of culture. Given all the meanings that have attached to the notion over time, it is necessarily somewhat arbitrary, and restrictive. It consists of two criteria: distribution and transmission. Culture is made of ideas and practices that have reached a wide distribution in space or time (or both), and did so essentially for being transmitted (not for being frequently reinvented). This way of seeing is meant to break away from models where culture is nothing but a distribution, transmission being only a sideshow. It excludes "evoked" culture: widely distributed ideas and behaviors are not cultural if their spread owes little or nothing to transmission (in other words, if their distribution is not a diffusion). If, for instance, the Lamalera are spontaneously given to sharing things, and have been like this for generations, for no reason other than their economic environment, this social phenomenon is not cultural to a degree sufficient to be covered here.

On the other side of the debate, this book's approach departs from approaches that consider "cultural" everything that is transmitted, even scarcely so, and even if no important diffusion follows from their transmission (Blackmore 1999; Aunger 2002). Our definition rules out things that are not transmitted abundantly enough to give birth to a diffusion chain that would reach reasonably far in space or time. A bit of whistling taken by a passerby from another passerby would not qualify, unless the song is a hit.

These two criteria (the distribution's size and the importance of transmission in creating it) are obviously not watertight. I would not have gone for a neater or less fuzzy definition. Culture, when seen as distributive, is a quantitative thing, not a separate class of ideas and practices. Whether something is cultural or not is not a question that will often bother us in this book: everything in human lives is more or less so. A more interesting matter is that of knowing to what extent some transmitted idea has become cultural: How far did its diffusion reach? What channels did it pass through?

Another notable peculiarity of the conception just sketched—culture as distribution and transmission—is that it does not mention cultural differences. I will try, when I can, to avoid pluralizing "culture." The rest of this book will not be dwelling on culture*s* as separate spheres, but on culture, without an *s* and without differences. In many ways this is a comeback to what the word meant to Victorian anthropologists like E. B. Tylor. Culture (singular) was to them the process whereby various know-hows, beliefs, and practices were transmitted. It did not matter whether it happened in one single, isolated society, or in thousands of related ones.

Imagine what would happen if there were only one homogeneous society in the entire world, with every human being sharing the same repertoire of traditions. These people would still need to find ways of passing their culture to the following generations. Such a world would interest me almost as much as this one. After all, the same basic problems that this book deals with would also be encountered there: How are traditions passed on? Why are some more successful than others? Why is it that our species has so much of them?

Do Traditions Exist?

Before we tackle those questions, let us say a word about traditions. I will use this word to refer to anything that is widely distributed in a population. Distributed, or rather, diffused; when traditions are concerned the words "diffusion" and "distribution" will be used interchangeably: the distribution of traditions is due to a diffusion process. Thus, it is a distribution.

This way of seeing traditions accommodates many widely shared intuitions, but not all of our intuitions. Our traditions, for instance, will not have to be long-lived: their diffusion chains have to be extended, but not necessarily in time. A craze that bursts on many people, albeit for a very short time, will be counted as a tradition. In Gabriel Tarde's words, "fashion-imitation" (*imitation-mode*) will interest us like "habit-imitation" (*imitation-coutume*). That said, most of the traditions that we will study are persistent ones, and their survival in time will draw more attention than their distribution in space.

Some Traditions Are as Durable as They Seem

This book's traditions look very much like what most people see in them: long chains of cultural transmission (Glassie 1995). They are a bit more remote from what usually goes under that name in philosophy or social science. To be sure, classical definitions do mention the importance of transmission. According to Mauss, for instance, techniques are traditional insofar as they are transmitted (Mauss 1934/1950; see also Pouillon 1991). In more recent works, however, no opportunity is missed to remind the reader that traditions need not come from lasting transmission chains (Hobsbawm and Ranger 1992; Boyer 1990). In this widespread view, traditions are defined as those things *believed* to be ancient and preserved, but reality can be quite different (Shils 1971, 133). Social scientists have increasingly shifted their focus away, from traditions in themselves, to the beliefs that surround them—for instance, beliefs in their immutability. Their actual persistence stirs little interest, when it is not simply denied (a point of view endorsed by Gosselin 1975).

This is even more true in philosophy, though there one finds as many definitions of the word as there are authors using it. When Alasdair MacIntyre spoke of traditions (1989), he most often had in mind certain families of thought in moral philosophy. Schools like Thomism or the Scottish Enlightenment are not frozen dogmas but ongoing arguments, involving competing positions. These conversations are, to a certain extent, closed: it may be very hard to translate disputes or ideas coming from one argument into terms that can be understood by another conversation. Why? Because philosophical conversations are more than mere ideas, more than mere arguments. They are, in his view, so adjusted to particular institutional and historical conditions that they may lose their intelligibility if uprooted. Must these conversations be transmitted and endure in time? MacIntyre seems to hesitate. He sometimes claims as much: "Some core of shared belief, constitutive of allegiance to the tradition, has to survive every rupture" (1989, 356). The sharing of ideas is not, however, sufficient to constitute a tradition. We may reject the most common opinions in the conversation we take part in, without ceasing to be a member. Thus, MacIntyre considers even Hume to be a continuator of the Scottish reformation: Scottish Protestantism, after all, is more than a stable corpus of doctrines and rituals. It is a living social context.

A closely related twentieth-century trend of thought used the word tradition as synonymous with "practice," an elusive notion that was usually intended to capture the implicit side of social rules: a set of habits that not only go without saying, but tend to lose their strength (their spontaneity, their apparent naturalness) when made explicit (Turner 1994 provides both an overview and a critique). The vision of tradition adopted here is cruder in comparison. It is, indeed, deliberately minimalistic. It bypasses many features of cultural life that lie at the heart of other definitions, interesting though they may be. It deals with what traditions really are, not with the way they appear to us; and it is chiefly preoccupied with continuity.

In a way, though, the reasons that have driven so many authors away from considering the continuity of traditions are excellent ones. Cultural persistence often *is* a myth. Mythical transmission chains tend to blossom around newly born traditions, like fairy godmothers over a princess's cradle. The European folk costumes craze, in the nineteenth century, is a case in point (Thiesse 2001). These costumes rapidly came to be seen as crucial elements of a local lifestyle bequeathed by countless generations on the people who wore them and had them made (with materials that were quite unavailable to previous generations). In this, European regionalists and patriots were following a very nineteenth-century-ish folkmania. Tartans remain a classic example: one savvy industrialist managed to sell off his stock of his fabrics by convincing his buyers that this was the traditional Highland dress, each Tartan pattern standing as the emblem of a distinct Highlands clan (Trevor-Roper 1983).

The point is not to deny that this tradition eventually spawned long diffusion chains—the survival of Tartan, and other European folk costumes to our days attests to the contrary; but these chains are less ancient than they appear to be. They are also more centralized. Their departure point is to be found in a handful of inventors (creative textile-mongers, for instance), not in a multitude of anonymous ancestors; but they were hailed as long-standing practices even when they begun. Many real traditions, thus, are so remote from the imaginary diffusion chains that have been made up around them, that one could be tempted simply to drop the issue of transmission chains.

Why, indeed, study cultural transmission, if it can be reduced to a collective illusion? Traditions would not be a phenomena to be explained, as much a misperception to be analyzed and cured. This is what makes cultural continuity, according to Pascal Boyer, "the least important and difficult question posed by traditions" (Boyer 1990, 8). Boyer has, by the way, written some of the best arguments against what he calls "the common theory of traditions"—the theory according to which traditions are characterized by a long-standing cross-generational transmission. His first reason for jettisoning this widespread theory is practical: ethnographers cannot directly observe traditions. The sort of data that allow us to judge the long-term continuity of culture is usually inaccessible to participant observation. (Things were somewhat different when the discipline had not yet completely taken the turn of fieldwork ethnography.) The ethnographer's experience is not readily transformed into the sort of data that can be used in a comparative or quantitative perspective. Stringent standards of comparison would need to be agreed upon—standards that dead ethnographers, to start with them, cannot be bothered with. To be sure, the Human Relations Area Files (among other projects) have found clever means of organizing ethnographic reports in ways that make comparative sense. Still, they suffer from the material's heterogeneity, from the need to interpret it, and from countless biases—what shall we do, for instance, when a tradition goes unmentioned in a report? Shall we consider this a proof of absence or an absence of proof? One issue among hundreds. Ethnographers as participant observers are decidedly not in the best position to observe the distribution of culture, in space or in time.

A second reason to abandon the common theory of traditions is the fact that anthropologists are not usually interested by lasting practices, as such. When a shaman recounts a vision quest, the words and syntax he uses are probably not much different from those he used thirty years before. In this, though, his tale does not differ from other tales that are not considered traditional. The shaman tale's conservation is not what grants it the kind of respect that one owes to traditions. Boyer is not the first to note that conservation across generations is not a necessary feature of traditions (of the kind of tradition that he is interested in, at any rate). He is joining views with some of the most careful students of folklore. Arnold Van Gennep, for instance, took much the same view in the rare instances when he discussed the historical continuity of folklore. He lamented the focus that many practitioners of his discipline put on the issue of conservation, thus forgetting other important properties of traditions.

> The lacunae in French folklore may well be due to the double meaning of the word "tradition." In one sense, the word denotes solely "that which is being transmitted" either from one being to another or from one generation to another, with no discontinuity. Another sense carries coercive undertones: "that which must be conserved as it is, with no alteration." To say that something is traditional means to many people that it is imposed, that it must be executed or admitted without a single change.
> (Van Gennep 1937/1999, 2940.)[3]

As Van Gennep stresses, conservatism (a social norm) and conservation (a historical fact) are two distinct (though compatible) phenomena. A traditionalist's conservatism in no way implies the existence of some extended transmission chain; but it is the authority that traditions are vested in (even when their conservation is dubious) that interests Van Gennep or Boyer. Both

---

3. My translation.

lament the focus that so many researchers have placed on stability. In Van Gennep's words, folklorists have shut themselves in "an overwhelming concern for trends towards stability" (Van Gennep 1937/1999, 2940). In so doing, they missed out on a wealth of social facts, the most important of them being that some practices could be invested with unquestionable authority and yet not be conserved through time. Students of culture forgot that conservatism need not imply conservation (and vice versa).

I have nothing to object to this view. In fact, I am tempted to go even further. Yes, the popular conception of traditions as transmission chains is often wrong. Yes, some practices are only thought to be ancient because they serve as tokens of worship or identity symbols, though they date from yesterday or the day before. There are also (as we shall see in chapter 5, on the topic of children's traditions) some practices without any special status or authority that nevertheless possess what Van Gennep called "folkloric tenacity." All these authors (from Van Gennep to Boyer through Hobsbawm et al.) were quite right to abandon the "overwhelming concern for stability." Stability is not, indeed, what marks out those customs that are taken to be traditional (traditionalist prejudices notwithstanding).

Here, though, our focus will be on culture as seen from the angle of its transmission and distribution. Stability (rather than any other mark of "traditionality") will be our concern, wherever we find it—in language, in technology, in rituals, or in children's games. Some of the traditions we'll study (Kwaio religion, for instance) are truly traditionalist: their ancient character is very present in their practitioners' minds, and they derive their status from it. Most, however, are not like that. Some are not ancient—just successful. Others are ancient indeed, but their antiquity goes unnoticed, or if it is known, there is no gain in prestige from it. These are traditions without traditionalism.

Culture Is Not an Undecomposable Whole

The choice to call traditions by that name is also meant to set them as more or less autonomous things, things that can be passed on independently of one another. This way of looking at culture does not subscribe to the view where all the things being passed on in a particular group hang together by a kind of preestablished harmony; where traditions cannot be detached from their common substrate; where they are fused into a coherent worldview. To be sure, there certainly are strong ties between certain traditions, and cultural integration is a reality, to a point; but what my minimal definition of culture wants to do is prevent us from taking such cultural integration as a given. The burden of proof rests upon the shoulders of those who think that traditions cannot be shaken off their cultural tree: cultural integration cannot be an axiom (a point already well made by Boyd and Richerson 1985, 37–38).

Let us consider a short and banal diffusion chain (hardly a tradition at all): a tune heard in the street, that one whistles to, that some other whistlers pick up on, repeat, distort. It can travel some distance this way. The quantity of information thus transmitted is slim, but this does not matter here: let us only look at the short tune's itinerary, at what pushes people to catch it. Passersby who come into contact with the tune differ in many ways. Their musical tastes, the other tunes they have in mind, and many other facets of their musical cultures—which cannot be perfectly homogeneous. If our tune is to become reasonably successful in a diverse population, it will have to be picked up on by different minds, each with a distinct musical repertoire. These repertoires need not be much altered when they include our small tune. This show that they are no unbreakable blocks. The small tune can be attached, or detached, without making much of a difference to the whole. This is even a condition of its being easily transmitted: a passerby hearing another whistling in the street lacks the means and inclination to upload (in a magical osmosis, as it were) the complete and exhaustive compendium of their thoughts, worldviews, memories, favorite colors, and so on—in a stranger's head. Only by breaking free of all this can our little tune travel at all. To be sure, not everyone who hears it will repeat it—and the choice to pick it up or not probably tells us a few things on a passerby's state of mind, music-wise. For us, though, who are interested in the tune's diffusion and the paths that it treads, it doesn't really matter to know what place it occupies in a particular someone's head, what meaning it has been vested with, what place it has made for itself in that particular mindscape, what personal memories it got tangled with or stuck to. Granted, if you look closely, everything in mental life is more or less connected to everything else: a small tune recalls a childhood memory, itself linked to a smell, and so on. Such linkages are of little help in knowing how far our tune will travel. If it is successful enough, it will appeal to a wide range of people. Each person may tie it to a different memory, in a different web of associations. We want to stay at a level general enough that we can account for the small tune's success in all these different minds. For that, we need to abstract away many a thing that could have been crucial to its success with such and such a particular adopter.

If culture can be decomposed into more or less independent traditions, we may like to know how far such decompositions may go. Some authors have suggested that it would stop at some sort of atomic entity, some elementary unit of culture. Dawkins's memes (Dawkins 1976; Dennett 1995, 344) are sometimes taken to play that part: cultural transmission would always entail the transmission of at least one such unit of information and replication, the cultural analogue of genetic transmission. Each tradition could thus be broken down and translated into a specific set of memes. Before the end of this chapter, I will explain why I do not endorse this view—why the transmission of a tradition need not entail the reproduction of one enduring mental representation.

For now, let us simply note that we do not need to endorse memetics' most ambitious claims, to know that culture can be decomposed. Cultural transmission does not require us to pass on an undivided world of feelings, ideas, and memories; yet just because it does not form a block does not mean it is made of discrete units—nor does it imply that cultural transmission would go through by replicating some fragment of an elementary code. You may borrow the tune that this passerby whistles; you may as well borrow a part of it, or just pick up a single note and improvise therefrom; or just whistle a related note that the other note evoked. Just like for the tune, there is no a priori limit to the decomposability of your musical repertoire: it is not a molecule whose atoms could be isolated.

Why Anthropologists Are No Longer Interested in Traditions

Today, one finds more interest for the approaches just described (culture seen as a package of distributed and transmitted traditions) on the margins of anthropology, less in its heart. Things were not always this way. Until fairly recent times, most anthropologists took it for granted that culture could be broken down into independent traits, called customs, folkways, traditions, or simply items. Lee Lyman and Michael O'Brien (2003) expose in detail the deep roots that this conception had grown. Here is how E. B. Tylor (yes, the one remembered for calling culture "that complex whole") opened his 1871 magnum opus:

> To the ethnographer, the bow and arrow is a species, the habit of flattening children's skulls is a species, the practice of reckoning numbers by tens is a species. The geographical distribution of these things, and their transmission from region to region, have to be studied as the naturalist studies the geography of his botanical and zoological species.... Just as the catalogue of all the species of plant and animals of a district

represents its Flora and Fauna, so the list of all the items of the general life of a people represents that whole which we call its culture.

(Tylor 1871, 8)

Fifty years later, that way of thinking still went without saying, or without saying much. The distribution and transmission of cultural traits was still the main concern of Kroeber or Boas. Cultural incoherence was little cause for wonder. As Lyman and O'Brien document, it was quite common, in the first half of the twentieth century, to look upon cultures as heterogeneous sets of discrete and independent traditions: "congeries of disconnected traits, associated only by reason of a series of historic accidents, the elements being functionally unrelated" (in Spier's words); Lowie called it "that planless hodgepodge, that thing of shreds and patches" (Lyman & O'Brien, 2003, 232).

Careful readers will have noticed how the needs of exposition force me to pack into a few simple viewpoints the complex history of a diverse discipline. Still taking a bird's eye view of its history, we can see that, a few decades later, culture as transmission and distribution was no longer the main focus of anthropological inquiries. Nowhere was this new orientation clearer than among British anthropologists. Radcliffe-Brown seized every opportunity (with more or less nuance depending on the occasion) to stress how different culture and social structures could be, as objects of study went (Radcliffe-Brown 1952; Radcliffe-Brown 1949). Anthropologists were to study those facts that were properly social: kinship, hierarchies, and so on. In so doing, they would, to be sure, come across culture; but they were warned not to lose their focus. As Radcliffe-Brown noted, the transmission of a language (for instance) could be studied while abstracting away (to a point) the social life of the people who spoke that language. That life, however, was the proper object of social anthropology: the web of economic, political, kinship-related ties that bind individuals into a group. Some social structures may be copied or transmitted, but this traditional mode is not what anthropologists should chiefly care about. They should worry even less about things like languages or technologies, which may be transmitted but cannot be directly studied as social structures.

This view was shared by a good number of Radcliffe-Brown's British colleagues, and famously by Leach:

> Culture provides the form, the 'dress' of the social situation. As far as I am concerned, the cultural situation is a given factor. It is a product and an accident of history. I do not know *why* Kachin women go hatless with bobbed hair before they are married, but assume a turban

afterwards, any more than I know *why* English women put on a ring on a particular finger to denote the same change in social status: all I am interested in is that in this Kachin context the assumption of a turban by a woman does have this symbolic significance. It is a statement about the status of the woman.

(Leach 1954, 16)

Statements like this one are somewhat extreme, but, however controversial they may have been in their day, they were influential. It may not have been followed in its letter (culture, not social structure, remains the official object of most anthropological research) but it often was heeded in its spirit. Today, there are still anthropologists dedicated to studying the distribution and diffusion of traditions (we have met or shall meet many such). Yet, they do not dominate the field as they used to do, and I am tempted to subscribe to this diagnosis posed by a recent review of the treatment of cultural transmission by the field: "transmission and its *modus operandi* do not constitute a starting point, a self-contained research topic" (Berliner 2010). Buttressing this diagnosis would be beyond the scope of this book. Neither will I try to explain why anthropology turned its back (as it seems to me) to its once-defining object of study. Let us instead explore some of the reasons that made that choice seem appealing. These were not bad reasons.

The anthropology that relinquished, little by little, the study of cultural diffusion and transmission, was increasingly drawn to the method of fieldwork-based participant observation (the advantage of which need no demonstration here). Fieldwork, however, is not necessarily the best vantage point from which to observe the distribution of culture. There, ethnographers lack access to many scales of space and time. This can be remedied by comparing ethnographies, but as we saw, the samples will be small, and their exploitation, uneasy. What they see is fragments of a distributed tradition, not the kind of data that historical linguistics or quantitative sociologists can use. If they want to see the distributional face of culture, ethnographers need to refashion themselves into historians—which, of course, they are most of the time, but the dominance of fieldwork necessarily outshines these other competences.

One other thing that might have contributed to pushing cultural traits out of the light was their use in ethnic classifications—the attempt to use the cultural repertoires of societies in order to build statistically sound categories, starting from the premise that societies are ethnically close to the extent that their cultural repertoires overlap. These attempts ran into two rather thorny problems.

The first one we have already met: societies are culturally heterogeneous; yet they need to be consistent enough to be distinguished from their surroundings—otherwise, culture would be a poor indicator to use to classify them. Fiji culture makes sense as an indicator of ethnic boundaries only insofar as we can expect two Fijians to resemble each other more than two random denizens of the Pacific. As we saw, however, only a small share of cultural variation serves to delineate social or ethnic boundaries in this way. The rest is just blurring the lines. Culture is not the worst of indicators for this task (it does better than genes, for instance); but that is a small consolation. The second problem was highlighted by Fredrik Barth (1969), among others. Even when we are given a clear-cut cultural boundary, we should not assume that ethnic loyalties will align themselves on it (or indeed pay any attention to it). Thus, according to Barth, the Pashtuns of Afghanistan may regard as fellow Pashtuns people from whom they are separated by abysmal cultural gaps, while they will deny Pashtun-hood to people with a very similar lifestyle that they have come to dislike for political or economic reasons. Culture does not carve social boundaries at their joints.

Such failures explain why traditions, in themselves, have lost some of their appeal for those social scientists who concern themselves chiefly with social, economic, or political ties. We could add on top of this the fact that cultural transmission is not very interesting as a social interaction. As Durkheim remarked, the transmission of a behavior can happen more or less in a social void:

> A man may imitate another with no link of either one with the other or with a common group on which both depend, and the imitative function when exercised has in itself no power to form a bond between them. (. . .) A cough, a dance-motion, a homicidal impulse may be transferred from one person to another even though there is only chance and temporary contact between them. They need have no intellectual or moral community between them nor exchange services nor even speak the same language, nor are they any more related after the transfer than before.
>
> (Durkheim 1897/1952, 123)

This argument was clearly aimed at Tarde, who replied that, on the contrary, imitation is always capable of creating rich social ties (Tarde 1897/2000, 224–225). I would love to prove him right here, but it seems that here again, Durkheim has the upper hand.

At first glance, the kind of interaction that allows transmission to occur can be very simple, to say the least. It may happen between two people for whom transmission will be the only social link. One may decipher epitaphs on the sarcophagus of an Egyptian king many millennia dead, or steal an invention whose inventor one will never know. In both cases the source of transmission is not aware of being a source (nor willing to be one), and this actually makes transmission easier. Considering similar cases, though, Tarde claimed that transmission always constituted a social tie of some kind, however tenuous (his favorite example involved French revolutionaries inspired by the writings of Thucydides). This is clearly a matter of definition, but we should note that the Egyptologist, the industrial spy, and the Jacobins formed no bound of trust, cooperation, domination, or enmity with their model. Cultural transmission does not seem to require or to favor a particular kind of sociability. It is not a social tie like other social ties—if it is a tie at all.

Traditions Do Not Exist Solely as Ideas

One last thing may explain the misgivings of contemporary anthropology when it comes to studying the distribution of traditions. Today, this approach is often championed by psychologists, by biologists, or by people who consider that traditions are ideas; that ideas are stored in our brains; that cultural transmission is an exchange of mental representations. This is indeed the standard definition of cultural transmission for the new approaches of culture (Boyd and Richerson 1985, 2; Laland, Odling-Smee, and Myles 2010; Mesoudi, Whiten, and Laland 2006). They take it for granted that culture is a set of socially transmitted representations (or bits of information). Not all of them mean to say that cultural transmission can be reduced to an information transfer, but little effort is made to dispel that impression. On top of that, memetics, the theoretical current that is known to the widest audience, has made much of the claim that culture can be seen as a set of informational units replicating from one brain to another (Dennett 1995; Blackmore 1999).

It is all the more important, then, to note that cultural epidemiology does not reduce culture to a set of ideas—nor does it boil cultural transmission down to a transfer of information (Sperber 1998). From this vantage point everything (including ideas) can be a tradition if it travels far enough; but not all traditions are ideas. Behaviors or techniques can be passed on as well as ideas, and the non-mental aspects of a tradition will often turn out to be the most important. Many traditions that will be studied in the next chapters—like initiation rituals or children's rhymes—are public manifestations. Something crucial would be lost to them if people stopped performing them, and just retained a knowledge of them. Being in our heads is one of their modes of existence, but cannot be the only one.

Geertz was quite right in this respect, when he remarked that most cultural things would not look like themselves at all if they were reduced to mental contents:

> If (...) we take, say, a Beethoven quartet as an, admittedly rather special but, for these purposes, nicely illustrative, sample of culture, no one would, I think, identify it with its score, with the skills and knowledge needed to play it, with the understanding of it possessed by its performers or auditors, nor, to take care, *en passant*, of the reductionists and reifiers, with a particular performance of it or with some mysterious entity transcending material existence. The "no one" is perhaps too strong here, for there are always incorrigibles. But that a Beethoven quartet is a temporally developed tonal structure, a coherent sequence of modeled sound—in a word, music—and not anybody's knowledge of or belief about anything, including how to play it, is a proposition to which most people are, upon reflection, likely to assent.
> (Geertz 1973, 11–12)

Geertz's argument does not consist in denying the fact that the performance of the quartet, and its transmission, involve representations of it. It simply states that these representations can be very diverse (from the visual signs on the score to a violin player's motor memory), and none of these representations can be said to *be* the quartet. (By a similar logic, the quartet can no more be reduced to the public, non-mental side of its existence: if all that was left off a Beethoven quartet were a few musicians' memories—no records, no sheet music—the quartet would be in peril, but it wouldn't be quite lost.) Geertz's point can perhaps be made more salient if we think of things, like race cars or satellites, which are so complex that probably no one possesses a complete representation of them. This is no obstacle to the making of satellites, or to the transmission of the know-how that makes their fabrication possible.

Culture, thus, is in our minds only up to a point. Two issues deserve to be distinguished here.

Does a tradition's transmission necessarily imply an exchange of representations? Yes; otherwise a virus hopping from a tree to another would count as a case of cultural transmission. Transmission as discussed here implies that at least one of the partners in the interaction acts upon the other's cognition, in a broad sense of that word (including emotions and motivations in addition to reasoning, perception, etc.).

Can traditions be identified with the information that is passed on when they are transmitted? No, not always. Just because cultural transmission involves an exchange of ideas does not mean that traditions themselves *are* the ideas that their proliferation relies on. Complex cultural forms can subsist through rudimentary interactions. Consider (to keep things simple, and without much regard for the entomological reality of the case) an ant that marks the path it follows toward a source of food with a chemical trace, so that other ant workers can follow in its steps. If these followers manage to make other ants follow the same path, it will set in motion a very short transmission chain (too short to count as a tradition, but that matters little here). At each transmission step, though, the ants may use any kind of information exchange. The first ant marks the road chemically, but the others, having discovered the source of food, may use different ways to invite fellow workers toward it—with their antennas, with stridulations, or by dropping bits of food along their way. All these means of transmission use different sensory canals and communicate different pieces of information. What the chemical marking communicates is a mere smell; antenna-tapping may elicit a following behavior; stridulation orients the ants' attention toward the food source; dropping bits of food is not in itself a signal but causes the ants to gather in the vicinity of the source; and so on. All along the transmission chain, a path to the food is reproduced by various and sundry means, but the information involved—the marking's chemical signature, the fact of attending to the food source, or the drive to follow another ant—is not itself transmitted. In this transmission could be compared to a monetary transaction. If I sign a check for twenty dollars to a friend, who cashes it in for banknotes, changes the banknotes for coins, and gives the coins to you, the twenty dollars have gone from me to you, but the banknotes, the check, and the coins have not. Means of payments are exchanged but the sum of money itself (being an abstraction) is not identical with the means of its transmission: twenty dollars is neither a check nor a banknote, nor a coin, nor the sum of all these. Likewise, the means that permit a behavior to be reproduced in a transmission chain do not themselves need to be passed on along the chain. Culture often differs from the ideas whose exchange allows it to get diffused (see Descombes 1998 for a similar argument).

Two Questions

Two issues will occupy the rest of this book: Why are there traditions, and why are they so numerous among humans? Outside the new approaches to culture, the social sciences seldom ask these questions, perhaps because they are implicitly considered settled. One frequent answer that is given, in passing, to the first question, is that cultural upbringing is simply infallible: children cannot help absorb the norms and practices of their society. The second question is often solved in a similarly sweeping way, by stating that humans are essentially cultural animals, as centuries of humanist philosophy taught us.

One goal of this book is to rob these answers of the aura of confidence that clings to them. The first answer should already look dubious: why should cultural acquisition be easy and automatic? Traditions are not invulnerable. Many die, many more are not born at all, either because transmission failed, or because diffusion did not follow. If this is true of traditions taken singularly, why wouldn't it be true for culture in general?

Why Are There Traditions Rather than Nothing?

Like everything that results from human effort, transmission can fail. It can fail for two very different kinds of reasons: because of a bug in transmission (we get misunderstood, we fail to imitate others accurately, etc.) or (more commonly, I will argue) because of a lack of motivation to transmit. If you tried (impracticable as it might be) to count all your thoughts and utterances of yesterday, you would probably find that few of them were picked up by you from somebody else, and that even fewer were reproduced by others from you. Even when transmission does occur, once, this does not suffice to create a tradition—a diffusion chain that extends long enough in time or space. Transmission needs to be repeated for such chains to emerge—but repetition is not guaranteed to happen. In everyday communication, we let out many ideas that are not relevant beyond a tiny local context: "a pen was dropped," "she is slightly tired today." They will not be retransmitted, or not much. In the same way, we sometimes imitate (without being aware of it) the accent, the postures, or some gestures of the persons we interact with. Such mimicry, though, typically does not outlast the duration of the interaction, and the few traces it leaves behind are soon gone. Even when they are not, mimickers are seldom mimicked back (van Baaren et al. 2004).

If transmission is neither automatic nor perfect, a concatenation of transmission episodes is even harder to obtain. As we shall see in chapter 4, most transmission chains collapse past a few links. To explain how certain transmission chains manage to reach far without breaking is the first problem posed by culture as it is looked at here.

Why Does One Species Monopolize Traditions?

Why are traditions more numerous among humans than anywhere else? The spontaneous answer is that our species is endowed with a special aptitude for having them, one that would form part of our genetic toolkit. This answer has been questioned by the discovery of traditions existing in other species, where foolproof cultural practices are rarer but well-attested. Certain dolphins, for instance, have the habit of using a sea sponge to go raking the seafloor, looking for food (Krutzen et al. 2005). This technique has spread in a group of dolphins sharing social ties (most often, mothers and daughters), but not in other dolphins found at the same place (and from the same genetic stock). Ethologists agree that behaviors like this one owe their diffusion to interindividual transmission. Their transmission can sometimes be observed in some detail, like the chimpanzee practice of breaking nuts on stones, studied by Christopher Boesch and his team (Boesch-Akerman and Boesch 1993). Centuries-old traces of the practice have also been found (Mercader et al. 2002), which could indicate a long-standing tradition, unless the practice was invented multiple times.

More or less durable or far-reaching traditions have been identified in dolphins, in tits, in small fishes, and so on. Most often the behavior that is being passed on is not very complex—as in tropical fishes, who follow the route that their conspecifics went through, to reach a mating site (Warner 1988). Sometimes the involvement of transmission is quite limited—the classic example being, in that regard, that of British blue tits, who are thought to have learnt to open aluminum-capped milk bottles simply from seeing opened bottles, their aluminum cap having been torn by other tits (Fisher and Hinde 1949; Sherry and Galef 1990). Since witnessing other tits directly was not necessary to its spread, that practice was reconstructed more than transmitted.

Yet it often cannot be denied that one is dealing with complex behaviors that would not have reached as far as they did without transmission. Many traditions are more dubious: they are merely differences in behavior observed from one animal group to another, which researchers cannot account for with environmental differences. They are called cultural by exhaustion of other explanations, but the possibility remains that the researchers' explanations might be incomplete, that certain causes may have been neglected. In any case, even if we lower the bar to accept such traditions, the richest animal cultures are astonishingly scarce when compared with their human counterparts. What keeps dolphin or chimpanzee traditions from going further? These are animal populations with rich social and cognitive lives. What keeps them from sustaining a greater number of traditions? Transmission there either fails to occur, or it fails to create extended diffusion chains.

Human traditions are not simply more numerous: they are qualitatively different from many of their non-human counterparts, in that it is often hard for a single individual, cut from the diffusion chain, to reinvent them single-handedly. This inability can have several causes: it might be because human traditions improve with time, solving problems no single mind could solve, or because human populations manage to conserve very good ideas that seldom appear and would be lost in other populations. We have already encountered this peculiarity of human cultures—cumulativity. Its students make much of its absence, or near-absence, in non-human cultures. These do not look like they are being fleshed out, or improving with time. Most of the skills they feature indeed seem within the range of a reasonably savvy animal to invent.

*

Confronted with these two questions—Why traditions? Why us?—we can rely on one tool: a quantitative and abstract view of culture, in which it emerges from interactions between individuals (culture is transmission), and is made of ideas and behaviors transmitted along extended diffusion chains (culture is traditions). Culture, thus defined, is somewhat more abstract than social life, somewhat more general than differences in lifestyle that may set two societies apart. This book was written on a bet: I am betting that the first of our two questions holds the key to the second. In other words, the causes of cultural stability as we can observe them today, in our species, are similar to those that make traditions live (or die) in other species, and in other times. We'll see in the last chapter whether the wager pays off. In any case, it guides the organization of this book. The next four chapters will try to understand why stable traditions exist. Two quite different things may explain this fact: efficiency in transmission, or success in diffusion. The next two chapters look at transmission mechanisms: imitation, learning, communication, teaching, social influence. The theories of cultural transmission that dominate today's new approaches to culture look into these mechanisms as though they held the key to cultural stability. Traditions endure, we are told, because they are accurately imitated. Do they really?

2 COMMUNICATION AND IMITATION

One word and one idea dominate theories of cultural transmission, at least since Tarde: *imitation* is the mother of culture. Imitation, one of Tarde's readers claimed, is "the key that unlocks every door" (Tarde 1893/1993, xxi), the fundamental mechanism that all culture springs from. This constitutes the imitation hypothesis.

For many authors, imitation is just a word that stands for cultural transmission, more or less as it was defined in chapter 1. Others, however, have construed it as a particularly powerful form of transmission, one that can account for the birth of traditions. In this view, imitation (and imitation alone) solves the two problems of cultural diffusion: the Flop Problem (how to sustain a transmission chain by eliciting multiple transmissions) and the Wear-and-Tear Problem (how to deal with the copying errors that accumulate along a transmission chain).

Imitation—that was Tarde's big idea—can solve the Flop Problem if it is compulsive. He saw no difference between what he called imitation and what the psychologists of his time called *somnambulisme* (a rough synonym of today's hypnosis). Imitation is "social somnambulism" (Tarde 1895/1903, 85): each one of us is unwittingly and permanently under suggestion from others; the spell is particularly strong when the others in question are numerous or prestigious. People around us offer an example that we are, somehow, compelled to reproduce. This neatly solves the Flop Problem. How, then, does imitation take care of the Wear-and-Tear Problem? By being faithful. Fidelity is often taken to be the key characteristic of human transmission, the one that explains the richness of our cultures.

(Tarde was often forced—e.g., chapter 6 of *The Laws of Imitation*—to soften the claim that imitation is unconscious and automatic. Even then, he downplayed these concessions as soon as he made them: even the most thoughtful decisions hide an unwitting obedience to suggestion and social hypnosis. Yet he does in several instances drop the claim that imitation must be compulsory, and this is what allows him to bring all kinds of transmission under the "imitation" label. Tarde saw even the absence of transmission as a subspecies in the general category of imitative behavior: not to imitate is to "counter-imitate"—Tarde, 1895/1903, 13.)

The ethologists and psychologists who study social learning (i.e., the kind of learning that takes place under the influence of other individuals, as opposed to solitary learning) take seriously two hypotheses that are closely related to Tarde's. The first hypothesis states that human cultures owe their stability to one uniquely human social learning faculty. According to the second hypothesis, what sets this faculty apart is its faithful accuracy: it allows us to reproduce a model's behavior, and what that model wanted that behavior to be like, in a very exact manner. That is why it is often called imitation (or "true imitation"). Others, who refuse to call it by that name (thus Heyes 1993) or who prefer to say that teaching, rather than imitation, is the key to culture, nevertheless concur that a mechanism of exceptional fidelity (whatever we call it) allows human cultures to be passed on.

The aim of this chapter is to convince you that, if human cultures do owe a great deal to a peculiar form of social learning, fidelity is not its chief characteristic. That mechanism is ostensive communication, not imitation.

Imitating and Understanding Others

Let us start from a paper by Tomasello, Kruger, and Ratner, which had a huge influence on the field of social learning. Their argument begins with two remarks: First, animal traditions are rudimentary and scarce. Second, humans do not learn from their conspecifics in the way other animals do. The conjunction of the two, they argue, is no accident: human cultures are richer because there is something special about human social learning. That something special, they think, is a psychological faculty proper to our species; their goal is to identify it.

It would need (the argument goes) to possess two characteristics. First, it would have to permit faithful, accurate, precise imitation: without such fidelity, humans could not stop their cultures from getting damaged as they pass from one individual to the next—in this book's terms, they could not solve the Wear-and-Tear Problem (Tomasello et al. 1993, 495). Second, this mechanism would have to be faithful to one aspect in particular of the model's behavior: its *intended* aspect, what the model wanted to do. For this the mechanism must be able to represent, or at least to track, the model's intentions.

The authors distinguish three types of social learning; to simplify, we might separate them into those that require a *simple* understanding of others' intentions or beliefs, and those that call for a *recursive* understanding.

To understand someone's intentions or their beliefs is to represent the goals and thoughts (the mental states) that guide their actions, in such a way as to be able to predict these actions, to reproduce them, and (if the action is an intentional one) to judge whether they have reached their aim (for instance, detecting in someone the intention to open a door allows you to make certain predictions and judgments concerning what will happen between that person and that door).

To understand mental states in a *recursive* way is to represent intentions or beliefs that are about other mental states (other intentions, other beliefs); these other mental states may, in turn, bear on yet other mental states—and so on. Imagine you are facing a closed door, your two arms burdened with grocery bags. I am there as well; I see you gesture at the door. I understand that you wish for me to open the door, and (in the same thought) I see that you want to share that wish with me. This thought may be seen as a set of recursively embedded mental states. You want me to open the door (willingly) for you: an intention that is about another intention. I recognize that you want me to open the door: a belief about an intention about another intention. You want me to understand that you want me to open the door: an intention to make me recognize that you intend me to do it. I understand that you intend me to understand that you want me to open the door: one additional degree of recursion. In spite of their complexity, we treat thousands of such embedded representations on an everyday basis (Sperber 2000).

This distinction can be used to differentiate two kinds of social learning mechanisms: those that require a simple comprehension of mental states, and those that use recursively embedded thoughts. The first category is where Tomasello et al. put what they call imitation learning, or "true imitation." Their view of it is quite specific.

Looking for "True Imitation"

Tomasello et al. define imitation by pointing out all the things that it is not. One cannot, to begin with, speak of imitation when an individual reproduces a behavior that she saw a conspecific perform, if that behavior was already part of her behavioral repertoire. This rules out the everyday sense of the word. Second, whatever information the spectator gets from observing her conspecifics must be about their behavior, not about their common environment. If, for instance, a monkey learns, from seeing another monkey pick up a banana from a box, that the box contains bananas, and acts in consequence, then the received usage in psychology rules imitation out. Psychologists would rather speak of "emulation" or "stimulus enhancement" for such cases. The conspecific merely helped to make the presence of bananas in the box more salient, but no truly novel behavior was taught. The emulator reproduced his model's behavior, but only insofar as it resulted in grabbing a banana from the box. No finer detail got mimicked. Had the spectator reproduced the precise, quaint sleight of hand with which her model opened the box, then and only then would Tomasello (and the many psychologists who followed his usage) accept to talk of imitation. Here, the word may signal at least three things: the model's action is reproduced at quite a fine-grained level of detail; a novel or unusual behavior is demonstrated; the imitator may be motivated by something beyond the immediate goal of grabbing the banana.

The standard experimental test to determine whether an animal readily imitates in this particular sense is the "two actions method" (see Heyes 1993 for a more complete characterization). It consists in presenting each spectator with a model who uses one of two ways of performing a given action (opening a box to fetch a banana, for instance). Other spectators are exposed to the alternative *modus operandi*. When, in a group of animals, the demonstrated method (whichever of the two it is) reliably influences spectators, the group is said to demonstrate, depending on authors and lingos, "true imitation" or "overimitation" ("overimitation" because the spectator did not need to be so faithful to grab the banana—she copied more than what was useful).

One of the most famous uses of this method (a not quite standard case, but a simple one) comes from one of Andrew Meltzoff's experiments (Meltzoff 1988). The subjects, toddlers, are faced with an adult model and a half-sphere of plastic that lights up when pressed upon. Instead of activating the toy with her hand (which seems the most direct and simple gesture), she does it with her head. For another group of toddlers (the controls), the regular hand gesture is used. Psychologists have deemed human toddlers willing and able to "truly" imitate, because toddlers in the test group use their head much more often than those of the control group. An apparently useless gesture was slavishly imitated.

The point of this method is to tell truly servile mimicry from merely opportunistic imitation; the most arbitrary and meaningless gestures are taken to be the most revealing in that regard. If correctly implemented, the two actions method reveals motivations that cannot be reduced to an instrumental motive, or explained by an environmental incentive: subjects must be led by some misunderstanding of the causality at work, by a desire to communicate something to the model, or by sheer playfulness. In addition, the imitator shows an ability to pick up a gesture directly from a model, without any environmental intermediation. This mix of motivations and competences is supposed to define "true imitation" (Tomasello et al. 1993, among others). That phrase is slightly unfortunate—other, completely different behaviors have as much of a claim to the title of "true" imitation—but it is convenient to use. "True imitation" is true, in spirit, to Tarde's conception of it: it is faithful and compulsive. Imitators must reproduce at a fine-grained level (fidelity) an action that they would have no reason to perform, had it not been demonstrated to them (compulsivity). As soon as a psychologist suspects that her subjects are not being completely servile, doubt looms; imitation is discarded in favor of emulation or stimulus enhancement. Reinvention is to be held in check by appropriate experimental controls: only faithful reproduction should be taken into account in our definitions of imitation (Visalberghi and Fragaszy 2002).

Why add such a demanding, almost contrived set of constraints to the definition of a simple word? The answer is clearly that researchers, at first, sought to discover a very special transmission mechanism, one so sophisticated that only humans could master it. Bennett Galef is one of the most explicit defenders of this strategy: his and David Sherry's 1990 study on the transmission of milk bottle-opening in tits set a new standard for imitation research, by showing that cultural transmission in these birds had little to do with imitation, and everything to do with reconstruction from cues. Each tit was put on the right track by the traces left by previous bottle-opening tits, nothing more. Likewise, Tomasello (2009, for instance) tries to prove that transmission behaviors exhibited by chimpanzees in the wild are based on emulation rather than imitation: chimpanzees do not try to mimick their conspecifics' action plans in a faithful manner (indeed, one may ask why they would want to do so). They are just improvising, on the basis of behavioral and environmental cues, actions that fit their purpose.

If tits or chimps are happy to reinvent new actions with the occasional help of cues left by their conspecifics, they have no reason to be particularly servile when they happen to reproduce a gesture. For most psychologists, this lack of servility is synonymous with a lack of truly efficient transmission; only when it takes the form of true imitation, they claim, can cultural transmission sustain lasting traditions; only then can it be called "cumulative."

> Cumulative cultural evolution depends on imitative learning, and perhaps active instruction on the part of adults, and cannot be brought about by means of "weaker" forms of social learning such as local enhancement, emulation learning, ontogenetic ritualization, or any form of individual learning.
>
> (Tomasello 1999, 39)

This point of view is shared by other important theorists of cultural transmission—Boyd and Richerson, for instance (1985, 34–35), who define culture as that which is passed on through imitation or teaching, not through weaker forms of transmission. We shall give, before the end of this chapter, reasons to doubt that teaching is indispensable to culture. There are other good reasons to doubt that "true imitation" is crucial. Let us examine them now.

Imitation Is neither a Human Privilege nor the Source of Our Cultures

Defenders of animal traditions, like ethologist Kevin Laland, note that those animal traditions that are passed on by non-imitative means (like bottle-opening in blue tits) nonetheless persist without much trouble. If they are stable, why should the fact that they are not "truly" imitated disqualify them from being called cultural?

> (. . .) neither imitation, nor teaching, nor any other sophisticated psychological process, is necessary for a socially transmitted behavioral tradition to be established. There is no evidence that simple processes such as local enhancement are any less likely than cognitively complex processes such as imitation to result in social learning, behavioral conformity, or stable transmission. On the contrary, numerous animal traditions appear to be supported by psychologically simple mechanisms.
>
> (Laland 2002, 234)

When faced with this sort of objection, authors like Tomasello, Boyd, or Richerson usually point out that rudimentary animal traditions may be preserved without true imitation, but cannot be gradually improved. Such progress is the privilege of cumulative cultures: cultural transmission only sustains cumulative traditions when it is based on true imitation or teaching (a view that chapter 6 will investigate more closely).

Why should true imitation have this effect? Because, the argument goes, true imitation retains "good tricks" that would vanish without it. This may sometimes be true; but it is also dangerously close to what we might call "the Hoarder's Fallacy." I once had as a neighbor a man who kept every single wrapping, box, tin can, old newspaper he ever had; the police eventually forced him to empty his basement (which had become a fire hazard). When asked about all this, he invariably replied that "those things might serve some day." Surely, they might—but it would not hurt to be a little more selective in keeping things. True imitation, as defined so far, is such a hoarder. Of all the social learning mechanisms that have been described, it is one of the stupidest. Suppose I am learning to crack nuts from a master of that trick. If I try to copy as many gestures as I can, I will reproduce many useless (but voluntary) gestures (like scratching my head in such and such a way). Of all the things that I reproduce, there will of course be useful gestures that I can recognize as such; there will also be, perhaps, a handful of opaque gestures, the use of which is not immediately perceptible. The key contribution of "true imitation" is supposed to lie in enabling the persistence of such opaque tricks; but what a wasteful form of conservation it is! The utter lack of selectivity implied by standard definitions of "true imitation" is not only inefficient: it is hard to see how such faithfulness could be sustained in a reasonably extended transmission chain. Some things just need to be dropped for traditions to travel. Imitation needs some way of selecting good tricks; but it is, by definition, incapable of selecting them.

Another argument undermines the claim that stable cultures are sustained by "true imitation": that mechanism seems to be present in species whose cultural life has little in common with ours. Experimental studies have thus claimed that "true imitation" could be found in marmosets (Voelkl and Huber 2007), in macaques (Ferrari et al. 2006), in rats (C. Heyes 1993) in gorillas (Stoinsky et al. 2001), or in chimpanzees (Whiten, Horner, and Marshall-Pescini 2003). These animals seem to imitate their conspecifics' gestures in a greater level of detail than would be justified by sheer instrumental motives.

This may be why Michael Tomasello and his team have gradually dropped the claim that imitation was a unique characteristic of humans and their cultures. They have turned to social learning mechanisms that require more than a simple comprehension of the model's intention. A truly sophisticated social learner must now be able to understand recursively embedded mental states. This, as we shall see, is probably a good bet: as it has become clear that chimpanzees are capable of understanding others' mental states and intentions (thus removing one obstacle in the way of true imitation), the capacity to handle embedded representations is attracting attention, as a crucially original feature of cultural transmission in our species (Thierry 1997; Thierry 1994). This preoccupation converges with some conclusions that have been reached by philosophers of language, most notably by pragmatic theories of communication developed in the wake of Paul Grice's work. Gricean theories of communication (Grice 1957; Sperber and Wilson 1995; Levinson 2000; Csibra and Gergely 2009) share the view that the transmission of ideas among humans is grounded in our capacity to express and understand recursively embedded intentions. What does this mean exactly?

Human Ostensive Communication

If I had to designate one social learning mechanism that trumps all others in our species, my bet would be on communication as characterized by Gricean theories: voluntary and overt communication, also known as ostensive communication.

To communicate with someone in an overt way is to try to change their mental life (instruct them, arouse feelings, orient attention, etc.) by making a communicative intention manifest. This so-called "communicative" intention (also sometimes called a Gricean intention or second-clause intention) is a peculiar kind of intention, in that it is fulfilled as soon as it is recognized. For example, suppose that Alice wishes to initiate communication with Bruno; she makes a gesture to Bruno manifesting that intention, and Bruno understands her gesture. By this very fact (Bruno's comprehension), Alice's intention is satisfied: communication has been initiated. This is not, far from it, the only way we can influence the mental life of others, but this one has two crucial characteristics: it is *voluntary* (ostensive communicators communicate deliberately) and *overt* (to communicate ostensively is to communicate by showing that one does). Voluntary + overt = ostensive.

Ostensive communicators desire to communicate, and manage to do so by making that desire visible (or audible). This does not mean that humans always transmit information deliberately, or never hide from the information's receptor. It means that they can, if they so wish, make their conscious intention to communicate public, and use this publicity to get their messages across. This very special way of passing ideas plays a crucial role in human transmission.

Is communication thus defined the same thing as teaching? Yes and no. It is not as broad as the acception of that term in ethology, yet it is less narrow than the range of phenomena that psychologists or anthropologists usually put under that word.

Ethologists Caro and Hauser (1992) call "teaching" all the voluntary behaviors whose sole function is apparently to help one individual learn a behavior. Like teaching thus defined, ostensive communication needs to be deliberate, and it can be used to assist behavioral learning in others (it can also serve other purposes: tell a story, draw attention on something, etc.); but unlike Caro and Hauser's teaching, ostensive communication needs to be overt. The target of communication must know that it is being addressed; more importantly, the target must use this knowledge to learn from the communicator. Merely voluntary but not overt teaching does not qualify. If I attach small wheels to a child's bicycle to help her learn cycling, I am "teaching" biking (in Caro and Hauser's sense); yet, in the Gricean definition, I am not communicating the skill of cycling ostensively. Why? Because the child does not need to recognize my intentions in order for me to help her learn cycling. She may or may not realize that I am trying to help, but that comprehension plays little part in her progress—the small wheels do all the work.

Ostensive communication is somewhat closer to what anthropologists or psychologists have in mind when they talk about teaching. Yet in these literatures too, the term teaching carries connotations that are absent from communication as discussed here. Communication can happen outside of any institution or organization; anywhere, at any time, from anybody to anyone (thus not necessarily between adult teachers and child receivers). Communicated contents need not be explicitly laid down: they may be reconstructed from thin cues, or hammered down by means of explicit instructions. They may not always have to be passed on by linguistic means: there is nothing, after all, in the definition of ostensive communication, specifying that it must coincide with language. Most human communication is linguistic, but uncodified gestures can be ostensive too; a capacity to communicate may be independent of language mastery, and develop earlier (Tomasello 2008). Human languages are the outcome of a protracted cultural evolution, while the cognitive capacities that allow us to communicate may well be innate (Csibra and Gergely 2009).

Let us now distinguish, in greater detail, ostensive communication from its immediate neighbors in the space of possible forms of social learning. It differs from several other types of transmission: involuntary transmission, voluntary but not ostensive transmission, and teaching.

Involuntary Transmission: When Behaviors Leak Information

The sort of cultural transmission that occurs in other animals often passes through cues that are made available more or less unwittingly by their sources. How are blue tits able to open milk bottles on seeing aluminum capsules torn by other blue tits? They are tapping into cues that other tits involuntarily left behind them—the open caps. Several animal cultures have been described whose members essentially feed on the information they can infer from their conspecifics' behavior—leaked or eavesdropped information (Danchin et al. 2004). These cues may bear on the state of the environment—for instance, when a crowding of buffaloes signals the discovery of a water pond. They may also afford the reinvention of a useful technique, like bottle-opening.

The most appealing feature of this form of transmission is that it is quite undemanding. It does not require any particular kind of social bonding, beyond the ability to perceive what others do. It can be observed in animals that hardly ever interact with their conspecifics. Red-footed tortoises are a case in point. They abandon their eggs as soon as the eggs are laid, and their lives are spent in utter isolation (outside short periods of reproduction). In the lab, they are nevertheless able to learn how to solve difficult problems (problems they could not solve on their own) by observing trained conspecifics (Wilkinson, Kuenstner, and Huber 2010). It is hardly likely that red-footed tortoises would have evolved sophisticated capacities to read other tortoises' intentions and moves; rather, what they are putting to use is nothing but a very general capacity to observe the cues provided by the actions of other animals. "Nor are they any more related after the transfer than before," as Durkheim would say.

We obviously share with tortoises a capacity to eavesdrop on the useful information that gets leaked around us. Certain societies have actually made it a norm, as we shall see, that children should acquire most of their know-how by quiet observation, picking up whatever filters through adult activities and patiently reconstructing what they are not told (Lancy 1996; Fiske 1996). Other forms of transmission are available to us, though, as they are to other species.

Non-Ostensive Voluntary Transmission

Cultural transmission outside of our species is seldom voluntary. Ethologists and psychologists who reviewed the evidence for animal teaching tend to converge on this conclusion (Caro and Hauser 1992; Csibra 2007). Many animals readily signal the presence of a predator or a source of food, most often to their close relatives; yet, as the psychologist Gergely Csibra notes, such information has only local relevance. It is not likely to help animals in other times and places. Thus it is transmission, but not *cultural* transmission: what gets passed on ceases to matter after a few generations have passed (at most). Cultural practices, those that are worth diffusing far and wide, and for a long time, are not usually transmitted in a deliberate fashion. When they are, transmission in the wild is voluntary but not ostensive: I mean that in the few cases when an animal sets out to help another learn a tradition in the wild, the teacher's intention is not (or at any rate need not be) overtly manifested and recognized for what it is. Teaching may take place covertly.

In the majority of the few cases of animal teaching documented by Caro and Hauser, teachers assist other animals in learning a behavior by changing their environment in a way that facilitates learning. Predation is a case in point. A tiger may wound a bull and omit to kill it off, to let her cubs train on it. Adult meerkats provide their young with sting-free or weakened scorpions to play with, but that is about all they transmit. We are close to what disciples of Vygotsky might call "scaffolded learning" (not his term) or the construction of a "zone of proximal development" (Wood, Bruner, and Ross 1976; Vygotsky 2012/1933): a learning-friendly environment is built, which canalizes the youngsters' explorations in a way that prefigures the things they will eventually learn. Humans, of course, also scaffold learning in this way, as anyone who learnt how to bike on small wheels knows.

Like other non-ostensive forms of voluntary communication, scaffolding is especially convenient in that it can work unbeknownst to its target: the small wheels on your bike worked their wonders even when you forgot about them. The tiger cub that makes its teeth on a weakened buffalo may or may not notice that its mother prepared the prey; this does not matter: it does not need this to become a better hunter. The contrary is true of ostensive communication: when an ostensive communicator's intention goes unrecognized, the transmission effort is lost entirely.

Christopher Boesch's observations of nut-cracking in Tai forest chimpanzees (Boesch 1993, 1991; Tomasello and Call 1997, 306–307) is currently one of the best-known examples of animal cultural transmission, possibly the one that comes closest to full-blown teaching. This observation has everything except, it seems to me, ostensive communication. The mother assists her young at every step of the nut-cracking process; organizes the workspace quite deliberately to make cracking her young's first nuts as easy as possible. What the mother does not try to do is catch her target's attention, or to show at whom her efforts are directed. This does not matter for the young chimpanzee, which does not need to attend to the mother's intentions fully to benefit from her guidance.

I also count as cases of voluntary but non-ostensive transmission the few instances of punishment ("coaching," in Caro and Hauser's terminology) that have been observed in non-human animals. These are rare and disputed. The clearest case has to do with alarm calls in vervet monkeys. Vervets are known to use a system of alarm calls, with a different call warning of the approach of a different species of predators. Punishment has been observed for young monkeys who rang the alarm bell when no danger lurked. A young vervet sounded a call to his mother, who started to run into hiding, but then, realizing her mistake, came back to hurt her child. This is one of the very few cases of "punishment" observed in the wild; rewards seem even rarer (Caro and Hauser 1992).

These episodes are tricky to interpret. Their rarity doesn't help. What is the vervet mother up to? Is she trying to correct the way her son uses alarm signals, or simply ensuring that she won't get disturbed in the future? Whatever the answer to this question, one thing is clear: the young monkey who gets corrected the hard way does not need to wonder about his mother's intention to grasp the lesson and stop misusing the alarm call. In general, punishments and rewards can influence learning even when they are not interpreted: they may or may not convey a message, but their impact is not exhausted by their communicative import. Positive or negative reinforcement (rewards and blames) influence behaviors directly, and sometimes, covertly: the target of these incentives may not know that they are being manipulated. Mothers who put chili on their baby's thumb to prevent them from sucking it are thus engaging in a kind of covert teaching.

Such implicit ways of canalizing learning, and other acts of non-ostensive communication, obviously exist in our species—including forms that seem not to be present anywhere else (not in the wild, at least). "Molding," used by dance teachers in Bali and famously described by Margaret Mead (1930), consists in manipulating the child's body, repeatedly and protractedly, to mold it into the right postures. These interventions serve a communicative purpose, of course: they achieve the same goal as a normal visual demonstration. In a normal demonstration the teacher would signal (in a slow, exaggerated, ostensive way) gestures that the child would grasp through her eyes. Molding, in a way, does exactly the same thing, except that it relies on the pupil's haptic and proprioceptive sense to get the teacher's message across to her brain. Yet molding is arguably more than a form of communication that would rely on unusual sensory modalities. I suspect that pupils benefit from molding in ways that go beyond what they can grasp by comprehending the teacher's message. Even if they had lost consciousness, their body could still gain a certain elasticity, a certain suppleness, certain habits of the body from the gestures they are puppet-mastered to perform. That particular effect of molding does not depend on overt transmission: the child does not need to know that she is being deliberately trained.

Voluntary and Overt Transmission: a Human Phenomenon

Transmission (to recap) can either be involuntary or voluntary. If (and only if) it is voluntary, the transmitter's intention can be overtly manifested. Transmission, in that case, is ostensive.

Involuntary transmission, by which animals let various kinds of information leak, is ubiquitous—indeed, one can hardly imagine how it could fail to exist anywhere. When starlings see a crowding of other starlings, they readily infer that some source of food or water is close by (Danchin et al. 2004). An animal does not need to possess sophisticated social learning capacities to exploit this sort of cue. Involuntary transmission requires no special skill whatsoever on the emitter's side, and only quite pedestrian abilities in receivers: associating crowds of animals and sources of food, seeing that a bottle can be opened. Involuntary transmission does not need to be particularly faithful (indeed, it need not result in imitation at all), but, as blue tits taught us, it may produce long diffusion chains.

To engage in voluntary transmission is to act deliberately to permit, improve, or canalize someone else's learning of a piece of information, a know-how, or a motivation. This can be done non-ostensively: in other words, voluntary teachers do not need their intentions to show, or to be recognized by those they are helping. Scaffolding (small wheels on a bike), positive or negative reinforcement, toy-making (including very simple "toys," like the meerkats' weakened scorpions) are all instances of transmission mechanisms that may work quite well with their target being unaware that someone is helping them learn. Such voluntary transmission, though rare, is not unheard of outside of our species.

Ostensive communication consists in using the recognition, by the receiver, of the emitter's intention to transmit something. Unlike other forms of transmission, it is overt by definition: one cannot communicate ostensively behind the target's back. In spite of its simplicity, it seems even more rare, in the wild, than voluntary transmission (itself already quite elusive). (Csibra and Gergely (2009) review potential candidates and find them all wanting.)

This does not necessarily mean that other animals completely lack the capacity for ostensive communication—the jury is still out on that issue. Few specialists would claim that any non-human species manipulates recursively embedded mental states with anything approaching human proficiency. Nonetheless, great apes are known to produce and understand informative gestures in the wild, and may learn to point in captivity. Whether these things count as ostensive communication is controversial, but it has been argued (Moore, unpublished ms.) that in certain circumstances, context and habit can supply much information that cannot be retrieved by inferring others' thoughts. Great apes could be occasional users of ostensive communication without having the cognitive wherewithal to be fully generalist users. Alternatively, one could argue that the problem is not simply cognitive—that social life in most species is not conducive to the use of ostensive communication for cultural transmission: the missing ingredient may not be a cognitive one—it could have to do with social motivations (transmission is a cooperative action, subject to all the restrictions that natural selection puts on the evolution of cooperative behaviors) or with social contexts (peaceful coexistence seems important). Whatever the case may be, the ostensive way of engaging in cultural diffusion looks like a human specificity.

Culture Did Not Build Our Communicative Skills from the Ground Up

A growing body of work in developmental psychology argues that the first rudiments of mind-reading abilities develop early, much earlier than previously thought, in the first two years of life (Baillargeon, Scott, and He 2010). This work should be seen together with the fact that ostensive communication appears to exist in all human societies—they all use language, and as we saw, even the simplest utterances need to be interpreted ostensively.

Yet not everyone agrees that the apparatus of ostensive communication mostly preexists culture. One of this book's reviewers attracted my attention to the growing popularity of three views that seem slightly at odds with the ones exposed here (Franks 2011, 216–238 provides a good synthesis of the first two).

First, our ability to "read" other people is not a purely individual achievement. The social world presents us with a wealth of information regarding the dispositions and feelings of others. This plentiful evidence is not to be found only in people's words or deeds, but also in cultural scripts and agreed-upon rules of conduct. In a grocery shop, I do not need to "read" the minds of the client in front of me, or the cashier's, to predict what they will do, or even say. Social regularities, in this view, contain a fair share of the information that in mainstream approaches must be inferred from scratch. Culture also contributes narratives, stories, rituals, standardized forms of explanation or justification, which all go to feed our mentalizing abilities (Franks 2011, 243–255). The critics thus come together to support a view of mind-reading where information concerning the mental lives of others is not painstakingly derived, but apprehended with little effort, in a process that resembles perception more than reasoning.

They also insist that mindreading does not take place in a social void. It is buttressed (the phrase in vogue is "scaffolded") by collaborative propensities (Moll and Tomasello 2007). This is not to say that full-blown thought sharing can never occur in a context of competition or antagonism (though some theoreticians of communication seem willing to go that far—see Carassa and Colombetti 2009). The claim seems to be that the emergence of mind-reading and communication (both in evolution and development) makes more sense in a society of cooperators than in a society of competitors (in contrast with "Machiavellian intelligence" theories of social cognition).

One last view that is gaining influence moots the possibility that our mind-reading abilities might be cultural through and through, just like, say, our capacity to read (Heyes and Frith 2014). The main argument presented in favor of this view is the existence of impressive cross-cultural variations in people's conceptions of other minds (as documented by, e.g., Lillard 1998). It is perilous (the argument goes) to postulate a uniform mind-reading faculty, when in some places the mind is seen as identical with the brain, while in some others it is a life force that leaves the body during sleep and persists after death.

The first two claims I happily take on board. Chapter 6 will explore in greater detail the view that human communication benefits from the exceptionally cooperative nature of our species. The third claim, that social learning is entirely built by cultural influences, seems much more dubious. It appears to rest on a conflation of two quite different phenomena: inferences about other people's mindsets as they occur in the flow of communicative interactions—rapidly, implicitly, silently—and the theories that people put forward, in philosophical conversation, when dwelling on things like the nature of thought or the limits of the self. The importance of preserving a clear distinction between public discourses or theories, on the one hand, and everyday mental activity, on the other hand, is wisely stressed by cognitive anthropologists (Quinn 2006; Bloch 2011, 117–142). Blurring this distinction is likely to result in claims that are embarrassingly implausible in their exoticism. One example is the view, criticized by Melford Spiro (1993), that the Burmese lack a notion of self because Theravada Buddhism teaches the non-existence of the self. As Spiro showed, the Burmese do attribute thoughts and actions to individual selves; incidentally, the Buddhist teaching that the self is an illusion can only make sense to people used to the concept of self. When discussing cultural variations in philosophy of mind, the pitfalls of a certain kind of relativism are never far.

Note that the sort of mind-reading capacities I am dwelling on here need not be verbalized. In this sense, it can remain implicit. To say that humans share sufficient mentalizing capacities to engage in ostensive-inferential communication is not equivalent to saying that they all have the same way of talking about mental matters. To be sure, a wide variety of philosophical views coexist on questions like the nature of minds, beliefs, or consciousness. Theories bearing on the philosophy of mind vary not just from one culture to the other, but inside one given culture. Likewise, the amount of attention given to abstract conversations about mental life, the available vocabulary, and the other intellectual tools devoted to these matters, are likely to show a lot of variety. None of this is proof that the basic capacity to make inferences on others' mental states (as it is put to use in ostensive-inferential communication) is a cultural creation from the ground up (like reading letters). Generally speaking, cross-cultural differences in the exercise of a capacity do not prove that this capacity has no innate foundation. Everybody agrees that our gait and posture is shaped, to a point, by our environment (our furniture—or lack of it—, our activities), which includes some cultural habits and norms. It does not follow that the capacity to walk and sit upright is entirely taught.

Ostensive Communication Is Not Particularly Faithful

Let us come back to the research program inaugurated by Tomasello, Kruger, and Ratner's 1993 article on imitation. Some of their proposals have failed (as they themselves admit), but others are spectacular achievements. The hypothesis that claims "true imitation" ("true" in the sense that it is based on the recognition of the model's intentions) as a human specificity has not, it seems, withstood the last twenty years of inquiry: other species are known to understand mental states, and to use this understanding in imitation (Buttelmann et al. 2007). In any case, elaborate traditions do not need "true imitation" to spread: blue tits need no deep understanding of their conspecifics' intentions to repeat their bottle-opening tricks.

Parallel to this, though, it has been difficult to identify, outside the human species, a clear equivalent of our capacity to comprehend embedded representations—what is sometimes called recursive intentionality. The contribution that this capacity makes to human cultural transmission is (as I will try to show later in this chapter) as massive as the importance of imitation is weak.

The research program sketched by Tomasello and his colleagues twenty years ago certainly bore fruit, in that we have become much more knowledgeable about what makes human cultural transmission distinctive; yet one mystery remains—why are these mechanisms not more faithful? As Tomasello, Kruger, and Ratner noted (1993, 502), humans can use their understanding of recursively embedded mental states to learn things together, but this collaborative learning need not take the form of imitation. We use our communicative abilities in many other ways, to invent or modify practices as much as to reproduce them. In this, ostensive communication does not seem to be particularly fit to solve the Wear-and-Tear Problem.

This point is somewhat obscured by the frequent association that is made between imitation and communication—in spite of the fact that they rely on very different mental abilities. All you need to do to imitate a model's gesture (as intended by that model) is grasp her intention and have similar motor capacities. Understanding a communicative intention takes a different toolkit: you need to be able to process recursively embedded representations. Having this higher-order ability means that you are also able to represent simpler intentions, and therefore to imitate them—but that is really the least of your talents.

Although separated by a psychological chasm, "true imitation" and communication often come together in reality. Communication may be used to facilitate the reproduction of certain gestures; conversely, imitation may convey communicative intentions. These interactions are the focus of the next section. We shall see how even the simplest forms of human interactions depend on the perception of recursive intentions.

Communicating to Imitate, Imitating to Communicate

Communication for Imitation: Demonstrations and "Rational" Imitation

In the two movies where Steven Spielberg films a first pacific encounter between mankind and a race of intelligent and benevolent aliens, his characters solve the problem of non-verbal communication in the same, very simple way. How? How could two clever animals share anything when they lack a common language, a common system of codified signs, a common cultural background, or even a common past experience? Spielberg's answer shows the problem to be less daunting than it appears.

When E.T. the extraterrestrial first meets young Elliott, his apparition gets the boy's attention. E.T. then gazes into Elliott's eyes and slowly lifts his long finger to his nose. For the viewers and for Elliott, it is obvious that this careful, deliberate gesture has only one apparent use: to capture Elliott's attention, and to show Elliott that E.T. is trying to capture the boy's attention. It works! In turn, the boy touches his own nose with his index. This approximate reproduction of E.T.'s useless gesture does two things. First, it shows that Elliott understands what E.T. was trying to do with his gesture—namely, nothing useful except demonstrating an intention. Second, it shows E.T. that Elliott also readily produces a gesture for the sole purpose of showing that he is ready to communicate.

The same trick is used in *Close Encounters of the Third Kind*: the only means of communication between the scientists and the aliens consists in reproducing alien signals. The film's leitmotif is the five-notes melody that goes back and forth between humans and extraterrestrials. For the only episode of face-to-face communication in the movie, the French scientist (played by François Truffaut) translates the melody into Curwen's musical sign language; the alien in front of him does not, of course, know the Curwen code, but still manages to show an understanding of Truffaut's communicative action, by imitating his gestures, with a direct gaze and a smile. From the aliens' point of view, Truffaut's gestures are meaningless; from the human point of view, the five-notes melody emitted by the spaceship is just as meaningless (though it could be meaningful for aliens). This does not prevent some limited kind of communication, even when signals have no agreed-upon conventional meaning. The only thing that passes between humans and aliens is an ostensive intention to communicate. That intention is fulfilled when recognized by the other party.

I am not arguing that one could handle intergalactic diplomacy with imitation as sole language. Yet if we compare it to other means of information transmission, this sort of ostensive imitation is already quite sophisticated. It allows both parties to know that others can deliberately send signals, that they can recognize in others the intention of sending such signals, and show that they recognize it. In other words, it allows for the mutual recognition of communicative intentions.

Such a capacity may not be a prerequisite for what developmental psychologists call "rational imitation," but it should make it easier. So-called rational imitation consists in reproducing, gratuitously, an arbitrary gesture that lacks any obvious function, when that gesture has been deliberately and clearly intended by the model. Psychologist György Gergely and his colleagues have explored it using a modified version of Meltzoff's experiment—the one where the model can light up a half-sphere with her hands or with her head. In Gergely's variant (Gergely, Bekkering, and Király 2002) the model always uses her head. In the first condition, though, using her head makes sense: her hands are busy keeping her shawl over her shoulders. In the second condition, the model's hands are free: she has no practical reason to use her head rather than her hands. She lights up the toy with her head nevertheless.

For Gergely and his colleagues, the model is "rational" in the second condition but not in the first. The word "rational" is a slightly misleading expression, but it has settled: a "rational" action, here, is one that is deliberate and unconstrained by circumstances—using one's head when one could decide not to use it. Gergely et al. show that infants imitate such "rational" actions more than irrational ones: they use their head to light up the toy when they can see that the models chose to use her head in a gratuitous fashion. Infants, in other words, imitate "rationally": they are sensitive to the unconstrained character of their model's gestures. Such rational imitation is a sophisticated variant of "true imitation": like "true imitation," it slavishly reproduces arbitrary and gratuitous gestures; but it is servile in a clever way, so to speak. It does not blindly reproduce the model's each and every move—only gratuitous moves that seem to correspond to the model's visible intention.

There are several good reasons to suppose that rational imitation tasks like this one tap into psychological mechanisms that are communicative more than imitative: rational imitation as these humans use it seems tightly bound with ostensive communication.

The first cue is the distribution of rational imitation in other species. Rational imitation is not uniquely human, but the animals that manifest it also possess special capacities to deal with ostensive communication, if only at the receiving end: captive chimpanzees that grew up among humans (Buttelmann et al. 2007), or domestic dogs, which are both evolved and trained to recognize and obey human orders (Range, Virányi, and Huber 2007). The second cue is that, rational imitation is driven by communicative signals, in human children (Király, Csibra, and Gergely 2013) as well as dogs (Virányi and Range 2009). Rational imitation is much more probable when the model catches the spectator's eye, waves at her, calls her by her name. These are what Csibra calls "ostensive cues." This is what E.T. does when he gazes at Elliott, or François Truffaut when he exchanges smiles and glances with his alien counterpart.

Communication, thus, seems to make imitation easier (and the other way around). How? Csibra and his colleagues (Southgate et al. 2009) argue that communication serves to specify which aspects of her gesture the model wants her target to reproduce. It is not indispensable for that purpose, but it helps. A gesture's useful or relevant aspects can be recognized without the help of communication: thus, when observing an adult who fails to perform an action (but does not try to attract the child's attention upon it), they can correct the adult's gesture and perform the action as it was intended to be, throwing away the wrong moves that caused the adult version of the gesture to fail (Meltzoff 1995). This requires them to recognize their model's intentions, but no communication is involved so far.

Communication, however, may facilitate intention recognition. Without words or gestures, the behavior of models in these experiments may well be baffling: a woman lights up a half-sphere-shaped toy with her head, though her hands are free. What is she trying to do? Is she trying to induce imitation? If so, what aspect of her action should the target reproduce? All this gets much clearer when the model displays communicative signals: children are much more likely to imitate her "rationally" when these cues are present (Király et al. 2013). By engaging in ostensive communication, the model does two things: first, she draws attention to certain aspects of her behavior, the gratuitous ones, that are to be imitated. Second, she initiates an interaction with the child: she is no longer indifferent or isolated.

Jacqueline Nadel, a pioneer in the study of the communicative use of imitation by young children (Nadel 1986), showed that, for two- and three-year-olds playing in a room, half of the time they spend interacting is spent on imitation. They play in similar ways with identical toys (provided by the experimenter), or, when there are no identical toys to be found, they manipulate different objects in synchrony. Imitation is reciprocal (every child is at least once imitated or imitating), with a different child taking the lead at different times. The time spent on imitation is correlated with the time spent on conversation (the limited sort of conversation that these young children are capable of). In later years, as language develops, it replaces imitation, which loses its importance for communication.

Psychologists Gergely and Csibra, who showed that toddlers imitate "rationally," also claim that rational imitation is the key to cultural transmission among humans. In their view, our capacity to handle communicative intentions evolved because it permitted rational imitation, and because rational imitation, in turn, allowed cultural transmission to be more faithful. They call this claim "Pedagogy theory." (It will be further discussed in chapter 6.)

The theory does not claim that all that is transmitted in our species gets passed on by means of rational imitation; it only claims that some traditions could not survive without it. Most cultural practices, from technology to ritual, are too complex for us to know what purpose they serve (if they serve one at all) merely by observing them. Csibra and Gergely call them "opaque." Since we cannot know which of their aspects are relevant to imitate, the best way to acquire them would seem to consist in reproducing as much of them as we can; but that, as we saw, is just the Hoarder's Fallacy. We simply cannot imitate without selecting some aspects, leaving others out. Selecting whatever is of immediate use for us is a solution to this problem, but, Csibra and Gergely remark, it will not help with opaque gestures. These gestures, they argue, grow in importance as technological sophistication increases. This is where communication comes into play: it allows models to guide imitation and focus their target's attention on relevant, if opaque, techniques.

When communication guides imitation in this way, it often takes the shape of demonstrations (we all know them, from YouTube tutorials to airplane safety instructions). Interestingly, most demonstrations include gestures that their targets are not supposed to reproduce. Suppose that you are teaching me how to fold a shirt: you slow down some crucial movements so I can see them, you point at certain parts of the shirt, you trace some imaginary lines on the shirt; and obviously, you talk. None of these behaviors is to be imitated: they are communicative devices, they are here only to guide imitation by making it more selective, and thus, more clever. If humans were born with a general proclivity to imitate everything their fellow humans do, that would prevent them from deriving any benefit from a demonstration (in addition to making their lives impossible). Fortunately, we feel no compulsion to imitate a teacher's pointing gestures; tellingly, the thought of reproducing communicative signals does not usually cross our minds, as we automatically separate them from the other gestures that they point at. We naturally look through the filter of ostensive communication, and see the practice we try to learn.

In other words, the kind of ability that permits us to profit from demonstrations is unlikely to take the form of a general drive to imitate. Such a thing would arguably harm social learning more than it would help. On the other hand, a general drive to produce and comprehend communicative signals would be extremely useful, not just to handle demonstrations but also to share ideas, feelings, preferences—in brief, all these things that are not behaviors, and so cannot be directly demonstrated or imitated. Of all the nuts and bolts that come into motion behind human imitation, ostensive communication seems the one with the most crucial impact on cultural transmission.

If so, why is its importance not better recognized by students of transmission? I suspect it is in large part because it gets easily confused with the various forms that it takes: linguistic communication, communication-assisted imitation, and so on. One such confusion is between communication and teaching: for many in the social sciences (English-speaking anthropologists in particular), the word "teaching" points at a form of transmission where culture is shared by institutionalized, deliberate, conscious, and explicit means, mostly through language, and with very little reconstruction or participatory learning. Teaching thus defined is a peculiar and recent form of cultural learning, one that Western countries have developed with an intensity that has few equivalents. With this view in mind, it is not surprising that anthropologists, and others, should be skeptical when they hear psychologists (like Csibra or Tomasello) claim that overt and voluntary information exchange is universal in our species. These points of view can nevertheless be reconciled.

Ostensive Communication Goes Beyond Teaching

Many misgivings in this domain spring from mere misunderstandings. Psychologists often use the term "teaching" in the sense it had in the early psychology of cultural learning (in Vygotsky, for instance)—that is to say, in a very broad sense, which includes not just what goes on in formal teaching institutions, but also many less formal interactions. Some disputes boil down to a semantic misunderstanding over the degree of formality ascribed to "teaching." On the other hand, this psychological tradition does tend to conceive of cultural transmission as a deliberate and conscious effort, on behalf of (mostly adult) teachers, to mold the minds of children. Language is taken to be the main vehicle of cultural transmission. On these points, disagreements between the psychological and the ethnographic tradition seem more genuine. Anthropological accounts of transmission stress that it can often be not just informal, but involuntary as well; that what is transmitted need not be put into words; that transmission may occur without parents and even without adults.

It Takes Place at Any Time, from Anyone, and for Any Reason

Just like ostensive communication does not need a well-defined institutional context to take place, cultural transmission is not attached to formal settings. As Atran and Sperber put it:

> In most human societies children become competent adults without the help of institutionalized teaching: there are no schools, no syllabus, no appointed teachers. Parents and other elders don't see their duty towards children as primarily one of education. They may, over the years, end up spending some time instructing the child in various skills, but actions carried with the purpose of teaching are rare. Most learning is achieved as a by-product, in the course of interactions that have other purposes.
>
> (Atran and Sperber 1991, 39)

This "institutionalized teaching" could be characterized as a combination of several elements. The first is organization: society (at least a sizeable part of it) coordinates to share the work of cultural transmission, and determine how it will be done. A second factor, which might be called centralization, implies that privileged times, places, and persons be set apart for cultural transmission. Lastly, transmission in these settings seems to be carried out as an end in itself, with no other immediate goal in sight. None of these things is included in the notion of ostensive communication that was sketched out earlier in this chapter. It does not have to be organized, or centralized, or to be an end in itself.

In any society (even those that have gone farthest in formalizing transmission) there are traditions that can be picked up anywhere, from anyone, without entering into any special plans—their transmission is not centralized, does not depend upon a group of specialists. What the word "car" and the green crossing sign mean is known by almost everyone, and they can explain it anywhere, to anyone, in most circumstances. Thus transmission need not be organized or centralized.

Nor does it need, I think, to be desired as an end in itself—but this particular claim may need some elaboration. Did I not claim, earlier, that ostensive communication was *overt and voluntary*? To engage with someone in this kind of communication, as we saw, I need to intend it, and to show that I intend it. Only by grasping these intentions can the target of communication understand what is being signified. If so, it would appear that ostensive transmission is necessarily deliberate; wouldn't it?

Yes and no. Ostensive transmission entails that something is deliberately conveyed, but many other things can be let out unwittingly in the same move. Sometimes, when communicating something, we leak many things besides what we wished to convey—including some things we clearly want others to ignore, and many other things that we did not specifically wish to express. Just because we want to establish communication does not mean we intend all the eventual consequences that will flow from it. When talking, we let out many signals (our accent, our lexicon, our knowledge—or lack of it) that can be tapped by others to make inferences that we cannot anticipate. Such leaks do not count as signals, yet they may be as useful to cultural transmission as deliberately conveyed information. Still, they are derivative on ostensive communication, not constitutive of it.

Much communication bears on the here-and-now, and is not intended to convey a tradition; it may serve to stabilize many, however. If, for instance, you happen to use a rare word in a conversation with someone who ignores it, you provide your interlocutors with cues that she may use to infer some of the word's meanings and the circumstances of its use. Still, you had no particular intention of doing this.

Thus, the contribution of communication to cultural transmission is twofold. There is a direct contribution—voluntary cultural transmission—and an indirect one. The habit, and the need of, communicating ostensively imply that the flow of information is particularly intense in our species. Two currents add up to make that flow. The first is made of deliberately communicated messages, the second of information made accessible unthinkingly, or even unwittingly. Both currents, the one that springs from deliberate intentions and the one that merely leaks besides the first, may feed cultural transmission. In chapter 6, I will argue that the rise of ostensive communication in our species coincided with the growth of the "human public domain"— which is how this book will call the stock of ideas and practices that are shared in human populations. This domain is the raw material of cultural transmission. Any element of it may give rise to a diffusion chain (though many will not).

For now, let us summarize. Transmission, just like ostensive communication, does not need specific institutions, times, places, or agents; neither does it require a specific set of motivations. It may take place at any time, anywhere, and be assured by anyone, for any reason. These are good rationales to avoid calling it "teaching."

It Requires an Active Reconstruction of the Transmitted Material

Another reason not to conflate communication with teaching is that communication can afford to be quite incomplete or sketchy: we saw in chapter 1 that traditions, in particular, may travel on a handful of cues that serve as bases for reconstruction.

In many societies (though no longer in ours, it seems), the education of young children is framed by norms that discharge adults from explaining much to them. The practice is often justified by the belief (more or less strong) that children are unable to learn or to think on their own before a certain age, typically six or seven—"the age of reason," as the phrase goes (that phrase itself being a probable vestige of a similar belief). That norm has been independently documented in a wide range of societies, where it applies at similar ages—five to seven (Rogoff et al. 1975 provide the classic survey; Lancy 1996 provides a detailed example among the Kpelle; Konner 2011, 287–289 summarizes the literature). Below the age of reason, children are not permitted to take part in certain tasks (or may take part under adult supervision only). Adults typically claim that children are incapable of learning anything; they are deemed to be playing. This is not to say that they are never given any responsibility—on the contrary, they can be quite exploitable; but, since they are thought incapable of comprehending even a simple demonstration, they are not instructed in the tasks they cannot spontaneously master—at least, not taught deliberately.

This is not to say they are not chided for their blunders. To cite anthropologist Alan Fiske's impression, both of his own fieldwork and of the literature on transmission in early childhood, "When children fail to perform adequately, adults say 'no,' tease, ridicule, punish or threaten" (Fiske 1996, 15). Being content with reprimanding children, without bothering to show them how they can avoid failures, could be seen as mere inadvertent negligence. It is arguably more than that. By refusing to instruct children, adults are defending a division of labor that is all to their advantage. They ensure that children's learning will not be too taxing before they reach a certain age. The link between the (convenient) belief that young children lack common sense, and the refusal to invest time and effort in teaching them, is often quite explicit. Anthropologists, being professionally inclined to take people seriously and at their word, naturally assume that, in the society they investigate, culture is not "taught": children learn by observation and imitation. Nobody instructs them deliberately.

Tempting as it may be, this conclusion arguably simplifies what goes on in such situations; we do not have to assume that people actually believe all the views they offer to justify a given practice. In this case, adults may occasionally refuse to expend their efforts on instructing the young, but they could be willing to do it in other instances; and they may still care a great deal about cultural transmission as well as desire that their children acquire useful skills. This is all quite compatible with the view that most of the time, it will be enough to let the children observe adults at work and perform menial tasks, with the occasional reprimand playing the role of explicit instruction (reprimand, after all, is a form of communication).

Thus, when one reads, in the ethnographic literature, that such and such society ignores teaching, there are reasons not to take such claims at face value. Sometimes the only form of teaching that is clearly ruled out is institutionalized, school-like teaching; sometimes the claim that "society X does not do teaching" coexists with precise descriptions of deliberate, adult-guided transmission.

The work of David Lancy, one of the chief anthropologists of childhood, who did fieldwork among the Kpelle of Liberia, is a case in point. One of the main claims of his ethnography is that "Kpelle adults do *not* see themselves as their children's teachers" (Lancy 1996, 79,); and it is true, in a way. The Kpelle are wont to say that they do not feel any duty to instruct their children, who can teach themselves most of what they need, and are not yet considered intelligent enough to understand the rest. Yet they can also be heard saying things that flatly contradict these claims:

> Third man: We will teach our children to work. We will tell them, "If one learns this type of work, one's life will be longer." If a child listens to you and you explain things to him, he will give you no cause for anger.
> (Lancy 1996, 76)

The explicit refusal to instruct children thus coexists with an explicit intention to teach. The contradiction is, arguably, only apparent. When the Kpelle say that children cannot and should not be instructed before their age of reason, they are stating a norm, buttressed by a dogma. The norm seems to permit a convenient division of communicative labor between adults and children. Like many norms, though, this one can be toted opportunistically as occasions demand, but disregarded in other circumstances. The Kpelle do seem to communicate some of their know-hows to their children:

> Second man: As the way I play Fanga [a type of drum] my children will learn it. If I'm cutting brush, I'll give him the machette for him to know how to cut brush. If it becomes hard, I'll show him how to make it easier.
> (Lancy 1996, 76.)[1]

It would be hard to argue that this kind of exchange does not involve voluntary transmission. Adult reprimands are as much a form of ostensive communication as explicit transmission. It is true, however, that the content to be learnt is not entirely made explicit in communication. Much has to be inferred or reconstructed from incomplete cues. Transmission, however, never goes without a modicum of reinvention.

It Can Bypass Language

When ethnographers claim, as they sometimes do, that culture on their field is not taught, but observed and imitated, one may be tempted to conclude that traditions are absorbed in an implicit way that has little to do with communication. Most of the time, though, the ethnographic data would not support that conclusion. They merely tell us that some things are transmitted by nonverbal means, which is quite a different thing from not being communicated.

This testimony of Alan Fiske's is a good representative of this literature. His paper reviews ethnographic evidence for the claim that "imitation is a core medium for acquiring culture in virtually every society that has been investigated (...) children learn most of their cultures on their own initiative, without pedagogy" (Fiske 1996, 12–13). There is truth in such claims, as we saw, and Fiske offers excellent support for them; yet it is easy to misunderstand what imitation truly means here. Here is one example:

> Three different diviners independently transmitted to me what they asserted was the capacity to see the moral meanings of misfortune in

---

1. I thank Gergely Csibra for pointing out these two quotations from Lancy's work to me.

the patterns of cowry shells tossed on the ground. They passed on to me the magical implements and legitimated my personal powers, anointing me and my implements in special rituals. But none of the diviners ever thought to explain or even demonstrate divination to me pedagogically. Nor did they recognize the point in doing so when I asked them to teach me.

(Fiske 1996, 4.)[2]

It is quite transparent here that the ethnographer is in continuous communication with the diviners, by means of words and non-verbal signs. The rituals are clearly performed in a way that is ostensive enough for the ethnographer to recognize them. Their meaning—the magical powers of the implements, the legitimization of the ethnographer's powers, and so on—must have been mentioned in previous or subsequent conversation. (The ethnographer may not be told these things directly, but an eavesdropped conversation counts as an instance of ostensive communication.) What Fiske rightly points out here is the fact that certain cultural practices do not fit into the neat format of an explicit dogma (of the kind that is taught in divinity schools): much of it is not linguistically encoded at all.

Two issues need to be kept separated: the linguistic encoding of a cultural practice (can it be delivered and retrieved as an explicit discourse, like a lecture, a theorem, or a recipe?) and the role that ostensive communication plays in its transmission. A failure to distinguish them may lead to misunderstandings in the anthropology of learning and apprenticeship: the ethnographer begins by echoing his informants' claim that culture in this society is not taught, but simply observed and imitated. A few pages later, though, the reader meets ethnographic descriptions that resemble nothing like teaching. Kayo Ohmagari and Fikret Berkes's description of traditional Cree knowhows (bush skills, tanning hides, etc.) is a case in point. It starts with the usual repudiation of teaching:

> Many elders pointed out that bush skills were not taught by formal education, in the abstract. Their way was "learning by doing" (...) through apprenticeship. The apprenticeship started as soon as a Cree child learned to walk; she was expected to help with and share in the work of the bush camp (...). The child was not usually given verbal instructions but encouraged to learn skills by playing and by imitating adults through participation in subsistence production activities (...). At the

---

2. Draft cited with the author's kind permission.

same time, the child acquired the Cree values of self-reliance, independence, and competence (...).

(Ohmagari and Berkes 1997, 206)

Two paragraphs later, real learning starts to look quite different:

In this process of trial and error, teachers were patient and supportive even if the apprentice failed many times, as long as she was diligent. The apprentice was told: "keep trying, never give up until you get it right." Furthermore, she was expected to follow the prescribed ways to master the skill. When she did it properly, the teacher praised her saying *ekute* ("that is the way"). In traditional Cree culture, parents taught their children adequate survival skills that allowed them to live in the bush by the time they reached their mid to late teens.

(Ohmagari and Berkes 1997, 206)

Suddenly, self-reliant Cree children have turned into apprentices; we meet a teacher where we had been told there was no formal education; "prescribed ways" have replaced free learning; verbal instructions supersede spontaneous imitation. Does this prove the Cree elders wrong? Not quite; but it shows how perilous it can be to take one's informants at their word when they describe cultural transmission. What we find in the many societies that reject teaching is not an absence of deliberate and ostensive guidance for cultural learners, but two other things: a set of norms that allow adults to avoid the instruction of children to become too burdensome an obligation, and a wealth of cultural knowledge that cannot entirely be put into words.

This last idea is the focus of much classic work in the social sciences, from Mauss's paper on the embodiment of culture (and the "techniques du corps") (Mauss 1934/1950) to Bourdieu's analysis of implicit social attitudes that cannot be objectified or rendered explicit (Bourdieu 1977). Their ambitious and elaborated theories won't be much exploited here, except to say that, indeed, there is much more to our representations of cultural practices than what may fit a linguistic format. Some traditions, therefore, simply cannot be explained through words alone. Does it follow, however, that they cannot be communicated? I do not think so, for two reasons. First, because communication does not have to be verbal. Second, because communicated contents do not have to be made entirely available by communicators: some things can be left for receptors to reconstruct (indeed, one could argue that some things *must* be so left out).

Non-verbal communication exists because linguistic encoding is merely a secondary and derivative form of ostensive communication. Communicative intentions can be retrieved from very simple gestures, like pointing. Drawing attention to an object, or showing blame or approval, all are things we can do non-verbally. The importance of communication in transmission is not measured in the number of words exchanged. Such gesture-based communication can, it is true, be excessively vague. It might often need to be completed with a great deal of individual learning and reconstruction; but that is nothing exceptional. Verbal communication itself can be quite sketchy; it sometimes needs some interpretative heavy-lifting to be meaningful. Consider the phrase "I have eaten already" (using an example of Sperber and Wilson's), uttered by someone. That person could mean infinitely many things by it: that she has eaten once in her life, that the last time she ate something substantial was yesterday, or five minutes ago. In most contexts, of course, she means she has eaten not so long ago, and sufficiently to not be hungry for a meal that could take place right now. Yet none of these elements ("not so long ago," "sufficiently," "right now," etc.) are encoded in the phrase; they need to be fleshed out. In a Gricean view of communication, that reconstructive step cannot be dispensed with: ostensive communication cannot be simply decoded like non-ostensive signals can be.

Even after all this interpretative work has been done, cultural transmission does not get by without some individual reconstruction, based on cues that canalize learning only approximately. Chapter 1 defended the view that cultural transmission is a continuum, with spontaneous reinvention on one end and heavily guided learning at the other pole. Seen from this angle, observational learning and teaching are not two different modes of cultural transmission, but two positions on the spectrum. The precision and quality of the cues left by others determine a learner's position on that spectrum. What is called imitation, in contrast to teaching, is very often nothing but a form of communication in which learners are deliberately provided with communicative cues, but these cues are so weak that learners are left to reinvent many things on their own. The conclusion that teaching is absent in such cases is tempting, but should be resisted. Misunderstandings lie ahead! Consider this claim made by a group of ethologists:

> There is surprisingly little evidence of teaching among modern-day hunter-gatherers, in comparison to learning by imitation (Bakeman et al. 1990). One study of !Kung infants noted that "adult tuition related to object manipulation seems minimal."
> (Hoppitt et al. 2008, 490)

The study cited by Hoppitt and colleagues (Bakeman et al. 1990) does indeed say that the !Kung take no interest in babies who play with objects, and do not try to explain their use. Yet they also note that !Kung adults often forbid infants from touching certain objects, and that "caregivers sometimes urge infants to look at interesting objects and hand objects to infants to calm or distract them" (op. cit., 796). Thus, they do step in to guide infant learning—favoring some object manipulations and preventing others; we are not dealing with mere imitation, although it is true that what adults show and tell infants is much too scarce to be sufficient. Individual baby learning (the study deals with adult-baby interactions, not with what goes on between children and adults, or between children and children) is a necessary complement.

To use studies like these to argue that children learn by observation and imitation, as opposed to teaching, is to suggest that imitation and communication are two distinct and self-contained modes of transmission. Imitation, though, is hardly ever observed in isolation: in every case we have seen in this chapter, it depends on communication.

Once such misunderstandings are cleared out, the ethnographic literature contains a wealth of observations that reveal the importance of ostensive (and also simply voluntary) transmission. In a review of the learning of hunting skills in small-scale societies, Katharine MacDonald (2007; Greenfield 2005, Hewlett et al. 2011 offer similar observations for other skills) shows that in most places, adults (and not just parents) instruct children, by building toys or small weapons; by giving advice; by going on hunting trips in easier (but less rewarding) spots; by organizing contests, games, and trainings; by answering questions (albeit sometimes grudgingly); by teaching animal traces and game trails; by sharing hunting tales.

Ethnographic data, thus, do not completely match anthropological interpretations. We should not be too quick to take them as evidence that cultural transmission is a matter of observation rather than communication. On the contrary, ethnographers are constantly bathing in a flow of ostensive communication. Perhaps the ubiquity of that flow, its permanence from one society to the next, makes it easier to forget when writing up reports from the field.

It Does Not Need Adults

The last misunderstanding between psychologists and ethnographers, concerning cultural transmission, has to do with the role of adults and parents. Psychologists tend to stress the importance of adults, parents and mothers chief among them. This focus seems misplaced to many anthropologists. They are quick to remark that parental involvement in children's education varies widely from one society to the next. These claims and the ethnographic work that buttresses them will be introduced in chapter 5. We shall see that ostensive transmission can build bridges in various directions: between adults, between children, as well as between generations.

One situation that illustrates the autonomy of generations is the indirect transmission of skills that are imitated by groups of children after observing adults—in games of pretense, for instance. Aristotle's famous claim, in his *Poetics* (IV, 2), that children learn the first things they know through imitation, arguably referred to pretense. The kind of imitation that is dealt with in *Poetics* is the sort that comedians engage in: a playful representation of social life. Pretense, like acting, is not an interaction with the pretend-players' models. All the same, children can teach themselves (voluntarily and ostensively) by rehearsing adult skills and habits with their peers. Such indirect transmission is likely to involve much reconstruction, with corresponding risks of unfaithfulness to the model. This is arguably the case whenever a group mimics a tradition without direct contact with its forebears—Hebrew as a living language, Druidic religion. All these cases could be said to rest on mere observational learning and imitation rather than voluntary transmission, but this would hide the crucial role played by ostensive communication between peers.

"A Light, Insubstantial, Fugitive Web"

In the rest of this book, no transmission mechanisms will be called upon other than those we saw in this chapter: involuntary transmission, voluntary transmission, and ostensive transmission. They seem sufficient to satisfy all the needs of the cultural animal that we are. We can pass on anything by one of these means, with the more-or-less important help of reconstruction and reinvention.

What about teaching and imitation, usually taken to be the chief engines of cultural transmission (Boyd and Richerson 1995; Tomasello 1999)? In chapter 1, we met stable traditions that did not seem to be transmitted with the help of either mechanism. The way modern English uses modal verb *was* one such example. When the new use started to grow, few people were aware of its novelty. Even fewer could explicitly represent the change in grammatical rules that lay under the mutation. All it did was eliminate old manners of speaking, not create new ones. For all these reasons, it could hardly be taught.

What that example suggested was confirmed in this chapter. Traditions, even the most stable ones, do not need to be taught or imitated. They do, on the other hand, often travel directly or indirectly through communication. The rule for modal use in English, for instance, is mostly reconstructed by speakers from cues left by their interlocutors in conversation where they do not intend or try to teach any rule at all. Teaching (conceived as organized and centralized transmission, undertaken without any other immediate goal) does occur, but it is best seen as a special case of communication, and quite an exotic one at that (many cultures seem to do without it). Imitation, when it produces interesting effects in our species, is supported by communication. Voluntary and overt communication thus appears to be the royal pathway for cultural transmission among humans.

This leads us to a difficulty that confronts the imitation hypothesis—the view laid down in the Introduction. In this view, traditions exist because (and insofar as) high-fidelity imitation can solve the Wear-and-Tear Problem. Unlike imitation (which is presumed to be faithful, if only because of its name), nothing in our definition of ostensive communication characterizes it as particularly fit for reproducing traditions with precision. Interpretation, reconstruction, and the occasional distortions they must induce, cannot be taken out of ostensive communication. Why, then, should traditions pass through such an unreliable medium?

Herder's *Outline of a Philosophy of the History of Man* perfectly exposed the problem (1791/2010, bk. 9, chap. 2). He drew a distinction between two mental capacities given by God to mankind, each of which could in principle serve to transmit ideas: language and imitation. Imitation is by far the most accurate, but its scope is quite narrow. Language, on the other hand, is more versatile—it can handle a wider range of contents; but how unfaithful it is! It seemed so ill-fitted for transmission that, Herder thought, we had to admit the Divine designer had simply blundered when he furnished the human mind:

> A little closer inspection, however, shows how imperfect this mean of our improvement is, not only considered as the instrument of reason, but as the bond between man and man; so that a more light, insubstantial, fugitive web can scarcely be conceived, than that with which the creator thought proper to connect the human species. Kind father! was no other less fallible modification of our thoughts, was no more intimate connection of men's hearts and minds, possible?
> (Herder 1791/2010, 421)

Herder puts his finger on a crucial difficulty for imitative theories of culture: nothing guarantees that our capacity for communication (which allows us to use language) is a reproductive mechanism. To communicate, he remarks, is to reconstruct, distort, or forget much of what we hear or say. Traditions travel through language at their own risks.

> This is the way of all sects of philosophy and religion. The founder had at least clear ideas of what he said, though probably erroneous ones: his scholars and followers understood him after their own manner; that is, they affixed their own ideas to his words, and at length reechoed nothing but empty sounds into men's ears. Manifest are the imperfections in the sole means of propagating human thoughts: yet to this our improvement is enchained, and we cannot emancipate ourselves from it.
> (Herder 1791/2010, 423)

Communication, in other words, does not seem to have been designed to deal with the Wear-and-Tear Problem; and this is only half of the problem for the imitation hypothesis. We still have to see how it deals with the Flop Problem. Tarde, and the research tradition that he started, solved it by positing that a variety of "social somnambulism" afflicted humankind. In this view, we cannot help but reproduce all kinds of ideas and practices under the influence of prestigious or numerous models. Conformity and deference would make traditions successful and thus solve the Flop Problems. Are they strong enough to do so? Is conformist and deferent imitation the engine of cultural transmission? That question is tackled in the next chapter.

3 THE MYTH OF COMPULSIVE IMITATION

Compulsive imitation, the tendency to reproduce behaviors simply because others exhibit them, is central to many theories of cultural transmission. This chapter will examine several of them. Some, like Boyd, Richerson, and Henrich's version of the dual inheritance theory of culture, study cultural transmission directly; others, like Herbert Simon's "docility hypothesis," defended today by economists like Herbert Gintis, are more interested in the consequences of culture on human behavior; yet others, like Christakis and Fowler's "three degrees" hypothesis, seek to study the social transmission of things like overeating, which are not typical traditions. These successful and popular theories have one thing in common. They take seriously the possibility that social influence could be sufficient, on its own, to ensure the stability of many traditions that we would not adopt, were we not in thrall to conformity and deference.

Social influence can be defined, for our purposes, as a form of cultural transmission that takes into account the number of models available for a given item, as well as their status. If the decision to reproduce a behavior is influenced by the number of people exhibiting it, social influence takes the form of conformity; if influenced by their prestige, of deference. These two mechanisms, theorized and explored in great detail by dual inheritance theories of cultural transmission (Richerson and Boyd 2005), make a lot of sense, especially when compared to simple imitation. They take into account many pieces of information that sheer automatic reproduction of everyone's actions would discard. A practice's success, and the status reached by those who manifest it, may be useful indicators (though indirect and unreliable, as we shall see) of how advisable it is to adopt it. The question we shall ask here is whether it makes sense to trust such cues over other, possibly more valuable pieces of information, in particular the many direct cues that we have about the costs, risks, or benefits associated with cultural practices.

Imitators will be called "compulsive," in this chapter, when they are indifferent to such direct cues, and only go by the prestige or number of their models. Conformity or deference are compulsive when the models' number or status trump all the other pieces of information we could use to decide whether or not to follow them. Though the compulsivity assumption may not always be endorsed explicitly, it is a crucial building block for some major results in the field (concerning, in particular, the cultural evolution of altruism). This chapter argues that compulsivity is not a reliable feature of human social learning.

Before I start, let me clarify what this chapter does not do. It is not a wholesale critique of the psychology of social influence, or of its use in models of cultural evolution. When learning from others, the number and status of our models is certainly a useful piece of information to employ. Everything else being equal, we should follow social influence. This chapter, thus, is not set to deny the existence of deference or conformity, but to counterbalance the simplifications that have grown around them—to begin with the notion that social influence could suffice to maintain traditions we would otherwise have good grounds to reject.

How Far Do We Follow Conformity and Deference?

An Ambiguity of Dual Inheritance Theory

One of the best illustrations of dual inheritance theory comes from an intriguing paper by Joseph and Nathalie Henrich (2010) on food taboos for pregnant women on the Fiji islands. Suppose you are one of these pregnant women: seashells, fishes, and squids are an important source of food for you. Some are harmless, others can have catastrophic consequences for your baby—consequences you would not notice until too late, when the baby is born. Such risky food is too big a part of your diet to be avoided altogether. Doctors, other women, provide you with advice, but they do not give reasons to back it up, and experimentation is out of the question. What should you do? The threat from contaminated seafood is hidden; this is clearly a case where other peoples' example and advice should be one of the chief sources of information you take into account. Indeed, women follow the food recommendations coming from respected elders (but not from doctors), and they are all the better for it. They follow other cues as well—some seafood seems intuitively more disgusting to pregnant women, for good reasons—but they cannot afford to ignore cultural examples. Of these they make a discerning use, trusting certain people but not others. The preferred models are chosen, not on the basis of their overall status or power (which would seem to place doctors and female elders on an equal footing, at least), but by more subtle and context-sensitive reputational cues that the study's authors capture with the word "prestige."

Such situations, where social influence leads us toward the better options, are numerous enough to make conformist and deferent imitation a strategy that is not just sensible but efficient. Dual inheritance theory argues that this was as true for our ancestors as it is for us: those of them who took into account such cues as the reputation and number of models had more descendants than others. We inherit from them a general propensity to imitate majorities and prestigious models. (I will use the label "dual inheritance theory" to refer to the collective work of Boyd, Richerson, and Henrich. The label is not perfect, since other people having worked on analogies between genetic and cultural transmission are often put under the same name, but no other label is widely used, as far as I know.)

By underlying the benefits of relying on such social cues, dual inheritance theory improves on earlier models of social learning. In these models, cultural transmission was as good as automatic, and its strategic dimensions were largely ignored (Cavalli-Sforza and Feldman 1981 is an example). Conformity and deference are more flexible and adaptive than random or unbiased transmission. In spite of their simplicity, they inject a great deal of information in people's choices. This information is mostly to the learners' advantage. When Boyd and Richerson's theory was first developed, it also had the great merit of stressing a fact that few people today would controvert: culture has many negative impacts on people's survival and fitness (even though its net effect has probably been positive, judging by our species' success, so far). Unlike sociobiology (or its rival, cultural materialism), dual inheritance theorists put an explicit focus on the many ways in which culture causes human behavior to depart from what a mere concern for survival, reproduction, or well-being would dictate.

Useful as they are, though, conformity and deference are highly idealized mechanisms. They started off as assumptions in mathematical models of social learning—reductive models that necessarily simplify the cognitive operations that make up people's decisions. Dual inheritance theorists never intended to say that cultural learning could be reduced to these two mechanisms. Still, the theory's models are overwhelmingly based on mechanisms of social influence; other mechanisms are acknowledged, but the ways they may interact or interfere with social influence seldom are. In many models that we shall study, social influence rules the fate of cultural practices without any rival.

This simplification could encourage some readers to think that, when social influence cues are pitted against other cues, the former are likely to win. Boyd and Richerson's most widely quoted examples of social learning do encourage that interpretation:

— *Kamikaze suicides* (Boyd and Richerson 1985, 4 & 24). Fighters who belong to units that engage in suicide attacks are often driven to follow the group's strategy at the cost of their lives. Many hypotheses have been devised to explain this. Some stress the fact that self-sacrifice is fundamentally compatible with the fighters' preferences and beliefs (nothing matters more than winning this war); family and friends will benefit; death is almost certain either way. Other theorists try to dissect the psychological mechanisms that enter into the making of a suicide attacker. Incremental commitment is one: by the time they give away their lives, suicide fighters have already gone through a long series of increasingly demanding sacrifices, each slightly more demanding than the one before (Gambetta 2005). Dual inheritance theory offers a completely different view—and a much simpler one. Suicide fighters are simply following the "majority bias": do what most people around you do. That psychological mechanism causes us to adopt useful practices most of the time, but occasionally produces terrible mistakes.

— *Michael Jordan's underwear* (Boyd, Richerson, and Henrich 2011, 10922). Another favorite illustration of the theory comes from advertisement. For many years Michael Jordan's image has been used to sell underwear. This is odd: Jordan's fame and reputation derives entirely from basketball; taste in underwear does not count among his most important (or public) achievements; and obviously, he does not advertise for free. Thus, we have every reason to disregard his recommendations.

It is indeed improbable that such campaigns have much effect on people: studies tend to show that celebrities influence us only in their domain of competence (Michael Jordan on basketball, Catherine Deneuve on aging gracefully, etc.) (Amos, Holmes, and Strutton 2008). Dual inheritance theorists disagree. Advertisers must know what they are doing (though customers may be stupid): we probably copy Michael Jordan, out of sheer deference. The habit of copying the prestigious is simply too hard for us to relinquish.

The popularity of these two examples shows that the possibility of compulsive conformity or deference is, at the very least, an open question for dual inheritance theorists. The overall picture is more complex, though: in other places, Boyd and Richerson emphasize that individuals should use simple imitation rules only when they have no better sources of information. For instance, conformist transmission can operate only if "individuals have difficulty evaluating the costs and benefits of alternative cultural variants" (Richerson & Boyd, 2005, 206; see also Henrich & Henrich, 2007, 66).

In spite of this, the idea that social influence would be capable of overriding even the strongest and most basic human preferences is taken quite seriously. In these two cases—Kamikaze suicide and Michael Jordan's underwear—deference rules even when the model's prestige is wholly irrelevant; conformity beats the will to survive. Richerson and Boyd justify this by saying that social learning is "built for speed, not for comfort" (Richerson and Boyd 2005, 187): it is a capacity that evolved relatively recently (on the scale of human evolution), because it allowed us to pick up adaptive behaviors. Like many recent adaptations, it is imperfect: evolution has not had the time to come up with better alternatives. Conformity and deference are coarse nets that catch a lot of junk.

> (...) fast and frugal adaptive heuristics such as conformist and prestige biases have specific, unavoidable, maladaptive side effects.
>
> ... individuals must adopt what they observe with only marginal modifications. As a result, we may often adopt maladaptive behaviors.
> (Richerson and Boyd 2005, 156 & 161)

"Simple Heuristics that Make Us Smart"—Really?

Boyd and Richerson like to relate this thesis to a popular view in psychology (defended by authors like Gerd Gigerenzer or Herbert Simon): human decisions rely on imperfect cues rather than exhaustive or perfectly rational procedures. Social learning is a "simple heuristic": its aim is not simply to make the right decision, but to make it at a reasonable cost (the cost being measured in processing time and brainpower). Using rough-and-ready indicators, like the number and prestige of models, can be a way of saving on these limited resources. It could be a way of solving what is often called a "cost-accuracy trade-off." For dual inheritance theory, the existence of this trade-off implies that social learning often produces suboptimal decisions (when one buys Michael Jordan's underwear for no good reason), and sometimes, disastrous ones (when one imitates a group of kamikaze suicides).

There are two problems with this view. First, it is at odds with most of the literature on simple heuristics. Gigerenzer, for instance, is quite clear that people do not just use any cheap and dirty heuristic. They have learnt (either as a species in the course of human evolution, or as individuals in their own lifetime) to spot cues that are so rich and so relevant that, most of the time, in the right context, they are just as reliable as more complex or expensive procedures. "Models of inference do not have to forsake accuracy for simplicity," says Gerd Gigerenzer; "the mind can have it both ways" (Gigerenzer and Goldstein, 1996, 666). The simple heuristics that we use, in this view, are a cognitive free lunch. We do not have to take the cheap and dangerous path: our decisions can be both inexpensive and reliable. In theory, the cost-accuracy trade-off still rules (without it there would be no point in choosing cheap heuristics over expensive ones); but in practice we elude it almost all the time. Speed *and* comfort.

Second, Boyd and Richerson do not explain what could prompt social learners to choose the cheap and inaccurate end of the cost-accuracy trade-off. Some choices, after all, are important enough that reaching a smart decision is worth paying some cognitive cost. Becoming a kamikaze suicide is a high-stakes decision if there is one. Should we trust the conformity heuristic on this, simply because we cannot be bothered to spend much time and thought over the issue? From an evolutionary standpoint, creatures that always go for fast and inaccurate decisions should be selected against. One possible answer to this objection would posit that conformity and deference simply cannot be used selectively; that we must follow them all the time, or not at all; that these heuristics are "hardwired" in our brains.

Thus, when considering the costs and consequences of social learning, we have to choose between three options:

— Option 1: Social influence is a simple heuristic that *always* makes us smart. That is the free-lunch view just sketched above, taken to the extreme. It would mean that deference and conformity never lead us astray: we are always better off following them.

— Option 2: Flexible imitation. Following social influence is not always a smart move, but when it is not, we simply turn to other cues, unless social influence is very cheap to follow, and the decision is not important enough to justify the cost of seeking more expensive cues.

— Option 3: Compulsive imitation. Social influence is a simplistic heuristic that makes us dumb, at least in some domains. In this view, conformity and deference cannot be used selectively, depending on the circumstances: they are hardwired, leading us to dramatic mistakes.

The literature almost unanimously rules out option 1: everyone can think of cases where the majority or the prestigious are not worth imitating, either because our models are misinformed, or because what is good for them is not good for us. This leaves us with a choice between options 2 and 3: is imitation of the many and the prestigious compulsive, or flexible? As we just saw, dual inheritance theory does not clearly opt for either option 2 or option 3. This chapter makes a case for flexibility. To see why this issue matters, it will be useful to describe the consequences of the compulsive imitation hypothesis in a field of research where it has served to back spectacular claims: the cultural evolution of altruism.

Docility: Does Compulsive Imitation Breed Altruism?

Evolutionary theory places some constraints on the type of helping behaviors that may exist without being wiped out by natural selection. William Hamilton's rule posits that helping others is adaptive only if one of the following conditions obtain:

— The individual who is being helped is related to the helper to such a degree that helping her is beneficial to the spread of the helper's genes.

— The helper herself somehow benefits from helping others. Hamilton's rule does not specify how this could happen, but there is no shortage of theories. Helping could be beneficial because help is directly reciprocated (A helps B, B helps A); because it is indirectly reciprocated (A helps B, B helps C, C helps A); because the helper would be punished if she did not help; because her reputation would suffer; or because defecting would alienate cooperators who could be precious in the future. In other words, cooperation with non-kin needs to be beneficial in some way if natural selection is to favor it.

We do not know exactly how, or to what extent, natural selection influences cooperative behaviors. To be sure, we know of many cases where an animal makes great sacrifices to help a complete stranger: lionesses have been known to care for antelopes (Hrdy 2009, 209 sq.). This kind of helping, Hamilton's rule tells us, is maladaptive, but it does occur. We know, however, that such cases are the exception rather than the rule; in general, Hamilton's rule predicts the allocation of investments in cooperation, at least in broad outline. Those who think that natural selection had nothing whatsoever to do with the evolution of cooperation in animals would need to explain why so many instances of cooperation are either kin-directed or ultimately beneficial to the helper. As far as I know, no other viable theory does this. Thus, natural selection seems to influence helping behaviors to a large extent.

How is that possible? Nobody is naive enough to think that genes determine behavior in a direct or automatic fashion, or that natural selection rules each and every detail of our thoughts and behaviors. Even if this were the case, the parameters that come into Hamilton's rule (degrees of relatedness to one's kin; costs of helping; expected benefits of direct and indirect reciprocity; reputational benefits; and so on) are abstract, multifarious, and elusive. In order to respect the rule perfectly, an animal would need to estimate every parameter with perfect accuracy. Such omniscient Darwinian robots do not exist. What we have, instead, is a set of imperfect heuristics that occasionally err. The standard Hamiltonian view does not claim that animal behavior should always be consistent with the rule. It admits the existence of uncompensated sacrifices to strangers, provided they remain rare. All it assumes is that natural selection tends, in ways often unknown or unexplored, to make animal minds sensitive to cues of relatedness and future benefits. This assumption can be rejected, of course, but there is a heavy price to pay—namely, to deny that cooperation is mostly kin-directed or beneficial to cooperators, or to find an altogether different explanation for these facts.

Few theoreticians are willing to pay this price, but there are exceptions. The docility hypothesis, first put forward by the maverick genius Herbert Simon, is one. Its claim: cultural transmission produces biological altruism as a by-product. Culture, in this view, is a package of practices that people acquire wholesale. Most of the package is worth getting, but some of it is detrimental to the adopter's fitness—in other words, maladaptive. We might think of it as a legacy, with many assets and some liabilities. Like a legacy, it has to be acquired in its entirety, or not at all: inheritors can't be choosers. They are docile. They do not pick and choose their cultural endowment any more than they choose their genes. The phrase "dual inheritance" (although Simon did not use it) says all: cultural transmission is as complete and deterministic as its genetic counterpart.

Docility thus allows cultural transmission to cause maladaptive behaviors. Some of these can be altruistic: they do not just decrease the agent's fitness: they increase someone else's. There are limits to the amount of altruism that can be produced in this way: on the whole, cultural learning should increase, not decrease, individual fitness. Even so, cultural learning engenders some altruism. Simon (1990) was the first to use the word "docility" in this connection, but the project of explaining human cooperation as a by-product of cultural learning is evident in some of Boyd and Richerson's earliest writings (Boyd and Richerson 1985—although their theorizing, since that book, cannot be reduced to the docility hypothesis, as we shall see). The view that social learning and cultural transmission have a lot to do with human altruism is also popular among experimental economists (Fehr and Fischbacher 2003). Simon's docility hypothesis is at the heart of gene-culture coevolutionary explanations of human cooperation (Herbert Gintis's modeling of Simon's hypothesis—Gintis 2003—makes the clearest case for it).

Does docility produce *more* altruism than other kinds of learning mechanism? That is far from sure. After all, there is no guaranteed way for an animal to make adaptive decisions day in, day out. Everyone has to make mistakes some of the time; and if someone exploits one of these mistakes, it is enough to make that mistake altruistic. Culture has no monopoly on altruistic mistakes: all sorts of learning are likely to produce some. Why would culture increase their importance?

Cultural group selection is the most frequent answer to this question. That hypothesis claims that the social norms and religious beliefs that set societies apart from one another play a crucial role in their survival. Culture, in other words, influences the fate of societies on timescales large enough to register in a Darwinian process. This requires the relevant traditions to be extremely enduring, to differ from one society to the next, and to be well shared inside any given society—sufficiently so, at least, to give some societies a competitive edge over others, in the protracted competition that is evolutionary selection. Cultures, thus, would be coherent and stable enough to qualify as evolutionary units of selection. Since altruism benefits its recipients, cultures that promote altruism (as opposed to other sorts of maladaptive behaviors) would get a competitive edge over others (Sober and Wilson 1999). As a result of this, reliance on cultural learning could make individuals better off in almost any domain except in the field of cooperation. As Simon put it, docile altruism is a tax paid on the benefits of cultural learning—a tax perceived by society, and paid by individuals.

There are reasons to doubt all this. (Why, for instance, would group selection favor altruistic behaviors, which benefit some people at the expense of others, rather than other forms of cooperation—those that benefit everyone, without resorting to the exploitation of altruists?) But suppose the docility hypothesis were right; then it would be a very powerful model. Other accounts of the evolution of cooperation and helping struggle with a basic problem: helping non-kin is maladaptive when others fail to reciprocate, which means it can only evolve under special conditions. The docility hypothesis does away with this problem: cooperation with non-kin does not have to be adaptive in order to evolve. Many authors welcome this conclusion. These are usually authors who were uncomfortable with standard evolutionary accounts of cooperation, or felt that it downplayed human kindness and the power of nurture. Even people who have never heard of the docility hypothesis look favorably on the view that, ever since culture, humans have escaped whatever evolutionary constraints might have weighed on cooperation.

On the face of it, this view seems to flow smoothly out of the current stream of research on gene-culture coevolution, an idea that has gained great respectability thanks to a mass of intriguing case studies (see Laland et al. 2010 for a review). They have uncovered a process whereby a population's genetic makeup evolves to fit the constraints of a traditional practice, or to exploit its benefits—as it would fit any other aspect of the environment. The evolution of lactose tolerance, a genetically determined capacity found mostly in populations with a history of dairy farming, is the least controversial example: the availability of fresh milk, the consumption of which requires a specific gene, maintained that gene in certain populations but not others. Dairy farming is, of course, a cultural invention. It depends on the regular transmission of a specific set of know-hows. Since the distribution of dairy farming is relatively well-documented, the influence of culture on genetic evolution is quite plausible in this instance (Holden and Mace 2009); but gene-culture-coevolution hypotheses often go much further.

According to David Sloan Wilson, one of cultural group selection's most influential theorists, the Christian tradition of charity toward their fellow Christians is what allowed Christian communities and dogmas to prevail over Paganism. That process, it is worth insisting, is presented as a demographic evolution, not a cultural one. The great plagues of Antoninus and Justinian wiped away many Pagans, but spared cohesive Christian communities whose demographic success allowed them to take control of Roman institutions. The spread of Christianity was, of course, a matter of cultural diffusion in most cases; but the decisive flick that precipitated its triumph was a demographic event. In the crucial days of the Pagan emperors, Christianity survived because Christians did—and they did because their religion, unlike Paganism, put a premium on solidarity (Wilson 2002, 204–215). This same propensity for charity, Wilson claims, had identical consequences in many historical circumstances, each time augmenting the community of believers. Whether the triumph of Christianity had a demographic component is not easy to know. One would need to ask: How was Christian charity implemented from one community to the other? Was it the same in every corner of the vast, cosmopolitan empire that Christianity was about to conquer? How biased was it toward fellow Christians? Who was counted as a fellow Christian? As for the Pagans (the many varied societies later described as Pagan), were they uniformly less generous than their Christian neighbors? Wilson's cultural group selection model assumes specific and clear-cut answers to these complex questions.

(To be fair, not all the hypotheses inspired by cultural group selection are as gratuitous. To begin with, dual inheritance theorists are more and more inclined to defend versions of group selection where selection does not bear on demographic groups, but rather on practices or forms of cooperation. Suppose that group A, which is loosely organized, loses members to group B, which is better at promoting cooperation: A members "vote with their feet" to swell the ranks of B denizens. In such a case, Boyd and Richerson would speak of "group selection," even if, demographically speaking, the original A lineage did not become extinct, and the original B population, as a biological entity, did not grow. In such a scenario it is people's choices, not demographic dynamics, that drive the evolutionary dynamic—Boyd and Richerson 2009.)

Cultural group selection (in its classic, demographic version) is a powerful, alluring theory; but it stands upon a huge, brittle pile of assumptions—namely, that social norms are sufficiently immobile to weigh on natural selection in the same way for a long time, sufficiently successful to be embraced by most members of a given group, but not so successful that they would spread outside of it (which would cancel the population's selective advantage). Theoretically, these assumptions are nothing impossible; yet, nothing one could rely on as a matter of course. Chapter 1 made a case against simplistic assumptions of cultural homogeneity. The real problem is even more fundamental, though. Underneath all this is one strong and debatable thesis about cultural transmission: that traditions are like a legacy that has to be accepted wholesale—debts and all. We cannot pick and choose from the cultural package.

Consider two models often cited to argue that biologically altruistic punishment evolves by cultural transmission: Andrés Guzmán, Rodríguez-Sickert, and Rowthorn (2007), and Henrich and Boyd (2001). Both papers model a population where norms of cooperation and norms of punishment are applied by some agents, agents whom others can copy. The norm of cooperation is a norm of mutual help, and whoever abides by that norm benefits in the long run. On the other hand, the norm of punishment (in those two models) is genuinely altruistic: agents punish other agents at a cost to themselves, without getting anything in return. Some agents are predisposed to copy others; some agents are not. Those who copy reproduce the norm of mutual help. As a result, they fare better than non-copiers, because mutualistic cooperation is beneficial. However, there is a catch: the agents who copy the (beneficial) norm of mutualistic cooperation *must* also copy the (detrimental) norm of punishment. Selectivity is not an option. In both models, free-riders are avoided by construction. An agent simply cannot share in the mutually beneficial norm without paying the cost of altruistic punishment. (Whether this altruistic cost is ever paid is debatable—in Henrich and Boyd's model, altruistic punishment might never have to be resorted to.) Likewise, in Gintis's version of the docility hypothesis, altruistic norms hitchhike the ride of other transmitted norms, only because agents are too docile to select against altruistic norms (Gintis 2003, 414). In all those cases, selection by individuals is implicitly or explicitly kept from interfering with the rise of altruism.

The dogma of compulsive imitation, then, is not just interesting in its own right. A lot rests on it. It matters all the more to examine this idea, an idea as ancient as theories of cultural transmission themselves. Herder would have seen eye to eye with today's dual inheritance theory on this ground; he often wondered at the many handicaps that we inherit along with culture. When God endowed humans with their powers of imitation, he condemned them to follow their peers in every way: "How poor must the creature be, who has nothing of himself, but receives every thing from imitation, instruction, and practice, by which he is molded like wax!" (Herder 1791/2010, 229). Sadly for us, imitation lacks selectivity. It allows the diffusion of harmful or useless traditions; that, however, is what Boyd and Richerson call an *unavoidable side-effect*: "From the means chosen by the creator, that our species should be formed only by our species, it could not possibly be otherwise: follies must be inherited, as well as the rare treasures of wisdom" (Herder 1791/2010, 230).

Is human social learning so undiscerning? Many disagree, on grounds both psychological and evolutionary. From an evolutionary standpoint, the claim made by dual inheritance theory, that the benefits of blind imitation (guided by conformity or deference alone) outweigh its costs, has been disputed (Mameli 2008). Psychologically speaking, we do not have to go by Herder's claim. We need not accept that our powers of imitation prevented us from learning in any kind of way but through others. Perhaps there is no need to choose between social learning and individual cognition: we may keep one eye open on what other people's example teach us, and a second eye on what we can guess by ourselves. That would be flexible imitation. The next section argues that flexible strategies of social learning are nothing complex or impracticable; they allow us to enjoy the benefits of cultural learning without paying the prohibitive costs of reproducing absurd or detrimental actions.

The Case for Flexible Imitation

This section examines the role of other people's example in our cultural choices. Cultural transmission depends on models by definition, but this does not mean that it should only be informed by what we know about these models. There is often a lot more to what we know and can use to choose a cultural practice. More importantly, we can use both kinds of information at the same time: we do not have to choose between observing our models and observing the rest of the world. We can give some weight to both types of cues.

Suppose you need to pick a restaurant on an unknown street—let us call it Social Influence Street. Here, most restaurants look more or less alike and offer similar prices. The only relevant information, therefore, is to be found by looking at where other customers go. This may not be a very informative cue: perhaps some shrewd restaurant owners moved their customers to the most visible tables; perhaps other people were no more informed than you were, and simply followed other uninformed people. We shall assume, however, that such things do not happen on Social Influence Street: other people, some of them at least, know things that you do not.

But let us walk on a little, and we end up on Personal Knowledge Street. Here, you know most of the restaurants through recent and direct personal experience (for the sake of this example, let us just abstract away things like food critics or crowd-sourced websites). On Personal Knowledge Street, restaurant frequentation is hard to observe (some waiters place patrons near the windows so they look more numerous) and it is a poor indicator of restaurant quality (other people followed other people, who did not know any better).

Personal Knowledge Street and Social Influence Street are fictions, of course. Many actual streets would be a mix of the two: you have some personal knowledge, but you don't know whether it is reliable or outdated; you have some social information, but you don't know how informative it can be. We can distinguish three basic ways of dealing with this uncertainty. *Compulsive imitators* always assume that they are on Social Influence Street: they tend to disregard their personal information whenever it is challenged by social cues. *Asocial learners*, on the contrary, believe themselves to have been walking Personal Knowledge Street since eternity: they pay no attention to their model's behavior. When they have no personal information to rely on, they simply choose at random. Models used to retrace the evolution of cultural learning usually consider only these two options: compulsive imitation or asocial learning. This is what makes the docility hypothesis work in the models that we have mentioned: agents have a choice between following others' example all the time (heedless to the costs of what they copy), or just doing without social learning and its benefits. There is no middle ground (a strange assumption that, if taken seriously, leads to a worrying conclusion, a classic example being Rogers's 1988 demonstration that cultural learning is not adaptive and cannot evolve). There would be much to recommend compulsive imitation if asocial learning were the only alternative to it. But it is not. *Flexible imitators* do not believe themselves to be on either street: they do not systematically follow either social influence or their personal knowledge, but try to give some weight to each.

The main objection to the flexible strategy is the difficulty of applying it. How do we assess the informative value of personal information, as compared to social influence? In many cases it would be easier simply to opt for one of the two inflexible strategies; that would be a cheap heuristic indeed (though not one that would make us smart). We should therefore expect people to keep the flexible strategy for those occasions where it is worth using—that is to say, when the stakes are high enough. Is there evidence of flexible imitation in such cases? Yes.

Abundant experimental evidence shows that, when it matters to them, human adults calibrate their trust in a careful way, and mostly for their own benefit. An example is provided by some replications of Asch's famous conformity experiment. As is well known, a substantial minority of people will systematically endorse the false opinion of a majority (Asch 1955). One should note, however, that in most versions of the experiment, imitating the majority entails no cost at all (on the contrary, pleasing others may be counted as a benefit). What happens when material rewards are introduced?

In a modified version of Asch's paradigm, Baron et al. (1996) asked subjects to recognize, in a lineup, an individual they had previously seen on a picture. They varied both the amount of information available to the subjects (by changing the amount of exposure to pictures subjects got) and the importance of the task (by introducing monetary incentives). Subjects blindly imitated a misleading confederate when the stakes were not high, or when their own personal information was unreliable (i.e., when the task was difficult because exposure to the pictures was short). They trusted their own judgments otherwise—in the condition where the stakes were high and the task was easy. It should be noted that, when the task was difficult and the motivation was high, subjects were much more likely to imitate the confederates than in any other condition. This makes perfect sense, since they had every reason to trust the unanimous confederates and few reasons to trust their own dubious perception. Of course, the experiment was rigged, so that trusting the confederates was always a losing strategy. Even so, mistakes in this condition were not more frequent than in the control condition (where subjects passed the difficult task alone). In other words, subjects followed the misleading confederates mostly when their own judgment would have been wrong as well. Their use of social information was flexible, indeed close to optimal given the constraints.

This result mirrors some interesting data obtained in the psychology of persuasion. People let others' arguments inform their own decisions to the extent that better and more direct sources of information are absent or mediocre (Conway and Schaller 2005). We endorse other people's opinion when the issue at stake is perceived as irrelevant, or when a lack of information makes it rational to do so, but not otherwise. This applies to the influence of prestige (Petty and Wegener 1998; Petty, Cacciopo, and Goldman 1981; Axsom, Yates, and Chaiken 1987; Rhine and Severance 1970). This also curbs the influence of conformity: Diane Mackie and her coauthors (1990) presented Californian college students with two short talks, one dealing with the issue of acid rain in New Hampshire, the other with a proposal to organize offshore drilling off the Southwest coast of the United States. Each argument was delivered either by a fellow student of the same college, or by one from a remote university. Conformity should push the subjects to agree with their fellow students, and that is what happened, but only when the issue at stake was of little direct relevance to them (acid rains in New Hampshire rather than Californian offshore drillings).

In such experiments, few things depend on the way the subjects behave. At worst, they may undergo a slightly disagreeable experience, quickly forgotten past the lab's exit door. The costs and benefits of imitation are negligible in Asch's conformity experiment; in Bandura's "Bobo doll" imitation experiments, where children tend to hit a doll after observing other children doing it (Bandura 1963); for passersby who tend to look up after seeing another passerby do so (Milgram, Bickman, and Berkowitz 1969); for students who are more likely to cover their computer keyboard after seeing others do it (Coultas 2004); and in all the literature dealing with our unconscious imitation of an interlocutor's pose, accent, or mannerisms (Dijksterhuis and Bargh 2001).

The situation is different in experimental economic games, performed with real money, where each move entails relatively important risks and gains. Still, research on social learning in economic games suggests that subjects rely on imitation (if ever) to the extent that it seems likely to improve their own payoff (Efferson et al. 2008; Efferson et al. 2007; McElreath et al. 2005; McElreath et al. 2008). Such examples do not support the view that imitation is, on average, more likely than individual decision making to yield maladaptive decisions regarding cooperation.

Some authors (most clearly Gintis, Bowles, Boyd and Fehr 2003, 22) have taken the existence of cross-cultural variation in economic games (Henrich et al. 2005) as evidence that culturally transmitted norms can be a cause of altruistic behavior. There are many reasons to resist this interpretation. First of all, there is no consensus on the motivations underlying altruistic giving in, for instance, the dictator game. It is increasingly clear that (guarantees of anonymity notwithstanding) some implicit concern for one's reputation still motivates most players (Dana et al. 2007). Framing effects and experimenter demands are also increasingly suspected to underlie altruistic giving (as argued by Winking and Mizer 2013, who find no donations at all in a dictator game played in a truly ecological setting). Second, the existence of variations from one geographical setting to another is not enough to prove that culturally transmitted norms are the cause. Important differences also exist among neighboring communities with no obvious cultural differences: adjacent Tsimane villages (Gurven, Zanolini, and Schniter 2008), different neighborhoods of Newcastle upon Tyne (Nettle, Colléony, and Cockerill 2011), and communities of horticulturalist-foragers less than 100 kilometers apart (Lamba and Mace 2011). Quantitatively speaking, those intracultural differences are quite comparable to intercultural differences (Lamba and Mace 2012).

This is not to say that a flexible imitator would *never* do anything costly under social influence, and there is indeed evidence that altruistic behaviors can be imitated, mostly by young children. In James Bryan's series of studies on imitative altruism (e.g., Bryan 1971), children are made to win a small reward in chips (which may be exchanged for real toys), and then told they may give a part of it away to a child in need by placing it in a jar. The setup resembles a dictator game, and just like in the dictator game, children are quite likely to show some generosity, with or without imitation. However, when the experimenter sets the example by giving away her own chips, children are more generous. The effect, however, is weak, and the authors argue that it can be explained away by a simple disinhibition effect:

> The effect of the generous model is hardly a strong one (...). A hypothesis that appears reasonable concerns the disinhibition of behavior. (...) For many children, set as they are in the novel contexts of both a laboratory and a helping situation, the witnessing of a "novel" behavior without reprimand would subsequently increase the likelihood of such behavior.
>
> (Bryan and Walbeck 1970, 346–347)

In other words, the model shows giving is permitted and has no unpleasant consequences. She may also reinforce the salience of the altruistic action by attracting the child's attention upon it (the same argument could be made about adult studies on model-induced giving—Bryan and Test 1967; Rushton and Campbell 1977). Most other effects attributed to costly imitation in children (like "overimitation" phenomena observed in three- to five-year-olds—Lyons et al. 2011) are weak and heavily context-dependent. The costs they involve are trivial compared to the costs of any important cooperation episode among adults.

The view just offered is nothing original: it just expects people to use social cues in a way that roughly aligns with what they personally know and desire. Thus, they do sometimes exploit information concerning the number of adopters for a given practice, or their social standing; but they use these cues in combination with others, and with an eye on their personal knowledge—especially if the stakes are high enough to reward a flexible approach. They might take cognitive shortcuts around some problems of little consequence, but, in many of the experiments just described, subjects are easily turned flexible, simply by making the task more interesting to them: by telling them that their decision will matter to some outcome outside the lab; by promising a few dollars; by engaging them in some locally relevant political issue.

The sort of decision that theorists of cultural transmission attempt to predict is of much more consequence: enforcing a moral norm, choosing a hunting or agricultural technique, and so on. With so much at stake, flexibility is to be expected. Yet most models of cultural evolution implicitly dismiss flexibility in favor of simpler mechanisms: conformist or deferent imitation. In so doing they follow an opinion that is widely accepted in social psychology, and beyond: prestigious or numerous models suffice to make even the most unlikely fad culturally stable. In the same way that fans will, it is said, kill themselves in numbers when their idol commits suicide, a huge literature claims that our cultural choices are compulsively swayed by the aura of the few and the weight of the many. The next section suggests a different take on fads and the madness of crowds.

Imitation: the Key that Unlocks Every Door?

Recent popular science books have made much to persuade the public that compulsive imitation can suffice to ensure widespread diffusion for just about any fad (Sunstein and Thaler 2008; Gladwell 2000; Christakis and Fowler 2009). The claim has received a lot of backing from peer-reviewed research, thanks to which the old literature on "popular delusions and the madness of crowds" (Mackay 1841)—collective hysterias, Saint Vitus dances, mass suicides, and so on—got a new lease on life. Once relegated to the margins of social science, the study of what Tarde used to call "somnambulism," or collective hypnosis, is back. The evidence is much less anecdotal than it used to be, but (I will argue) still does not suffice to show that social influence easily sways us.

Conformity and Deference: Psychological Mechanisms or Social Facts?

One big reason for the exaggerated importance of conformist and deferent imitation in the social learning literature is its unclear status: one does not always know whether imitation is treated as a psychological mechanism or as a social phenomenon. The psychology of deference and conformity is what we are concerned with here, what the compulsive imitation hypothesis was always about; but sometimes we happen to imitate numerous or prestigious sources for reasons that have nothing to do with their number, or prestige. The number and social standings of the models who carry a tradition also affect the accessibility of that tradition—how easy it is to encounter it—as well as (sometimes) the costs and benefits of adopting it.

Let us start with accessibility (a notion to be more fully developed in chapter 4). If a friend of yours starts to smoke beedis, you are slightly more likely to smoke beedis as well. Why? Simply because your friend makes beedis more conspicuous, easier to experience or to get a hand on, than they were before—thus amplifying whatever preexisting taste you had for it. This effect will obtain even if you do not care a whit about following your friend's example in any domain. All that matters is that it makes beedis salient. It pushes them closer to you.

Accessibility obviously favors cultural transmission, but not because of conformity or deference. Yet there is a risk to mistake the effects of accessibility for the effects of a compulsive imitation mechanism like conformity. Take one of the most influential papers of dual inheritance theory: Henrich's reinterpretation of the S-shaped diffusion curve (Henrich 2001). Anticipated by Tarde and documented in great detail in the "diffusion of innovations" literature (Rogers 1995), the S-curve shows that, when an innovation spreads inside a population, it runs a slow course at first, being picked up by a few early adopters, then gathers momentum and spreads at a much quicker pace, slowing down again when the pool of potential adopters is saturated. The textbook case of an S-curve is the diffusion of hybrid corn among Midwestern farmers; there are many others. As Henrich notes, the S-curve implies that for everyone in the population, the probability of adopting the innovation rises slightly each time someone else adopts it. This Henrich interprets as proving that people are following a conformist imitation strategy, assessing the proportion of adopters around them and using this information to make a decision. Accessibility, however, explains the S-curve just as well as conformity does: the more widely spread an innovation is, the more likely we are to come across it, to know about it, to see its uses.

The number of models, or their social standing, also influence the costs and benefits that attach to cultural practices. Some things become useful to imitate simply because they have been endorsed by an authority or a majority. This is enough to explain why people's adoption of certain technologies (like Macintosh computers or, in their time, LaserDiscs) depends on the level of adoption in the population at large—without conformist motivations having anything to do with it. Here again, dual inheritance theorists tend to discount this possibility. In their study of Chaldean Christian immigrants in Chicago, Henrich and Henrich (2007) note that this small community has found an economic niche in running grocery stores: most newcomers start off as clerks in such a shop, and eventually try to found one. The authors consider only one explanation for this: newcomers align themselves on what the majority of Chaldeans (encouraged by community leaders) deems advisable. That explanation may be true, but it dismisses many others that are equally likely: for a Chaldean, entry costs into the grocery trade are likely to be much lower than they would be in a field with fewer Chaldeans in it; training will be easier, for similar reasons; insider information (on supply chains, stocks, etc.) will be readily available, and so on. Conformity, deference, and other mechanisms of compulsive imitation should be considered alongside alternatives.

Cultural Diffusion in a Population of Flexible Imitators

Baron et al.'s replication of Asch's conformity experiment nicely tested the flexible imitator hypothesis: it shows that, when it matters, people weigh what they know about their models carefully, in a way that approximates the true value of that information. What does this imply for cultural diffusion? For one thing, we do not expect majorities to make or unmake traditions by themselves, irrespective of the material's intrinsic qualities, when people have any personal experience of these qualities. If people have any personal preference for or against a tradition, these preferences should be able to override conformist biases, when it matters.

A recent set of studies by Matthew Salganik and colleagues (Salganik, Dodds, and Watts 2006, Salganik and Watts 2009) makes precisely this point. What the authors did is create a small, experimental cultural market, in the shape of a "virtual jukebox." Subjects are presented with a selection of pop songs from fledgling rock bands (all entirely original and previously unheard). They can click on a song, listen to it, and download it, in that order. Several sessions were organized, with a different group of subjects in each. There are two kinds of sessions, one in which subjects are just given a list of songs (control condition), and one in which songs are arranged by popularity, with the most downloaded ones coming first (social information condition).

Song selection thus takes two steps: first, click and listen; second, download. It should be no surprise that social information makes a difference in the first step, when subjects are faced with a series of tunes by an unknown band they could not listen to. Other people's behavior is clearly the only relevant cue in this instance, and it is followed. Some readers retained only this aspect of the experiment, which they cite as an illustration of the powers of conformity.

But what happens in step two? Here, subjects have listened to the song: they know whether they like it or not. In the social information condition, they also know (from step one) how popular it is with others. This is the only condition where personal and social information are pitted against one another. If subjects showed a strong conformist bias, we would expect social information to override, at least partially, the quality of the song. It does not. Other people's choices have no discernible effect on the probability of downloading a song once it has been listened to (Salganik et al. 2006—supp. mat; Salganik, personal communication). The song's quality (as measured by the average grade it gets from subjects in all sessions) is the best predictor of subjects' choices at this stage.

Most subjects listen to a handful of songs only, but they frequently download those they had listened to; this is probably to be explained by the peculiarities of the experimental setting, the nature of the songs, and the way they are presented. As a consequence, the lion's share of a song's success was determined in the first step, where subjects had no first-hand experience of the songs. Given this, the experimentally generated "charts" should have been ruled over mostly by conformist dynamics: all it took for a mediocre song to take off was for a few downloads to propel it to the top, where it would have gotten most of the clicks, beating other songs at the stage that mattered the most, its success snowballing into a conformist dynamic.

Such evolutions do happen, but their scope is surprisingly limited. A song's quality (i.e., average ratings over all sessions) remains, by far, the best predictor of its success in the "social information" condition. The effect of social information is quite real (as we should expect, given that most of the selection happens on step one): different songs reach the top of the charts in different sessions, and their success is not as easy to predict, on the basis of their quality, than it is in the control condition. Yet this unpredictability mostly affects top-quality songs: social influence may turn a good song into a super-hit, rather than a success, or the other way around. What it does not do is condemn a good song to oblivion, or push mediocre songs to the top: those rated two stars or less (five stars being the maximum) are almost never downloaded.

In a follow-up study, Salganik and his coauthors showed that the disruptive effects of social influence—its capacity to wreak havoc with the links between quality and popularity—increased when the number of subjects per session decreased. This reflects the fact that small groups collectively process less information than bigger groups: they have fewer opportunities to scout for good songs. Their downloads are but a mediocre indicator of a song's quality. More subjects would mean more occasions to explore the library of songs, and more information injected into the collective average of their choices.

These beautiful experiments give us a sketch of what cultural diffusion may look like in a world of flexible imitators: conformity and deference modulate the success of traditions, but they do not, by themselves, stabilize things that would not otherwise have become stable traditions. They do not make or unmake traditions when the material does not lend itself to it. We just saw, however, an important caveat to this principle: it loses its validity as populations become smaller. This idea will be explored more thoroughly in chapter 4: group size is a barrier against the arbitrariness of social influence. Conformity and deference (being what will be called "local attractors") may stabilize traditions only in some places and in the short run.

This principle is not based just on experimental observations alone: it is one of the main conclusions of the theory of informational cascades (Bikhchandani, Hirshleifer, and Welsh 1998), which was devised to determine the conditions under which irrational behaviors can spread, by imitation, in a population of rational agents. Much of what you just read about flexible imitation is inspired by that theory. (I do not, however, aim to take on board all the axioms of rational agent theory; flexible imitators are simply prudent: they do not imitate any costly behavior without a motive.) The theory of cascades is most famous for showing that, even in a group of well-informed rational agents, practices may spread that everyone personally knows to be bad, because everyone thinks that everyone else knows better. These are called negative informational cascades. Negative cascades are the theory's most famous implication, and the reason why it is so often cited in support of the view that social influence can stabilize the most egregious fads. A somewhat less famous prediction of the theory is that negative cascades should be short and rare; as we shall see now, they are.

Negative Informational Cascades Are Short or Rare

Negative cascades happen when social influence pushes people to make choices that they have good personal reasons to reject. The conditions specified by the theory for their formation are rather drastic. Being flexible imitators (by hypothesis), the agents choose to rely on their personal information, unless it seems to them less reliable and more ambiguous than what they can infer from others' behavior (unless they believe themselves to be on Social Information Street). The key signal that pushes agents to conform, according to the theory, is unanimity, or near-unanimity, in others, along with evidence of unreliability in one's own information. The first condition, unanimity, is particularly fragile: a few people following their own private information instead of the crowd (like the little boy in Andersen's tale) or simply behaving randomly, are enough to throw the cascade into disarray. Because of this, the theory predicts that cascades should be infrequent and confined to small scales: "cascades are born quickly and idiosyncratically, and shatter easily" (Bikhchandani et al. 1998, 158—see also Bicchieri and Fukui 1999). In this negative informational cascades differ from positive ones, in which agents share beneficial practices that they could probably have produced without the cascades, only less rapidly.

The theory is one thing; the way it is applied to real-world examples is another. The mere existence of negative cascades is a most spectacular prediction of the model, and its proponents understandably want to make the most of it; as a result, empirical illustrations of informational cascades often go far beyond what the theory says, and negative cascades are typically presented as a substantial problem, one that may affect millions of people (according to Bikhchandani et al.; see also Kuran and Sunstein 1999; Bicchieri and Fukui 1999). Real-life examples of negative cascades, though, are difficult to come by, and those that have been put forward are controversial. The irrational behaviors that are said to have spread through a cascade are usually either not very successful or not nearly so irrational as they are portrayed to be.

Among the cascades that were probably much less stable and widespread than commonly thought, one may count the famous Tulipmania of the Dutch Golden Age—the textbook case for the madness of crowds, already dissected in Mackay's 1841 book. The "negative cascade" version of the story goes like this (Bicchieri 2006, 204 sq.). Thousands of tulip lovers wasted fortunes on worthless flowers for many years, because the collective craze had induced them to believe the flowers had more value than they really had. Today's historians concur that the speculative bubble around tulips lasted only a few months before prices came back to something like their current (and not inconsiderable) value (Goldgar 2007); but more importantly, market bubbles should be distinguished from negative cascades. There is no sign that tulip buyers were deluded about the true value of tulips. Instead, they had good reasons to believe they could make a profit from the increase in prices—a risky bet, obviously, but not for that an absurd one. (Incidentally, it could be the case that the clonal varieties of the Dutch Golden Age, rare, instable, and now extinct, were actually much more beautiful than those of today.)

The plank roads craze that seized the northeastern United States in the first half of the nineteenth century is another favorite of the literature. Plank roads do not last more than a few years; yet they were sold to many towns and counties as permanent pieces of equipment. This would be a case of negative cascade if buyers had based their decision on the purchases of other buyers ("if our neighbors bought plank roads, why shouldn't we?"), rather than their personal information. This, however, cannot be known for sure. Shrewd lobbyists downplayed the drawbacks of plank roads (unknown to buyers at the time); also, we don't know to what extent buyers had to suffer the future consequences of their mistake (which would be faced by the next mayor). Whether other buyers' decisions were a factor at all, we do not know. Whatever the case may be, the plank road fever as a whole lasted a decade at most, always traveling from state to state, as the scam got uncovered quickly, by the decay of plank roads themselves. Interestingly, the warm and damp southern states, where wood decays faster, eluded the craze (Klein and Majewski 1994).

Much of the success of informational cascades has to do with the fact that they allow many apparently absurd decisions to be dealt with easily within a rational choice framework; as a result, though, authors are sometimes tempted to pin any and all kinds of irrationality on a cascade. Timur Kuran and Cass Sunstein's interpretation of mass panics as informational cascades (1999) is a case in point. They start with the well-documented fact that people tend to overestimate the probability of unlikely events: plane crashes or hurricanes are feared out of proportion with the likelihood of their occurrence. Kuran and Sunstein argue that these illusions can be amplified by media attention into full-blown collective illusions, thanks to the mechanism of cascades. If other people worry that airbags might kill babies, or that vaccines cause autism, then surely my own worries are justified. This may turn out to be true, but we do not know to what extent these crazes are put into motion by sheer conformity. In any case, not everything that is irrational about us demands to be explained by social influence; we can find within ourselves plenty of motivations to behave weirdly. The urge to appeal to social influence and the madness of crowds when dealing with things like Cargo cults or witch hunts is understandable: after all, these obviously depend on some kind of cultural transmission; this, though, does not mean that people were pushed into these crazes by blind imitation, compulsive conformity, or because "culture made them do it." Assuming that they did is just a way of avoiding a deeper consideration of the underlying psychology.

Waves of Compulsive Imitation: Often Evoked, Seldom Documented

Studies on the diffusion of unhealthy behaviors (alcoholism, crime, or suicide) is in full health (Bikhchandani et al. 1998; Christakis and Fowler 2009; Mesoudi 2009), thanks to new statistical techniques allowing their users to disentangle social transmission from other causes. Among them is the "clusters method" that has been briefly presented (and criticized) in chapter 1: it aims at identifying points—in time, in space, or in a social network—where a behavior is abnormally present, once most of the usual predictors for it have been controlled for. These abnormal "hot spots" (of obesity, tobacco use, suicide, etc.) are taken as evidence that imitation was involved.

The fact that these studies usually concern conducts thought to be pathological, as well as the rhetoric of contagion that pervades them, would have made a nineteenth-century criminologist like Tarde quite happy. In any case, the high costs associated with these behaviors means that, if these studies were true, the flexible imitator hypothesis should not survive it: these actions are too costly for compulsive imitation to cause much of them by itself.

(Note that, while suicide or obesity are obviously costly, that is not true of everything that we can imitate about them. Flexible imitators would not be readily pushed to commit suicide just by knowing others did; if, however, they had already decided to commit suicide, they could very well imitate someone else's method for it, as distinct from the act itself. The fact that the means and places of suicide are highly cultural—think of Golden Gate Bridge, the Aokigahara forest, or the sentry box in the Boulogne camp that Durkheim studied—is not a problem for my view. Incidentally, all the examples Durkheim uses to establish that "no fact is more readily transmissible by contagion than suicide" (1897, 141–142) are cases where nothing is imitated except the location or means of self-harm.)

This is not to deny that, in some particular contexts, social influence can be clear and relevant enough to tilt people in the direction of costly choices. In a tightly knit group of soldiers, for instance, if there is unanimity to decide on a suicide attack (high costs, but also high benefits from the point of view of a committed fighter), it might be powerful enough to sway. The point is, such influence does not scale up to bigger or looser groups. Like conformity in Salganik's jukebox experiment, its effects only go so far. Anthropologists working on suicide terrorism seem to concur. Scott Atran (Atran 2003) argues that kamikaze warriors do not, as is sometimes thought, come from a solitary crowd of desocialized desperados, drawn into a mass movement by charismatic leaders. Quite the contrary: they usually share their ideals and actions with small groups of friends—football teams, student organizations, and so on. If they follow a model, it is not one that they saw on a television screen or at a mass rally. He would be someone they have known since childhood. As Atran notes, today's terrorist franchises seem to understand this better than the states that fight them: the urge to die for a cause does not travel far and wide. It grows locally.

Such close-range influence falls within the scope of flexible imitation; waves of collective madness on a large scale do not. Yet there seems to be a lot of evidence for such waves, starting with the widespread view that high-profile suicides put crowds of copycats into motion; not only that, but new network approaches to social transmission (Christakis and Fowler 2009) claim to show that we are compulsively drawn to imitate, not just what our friends do, but what their friends, and the friends of their friends do. I won't give here an extensive summary of the many criticisms put forward against the literature on waves of imitation (Baron and Reiss 1985; Steglich, Snijders, and Pearson 2009; Lyons 2011), but simply mention the most pressing problems facing the field, according to critics. The difficulties attached to the "method of clusters," which was introduced in chapter 1, will serve as a guide, although the method is slightly outdated and has been refined since, as we shall see.

The task of trying to identify anomalous concentrations for a certain behavior, and show the influence of imitation by controlling other causes away, is vulnerable to two well-known mistakes. Suppose we know of a building where people smoke much more than in the whole surrounding street and neighborhood. Even after controlling for the variables that usually predict tobacco use (say, people's social or financial standing, their age, etc.), it stays abnormally high. Two questions need answering before we put the blame on imitative transmission. First, do we know all the relevant predictors? There might be some factors we overlooked. The building, for instance, may harbor a tiny micro-traffic in smuggled cigarettes, bootlegged by some foreign neighbor. This is often called the *common environment* problem. Second comes the problem of *homophily*, which is really about directions of causation: we think the building's dwellers smoke more because their neighbors smoke; but could it be the other way around? Perhaps they settled in this building because they knew they would find fellow smokers there. Perhaps they were not looking for fellow smokers, per se, simply for people who enjoy partying, or who do not have children—traits that happen to be correlated with smoking. These two problems are not beyond the reach of newly developed statistical tools (see, for instance, the work of William Hoppitt and his team, who apply their tools to animal cultural transmission—Allen et al. 2013), but most claims made about behavioral contagion are backed by different tools, which (critics argue) fall short of solving our two problems (Steglich et al. 2009).

The common environment problem can be solved in two ways: by comparing two situations that differ as little as possible, or by comparing the data to a simulation. Both solutions fall prey to specific problems. The first can be illustrated by the sociological studies that were led in the 1970s and '80s on suicide contagion; the second, by contemporary work on the spread of obesity, happiness, or depression in social networks.

The first systematic studies on the spread of suicide (Stack 1987; Phillips 1974) have been much criticized for their approximations, in particular for the comparative methods they used (Baron and Reiss 1985). To explore the impact of publicized suicides on the overall suicide rate, they compared the ten days that follow a publicized suicide to the ten days that preceded it. The comparison would work only in the absence of seasonal effects: suicide rates, at the times of the year where suicides get media attention, should not differ (suicides-wise) from other times of the year. But that is not certain. Critics argued that the press tended to report suicides at certain times of the year more than others: periods that coincided in seasonal suicide peaks, due to various things (from the weather to economic activity). When it comes to documenting the effects of celebrity suicides, comparisons are more questionable still. The brute data speak in various directions, with some studies showing suicide increases after a celebrity ends her days (Yip et al. 2006), while others evidence a slight decrease (Baron and Reiss 1985). None of this can teach us much about the contagiousness of celebrity suicides, though, without a proper basis for comparison. Such a proper baseline would be, in this case, the suicide waves that follow when a celebrity dies a natural or accidental death—as happened, for instance, after Lady Diana disappeared in a car crash (Hawton et al. 2000).

To avoid problems of this sort—problems posed by the comparison of two real situations, each slightly different from the others—testing the data against a simulation can be a solution. This is what Nicholas Christakis, James Fowler, and their colleagues do in a series of papers, as remarkable as they are controversial (Christakis and Fowler 2007; Christakis and Fowler 2009). They try to spot clusters, this time not simply in space or time, but in social networks. They start from a partial, detailed map of the social relations of thousands of people. They trace the circulation of obesity, smoking cessation, or loneliness, in the network, as time goes by. They claim to rule out homophily and common environments by comparing their data with a simulation that models the effect of both mechanisms, plus randomness, without social influence. This method has many advantages over the methods of clusters; it permits distinguishing between social and geographical proximity. Critics (a useful, though strongly worded, summary can be found in Lyons, 2011) have found fault both with the simulations and with the way the authors compare them with the data, claiming that homophily and a common environment could explain away most of the alleged transmission. A reanalysis of the data produced more nuanced conclusions, but agreed that taking homophily into account leads to reduced estimates for the strength of social contagion (VanderWeele 2011).

There is, however, one astounding result in this research program that this debate does not touch: the "three degrees rule" that obtains in all the studies performed by Christakis and Fowler—on the spread of obesity, of happiness, of loneliness, and so on. The rule states that these things may jump as many as three degrees of separation in a social network. Suppose that I am obese, but my son is not. Neither is his secret lover (whom I do not know). The three degrees rule states that my obesity can influence my son's secret lover's *mother*, in spite of being completely absent in my son, and in his lover. If this is true, the consequences are daunting: the friends of the friends of the friends of your friends amount to an impressive number of people, and (says the rule) you can influence them all, even if you fail to influence your friends directly. This should be enough for anyone to spark awesome cultural epidemics.

Reality is less magical. Christakis and his team work with incomplete data, and their reconstitutions of social networks are not comprehensive. The way their medical data are collected means that most subjects belong to closely overlapping networks (see introduction in Christakis & Fowler 2007). As they acknowledge, it is quite likely that, in their reconstituted networks, people may look like they are separated by several degrees, while in reality they are simply friends—only that friendship is not recorded in the data (as argued by Lyons, 2011). This easily explains the "three degrees rule": if my obesity can influence the weight of my son's lover's mother, that may simply be because I happen to know the mother directly, unbeknownst to the researchers who map my social network. My son and his lover have nothing to do with the process. Behind the spooky action at a distance lies nothing but a very banal, one-to-one direct influence, hidden by lacunas in the data. Even that influence may still be a mere reflection of the confounding effects of homophily and common environment.

These issues may be technical, but their consequences are not. Together they may account for a large overestimation of social influence's influence. Sinan Aral and his colleagues (2009) estimate that a failure to control for homophily and common environment is responsible for a three- to sevenfold overestimation of the impact of imitation dynamics in the literature. Along with other biases that social psychology, and to a lesser extent social science, inherited from its nineteenth-century past, these results feed a habit of thought that consists in mistaking any unexplained cluster of traits or actions as a fruit of social transmission. The literature dealing with the contagion of costly behaviors appears more often than not to show the reverse of what it is taken to prove: compulsive imitation may tilt people in various ways on small scales, but its effects dissolve before sizeable waves can form from it. This argument, used by Durkheim against Tarde's theories, remains powerful today.

The Influence of Influentials: Tautology or Misunderstanding?

Noxious behaviors may not spread as easily as usually assumed, but this leaves the case of other sorts of cultural practices quite open. In many fields, from the "diffusion of innovations" literature (Rogers 1995) to sociolinguistics (Labov 1980), deference seems to rule. The claim that prestigious models make or unmake the spread of cultural variants seems well grounded. When one takes a closer look, however, prestige and influence, as these literatures construe them, appear to be rather hazy notions that have little to do with deference as we have been studying it so far.

Consider William Labov's widely echoed claim that phonological changes (changes in pronunciations or accents within a language) trickle down from the most prestigious speakers to the least prestigious ones. This does not mean to say that it is the higher or best-regarded sections of society that influence the rest. Like most of his sociolinguist colleagues, Labov takes the reverse to be the case.

> (. . .) the theorist focuses on the laws of imitation (Tarde 1873 [sic]), and the borrowing of prestige forms from centers of higher prestige, then it would follow that new sound changes will be the most advanced in the highest social classes (. . .) [However] Kroch (1978) pointed out (. . .) that no case had been found in which the highest social group was the originator of a systematic linguistic change, and argued that systematic (or "natural") sound changes would always be expected to originate in the working class. A wide variety of sociolinguistic studies carried out since 1965 showed no case contrary to Kroch's position (. . .) Whenever age distributions and earlier reports indicate that there may be sound change in progress, the highest social class lags behind.
>
> (Labov 1980, 253)

Tarde's mistake, which Labov and his colleagues discovered to their surprise, has been uncovered in other fields as well. Stanley Lieberson's work on the spread of first names (2000) concludes that there is less to the contribution of upper classes or prestigious characters to the success of first names than what appears at first. The Christian names of movie stars make popular first names, yet the causality does not necessarily run from stars to the rest of society. It often works the other way around, for stars do not choose their names at random. They are carried by the tides of fashion like anyone else. The name "Marilyn" was already peaking when Norma Jean Baker chose it, thus feeding a cultural trend that was taking place without her. When Lieberson looks at prosperous classes instead of celebrities, he also finds that simple trickle-down mechanisms fall short of explaining the complex interactions that go into a first name's diffusion.

Yet these discoveries have not demoted prestige. It remains a key explanatory category in studies of social diffusion. How so? The word's meaning simply shifted. What Labov calls "prestige" is the reputation that attaches to certain groups, those most likely to be imitated. The permanent inhabitants of Martha's Vineyard (home, in the summer, to the rich and famous), wishing to go local and be identified as natives, tend to imitate the accent of the Vineyard's fishermen. Why? Because (Labov supposes) fishermen are taken to embody the authentic spirit of the place. They are locally prestigious. In Philadelphia, on the other hand, the true heart of Phillyness is to be found in middle-class working women, the group where phonological changes tend to find their origin. This way of using prestige allows Labov to save Tarde's claim, which his and others' investigations seemed at first to condemn.

> Once we are willing to refine our notion of prestige to give full weight to the local prestige associated with the Philadelphia dialect, Tarde's laws of imitation gain in respectability. But we must be ready to recognize that such a local prestige, which appears primarily in behavior and rarely in overt reactions, is powerful enough to reverse the normal flow of influence, and allow the local patterns to move upward to the upper middle class and even the upper class.
>
> (Labov 1980, 253)

Prestige so defined is thus completely distinct from wealth, authority, or status. In this Labov agrees with traditional sociological views of charisma and influence. To cite just one famous study, Robert Merton's work on influentials in the small town of Rovere (1968) shows that there is no perfect overlap between scales of status and scales of influence: people do not always look to the top of the social ladder to ask for advice. This decoupling of prestige from other forms of social superiority would not be a problem if there were other ways of measuring prestige, or clear criteria to define it. Unfortunately, cues of prestige are quite elusive—so hard to grasp, in fact, that sometimes, prestigious groups are known only by the cultural trends that they start. How do we know that Philadelphia's working women are prestigious? Because their accent got imitated. Why were they imitated? Because they were prestigious.

Labov's work has tremendous descriptive value, and was revolutionary in his time; yet his explanations by prestige look like ad hoc, a posteriori constructions—I mean that one can easily imagine how the same theory could accommodate quite different data, simply by tweaking the notion of "local prestige." Once a cultural trend has been traced down to a particular group identified in this way, that group's reputation is easily interpreted in favorable terms. This may not make prestige-based explanations of cultural diffusion wrong, but it makes them very difficult to falsify. Take any episode of cultural diffusion from the poor, the obscure, the humble, to the highest reaches of society: nothing is easier than turning it into a triumph of a prestigious minority over a fascinated majority. How did Christianity, a religion born from an oppressed minority in a remote corner of the Roman world, climb its way up to the emperor? Because of the moral prestige of women and slaves. Tarde was particularly fond of this kind of argument, which he uses, for instance, to explain the diffusion of Roman law and customs. These laws endured in the Western provinces, but not the Eastern half of the Empire. Why? Because Rome's military triumph made more of an impression in the West than in the East. The Eastern provinces were invaded with as much success, and for a longer time, but all they saw in Rome was one invader in a long list.

Such ad hoc uses of prestige are also familiar in the diffusion of innovations literature. In Everett Rogers's textbook, the diffusion of an innovation is chiefly due to opinion leaders; but what is an opinion leader?

> Opinion leadership is the degree to which an individual is able to influence informally other individuals' attitudes or overt behavior in a desired way with relative frequency.
>
> (Rogers 1995, 27)

Opinion leaders, in other words, are nothing but people who participate in the diffusion of an innovation. The innovations in question are mostly technologies: drugs, seeds, or machines. What drives their diffusion? The first thing that comes to mind is not the charisma of a few influential doctors or farmers, but sheer practicality. This literature chooses to focus on innovations representing "a major change in previous behavior, whose results (in terms of relative advantage) [are] strikingly evident" (Rogers 1995, 300). Should not we look there first?

Without denying this, Rogers, echoing Tarde, claims that it is the elites (defined by their status or reputation) who tend to fulfill the function of opinion leaders (Rogers 1995, 288–294); yet the works he cites do not support this claim. For instance in Coleman, Katz, and Menzel's study (1957) on the diffusion of tetracycline antibiotics among doctors (a model for much subsequent work), the ones who matter are not the most powerful, the wealthiest, the most senior, or those who enjoy the best reputation, but simply the best connected. Having many friends, belonging to many networks, may correlate with status or reputation, but prestige is not key to it.

That said, there could be another way of fleshing out the notion of social influence. It could be the case that some people, irrespective of their standing, status, or reputation, happen to be very good at all kinds of cultural transmission. They would influence their colleagues on the choice of new drugs, give their friends welcome advice on a car purchase, their coreligionist on matters of faith, and so on. If such generalist influentials existed, the elusive notion of cultural prestige could turn out not to be a tautology after all. The sociology of cultural influence, however, speaks against this idea, showing most opinion leadership to be domain-specific. In Merton's study of cultural influence in Rovere, two-thirds of the influential people they study are strictly "monomorphic," which is to say their opinion is decisive only on certain matters (Merton 1968; see also Katz and Lazarsfeld 1955, 332–334, defending the same conclusion). What Katz, Merton, and others had observed in American society has also been observed by anthropologists working in quite different settings. A study of reputational cues produced by Victoria Reyes-Garcia and her coauthors (2008), among the Tsimané of lowland Bolivia, shows that intellectual prestige (one's overall reputation for knowledgeability, as established by other people's ratings) is not substantially correlated to one's expertise concerning medicinal plants; neither is seniority. The Tsimané manage to find good experts on herbal medication, but do so by using subtler cues. Such indirect cues are arguably more difficult to build than general-purpose prestige. If they fail, direct observation may be a better way to spot experts. A hunter's successes and failures, for instance, should be quite informative; and yet they are surprisingly difficult to document and exploit. Among the Aché of Paraguay, where hunting is an important everyday task, it took researchers twenty-seven years of observations (following thousands of hunting parties) to get reliable data, cleared of chance or confounds, on who the best hunters were. In big-game hunting societies where hunters work as a group, assessing individual skills seems to be even more of a headache (Hill and Kintigh 2009). With generalist influentials being so hard to find, opinion leaders turn out simply to be people who happen to start trends for unknown reasons; we may want to call them prestigious, but this label is not by itself very helpful.

We should not make too much of the fact that prestige, as an explanation for cultural diffusion, has been such a slippery notion in the past. More rigorous construals of prestige and deference (as attempted, for instance, by Henrich and Gil-White 2001) could put these notions to work in more fruitful ways. Nor am I arguing that flexible imitators should pay no attention to their models' reputation: it should be, after all, quite an informative cue. The question is, how informative—and how easy to retrieve? Dual inheritance theory routinely assumes, as we saw, that prestige is a transparent and straightforward indicator, readily obtained and easily translated into decisions. There is no denying that some societies manage to build reputational systems of great reliability; but such achievements cannot be taken for granted. Reflecting on prestige cues and the way they are used in models of cultural evolution, the philosopher Catherine Driscoll (2008) remarks that useful reputation systems cannot be built by one person alone: they require many people to pool their knowledge together. This takes the form of constant updating through everyday gossiping and observation; at the same time, collective reputation systems need to be maintained against error and dishonesty. Nothing impossible in all this; but nothing a theory could take for granted either. A good reputation system is no trivial cultural achievement. It is itself a tradition.

Closing the Case against the Imitation Hypothesis

This chapter started with the widespread view that conformity and deference are "cheap heuristics that make us smart." As we went, it became increasingly difficult to keep the cheap part and the smart part together. Authors who put the stress on the cognitive frugality of imitation end up predicting that it will push people to accept all sorts of sacrifices they would not have consented, had it not been for social influence. If, on the other hand, they insist on the smart side of the trade-off, they soon realize that imitation cannot be the simple mechanism that models of cultural evolution depict. Learning from others in a smart way is a demanding, information-hungry task; the cues we get from our models need to be interpreted, integrated, and used in flexible ways, along with other pieces of information. The resulting process is so unlike compulsive deference or conformity that the name "imitation" is not really adequate.

This chapter and the one before allowed me to argue that imitation, defined either as a capacity to reproduce behaviors in a faithful way (chapter 2), or as a compulsion to follow social influence (this chapter), is not the engine of cultural transmission. If imitation appears to be "the key that unlocks every door," that is mostly because the concept is slippery enough to be applied to any case of cultural transmission. The idea is plastic enough to enter any lock (sometimes jamming them in the process) but it does not open many. Why, then, does it fascinate so much? Why have more-or-less all theories of cultural transmission since Tarde been theories of imitation?

The appeal derives, I think, from the prospect of explaining large-scale diffusion with small-scale transmission—culture with psychology. If the rise of stable traditions depended on a handful of efficient transmission mechanisms, then we could focus all our efforts on identifying those mechanisms—relatively simple cogs and wheels, already cut out to dry by social psychologists. We could bet everything on solving the Wear-and-Tear Problem, and ignore the Flop Problem. This satisfies an understandable scientific taste for simple explanations. It also speaks to the temptation to reduce big anthropological issues to problems of cognitive engineering. There is nothing wrong with such reductionist aspirations: they may work out.

In the case at hand, though, imitation as classically understood—that is to say, faithful and compulsive—seems too weak and not specific enough to explain much about cultural diffusion. Social influence does not have such a hold on our minds that it could induce us blindly to reproduce anything that goes around our society: it does not solve the Flop Problem. Nor is cultural transmission underpinned by faithful or conservative mechanisms: there is no imitative capacity to solve the Wear-and-Tear Problem. Both parts of the imitation hypothesis fail.

Fortunately, the two problems of cultural transmission can be solved without appealing to compulsive or faithful transmission mechanisms. The trick is to put the Flop Problem first, and the Wear-and-Tear Problem second. The next chapter explains how this can be done.

4 A THEORY OF DIFFUSION CHAINS

Most of the authors studied here would probably endorse the following claim, made in the first few pages of an edited book representing the state of the art in various disciplines on the topic of cultural transmission:

> Cultural persistence is essentially a question of transmission, the passing on of information from individual to individual or from groups to other groups.
>
> (Schönpflug 2009, 2)

That claim seems innocuous enough. Cultural diffusion, after all, is nothing but a set of transmission episodes. When the distinctive features of a tradition are preserved in space and time, some information needs to be preserved every time it gets passed on. Symmetrically, it seems obvious that a series of efficient and faithful transmission episodes must form a stable transmission chain.

Yet the idea that preserving information through faithful transmission is the way to make traditions last is deeply misleading. That intuition springs from the excessive importance that we grant to the Wear-and-Tear Problem, as opposed to the Flop Problem. This chapter will try to convince you that the Wear-and-Tear Problem should not be taken as seriously as it is. Solving it leaves the Flop Problem unsolved. Solving the Flop Problem, on the other hand, will often render the Wear-and-Tear Problem negligible. Why? Because the persistence of traditions does not chiefly depend on the quality of their transmission. Accurate transmission is, in fact, neither sufficient nor necessary. Transmission needs to be plentiful—that is, abundant enough to create redundant, robust, and repairable diffusion chains. In this chapter, I explain how cultural success allows the Wear-and-Tear Problem to be overcome, even in the absence of faithful transmission. I will then outline the causes of cultural success. There will be different causes, depending on the scale one considers. Cultural diffusion does not work in the same way when it is observed over ten years or ten centuries, in a village or on a continent.

Transmission Is Easy, Diffusion Is Hard

There Is No Inertia for Transmission

The experimental literature on cultural transmission tends to hide the Flop Problem behind the Wear-and-Tear Problem. Reading it, one gets the impression that cultural transmission is endowed with a kind of momentum—that once transmitted, a practice has a spontaneous tendency to keep going and transmit anew. In adequate conditions, this momentum creates traditions by itself:

> Culture emerges as a natural and inevitable consequence of interpersonal communication.
> (Conway and Schaller 2003, 110)

> Imitation is an important type of social learning that can readily lead to stable cultures.
> (Marino 2007 cited by Claidière and Sperber 2010, 651)

Tarde's entire theory rests on this postulate: cultural transmission obeys a law of inertia. It is self-perpetuating.

> The fact that a new taste or idea has taken root in a mind which is constituted in a certain fashion carries with it no reason why this innovation should not spread more or less rapidly through an indefinite number of supposedly like minds in communication with one another.

> It would spread *instantaneously* through *all* these minds if they were absolutely alike and if their intercommunication were perfect. (...) When wants or ideas are once started, they always tend to continue to spread of themselves (...).
>
> (Tarde 1895/1903, 114–115)

Obviously such ideal conditions are never exactly met. Transmission depends on human vehicles; if they fail to live long enough, or to travel far, or to be sufficiently accessible, their traditions will not travel much farther than they do. Many oral traditions that flourished thousands of years ago are lost to us, not for a lack of efficient transmission, but because their carriers died without offspring and without having come into contact with the ancestors of modern humans. Others faded away because they circulated in populations that were too small to exist in a sufficient number of exemplars to avoid accidental extinction. Yet denying all this is not what Tarde had in mind. He claimed that, once these problems are abstracted away, the momentum of cultural transmission spawns lasting traditions. Well-functioning transmission mechanisms produce culture as a matter of course: cultural transmission has inertia.

(As Bruno Karsenti notes in a commentary of *The Laws of Imitation* (Karsenti 1993), this inertia assumption got Tarde into trouble. After all, some cultural practices remain stable through time: they neither expand nor regress. Tarde's theory would predict that the diffusion of any idea or practice should extend continuously, if left to its own devices. Why, then, are so many traditions not spreading? This problem is what led Tarde to postulate mechanisms of competition between practices, and, above all, mechanisms of "counterimitation"—what researchers today would call "anti-conformity.")

Nothing illustrates this postulated inertia of traditions better than the popular virus metaphor (used at least since Dawkins 1976, see also Dennett 1995). The image likens cultural transmission to an infection, and diffusion to an epidemic. When a population is sufficiently large, interconnected, and replenished at a rate that compensates mortality, viruses spontaneously spread. The selection pressures under which they evolved shaped them to do so. They are equipped with a small number of highly specific, highly sophisticated transmission mechanisms that (in ideal conditions) ensure their diffusion. Conditions, of course, are seldom ideal: interactions between individuals may be too rare; populations of carriers may grow scarce, or go extinct; there may be competition from other viruses, and so on. Still, epidemics are fed by a virus's spontaneous tendency to get transmitted over and over again, if unimpeded. On a perfectly smooth and frictionless surface, Galileo argued, a ball would go around the Earth, preserving its momentum for eternity. In the same way, imitative theories of culture predict cultural diffusion as an inevitable consequence of transmission's inertia.

This seems too easy. Of all the things we say, do, repeat, or imitate, very few get transmitted beyond a restricted context (as this chapter shall illustrate). Many practices that do get transmitted from one individual to another are too insignificant to be transmitted once more. They do not give birth to a genuine diffusion chain. We saw in the last chapter that, while social influence might compel us to adopt certain practices, it usually failed to beget full-blown social epidemics. This was just another way of saying that the Flop Problem does not take care of itself.

In this, traditions do differ from epidemics. A virus relies, for its contagion, on mechanisms of transmission that characterize it uniquely. The virus's diffusion depends on the sophistication of its unique transmission mechanism. Our ideas and our actions are different. Their transmission passes through a variety of channels—some of them rudimentary, most of them not tailor-made for this or that particular thought or action. They do not spontaneously reproduce (as believers in compulsive imitation would have it). Having been transmitted so many times does not give them a further push. Nothing keeps us from distorting or relinquishing them.

Why is that? The inefficiency of transmission is not to blame. Transmission could be as faithful as we want, but this in itself would not enable it to create stable diffusion chains. Even the most reliable transmission mechanisms are not perfect—some errors must be let through. In a certain type of diffusion chains (sequential chains), these errors accumulate rapidly and irreversibly. That loss of information is not something that accurate transmission, however faithful, could prevent.

Why a Few Transmission Episodes Do Not Make a Diffusion Chain

The best place to see this is the social-psychological literature on diffusion chains, first studied experimentally by Frederic Bartlett (1932) and recently put back in fashion by new approaches to cultural transmission. Bartlett tried to evaluate the conservation of different kinds of material in diffusion chains that resembled a Chinese Whispers game. One of the traditions he studied was a Native American legend, *The War of the Ghosts*. Having read the legend once, a subject had to render it in writing. That rendering was then read by a second subject who did the same for a third subject, and so on. This simple technique has since been taken up by many experimental studies that simulate cultural diffusion in humans and other animals (Mesoudi and Whiten 2008, 2009).

Synthetic diffusion chains are quite an appropriate tool to determine whether transmission mechanisms suffice to solve the Wear-and-Tear Problem. In such chains, diffusion is reduced to a sequence of transmission episodes, abutted to other transmission episodes. Most other aspects of diffusion are excluded. In Bartlett's prototypical experiment (a widely followed example) diffusion chains are strictly sequential: A passes something on to B, who passes it on to C, and so on. Each individual receives the transmitted material from one single other individual, once. In those sequential chains, each link stands or falls on a single transmission episode. Thus, the only thing that determines whether the material will be preserved is the quality of transmission mechanisms at work. Outside the lab, however, diffusion chains are not sequential. This changes many things:

— Transmission in real settings can be *repeated*: A passes something on to B one day, and again the next day, and the day after. However weak or inefficient a transmission mechanism, its effects can be compounded by frequent use.

— Transmission can come from several distinct individuals, and not just one model: A, A' and A" pass something on to B. In other words, transmission can be *redundant*. Learning from several sources is more accurate than learning from only one: confronting several redundant sources, each giving its own version of a given tradition, prevents B from copying of errors and variations that A, A' or A" could introduce. Here again, this effect is independent of the quality, faithfulness or efficiency of transmission mechanisms. It relies on B's abilities to synthesize a variety of cues, and use them to reconstruct a tradition.

— A single diffusion chain can, at any point, branch out into multiple chains: A passes something on to B and B,' who pass it on to C, C' and C", and so on. Diffusion chains *proliferate*. A chain gains stability from branching out into parallel sub-chains, for each sub-chain is an additional chance of surviving. Sequential chains, on the other hand, hang by a single thread. Even extremely faithful and efficient transmission mechanisms, if arranged in a linear fashion, are vulnerable to the accumulation of errors that must occur if transmission is less than perfect.

The powers of repetition, redundancy, and proliferation will be further explored later in this chapter. For now, let us remember that Chinese-whispers-type sequential chains exclude these three mechanisms by construction, leaving only the sheer faithfulness of transmission episodes to bear on cultural survival. (I will use the word *sequential* to refer to chains where repetition, redundancy, and proliferation are impossible, allowing no parallel transmission whatsoever; chains that exclude proliferation, but allow repetition and redundancy, will be called *linear*).

If you ever played Chinese Whispers, you will not be surprised to learn that sequential diffusion does not go far. Bartlett showed as much: it took only six transmission episodes for *The War of the Ghosts* to be eroded by half its length, the last version being 180 words long while the original was 330 words long. Some essential themes of the tale disappeared, starting with the ghosts in the title. Replications of Bartlett's experiment yielded the same observation (for instance, Kurke, Weick, and Ravlin 1989 found that 20 to 30 percent of the story, depending on groups and measures used, had disappeared; see also Northway 1936). Using more familiar material does not change this. Gordon Allport and Joseph Postman's experiments, designed to study the spread of wartime rumors (1947), circulated descriptions of drawings depicting everyday situations. After five or six transmission episodes, descriptions lost on average 70 percent of their distinctive elements. In Alex Mesoudi and Andrew Whiten's (2004) study of narrative retransmission, four retellings of a banal story leave it with the content of three sentences (at best). In none of these cases is the material reinvented or interpreted in innovative ways: the output of sequential diffusion is much shorter and poorer in content than the input was. Lost information is not recovered. Similar results can be found in (Bangerter 2000; Ward 1949; Hall 1951) (the last two studies used drawings instead of stories).

Three experiments (Mesoudi, Whiten, and Dunbar 2006; Kashima 2000; Higham 1951) attempted to curb this tendency by making some stories more interesting than others. In T. M. Higham's experiment, one of the stories provided the subjects (undergraduate students) some cues of what the next exam would be about (the ethics of 1950s experimental psychology was notoriously broad-minded). These three studies do show that intrinsic interest improves a story's chance of survival in a sequential diffusion chain—but not to the point where information loss could be stymied. Even the most eye-catching stories have a hard time getting through very short chains. After five (Kashima) or four transmission episodes (Higham; Mesoudi et al.), authors report conservation rates that range from 0 to 50 percent of the original content (their own figures); never more.

Such conservation measures are necessarily crude and limited. A story's preservation can be assessed in many ways: one could prioritize the retaining of some characteristic themes, the reproduction of a narrative structure, or the fact that some rules of composition are being respected. The works reviewed here give us reasons to think that all these things suffer on the sequential treadmill. Oral traditions are different—at least those whose conservation has been measured (Rubin 1995; Lord 1960). For sure, long epics and ballads are not preserved *verbatim*—as Albert Lord showed, word-for-word identity is usually not a criterion that epic singers and audiences use to assess the similarity of two tales. Still, when two versions of an epic (or ballad) are compared, formulas, narrative structure, themes, and so on display an impressive continuity (see Rubin 1995 for a more quantitative assessment). Nor is *verbatim* recalling rare: children's rhymes are a case of oral tradition preserved word for word for decades, sometimes centuries.

Like other traditions of its kind, *The War of the Ghosts* (the tale used by Bartlett) presumably enjoyed a high degree of stability when it was collected in America. Yet sequential diffusion chains failed to reproduce this conservation in experimental conditions. What went wrong? The answer is to be found in those experiments that manage to create stable diffusion chains in the lab. Such chains usually present two properties: they are not strictly sequential, and subjects have a direct interest in reproducing what passes through the chain.

In these experiments, small groups are asked to test different ways of solving a technical problem (Baum et al. 2004; Caldwell and Millen 2008; Weick and Gilfillan 1971). Good solutions are rewarded. Groups are renewed, little by little, so that each newcomer can learn several techniques, from several models. Typically, subjects do not try to copy their models for the sake of it, but they reuse the most efficient techniques. Good ideas last until the experiment stops, after eight (Weick and Gilfillan), ten (Caldwell and Millen), or twelve (Baum et al.) generations. At that stage, the good ideas are widespread in the group, and would have been passed on to the next generation, had it existed.

What if the chain is still non-sequential, but the material being passed on is useless, uninteresting, or unpractical for participants? One of Weick and Gilfillan's experiments is relevant to this issue. The authors gave their subjects a choice between two solutions to a coordination problem, one of which required more effort than the other, for an identical payoff. Unsurprisingly, the easy one got passed on over eight generations, the hard one not at all. In two other experiments (Jacobs and Campbell 1961; Zucker 1977), the material that circulated inside the chain had no appeal whatsoever for the subjects. These experiments tried to bring the subjects to induce a subtle and unconscious optical illusion in one another (the illusion consisted in misrepresenting the location of a tiny dot of light, under the influence of other people's testimony). Groups of subjects that had been conditioned to show the illusion were gradually renewed with unbiased subjects. As experimental generations came and went, the illusion rapidly faded. It was completely extinct after eleven (Jacobs and Campbell) or eight (Zucker) partial renewals of the groups.

Tiny as those chains might be, most laboratory micro-traditions fail to reach across them. Those that do benefit from two favorable conditions: First, they are interesting and useful enough for subjects to reproduce them. (Readers of chapter 3 will not be surprised to see that, unlike compulsive imitators, we do not copy anything and everything.) Second, the traditions get several shots at hitting their target—they travel on non-sequential chains.

These two conditions are not strictly necessary to the stability of transmission chains, but the exceptions actually prove the rule. In an elegant series of experiments, Tom Griffiths and his collaborators have shown that some stimuli are reproduced almost indefinitely along sequential chains. Their subjects are typically asked to learn and transmit statistical relations between variables (Kalish, Griffiths, and Lewandowsky 2007). Some are simple and intuitive, like a linear relation (when X grows bigger, Y grows bigger); others are much harder to grasp (as, for instance, bell-curved functions, or sheer noise). Intuitive patterns never fade away in the course of transmission; however, non-intuitive patterns do not just disappear. They always turn into intuitive patterns, usually in a few steps. As the authors argue, this demonstrates that intuitive patterns are not exactly transmitted. Rather, they are reinvented alike at each transmission episode—and they spontaneously reappear without any transmission. The arbitrary traditions that are seeded at the start of each chain rapidly fade, unless they fit the most intuitive pattern. In a way these patterns last in spite of sequential transmission, not because of it.

Later in this chapter, I will argue that the two conditions under which laboratory traditions prove stable—intrinsic appeal and non-sequential transmission chains—are key to the stability of culture in general. For now, suffice it to say that, in the laboratory, one does not automatically breed a stable tradition, not even a small-scale, artificial one, simply by asking subjects to copy a practice. Successes do happen, but only for appealing material.

Transmission Fidelity Is Not the Problem

If transmission, as studied in these experiments, fails to create lasting diffusion chains, couldn't that be because it is not faithful enough? In some of the experiments we just reviewed, this appears to be the case: subjects are simply not up to the task of reproducing what they are given. An important proportion of the story featured in Kashima (2000)'s experiment (three quarters of it, or the whole story, depending on conditions) disappears as early as the first link in the chain. Perhaps one might get better results by exploiting more efficient transmission mechanisms?

Quite possibly—but that would solve nothing. Sequential (or linear) diffusion chains would not solve the Wear-and-Tear Problem by means of unerringly faithful transmission. That is what Nicolas Claidière and Dan Sperber argue in a paper (2010) dwelling on diffusion chain experiments performed with animals. These experiments attempt to measure the diffusion of behaviors in regularly renewed populations. Most of them use the two actions method that is described in chapter 2. The subjects (for instance, monkeys) are given an occasion to grab a bit of food, and two ways of grabbing it—one way being demonstrated by the monkey's neighbor in the chain. Both techniques are roughly equal as far as efficiency is concerned: imitating a conspecific's gesture is of no particular help to grab the piece of food. There is no rationale for preferring one to the other, and therefore, there is something arbitrary about the kind of imitation that the two-actions method is supposed to elicit. Most chains are sequential, the individual exposed to the model becoming a model for the next in line, and so on. Sometimes, the chain is not strictly sequential; it is made of populations with a high replacement rate, allowing for repetition and redundancy, but very little proliferation.

All these experiments follow the general rule: they fail to create stable diffusion chains of more than ten links. Interestingly, their evolution can be captured by a model in which every animal has a very high probability of imitating previous generations. As Claidière and Sperber's model shows, a tiny number of non-imitators is enough to give birth to a lineage of increasingly frequent non-imitators. Even if the great majority of animals choose to imitate their model with high fidelity, a minority of oblivious subjects is enough to undermine diffusion. Of the two techniques used in a two-actions experiment, the one that was seeded at the start of the diffusion chain has no more than a few links to go before it loses its initial advantage.

The same reasoning could be applied to all the diffusion chains where traditions have little interest for those who pass them around. Whether it is dealing with an obscure legend or with a technique that offers no special benefit, transmission, however faithful, will not prevent the material from losing ground to the imperfections of imitation. Thus, even when behavior transmission is easy and faithful, diffusion does not follow suit. There might be a momentum, but no inertia to preserve it. The momentum needs specific mechanisms that will preserve, accumulate, and distribute it. It needs diffusion mechanisms.

For Transmission, Quantity Matters More than Quality

These diffusion mechanisms are those we have already met: repetition, redundancy, and proliferation. They are simple and well known. This section explains how they support cultural diffusion, and how they influence one another. We start with a short literary illustration.

Cultural Transmission Is No Chinese Whispers Game

In a passage from *In Search of Lost Time*, the narrator (whose fascination for the atavisms of old-stock French aristocrats is one leitmotiv of the novel) reflects on the Baron de Charlus's signature laughter:

> And he gave a little laugh that was all his own—a laugh that came down to him probably from some Bavarian or Lorraine grandmother, who herself had inherited it, in identical form, from an ancestress, so that it had tinkled now, unchanged, for a good many centuries in little old-fashioned European courts, and one could appreciate its precious quality, like that of certain old musical instruments that have become very rare.
>
> (Proust 1922/2000, 425)

It is hard to know what kind of transmission mechanism Proust has in mind here (heredity or culture). Suppose that he is dealing with cultural transmission. In that case, the preservation of the Baron's laughter is nothing short of miraculous. In his lifetime, Charlus had occasions to hear dozens of different laughs from kin and non-kin. Of all these he retained and copied only one—his grandmother's. She herself had learnt how to laugh from one source only, and so on. Any link in this diffusion chain could have spawned a reproduction error. The chain's sequential shape keeps these errors from correcting and, since every relay only has one model at their disposal, lost or conflicting sources can neither be compared nor recovered. Idiosyncratic variations or personal errors introduced by a creative grandmother cannot be detected or rooted out. They will be transmitted along with the rest, as long as the chain lasts. Why are models so scarce? Perhaps because the ancestresses' laughter does not proliferate very much (barely enough, indeed, to make it to Charlus's time). It seems clear that transmission does not take place much more often than once every two generations, exclusively among the Baron's kin.

Like Proust, people seem fascinated by simple, linear diffusion chains that resemble a Chinese Whispers game. The stories we like to tell around traditions often fit this schema: we like to think that their continuity hangs by a single thread. Perhaps that is partly because that thread is easy to follow. It connects in a direct line a handful of privileged ancestors to a lineage of faithful heirs. Sadly, when transmission hangs by a thread, it is a matter of little time before the thread starts to unravel. When stability hangs by many threads, on the contrary, a lack of fidelity, a vagary of memory, a death, or a departure may break one thread with little damage to cultural preservation. These are the diffusion chains most likely to survive.

Two engines of diffusion are absent from the transmission of the Charlus family laugh: redundancy and proliferation—that is to say the ability to compare several models or to train several others. These diffusion mechanisms, like repetition, depend on the number of transmission episodes that a given tradition undergoes. They ground the stability of diffusion chains, by making them robust and repairable, and by multiplying them, thus diluting the risks of extinction. Like the legendary hydra, culture is hard to kill because its heads grow back, and because it has several of them. These mechanisms are neutralized in classical diffusion chains experiments, as in the story of the Baron's laugh.

A Tradition Must Be Carried by Many Robust Diffusion Chains

If the hypothesis that has just been sketched out is accurate, we should observe a strong relation between the quantity of transmission episodes that a tradition benefits from, and its survival. In other words, we should see in the real world the exact inverse of what happens in sequential diffusion chain experiments, where cultural survival decreases with each additional transmission episode. Redundancy and repetition should make a difference. So should the proliferation of transmission chains.

How can one show substantive correlations between the frequency of an item's transmission and its survival? Historical linguistics has access to abundant and relevant data. Language is an interesting object for yet another reason: every public utterance of a word can be counted as an occasion to transmit it (or repeat it) to hearers. As anyone who has learnt a language knows, new words are not transmitted once and for all. Each additional use of a word stabilizes that word a little more. This sentence that you are reading adds a little something to the stability that the verb *to stabilize* enjoys in your mind. Reading it makes it a little more likely that the word, its uses, its spelling, its connotations, and so on will be present in your mind for you to reuse it (see Bybee 2010 for a thorough exploration of such usage effects on language learning).

A word's frequency in the lexicon is a good approximation of the quantity of transmission episodes that it enjoys—and it is easy enough to evaluate it quantitatively. In a 2007 paper, Mark Pagel and his coauthors showed that a word's frequency of use in Spanish, French, Greek, English, and Russian predicts the word's longevity. Such effects of frequency on the rate of lexical change are well known in linguistics (Bybee 2010, 17–19), and such a correlation is exactly what one should expect. What is more surprising is its importance: according to Pagel et al., frequency of use predicts more than half of the variance in longevity—making it the best predictor of a word's survival by far. Linguist Nicholas Ostler came to the same conclusion in quite a different way, in an investigation of language survival (2005). Two factors, according to him, best predict it: Being included in the liturgy of a written religion (like Greek or Sanskrit), and being spoken in a dense population (like Egyptian or Chinese). Of all the causes examined by Ostler, these two are the most tightly linked to transmission frequency, that is to say, to the number of occasions one has to come across someone who speaks the language and to hear it employed. Here again, what is surprising is not so much the fact that these things make a difference; it is how important that difference is, compared to the other factors that spring to mind when one thinks about language survival—state sponsorship, literary culture, colonies, and so on. Of course, word frequency and other such indicators are somewhat imprecise. They do not allow us to distinguish repetition from redundancy or proliferation. They capture a motley set of parameters. Still, they help us see that the same transmission mechanism—verbal communication—can give rise to a wide range of diffusion chains, some much more stable than others. A spoken word owes the greater share of its survival not to the fidelity of its transmission, but to the frequency of its use, and hence, of its transmission. A great many factors may influence that frequency—the word's memorability, its everyday utility, the density of the population where it circulates, its possible use in writing, and so on.

Redundancy and Repetition Make Diffusion Chains Less Fragile

The stabilizing effects of repetition and redundancy are well-explored (Eriksson and Coultas 2012). Not only do we know that they can stabilize traditions in the absence of faithful transmission, but they cannot be done without. If a cultural item can only be learnt from a single model, in one go, that item will go extinct even if it carries an evolutionary advantage for its adopters, and even if it can be easily recovered through individual reinvention (Enquist et al. 2010). The fact that we are more likely to memorize an item that we are frequently exposed to is one of the first discoveries of the psychology of memorization (Ebbinghaus 1885). The impact of repetition on cultural stability is likewise well known (Rubin 1995). What is well memorized stays longer in our minds, and thus remains available for transmission, which cannot harm a tradition's survival.

The work of the anthropologist Harvey Whitehouse on the transmission of religious rituals applies this principle in a clever way (Whitehouse 2000). According to his theory, the memorization of rituals obeys different constraints depending on how frequently they are repeated. If I want to remember a ritual that took place ten years ago, I need vivid and striking images: seldom-repeated rituals will include elements designed to leave a lasting sensory trace, like physical pain (Whitehouse's theory is meant to apply to violent initiation rituals in Papua New Guinea). If, on the contrary, a ritual is frequently celebrated, then it may tap into a different kind of memorization—the kind of memory that registers routines, repeated gestures, formulas. That type of memory is relatively indifferent to strong emotions, but unlike the first, it retains arguments and narratives. Whitehouse then predicts that these two kinds of memory select distinct types of ritual: infrequent but striking rituals, eliciting strong feelings, and routinized rituals, boring but stable by virtue of their procedural and discursive content. Thus, transmission quantity saves rituals that could never last if they were rarely performed.

The intuition behind all these theories seems quite accurate: repetition and redundancy give robustness to diffusion chains that would otherwise risk collapse. Few of the things that have been said so far would have surprised Tarde, who put repeated transmission and its links with cultural stability at the heart of his doctrine. This led him, for instance, to predict that frequently celebrated rituals should last longer than the religions they are attached to. In general, the view that repetition and redundancy make diffusion chains robust and repairable does not lack proponents (Enquist et al. 2010). Proliferation, however, has attracted less attention.

Traditions Must Proliferate in Order to Survive

In his theory of ritual transmission, Whitehouse observes that rare rituals (meant to strike memory once and leave a vivid trace) differ from routine rituals in another respect—their diffusion in space. Their distribution in time also differs: when they change, routine rituals change abruptly and all together. With the exception of a few messianic fevers, routine rituals meet with greater success than rare ones. That difference is one that, in my view, the hypothesis sketched above fails to predict or explain: routine rituals are better distributed in space than rare rituals; the latter often belong in small communities. Couldn't there be a link among the repetition of routine rituals, their success, and their diffusion?

The frequent reproduction of a ritual cannot harm its diffusion. What is often transmitted is not just better remembered and easier to reproduce in a faithful way. Frequent transmission also helps diffusion by creating chains that are more numerous, in addition to being resilient. Since routine rituals are often celebrated in front of some kind of audience, and such public displays create as many occasions of transmission as the audience is numerous, one should be more likely to encounter routine rituals, and thus to adopt them. As they cover more ground than other rituals, as they travel faster, they can also change at a faster pace, and on a larger scale.

A good diffusion may feed back on a tradition's stability. When a ritual has settled in a number of different villages, it may have started an independent diffusion chain in each of those villages. This dilutes the risks of extinction. As fragile as each diffusion chain may be on its own, it may break down without jeopardizing the stability of the tradition as a whole—while an isolated chain concentrates all the extinction risks on itself. This could explain why many New Guinea initiation rituals, performed once in a generation and owned by tiny village communities, are on the verge of extinction in spite of being extremely well memorized (Barth 1975).

Stability and Success Go Together

Diffusion (as defined in chapter 1) is, for a tradition, the fact of being found in roughly similar forms in distant points in space and time. Stability, which we could define as diffusion through time, is only one aspect of it. Diffusion may also take the shape of a massive wave reaching a wide audience in a very short time frame. Such traditions enjoy great success but little stability. Early research on cultural transmission set great store by this distinction. Tarde sharply differentiated "fashion-imitation" ("*imitation-mode*"), the mechanism behind fads and short-lived fashions, and "habit-imitation" ("*imitation-coutume*"), which he used to explain why long-standing traditions endure. I do not believe there are distinct transmission mechanisms for huge but ephemeral successes and forms of diffusion that are more lasting, though less spectacular. This being said, there is evidence that people are sensitive to the difference between the two. Parents choosing a name for their baby, for instance, can tell the fads from the stock-in-trades. They can do this in part because the two have very different life cycles (Lieberson 2000). Names that rise fast are likely to fall out of fashion with the same swiftness; parents are surprisingly good at perceiving and predicting this dynamic (Berger and Le Mens 2009).

Overly abrupt success may be a hindrance to stability. On this point, Tarde's sharp distinction between fashion and habit is vindicated. We should note, however, that what hinders stability here is not success per se, but rather the speed with which it occurs. As Jonah Berger and Gaël Le Mens show in their study of baby names, success foreshadows failure only when it is too sudden. Success as such is, on the contrary, a boost to stability. Thus the contrast of fashion and habit, howsoever intuitive it may seem, hides the fact that the two aspects of cultural diffusion go hand in hand (a few exceptions notwithstanding). Success is crucial to stability.

Our tendency to neglect the quantitative dimension of cultural diffusion seems common enough, particularly among traditionalists. Their homemade cultural histories tend to emphasize stability and conservation at the expense of success and proliferation. This testimony of a Turkish calligrapher (as reconstructed by a folklorist) is typical:

> Yusuf Sezer describes his life's duty as passing his art unspoiled to the future. Born to be a farmer in a mountain village in northern Turkey, Yusuf encountered the art of calligraphy by chance. It changed his life. Seeking deeper masters, he moved to Istanbul and received his *icazetname*, the diploma empowering him to sign his works, from Hattat Hamid Aytal, the greatest calligrapher of his generation (. . .). Through Hattat Hamid Bey, Yusuf Sezer connects to an unbroken succession of teachers and learners, stretching back to the great master of the 16th century, Seyh Hamdullah. Proud to belong to this noble genealogy, Yusuf says it is his duty to practice correctly and bequeath a robust art to the future.
>
> (Glassie 1995, 408)

The diffusion chain that ends with Yusuf Sezer is a purely linear, Bartlett-style sequence of transmission episodes. We are not told about any other student of Hamid Bey—nor is there mention of other, possibly competing schools, which would have been inspired by the teachings of master Sey Hamdullah, or would boast an affiliation with him. Many traditionalist narratives are built according to this pattern. They have erased the traces of the successes and proliferations of the tradition.

The three diffusion mechanisms—repetition, redundancy, and proliferation—allow traditions to prevail where a simple sequence of transmission episodes would fail, and enable cultural transmission to succeed even with inefficient or inaccurate transmission mechanisms. If transmission is poor on any given episode, this can be remedied by multiplying episodes—by learning several times (thanks to repetition), by combining several sources to mute transmission errors (thanks to redundancy), and lastly, by launching several diffusion chains, in the hope that a few of them may be robust enough (proliferation). All this means that high fidelity in transmission mechanisms is not necessary to diffusion. As we saw earlier, it is not sufficient either. For transmission, quantity beats quality.

Absent quantity, however, even the best kind of transmission will not compensate a lack of success. Diffusion chains that start on too small a scale may briefly take off, but must eventually taper. The old judiciary motto applies: *Testis unius, testis nullus*—one witness is no witness. When a tradition goes through only one intermediate, it depends on him in every respect. It becomes vulnerable to every accident, and any distortion.

Why Do Traditions Proliferate?

Behind repetition, redundancy, and proliferation lies transmission quantity. Why are certain things abundantly transmitted? Thanks to three things. First, they spread because they have spread before—they are known by a number of individuals, scattered in space and time. Second, because they possess what could be called (for lack of a better word), attraction: people want to transmit them when they carry them, and they want to adopt them when they encounter them. Lastly, an oft-transmitted tradition needs its carriers to interact with other individuals, so as to create diffusion chains that will extend farther than the places and times that each one of them is attached to. Individuals, of course, are not necessarily accessible to one another. Time or space may separate them. This third factor, accessibility, will be dwelt on first.

Accessibility: Certain Populations Make Contacts Easier

In any population there are sets of individuals that can interact, and other sets that are more or less deprived of that possibility. Many things can prevent communication between individuals: they may not be contemporary, they may not be near enough to one another, and so on. Any population can thus be characterized by the average *accessibility* of its members—their ability to be reached by a greater or lesser number of other individuals. In the tiny diffusion chains that get synthesized in laboratories, for instance, each participant only has contact with her two neighbors on the chain (and there can only be one episode of contact per neighbor). Such circumstances are, of course, unusual. Your own society generally gives you access to a vast proportion of your contemporaries (and these circumstances are unusual too).

A wide array of parameters influences accessibility in a population: average lifespan is one. In a population where people live longer, they will have, across their lifespan, more contemporaries than they would have had if everyone had lived less. This means that a greater fraction of the population will be accessible to most people. In this respect, a long life is like a long journey—the equivalent in time of accessibility in space. Like a population of short-lived individuals, a sedentary population that is widely spread out on a rough land has poorer accessibility than one concentrated in dense habitats. The notion of accessibility seeks to capture this kind of contrast—to give a rough idea of what share of his population the average individual can reach.

This is not exactly what social networks, as they are usually used in social science, are made to capture. They are designed to represent populations that are well known, and change little. The populations that will interest us here (for instance, in chapter 5, children's peer groups as they existed in Europe in the last four or five centuries) are rapidly renewed, and the specifics of their social organization remain unknown to us. Accessibility is not so much about social ties as it is about distances in time and space. That is not to say social networks do not affect accessibility. We should expect the populations where people have tight links with one another to make interactions easier, all else being equal. Institutions, too, can organize accessibility in a more formal way. Institutions are, among other things, ways of ensuring that their members stay in touch: post offices, churches, or journals are accessibility factors, and thus auxiliaries of cultural transmission.

Important as such sociological factors may be, they are not the only ones that determine a population's accessibility. One other factor that matters in this respect is the scale at which populations are considered. The larger the scale, the poorer accessibility becomes. If a population inhabits a vast territory, this reduces the fraction of the population that is accessible to its members: the population either gets larger or becomes less concentrated. Likewise, when we observe a population for a long stretch of time, it gets renewed many times, making it harder for its members to reach one another.

As we shall see in the next chapter, the rhythm and the workings of generational turnover vary from one society to the next, with interesting cultural consequences. Aside from this, new technologies, most of them relatively recent (like writing), can remedy a lack of accessibility. As a result of all this, the accessibility of a population for its members may undergo considerable variations depending on the scale one considers, but also on the population's demography (its density, its members' longevity, the rate of generational turnover); on what uses it makes of information storage technologies; on how its social networks are structured; on what institutions it sets up to organize accessibility.

The influence of demography on cultural transmission will be examined in the next two chapters; however, little will be said in this book about technologies and institutions. That is because I found little to add to the amazingly rich anthropological literature on these topics. We know a lot about the cultural impact of material techniques like writing (Goody 1977; Severi 2007; Bloch 1997), or cognitive techniques like the arts of memory and the other parts of rhetoric (Yates 1974). As for institutions, the issues that they raise are even thornier than those considered here.

A consequence of this omission is that most of the traditions that will interest us here are orally transmitted, by which I mean that their diffusion is not, most of the time, supported by complex techniques or supported by institutions. This word, *oral*, is deceptive in many respects (as its many detractors have not failed to note). It will serve here to point at traditions that are not even verbal (like techniques), and whose transmission need not rely on language (as we saw in chapter 2). It is also worth noting that some verbal traditions, like ritual formulas, rely on sophisticated memorization techniques to be passed on. Some of these techniques resemble writing in many respects (Severi 2007). Such traditions that rely on sophisticated tools for their transmission will not be our primary focus here.

Many Ways to Proliferate, Several Types of Diffusion Chains

Better accessibility stabilizes diffusion chains in two ways. First, in accessible populations, chains link several points separated by a lot of space, or a lot of time, and thus cross vast distances in a few steps. Such chains go through few transmission episodes, and few people. We will say they are *short*, and yet *extended*: they go far, as if walking on seven-league boots. By allowing a few individuals to reach many others, they foster traditions that consist of many chains radiating from a few focal individuals—branching-out, ramifying chains, mounted in parallel rather than sequentially. We shall say that they are *wide*.

When accessibility is mediocre, on the other hand, distances are harder to cross with a few transmission episodes, and wide diffusion chains are hard to grow. In poorly accessible populations, the chains most likely to arise are short, but not extended. They do not go far. A few long chains might arise, but those will be narrow and compact. *Long, narrow, and compact* chains cover important distances in space or time, by going through many transmission episodes. They do not proliferate very much.

Here is an analogy. In one country, whose every major city is well connected by planes, there are direct connections even between distant cities. Here, one can have a long journey passing through few cities. Here, one can reach many cities by radiating from one single point. Now imagine another country, where air transportation is less developed. There, one can hardly go very far without stopping at many other cities. From a given city, not many cities can be reached by a direct flight. Rather, they are accessible indirectly, through other cities. In that country, the length of a journey is likely to reflect the number of stopovers that it contains: a journey that includes few or no stopovers will be a short one, but long journeys will be *compact*—they will include many stopovers.

Or imagine that each individual in a diffusion chain is a node, linked to other individuals in the chain by a rope. A sequential chain, like those of Bartlett's experiments (A to B, B to C, C to D, etc.), will look like a simple knotted rope. A less sequential chain (one that branches out more) will look like a work of crochet. Narrow chains do not branch out much (though they are not completely linear), while branching-out chains, joining many parallel threads, are wide. One can easily visualize most parts of a narrow chain by having it hanging from one's hand: it mostly occupies one dimension. To see a wider chain, however, one needs to spread it out on a table: it fully occupies two dimensions. Imagine now that distance is represented by the length or rope linking each pair of knots. Some chains link great distances with a few knots: they are extended. Others are compact, covering a comparatively small distance with many knots.

In a very accessible population, diffusion chains come in many sizes and shapes, their shape being relatively unconstrained by their size. There, we will find long and wide chains; long and narrow chains; long and compact chains; long and extended chains; and here again, short chains of all varieties. In a less accessible population, however, the size and shape of diffusion chains is more constrained: wide or extended chains tend to be short, long chains tend to be compact and narrow. When accessibility is poor, the length that a chain may reach is tightly tied to the number of its knots. Long chains need to be compact and narrow.

There is little exaggeration in saying that most human populations underwent, in the course of their more or less recent history (sometimes since Neolithic times, sometimes much more recently) a series of explosive increases in accessibility. The density of populations, the importance of information storage, the evolution of institutions—all these things boomed several times in the history of our species. Today's accessibility, a legacy of all these upheavals, is somewhat abnormal. Still, the accessibility increase was neither general nor uniform. Not every population, not every kind of cultural diffusion was affected in the same way. It remains impossible for many people to reach their fellow humans, who live several centuries or hundreds of kilometers away. Aside from the traditions that are supported by sophisticated technologies, by a state apparatus or by religious institutions, many cultural forms still follow the well-worn road of long, compact, and narrow diffusion chains. This is especially true for the traditions that have been around for a very long time. Accessibility is less important if one considers five hundred years in the life of a population rather than fifty, since it is harder to reach people five hundred years away. As a consequence, compact and narrow chains were arguably the only way for lasting traditions to travel before accessibility exploded. As we go back in time (like we will do in chapter 6 when speculating on the early cultural life of our species), recent increases in accessibility will seem more remote and less relevant.

Cultural Selection—Many Are Called, Few Are Chosen

After accessibility, the second root of a tradition's success is its intrinsic appeal. The best way to introduce it is to look at cultural selection.

Diffusion is difficult. The main bulk of what gets transmitted does not get diffused. There is (to use the popular phrase) a cultural selection that invites many and selects but a few. Success is not evenly shared among traditions: there does not seem to be any upper limit to the fame of the most popular, but little is left for the obscure majority. Such distributions of popularity have been shown to obtain for first names (Hahn and Bentley 2003), for the frequency of word use (Zipf 1935), for languages (as we saw earlier), even for the success of dog breeds (Bentley et al. 2007). It seems intuitively true of the spread of religions as well: a handful of creeds, all originating more or less from the same stock, share the souls of most believers between themselves.

In many such cases, researchers try to identify a power law, a well-known type of statistical distribution studied by social scientists since Pareto. If the success of books, dog breeds, or first names follows such a law, it means that if we rank books, dogs, or names according to their success, we will find fewer dog breeds, first names, or books in the more successful categories, the number of items in the category being a power function of success (however we measure it). If we want to know, for instance, how many books have sold a million copies, we have to divide a million by itself a certain number of times. Power laws are extremely unegalitarian. Unlike other distributions, they specify no upper limit to success. Power law distributions, in other words, are extreme. They are not, however, the only extreme distributions. Most of the distributions we have just cited are merely extreme. They follow power laws approximately, or locally. The phrase is often employed in quite a lax sense—for instance, when used to describe book sales, there is a tendency to call a power law any kind of scale free distribution (Clauset, Shalizi, and Newman 2009). The nuance will be of little concern for us here. I am only interested in extreme distributions, marked by extreme inequalities, where the upper limits of success are hard to know—with or without power laws.

Inequalities of cultural success should not be surprising. They are the trademark of all diffusion processes. Whenever something's success depends on any kind of transmission, this makes it very variable (Simon 1955). The most widespread flu epidemics are also the rarest, small epidemics being vastly more numerous; and we can hardly predict how lethal the next big one will turn out to be. The number of birds falling to the avian flu thus follows an extreme distribution (Small, Walker, and Tse 2007).

Cultural success is extreme in all the cases we considered. Is this true of cultural stability as well? Relevant data being relatively less easy to find, that hypothesis is only plausible. Theoretically, unequal success should translate into unequal longevity, since the stability of traditions is an aspect of their diffusion and a consequence of their success. As we saw, the most popular first names are generally the most durable (though the correlation is far from perfect). There are at least three additional reasons to expect such a relation. The first is that diffusion has self-perpetuating qualities: traditions that are already much represented in a population are more likely to be transmitted there. Second, chances are that those traditions did not owe their diffusion to random chance alone, but also to a form of appeal that will boost their future diffusion.

In practice, though, cultural survival is harder to measure than is success at a given point in time. One needs data that cover a time-span wide enough to spot the longest-living traditions, yet fine-grained enough to spot the short-lived ones, and homogenous enough to make sure that one is measuring the same thing at various points of time. The data on children's games that will be presented in chapter 5, or those of Pagel et al. (2007) on the survival of Indo-European words (this chapter), do not quite meet these demands. Still, interesting data exist, bearing on the survival of firms (Ormerod 2006) or utopian communes (Stephan and Stephan 1973). As predicted, it follows extreme distributions: most firms or communes do not survive their first few years, but the few survivors may endure indefinitely. These institutions are rather far from the kind of tradition that will be studied here (although their survival often implies the transmission of several traditions).

Some of the best data are about a rather curious example, the diffusion of black-capped chickadee songs (Ficken and Weise 1984; Ficken and Popp 1995; Baker and Gammon 2008; Baker, Baker, and Baker 2001). Ornithologists know that these birds learn their songs at least in part from their conspecifics: chickadees raised in isolation have abnormal vocalizations (Ficken and Weise 1984). Some songs are culturally transmitted: they are known by every bird in a given region, but otherwise unknown, even in neighboring regions distant by a few kilometers. The majority of songs, however, are individual innovations that other chickadees never take up. This last fact explains a big share of the inequalities in success between songs. Out of 184 types of gargles recorded by Ficken and Weise (1984), the majority (104) account for less than 0.1 percent of the total of recorded gargles. Even if one chooses to ignore all the idiosyncratic, merely individual gargles, and focus only on those gargles that have been adopted by different birds, inequalities do not disappear. Two very frequent gargles, each covering a large territory, dominate all other gargles, at every recording point. Other gargles are usually limited to one or two observation points (Baker et al. 2000 present similar data). Analogous observations have been made for chimpanzee cultures. In an observation of transmitted know-hows, Hans Kummer and Jane Goodall thus remarked that "of the many such behaviors observed, only a few will be passed on to other individuals, and seldom will they spread through the whole troop" (1985, 13).

Does the distribution of longevity follow that of success? Apparently so. When Baker and Gammon (2008) analyzed the survival of eighty-nine transmitted gargles, they found that a third of them lasted no more than one season. The second third lasted between two and seven seasons (with some lapses), while the last remaining third lived as long as could be measured. These last songs were also the most popular, being shared by two to six times more birds. Their success may not entirely be a matter of chance: it appears to be linked to certain acoustic properties. How long could these survivors last? Probably a great deal longer than the observation period. Ficken and Popp (1995) recorded eleven gargles that had not changed over a nineteen-year interval (before they stopped recording); in that interval a typical black-clapped chickadee population will have been renewed six or seven times. To extrapolate, the human equivalent would be four centuries at least.

Similarly sophisticated work on the survival of human tradition is hard to come by, but some traditions, like first names, are well documented and easy to treat statistically. Wherever it has been measured (in Europe and the United States—Hahn and Bentley, 2003; Lieberson, 2000), the success of first names follows extreme distributions—and so does their stability.

In their 2009 study of French first names (already alluded to), Berger and Le Mens note that, during the twentieth century, half of the first names they study become very rare in less than forty years after their popularity peak. If all the twenty thousand first names in the INSEE (French National Institute for Demography and Statistics) repertory had a forty-year half-life, very few of them could last several centuries; but of course, many did. Most of the dominant first names (for boys at least) date back to medieval times (Lieberson, 2000). The INSEE data necessarily underestimate the longevity of some first names—those that will come back from the cold in a few decades, those that barely survive in obscurity. On the other hand, they are forced to overlook very rare names (personal information protection laws forbid the analysis of first names that have been given less than three times). Presumably, the two biases should roughly balance one another, leaving us with a plausible estimate—enough to see that survival is distributed in a very unbalanced way.

More often, the gap that separates the minority of survivors from the rest seems so obvious that nobody takes pains to measure it. Thus, historians of literature agree that only a tiny proportion of published novels from the past is being read today—a tiny share even of noticeable successes, not to mention the manuscripts confined to file-drawers. Here is what Franco Moretti wrote after analyzing the catalogues of a dozen traveling libraries in the British empire (Moretti 1998, 2000):

> *Alice Grey, Astrologer, An Old Family Legend, Anna, Banditt's Bride, The Bridal of Donnamore, Borderers, Beggar Girl* . . . It was the first page of an 1845 catalog: Columbell's circulating library, in Derby: a small collection, of the kind that wanted only successful books. But today, only a couple of titles still ring familiar. The others, nothing. Gone. (. . .) The

majority of books disappears forever. And "majority" actually misses the point: if we set today's canon at two hundred titles (which is a very high figure), they would still be about 0.5 percent of all published novels.

(Moretti, 2000, 207)

Moretti overstates his case only a little: not all the novels he mentioned really disappeared. Some did not make it into the academic canon, but still won over a few amateurs. Others had no such luck, but left a few copies that might find readers some day, and today suffice to grant them a form of virtual survival. Not all of them fell as low as *The Bridal of Donnamore*. Still, all of them owe everything to technologies and institutions that allow them artificially to overstay their welcome among readers. This is a rather poignant illustration of the lack of inertia for cultural transmission: what gets transmitted once seldom gets transmitted once more. Yet even for those traditions that do give rise to a diffusion chain (like the novels of this catalogue, read by thousands), past survival is no guarantee of future survival. The momentum dissipates. Only for a handful of items is diffusion sufficiently wide to avoid this fate.

These traditions certainly had luck—I mean that their success is not simply due to their own merits. Diffusion phenomena naturally produce extreme distributions, and they would favor certain traditions over others even if all traditions were identical (Bentley et al. 2007); still, there are reasons to suspect that the success of certain traditions involves more than luck.

Traditions Survive Cultural Selection by Being Attractive

Is cultural selection a matter of chance? Not entirely. Some traditions are more likely to withstand it because they are more attractive. A curious phenomenon, documented by historians of books, allows us to see cultural selection at work.

In his work on traveling British libraries, Franco Moretti noticed that smaller libraries (as compared to bigger ones) offered more classics to their readers, as a proportion of their other titles. (Classics were defined as the books featured in Richard Bentley's "Modern novels" collection, or written by an author featured in the *Dictionary of National Biography*). In big libraries, the classics are surrounded with a large proportion of lesser-known, lesser-diffused books. In spite of this, small libraries do not seem to harbor more conservative tastes. For instance, they offer as many foreign language books as do bigger libraries, relative to the size of their collection. Big libraries also buy classics—they buy more of them in absolute numbers (though never as many as they could). Why do they have fewer classics, relative to the size of their collection? Because they are wealthy enough to go further down their priority list, and diversify. Other examples of this effect can be found. In Amiens, in the sixteenth century, an analysis of post-mortem inventories shows that the most successful books (books of hours) are twice more represented in the libraries of small shopkeepers, who possess few books, than in the belongings of wealthier book owners (Chartier 1982). This relation between a library's size and the proportion of classics in it is a signature of cultural selection. If books were randomly acquired, with any book being worth the same as any other book, a classic would be as likely as any other piece to enter any catalogue, or to be left out. Classics would be as numerous, relatively speaking, in big libraries as in smaller ones. Our failure to observe this shows that classics are somewhat more appealing (which could be due to their reputation, literary worth, or simply cheaper prices).

One might use this repertoire-size effect to reveal the preferences that guide cultural selection. The fact, for instance, that the effect obtains for classics but not for foreign authors—foreign language books being as numerous, in relative terms, in small libraries as in big ones—suggests that an author's nationality is not much of a constraint on librarians' choices. British authors are neither in front of others nor behind, on the priorities list. This is not trivial since, as Moretti notes, the share of British authors in the libraries that he studies was rather small, and waning. Yet the absence of a repertoire-size effect suggests that these books were as much in demand as others (as far as librarian demand was concerned).

The selection that acts on books in traveling libraries seems inversely proportional to purchasing power. With money and space to buy and store more books, big libraries are somewhat spared the task of choosing. In a world of rich libraries, the success of books does not depend on their appeal as much as it would in a world of small traveling libraries. More generally, we can assume that a tradition's intrinsic appeal will be more advantageous when proliferation is hindered. The more accessible a population, the easier it is for diffusion mechanisms (proliferation, repetition, and redundancy) to work. When things are easy, a tradition can transmit abundantly without being very attractive. Only in more difficult circumstances should attraction kick in. Some institutions, some techniques, some demographic conditions will yield success for nothing, and diffusion for free. To take a random example, the authorized biography of Leonid Brezhnev, a collective brainchild of the

Marxist-Leninist Institute of the CPSU's Central Committee, was not exactly a crowd-pleaser. As Clive James put it in his review:

> Here is a book so dull that a whirling dervish could read himself to sleep with it. If you were to recite even a single page in the open air, birds would fall out of the sky and dogs drop dead.
>
> (James 1978)

Whether James was being fair or not is beside the point, as far as the diffusion of Brezhnev's biography was concerned. It was backed by an institutional and technical machinery that made large-scale diffusion inevitable in the short run. It was bound to hit some easy targets: those who were more or less coerced to pay attention to it; the ideologically committed; the historians; those with nothing better to read. Of all the individuals ever exposed to the biography, these readers probably constituted only a tiny share; but, thanks to the disseminating power of the Soviet complex, a tiny share of the total was still a huge number, considering the work's quality.

Most traditions have no such luck. They are not born in the middle of a dense web of accessibility. What happens to them? They will not go far without help from our three diffusion mechanisms—repetition, redundancy, proliferation. All three need to be fueled either by accessibility or by attraction: disfavored traditions need some intrinsic appeal to make up for unfavorable circumstances.

Attraction Can Be Linked to a Restricted Context, or More General

A practice or an idea possesses attraction when it is more likely than others to be taken up or retransmitted. This notion does not do much more than point at a motley bunch of factors. So many things can make a practice attractive! Its success often consists of a variegated set of contingent causes, specific to a particular setting. Legend has it that the Manchu haircut (a tight braid in the back behind a shaved head) had been adopted because it freed the field of vision of steppe raiders. Others say the braid could be used as a pillow to sleep on the rough. Unsatisfying just-so-stories, perhaps: there are many other ways to get one's hair out of one's eyes, or to improvise a cushion. The braid haircut probably served for a while as an ethnic marker of Manchu-ness (though here again, many other signs could serve the same purpose, and did). Either way, it was such a strong symbol for the Manchu Qing dynasty that it decided, upon its accession, to make it mandatory for all the emperor's subjects, on pains of death.

Is there any commonality that could link all the things that made it desirable, for so many people, to cut their hair in the Manchu style? The wind of the steppe in the horse-riders' hair; a desire to self-identify as a Manchu; the fear of capital punishment—the list hardly suggests a general formula that could predict the success of the haircut in all circumstances. Cultural attraction is often like this. It hangs by too many threads; too many variegated, heterogeneous, contingent, tangled threads. It beggars description. At first glance, there is little to be said of it that would be general and specific enough to catch a theoretician's attention.

Proponents of cultural epidemiology, and some other psychological approaches to culture, do not see things in quite this way. These researchers have no trouble acknowledging the fact that traditions usually succeed for local and contingent reasons, in unique contexts. Some practices, like the Manchu braid, owe almost everything to a local factor of attraction (the Qing edict) that is best studied in the usual historical fashion. Other factors of attraction, however, are much more general. They weigh on the choices of a great variety of human beings, in a wide array of contexts. Their existence implies that some ideas or practices almost always enjoy a slight advantage in diffusion: they appeal to almost everyone (Sperber and Hirschfeld 2004; Atran 2003b; Boyer 2001).

Such phenomena have been studied for a long time. Sound symbolism is one example. According to a hypothesis that dates back at least to Plato's *Cratylus*, certain sounds are more appropriate than others to express certain meanings; indeed, psychologists have long known that people in very different places use rather similar sounds to designate certain things. You are more likely to give the name *Buba* to a round shape, and the name *Kiki* to a spiked shape, rather than the other way around (even if you cannot read or write—Köhler 1947). It seems that languages are like people in this respect: different languages tend to converge on similar meanings to name similar things. Native speakers of English are capable of guessing (above chance levels) which one of those two Yoruba words, "tuun" and "luk," means "deep," and which one means "superficial" (Slobin 1968).[1] Such findings have been extensively replicated. One could interpret these results by saying that human languages have a tendency to evolve toward those sounds that intuitively seem to have a natural fit with a given meaning. Word sounds, in other words, are subject to a very general factor of attraction that favors some sounds over others.

---

1. "Tuun" is "deep," "Luk" is "superficial."

Traditions Are Appealing in Many Ways, Not All of Them Cognitive

One may raise a distinction between two kinds of properties that help the transmission and diffusion of a tradition: *cognitive* attraction versus *motivational* attraction. A tradition has cognitive appeal when it fits our information-processing capacities. This makes it easy to store and reproduce. It is motivationally appealing when it taps into emotional or decisional mechanisms that make us want to use or transmit it. The first kind of appeal has to do with the ease of communicating, recalling, and reproducing it. The second kind bears on whether or not we want to do all these things.

On top of this, attraction (of the cognitive or motivational kind) is more or less *local* or *general*. Some traditions are easy to understand or remember for some people only: the rules of English for modal verbs, which we met in chapter 1, are easier to learn for today's English speakers. This, however, was not necessarily true of previous speakers of English, for whom other rules seemed more intuitive. The same can be said of motivational attraction: its scope can be quite restricted. Qing dynasty law was a strong incentive for its subjects to wear the Manchu haircut, but it had little effect beyond the borders of the Empire or after its downfall.

(The distinction between local and general factors of attraction might be misunderstood, especially by people taught by dual inheritance theory, as a mere restatement of Boyd and Richerson's distinction between "content biases" and "context biases." The two are not equivalent, however. "Context biases" essentially capture phenomena of social influence, like conformity and deference. (As we saw in chapter 3, Boyd and Richerson view these in a way that is quite different from the one proposed in this book.) Local attraction is much more general. For instance, the reasons that made the Qing braid attractive had little to do with the prestige or numbers of those who wore it, and everything to do with local politics.)

Among new approaches to cultural transmission, cultural epidemiology (the chief inspiration for this book) is probably the one that has given the most thought to cognitive attraction. Traditions are not just ideas: they also exist as behaviors and public manifestations. Nevertheless, cultural epidemiology chiefly studies them in their mental form, asking such questions as: How do we represent religious beliefs? Why are certain myths better remembered than others? And so on.

How do cultural epidemiologists explain the success and survival of traditions? Primarily by studying the way our mind deals with them. Not every tradition is equally easy to represent and retain: some tales are simpler to remember, some scientific theories are more intuitive. Those traditions get a more robust diffusion: they are more likely to endure through time and space.

Cultural epidemiology sometimes presents itself as a purely cognitive approach to culture—a study of the role of memory, categorization, reasoning, and other ways of processing information, for cultural transmission. Its toolbox was not originally meant to include other mechanisms, like emotions or motivations (Sperber 1998). In reality its current practitioners are more opportunistic, and they do not look at culture through the lens of communication or memory alone. They do not think culture is made of packs of stored information—they make some room for the fact that traditions also elicit emotions and motivations in their carriers. This interest for non-cognitive factors could, it is true, be a little more conspicuous; in general, psychological theories of cultural transmission tend to have eyes only for our capacity to transmit or to memorize traditions efficiently. They have very little to say about our desire to pass them on—to pass them on *abundantly*.

If human traditions were simply stored on a hard drive, somewhere in some kind of digital collective conscience, they would need to be accurately entered into the machine, and faithfully retained. It would take nothing more. Their preservation would ensure their survival. Real traditions are different: they are carried by thousands of human beings, who live, who die, who travel. If they are to reach the times and places that these carriers inhabit, they need to be transmitted many times to human beings. Unlike computers, humans are subject to desires and aversions. If they like a tradition, they will transmit it abundantly: they will find ways of remembering and understanding it even if it is hard. If they dislike it, they will neither transmit nor retain it, even when it would be easily done. Diffusion, thus, would not take place if traditions did not awaken a desire to spread them.

What characterizes cultural epidemiology (or should, at any rate, characterize it) is not that it studies cognitive rather than motivational attraction. Rather, it is an interest for general as opposed to local attraction. Some traditions owe their success to very general cognitive mechanisms, but there are general motivational mechanisms that play a similar role. Some emotions are surprisingly uniform from one society to the next (we will study disgust as an example), and the traditions that rely on them may thus be stabilized. Certain techniques reliably give a useful result, whatever the context, which motivates their users to make them into stable practices.

If cognitive attraction draws so much attention, it might be because the "cold" psychology of information processing is more accessible to today's cognitive science than "hotter" mechanisms like emotions and desires. Specialists of the latter would probably beg to differ. Whatever the case may be, the relative neglect of motivation has at least one other cause. That cause is the prejudice according to which, when cultural transmission is concerned, quality matters more than quantity. The storage of cultural information, the faithfulness of communication and memory, are all related to cognitive capacities. The motivation to reproduce or to adopt a practice contributes to its proliferation, but not to its faithful preservation. It falls outside the scope of the Bartlettian vision of culture, in which everything rests on the fidelity of transmission and the stability of memory.

For a narrative to survive a Bartlettian diffusion chain, it does not really matter whether subjects are motivated to reproduce it in great quantity—as long as the narrative can be stored, and passed on. Experimenters solve the motivational problem of transmission in the simplest fashion. They pay their subjects (or they find other ways of securing their good will) to follow their instruction: transmit the story once and only once. In a more realistic setting, subjects may not want to retell some stories even once, while other stories would prompt endless repetitions. This limit of the experimental design was recognized early on by two pioneers of the experimental study of rumor transmission:

> In place of the deep-lying motivations that normally sustain rumor-spreading, we find that the 'Go' of the laboratory rumor depends upon the subject's willingness to cooperate with the experimenter. In the experiment the subject strives for accuracy. His own fears, hates and hopes are not aroused. He is not the spontaneous rumor agent that he is in ordinary life.
>
> (Allport & Postman 1947, 64)

Cultural success is neutralized in Bartlettian transmission chains. So are the forms of attraction that bring it about. The only mechanisms left are cognitive constraints on memory and transmission. My point here is not to dismiss these constraints—far from it. A tradition that cannot proliferate absolutely needs to be accurately transmitted and safely stored if it is to survive for any length of time. A tradition's survival, however, is but one dimension of its diffusion. Its second dimension, success, is flattened in laboratory-made diffusion chains. In a way this makes sequential chains a superb tool to study memorization and learning biases. Sooner or later, the distortions that any material undergoes accumulate to give us a very accurate picture of the subjects' cognitive proclivities and biases. Tom Griffiths and his team have shown it many times (Xu and Griffiths 2010; Reali and Griffiths 2010). They have also shown, however, that the effects of such biases can be blunted by making the transmission chain redundant (Griffiths, Lewandowsky, and Kalish 2013). In other words, the power of cognitive constraints gets diluted as we move toward more realistic transmission chains.

I am not trying to establish a rigid separation between cognitive mechanisms (which would be free of any connection with their motivational or emotional counterparts) and motivational mechanisms (which would not process any information). The distinction is obviously not watertight. That the two aspects interact is evident in the very first stages of perception: visual or auditory information is processed in ways that reflect differential allocations of attention, motivating us to devote more or less effort to certain perceptual tasks. Conversely, emotions are complex bundles of mental functions that include the perception and memorization of specific sitmuli. Disgust is a case in point, as we shall see. The motivational and the cognitive do go together. Ideas that are easy to treat and store may often also be the ones eliciting strong motivations, making them relevant and more likely to spread.

Why (by the way) should we expect the two to go hand in hand? First, because specialized emotional mechanisms (like fear or liking) may be better equipped to treat certain pieces of information, and to direct attentional resources to them. Second, stimuli that are easy on the mind are also experienced as emotionally rewarding, simply because they impose a very light cognitive load on us. Psychologists Reber, Winikielman, and Schwarz (1998) have shown that their subjects deemed more pleasant, attractive, or beautiful the stimuli that presented neater contrasts—a black dot on a white background is rated as better-looking than a black dot on a gray background—or stimuli that had become more familiar for having been observed many times. Similar results obtain with stimuli that are easy to treat for other reasons. Blurred images, for instance, are less appreciated, even when the blurring is so faint as to slip beyond conscious awareness.

Although they do overlap in many cases, motivational attraction (a rather overlooked cause of cultural success) is best thought of as separate from its cognitive counterpart. This distinction is meant to avoid reducing cultural transmission to its sole cognitive dimension—a frequent temptation that is illustrated below by the confusions surrounding the idea of cultural memory.

Transmission Is Not Memorization, Culture Is Not Collective Memory

There is no shortage of best-selling books, from psychology to marketing, trying to explain cultural diffusion. On reading most of them, one gets the impression that diffusion is caused by two things: Its being promoted by prestigious influentials, and its compatibility with human memory. Here is Malcolm Gladwell's *The Tipping Point* (from a passage where the author likens cultural diffusion to an epidemic):

> In epidemics, the messenger matters: messengers are what make something spread. But the content of the message matters too. And the specific quality that a message needs to be successful is the quality of "stickiness." Is the message—or the food, or the movie, or the product—memorable?
>
> (Gladwell 2000, 92)

This deceptively simple claim plays on the ambiguity of the word *memorable*. A memorable meal is a very good meal, but not necessarily an easily described meal, let alone a set of easily replicated recipes. The kind of food that lends itself to global diffusion is not so much memorable as it is pleasant. There are, to be sure, conditions where recipes must be easy enough to describe and memorize, if they are to propagate and survive, but today's globalized food culture is nothing like that. We have all the institutional and technological means at our disposal to solve the problem of storing and disseminating millions of recipes (some of them secret, some of them dauntingly complex). Memorizing a good macaroon recipe is no small feat, but this difficulty is of little consequence for the success of macaroons.

It will not always be relevant, to be sure, to distinguish macaroon-memorability from poem-memorability; the two things may go hand in hand. What we risk in merging the two is to end up believing that cognitive memorability is the key to cultural diffusion, and to jettison motivational attraction as a consequence. This sometimes happens to cultural epidemiologists—here, for instance:

> In oral traditions that characterize most of human cultures throughout history, a narrative cannot be transmitted and achieve cultural success unless it stands the test of memory (Rubin 1995, Sperber 1996). Therefore, all else being equal, a more memorable narrative has a competitive advantage over a less memorable one. (. . .) Minimally

counter-intuitive folktales are more memorable and easier to understand and transmit to others. As a result of their superior memorability and understandability (but not necessarily other characteristics) they are more likely to become culturally popular.

(Norenzayan et al. 2006, 531–32)

In this article, the anthropologist Ara Norenzayan and his colleagues demonstrate a correlation between the memorability of a certain type of story (the type that includes some counterintuitive elements, but not too many) and its cultural success. The attraction of "minimally counterintuitive" stories was first explored in the lab, by comparing their memorization with that of other stories. The team then went online to show that, in the Grimm brothers' collection of tales, those that fitted their description of minimal counterintuitiveness got more hits on Google. This effect is what backs the authors' claim: a story's memorability explains its success. In the case at hand, though, it is quite dubious. Google-fame is not linked to memorization in the same way that diffusion in oral culture depends on remembrance. An orally transmitted tale (I use the word "oral" merely to refer to the sort of transmission that is unsupported by high-capacity information storage technologies) needs to be preserved and reproduced by storytellers; but Google users have the means to preserve and transmit cultural items without memorizing them (individually or collectively). As a result, the engines of success on the Internet (and in all places where information is cheaply stored) are not strictly cognitive.

Granted, motivational attraction cannot be entirely dissociated from memorability: there is a link among a tradition's being interesting, its attracting attention, and its leaving a vivid mark in memories. As Pascal Boyer and Charles Ramble (2001, 538) remark, a tradition's memorability may not cause its cultural success, but the causality might be reversed. Memorability could be enhanced by attraction. It could even be studied as an indicator of attraction. This makes sense, but in this case memorability is only a reflection of attraction, not a cause of success in its own right.

Even in oral cultures, memorability is not the key to cultural diffusion, for two reasons. First, memorization and memorability need to be distinguished. Not everything that is memorable gets memorized, and many things are hard to retain but are remembered nevertheless. Ebbinghaus, who trained himself to rote-learn lists of numbers, showed that repetition and redundancy can fixate the most arid material; even very coarse mnesic tricks can turn the dumbfounding into the memorable. I am not denying that some traditions are intrinsically worse than others as far as remembering them is concerned—but there are ways around these difficulties. Genealogies, lists of gods and ancestors, and other staples of traditional oral cultures seem, after all, as memory-friendly as a phonebook.

Second, the links between a tradition's success and its more or less accurate retaining vary from one population to the next. Two conditions need to obtain if diffusion is to reflect memorization: those who do the remembering need to live long, and to be accessible to others. Though simple, these conditions are nothing trivial, as shown by an article by model-builder Pontus Strimling and his colleagues (Strimling, Enquist, and Eriksson 2009). They compared the effects, on the spread of a cultural item, of two parameters: transmission probability and retention probability. When a population is never renewed (meaning that no one ever leaves or dies), everyone eventually gets exposed to every tradition, however poorly transmitted. Retention makes all the difference. When the model is made more realistic, however, by letting the population lose or gain members at regular intervals, things change. The faster a population gets renewed, the more weight is given to transmission probability (as opposed to retention): stable traditions need to be adopted by newcomers frequently enough to compensate for the loss of their former carriers. (This effect is modulated by the frequency of interactions between individuals. When possibilities of interaction are numerous, every tradition eventually reaches a certain level of diffusion, even traditions that are not particularly likely to be transmitted.)

A population thus needs a certain degree of accessibility for memorization to foster cultural stability. If people have few interactions, or if generational turnover keeps them away from other generations, accessibility will be mediocre. Memory will then lose some of its importance, for the benefit of another diffusion factor: the kind of motivational appeal that elicits an urge to transmit and adopt traditions.

We have been taught by the classics of social science (mostly its French, Durkheimian current) to see culture as a society's "collective memory" (Halbwachs 1925/1992). The idea is alluring, but even if we take it figuratively, it is as misleading as it is evocative. The problem is not simply that societies are too fluid and difficult to grasp to be ascribed the kind of memories that we attribute to individuals. The real problem lies deeper. The metaphor of collective memory asks us to reduce cultures to sets of mental or public traces, stored in monuments, books, computers, or brains. Culture, however, does not last by staying stored in quiet preservation. It lives by proliferating and disseminating. Memorization is but one phase of this process, and not the most challenging or important step at that. Traditions may, of course, be used to learn things about the past. The past, after all, is where they come from. Carrying information about that past is not, however, their function: their history did not shape them to be retained faithfully, let alone to preserve a people's memory.

When Does Psychology Drive Culture?

Cultural epidemiology thus studies the psychological factors (cognitive or not) that influence cultural diffusion by endowing some traditions with attraction. Among these factors, it prefers to focus on the most general—the most robust and least variable aspects of emotions, memory, perception, and so on. It aims to explain very general trends in cultural evolution, using hypotheses that are wider in scope (and thus more risky) than the sort of theorizing most anthropologists are comfortable with. Following in the wake of Lévi-Strauss's ambitions, it looks at cultural forms as reflections of universal structures of the human mind. In a word, it has a habit of thinking big.

This theoretical ambition also carries with it a kind of remoteness from the specifics of cultural history. By concentrating on the most generally appealing aspects of traditions—those that affect almost everyone, almost everywhere—one chooses to neglect local factors that might be much more important, albeit on a smaller scale. One also invites skepticism. Many doubt that there is any such thing as a universal structure of the human mind, beyond vague or trivial commonalities. Its existence seems at odds with the daunting variability of human cultures; its study incompatible with the concern for contextualization shared by most human sciences. Does it have any impact, when measured against constraints of a more local kind—political, economic, or social? Even when they admit that universal psychological constraints could weigh on cultural history, the skeptics suspect that their action would be too diffuse to be of any interest. All we can hear from listening to universal mechanisms is a weak, monotonous background hum. What we want to listen to are the specific melodies that stand out against that background.

This section tries to address these concerns. Yes, we need to think big, even when this entails a risk of losing sight of specificities. That research program is not the only possible one, or the most adapted to the usual objectives of social science; but it is the most appropriate to address the big questions that concern this book: why are there stable traditions at all? Why are humans so cultural? The cultural impact of the most general psychological mechanisms is not as weak or as uniform as critics suspect it to be. More precisely, it is not uniformly weak. In some cases it is truly nothing more than a negligible background hum, but it can grow loud and distinctive under certain conditions. It all depends on the kind of transmission chain that one considers. In long, narrow, and compact diffusion chains, general attraction is strong. Its effects are diluted in other chains. Let us illustrate this point by a handful of case studies, showing how very general psychological factors may influence diffusion.

Politeness Norms Last Longer if They Tap into Our Sense of Disgust

In one article on the evolution of social norms, philosopher Shaun Nichols (2002) makes a prediction concerning the history of European manners. Many etiquette norms (table manners, norms of posture, ways of behaving in polite society) seem arbitrary or pointless, but blind conservatism is not the only thing that keeps them alive. A sizeable fraction of them owe their stability and success to the emotions that are elicited when they are broken (or when one figures that they could be). Nichols believes, along with many psychologists, that some features of disgust ("core disgust"—Rozin and Fallon 1987) are well preserved across cultural boundaries. He thus predicts that etiquette norms prohibiting actions that elicit "core disgust" are more likely than others to be sustained and enforced, and less likely to be displaced. Inspired by Norbert Elias's work on the evolution of manners in Renaissance Europe (Elias 1939), Nichols examined the rules laid down in Erasmus's widely read guide, *On Good Manners for Boys*, and asked independent coders to state, for each rule in a sample collected from representative sections of the book, whether the conduct it prohibited could elicit "core disgust," as defined by a checklist (first group of coders), and whether it was still part of the rules of etiquette that they were used to (second group of coders). The study found that most etiquette rules prohibiting some core-disgusting behavior made it to our own time, while most of those that did not failed to stay the course. Elias argued that the slow rise of "clean" manners in Europe was due to "an expanding threshold of repugnance" (Elias in Nichols 2002, 20). Nichols disagrees: the "threshold of repugnance" did not expand by an inch. Instead, European etiquette slowly rose above that threshold, because cultural diffusion worked best for the rules that seemed the most intuitive and the least arbitrary.

In this case, it is hard to judge whether Nichols's interpretation fits the facts better than that of Elias; but other studies show that cultural diffusion travels a longer way when a tradition recruits our sense of disgust.

Anthropologists Daniel Fessler and Carlos Navarete (2003) showed, in a comparative study of seventy-eight cultures, that meat is the most tabooed kind of food, by far. In the twelve cultural areas that they studied, meat-related taboos are more—usually much more—numerous. Having considered and dismissed a range of alternative explanations, they conclude that the reason why "meat is good to taboo" is because it is a privileged target for the human sense of disgust. These studies are not the only ones that show how disgust can help cultural diffusion. The Heath brothers, who studied urban legends, noticed that modern scary tales show an uncanny predilection for nauseating rumors: dirty restaurants that steal your organs, or epidemics where victims see their brains occupied by colonies of tiny worms. The popularity of these tales is immense even when they are compared to stories that induce other strong emotions (like fear or compassion) (Heath, Bell, and Sternberg 2001).

Among the Kwaio, Beliefs about Spirits Survived by Being Intuitive

Among the Kwaio who live in the mountainous center of Malaita Island (Solomon archipelago), almost everyone claimed (at the time of Roger Keesing's fieldwork) to have interactions with ancestral spirits called *adalo* (Keesing 1982, 33–59). They can be met in dreams or prayed and sacrificed to, and divination yields information as to their intentions and ways of action—crucial information, since *adalo* are behind many significant events of daily life. When taro crops are bad, when someone falls ill, one will try to find out which *adalo* caused the trouble, and why; for *adalo* do no gratuitous harm. They use their omniscience to prevent, detect, and punish all sorts of misdemeanors (Keesing 1982, 42). Relations with *adalo* are highly strategic since their intentions, however menacing, are seldom obvious. One needs constantly to bear them in mind and think ahead of them. What *adalo* know or ignore about mortals, what they might learn that could bring punishment down on a Kwaio, is a constant concern. Yet apart from the way *adalo* get and use strategic information bearing on human perils and rewards, most Kwaio show very little interest in the properties of *adalo*, their nature, or their place in the universe. Ideas become extremely vague when conversation drifts away from immediate strategic interaction with the spirits.

According to Pascal Boyer's interpretation of Keesing's ethnography (Boyer 2001) belief in *adalo* (as happens with many other ghosts, spirits, and ancestors) owes its stability to a universal human propensity to search for intelligent agency. Detecting intentional agents, the theory goes, is a crucial task for us, and evolution has equipped us with a specific psychological faculty for that purpose. Given the importance and complexity of this task, given the costs of failing to detect intentional agency when it occurs, our intention-detection devices tend to get activated too readily. Still, when they do, we do not simply dismiss the signal as a false alert.

Attributing an event to an intentional agent, real or not, authorizes many interesting inferences on matters of strategic importance, like the agent's dispositions toward us, its overall plans, its future actions, and so on. The appeal of strategic information, combined with the ease of inferring it, can easily trap attention and defuse skepticism. All other things being equal, a belief that allows us to make sense of events by appealing to a form of intentional agency will enjoy a favorable prejudice. Boyer puts forward this hypothesis as a means of explaining the popularity and longevity of *adalo* beliefs. It also sheds light on some features of those beliefs: why they leave so many properties of the spirits unspecified, and why they focus so narrowly on strategically relevant information at the expense of everything else.

Generally Attractive Traditions Do Not Always Prevail

Let us suppose that all the authors just cited were right. Meat taboos, belief in *adalo* spirits, some rules in the canon of European manners, are successful and stable mostly because they appeal to universal properties of the human mind. Are these cases typical of cultural transmission in general? Or must some special conditions be met if we want cultural items to survive by means of their universal psychological effects? I think that cultural diffusion, in the cases we just reviewed, takes place in special circumstances—not weird, not uncommon, but special.

What makes diffusion special in the case of European norms of etiquette is indeed quite banal: Nichols was able to measure the differential survival of Erasmus's prescriptions because enough time had passed for many of them to die out. The fate of cultural habits is not so often measured at an interval of several centuries. Had Nichols carried out his experiment with European students a few years after Erasmus's book was published, the results would probably have been quite different. In particular, the impact of core disgust might have been harder to detect, as Erasmus's authority would have carried more weight. After all, *On Good Manners for Boys* was not just any manners guide. The Renaissance equivalent of a modern best seller (130 editions, translated in four languages soon after its publication), it was written by one of Europe's first intellectual superstars. Here, we meet a triviality that has many important consequences: selection, when it assumes the form of differential survival, takes some time. On shorter timescales, the effect of people better remembering and transmitting disgust-related rules may be too noisy to be detectable. It may also be blurred by local accidents, like the influence of Erasmus.

The same is true for *adalo* worship, which by Keesing's estimate (based on archeological data) has been alive in one form or another on Malaita for two millenia at least (Keesing 1982, 217–218). In addition to the considerable length of time that *adalo* spirits had to cross, there were the perils of traveling in a very sparse population, living in tiny, scattered settlements, in the most rugged and mountainous sector of Malaita (Keesing 1982, 9–10, 13). Diffusion was probably as arduous across generations as it was across time and space. Kwaio culture was confronted with a problem that one might call *demographic scarcity*: when groups are so small and scattered as Kwaio groups are, some of them at some moments in time will lack entire demographic categories, like middle-aged women or elderly men (Keesing 1982, 17). As a result, some cultural forms that have to be passed on from one demographic category to another (e.g., elderly grandmother to adolescent daughter), because of some taboo, ritual necessity, or special interest in the other category, cannot be transmitted adequately. A fair proportion of Kwaio religious practices are subject to a transmission restriction of this kind (Keesing 1982, 198–202). The problem is all the more acute since, as Kwaio traditionalists know but too well (Keesing 1982, 85, 90), only a few members of a given demographic category will make good learners. Not all youngsters with the appropriate background also happen to have the skill and dedication required to master the most complex forms of lore. (We will look at such obstacles to transmission in greater detail in chapter 5.)

Demographic scarcity, combined with unfavorable transmission rules, must have proved fatal to many Kwaio traditions. Many were probably swallowed by a demographic glut before they could reach the Kwaio of today; others would have died out for lack of reliable and abundant carriers. One thing is sure: those that managed to reach twentieth-century Kwaio had to proliferate in order to survive. That means they had to be memorable and easy to transmit—but not only that; they proved enduring because everyday events did not make sense without them.

Adalo lore, European manners, urban legends—all these things traveled on long, narrow, and compact transmission chains. In other words, each went through carriers who were numerous and diverse, and were arranged in a chain that was not wide enough for one carrier to guide their diffusion on his own (even one as influential as Erasmus). They were tested by a great number of different, more or less independent minds. Had they been less numerous, or less independent, general attraction may not have prevailed. Its effects can be thwarted in two ways—the vagaries of diffusion, and local factors of attraction.

How the Vagaries of Diffusion Dilute General Attraction

Let us focus on the contingencies of diffusion first. Imagine two traditions, both equally appealing. Chance may arrange things so that one is better diffused than the other. This is all the more probable when opportunities for transmission are rare, and when they are concentrated in a few hands. When two equally attractive traditions are given the same number of transmission opportunities, the smaller that number of opportunities is, the greater the probability that the resulting diffusions will be unequal. That is a simple application of the central limit theorem: if you flip a normal coin ten times, your chances of drawing tails roughly as many times as heads are lower than they would be if you had flipped the coin one hundred times.

The influence of chance on cultural diffusion does not stop there. Traditions are not, as a rule, all equally likely to be transmitted. The vagaries of geography, demography, or social connections may allow certain traditions to spread more than others, even if they are less attractive. In very accessible populations, some traditions (like Brezhnev's biography) will be supported by powerful institutions, by information storage technologies, or by individuals who happen to wield more cultural influence than others—because of their influence, their longevity, or their mobility. All this creates numerous transmission opportunities, which are typically within the reach of some traditions, but not others. The resulting inequalities of diffusion are not necessarily linked with differences in intrinsic appeal.

Local Attraction Can Override General Attraction, Locally

We must add on top of all this the influence of local attraction. The Manchu haircut had little intrinsic appeal for the Chinese (far from it), yet this disadvantage was offset by imperial decree, for a time, within the Empire. Being restricted to particular times and places (quite important chunks of time and space, in that case) does not make local attraction weaker than its general counterpart. Locally, in certain specific contexts, traditions that tap into mechanisms that are quite generally shared may be overridden. General attraction is set apart not by its strength but by its reliability and constancy across a wide range of contexts. Mechanisms like the intention-detector that Boyer appeals to in his explanation of beliefs in spirits, or the "core disgust" postulated by psychologists, are not iron laws of human thought. Of all the mental mechanisms that influence our cultural choices one way or another, they are not the most powerful; but they make up for their weaknesses with two properties. They are reliable—we have reasons to suspect their presence in most people, in most contexts—and they have constant effects: they tend to weigh in the same direction whatever the circumstances.

Locally, ubiquitous and reliable mechanisms are mixed up with local factors of attraction that are less reliable or constant, but still capable of prevailing. When the emperor forces the Manchu haircut on his subjects, he gives them a strong motivation to adopt it, but that motivation is neither reliable (it is confined within the empire) nor constant (for opponents of the state, the decree could be a reason *not* to wear the braid). These unreliable and transient causes still predict Chinese choices much better than factors of a more abstract or general nature, like the braid's æsthetic properties.

The first authors who started to apply statistical thinking to diffusion had seen this contrast between two types of forces acting on cultural history. Here is David Hume's *Essay on the Rise and Progress of the Arts and Sciences*:

> *What depends upon a few persons is, in a great measure, to be ascribed to chance, or secret and unknown causes: what arises for a great number, may often be accounted for by determinate and known causes.* Two natural reasons may be assigned for this rule. First, if you suppose a dye to have any biass, however small, to a particular side, this biass, though, perhaps, it may not appear in a few throws, will certainly prevail in a great number, and will cast the balance entirely to that side. In like manner, when any causes beget a particular inclination or passion, at a certain time, and among a certain people; though many individuals may escape the contagion, and be ruled by passions peculiar to themselves; yet the multitude will certainly be seized by the common affection, and be governed by it in all their actions. Secondly, those principles or causes, which are fitted to operate on a multitude, are always of a grosser and more stubborn nature, less subject to accidents, and less influenced by whim and private fancy, than those which operate on a few only. The latter are commonly so delicate and refined, that the smallest incident in the health, education, or fortune of a particular person, is sufficient to divert their course, and retard their operation;

nor is it possible to reduce them to any general maxims or observations. Their influence at one time will never assure us concerning their influence at another; even though all the general circumstances should be the same in both cases.

(Hume 1744a/1998, 7–8)

The mechanisms that Hume describes in this passage are the ones we have just been dwelling on. They modulate, or distort, the influence of general factors on cultural transmission. General attraction may be diluted because the sample being considered is too small to carry any signal, or because attraction is masked by transient, unreliable factors. These two problems diminish in severity as the sample gets bigger; first, because any factor becomes easier to detect; second, because constant factors, since they work in the same fashion for everyone, will evince a coherent pattern while local factors cancel each other out. Regarding this second point, however, Hume's recommendation to focus on big numbers to seek the most general causes is not entirely satisfactory. As the Manchu braid shows, hundreds of millions of men may behave in a way that is just as contingent as it would be if they were a small group—just give one man enough power to bind them all to one arbitrary choice. The impact of contingency on a cultural diffusion chain is not simply a function of the number of individuals in it. What matters, as we shall see now, is the shape of the chain.

General Attraction Prevails in Long and Narrow Diffusion Chains

One cannot be sure that a tradition's success reflects a general factor of attraction, lest that tradition has stood the test of transmission across a wide range of conditions. For that reason we cannot know whether the preservation of some European etiquette rules was due to the universal appeal of norms against disgust-inducing actions (as Nichols thinks it was) or to a gradual increase of disgust-sensitivity in Europe (as Elias had it). A tight bundle of traditions and institutions held Europeans together throughout that period, so much so that they might have shifted together in their sensitivity to disgust.

Such things muffle the influence of generally attractive traditions. Culture is not tidily molded on cognitive universals. Specific conditions need to be met for general attraction to prevail against local attraction and against the vagaries of diffusion. What is needed is a large number of transmission episodes. These episodes should not be concentrated around a few individuals or a few situations. They should be dispatched over a range of very different times, places, and social contexts. Long, narrow, and compact diffusion chains fulfill these conditions. Theirs is the shape that diffusion assumes when stable traditions endure in populations with poor accessibility: chains that go far by means of many small steps, connecting distant times and places in a very indirect fashion. No single link in the chain carries the tradition over a long distance; none is connected to more than a tiny fraction of all the other links.

These chains are fed by many individuals, each coming from a different context. We should thus expect them to be more sensitive to general attraction. Short chains have fewer links. Extended chains reach far without going through as many different individuals. Long and wide chains, those that include many parallel sub-chains, are commanded by a few leaders for whom the chain is much more accessible than it is for others. Those chains risk reflecting only a few individual decisions rather than the cumulated choices of many diverse individuals. By contrast, when an idea travels on a long, narrow, and compact chain, it passes through thousands, millions of different heads. That means as many thousands or millions of psychological filters, all different, yet with a small cluster of features in common. Along the chain, idiosyncratic and local features pull in different, inconsistent directions. Their effects will average out as the chain grows longer. Reliable and consistent features will show clearly through the chain, as idiosyncratic features are washed out.

Engineers say there are two ways to bring down a bridge. The first technique is rather crude, but convenient if what you want to destroy is a small bridge (or a small fragment of a longer bridge). Take a crane, wielding a wrecking ball. Hit whatever it is that you want to pull down. The frequency of the shocks, their exact momentum or location, do not matter as long as the target gets hit hard enough. The second method, a bit more elaborate, is appropriate to lay down long bridges on their whole length, in one go. The trick: Apply a series of repeated and synchronized shocks along the length of the bridge. Impact points should be numerous. Together, they should cover as much length as possible. With this method the force of each individual impact does not have to be so strong. (It is said that the rhythmic steps of soldiers caused a chain bridge in Angers to tumble down.) The rhythm and location of the impacts, on the other hand, are crucial. If the shocks are sufficiently spread out, sufficiently synchronized, a resonance wave forms and dislocates the bridge.

Likewise, there are two ways to preserve a tradition on a long, narrow, and compact chain. There are factors that may, if they prove strong enough, stabilize it on a small portion of the chain; and there are those (weaker perhaps, yet ubiquitous and reliable) that can carry it along the whole length of the chain.

Locally, these may not be the easiest to detect—they tend to fade into background noise. Only on large scales of space and time is their influence perceptible.

For Instance, Widely Diffused Languages Tend to Be Easier on the Mind

To summarize, traditions and their distribution rely on context-bound mechanisms that the social sciences are used to studying, but also on mechanisms of a more general kind that psychologists focus on. Mechanisms of the second kind start to matter when diffusion chains are long and narrow. Some empirical confirmation for this hypothesis can be found in a sub-field of linguistics that has recently seen interesting developments. According to a growing body of work, some formal differences among languages can be linked to their diffusion. The most widespread languages, those that have been acquired by the greater variety of learners, may be simpler and, so to speak, more learnable by second-language learners. To make their point, the authors behind this conjecture need to do two difficult things: identify difficult constructions that are likely to be hard to learn, and relate their presence to demographic variables.

The first point is not the easiest to make, since the view that all languages are equally complex has deep roots in anthropology and linguistics (Sampson 2009). That view seems to be based on three very different preoccupations. First of all is, I suspect, a concern that ranking languages on a complexity scale might encourage all sorts of ethnical prejudice. This fear can, perhaps, be laid to rest, since according to the arguments that are being developed nowadays, "bigger" languages should be less sophisticated than smaller ones, a view that language preservationists could turn to their advantage. Whether or not this line of thought turns out to be persuasive, the political concerns around the study of language complexity are extra-scientific. There is also the popular axiom that holds that whatever complexity is removed from morphology must be reintroduced in equal measure into syntax—about which more below (see Deutscher 2009 for a critique). Lastly, the idea that all languages share the same deep structure, popularized by generative linguistics, does not encourage the explorations of complexity differentials.

The search for measures of linguistic complexity might well be a red herring (like the search for complexity metrics have proven to be in so many sciences), but second-language learnability seems easier to handle. Some features at least appear to add to the difficulty of mastering a language, without compensating in any obvious way for the loss of cognitive comfort they impose on speakers. Grammatical gender (a set of ad hoc rules that causes even proficient non-native speakers in German or French to stumble on "*das Türe" or "*le chaise") is a case in point. Having an extremely small phoneme inventory is another feature that may complicate comprehension and communication (Trudgill 2011, 122–129). A lot of research on linguistic learnability focuses on the complexity of morphological rules (like grammatical gender rules). Word formation rules vary widely in their difficulty. Some languages have inflection rules for substantives or verbs that are completely lacked by others; some encode much more information in affixes; and so on. Speakers of morphologically complex languages are often required to encode explicitly certain bits of information that could have been kept silent or merely implicit, had the language been different: how far I am from the chair I am talking of; what gender I associate chairs with; how I came to learn what I am saying about that chair. In this respect their expression is not as economical as it could be.

Linguistic history offers examples both of morphological simplification (of which we saw an instance in chapter 1, for Middle English) and complication. In cases of simplification, some of the complexity lost by the morphology arguably creeps back into the syntax. Latin languages, for instance, jettisoned a rich system of inflections in the course of their evolution, but had to make up for it by respecting strict rules on word order in sentences. It used to be taken for granted that whatever complexity was reintroduced in this way precisely balanced the amount of complexity lost by morphology. Indeed, the view that all languages are equally complex stands on this argument. Today's theorists of linguistic complexity doubt it. Syntactic constraints born as by-products of morphological complication, they argue, are more parsimonious and transparent than the morphological rules that they replace. Why? Mostly because morphological inflexions are attached to words, meaning that, when words undergo phonological changes, rules are easily distorted along with the sounds. Words become irregular (Trudgill 2011, 95–104). Theory thus predicts that morphologically complex languages should get much more than their share of the ensuing irregularities.

Why are languages so variable in this respect? Two closely related answers have been proposed. According to some, morphological simplification is an effect of acquisition by adult second-language learners. Being notoriously bad at learning second languages, they jettison complexities that children would retain. They also seek to impose simple rules on a complex material (Wray and Grace 2007). Another hypothesis, which can be considered an enlargement of the first, holds that languages simplify when they are spoken, not just by adult second-language learners, but by diverse individuals—people with few habits, traditions, or knowledge in common. It is easier to sustain a rich and complex language inside a small community of people who know one another well and share a substantial background, than to teach it to many strangers. This, in a nutshell, is the view defended by Peter Trudgill (2011), who tested it on insular dialects of Scandinavian languages, as well as dialects of English: small, isolated dialects are less regular; they present less transparent constructions; they tend to be more redundant. Trudgill admits that size and contact do not strictly determine linguistic complexity. In some cases, indeed, languages surrounded by many others will become more complex, not less. Contact, after all, allows new linguistic inventions to spread and add to a language's repertoire of forms. This kind of complexity, however, does not necessarily harm learnability; moreover, the kind of contact that brings about this type of change is different from the kind that causes simplification. Learnable complexity grows when language contact involves many bilingual children; simplification occurs when contact is mostly due to adults.

Trudgill's views have been tested quantitatively, and the results are suggestive. Gary Lupyan and Rick Dale (2010) show a weak correlation between a varied set of traits thought to relate to morphological complexity, and three demographic variables: the size of the community of speakers; the geographic area it occupies; its contacts with other languages. These relations hold when controlling for relations to language families or geographical proximities. These non-linguistic variables seem to have something to do with the complexity of a language's possessive pronouns, the richness of its inflexions, whether or not it is agglutinative. Likewise, Daniel Nettle (1999, 130–148) shows that rare and unwieldy sentence constructions that put the object before the verb and the subject are more likely to be observed in languages spoken by very few people.

How exactly one should interpret these correlations is debatable, but the theory of diffusion chains that has been laid down here seems to fit nicely with these findings. When a language is spoken by small, culturally isolated populations, on a small territory, it travels on short and wide transmission chains. A population of a hundred or a thousand people is accessible in large part to anyone. Few individuals will feed the chain, and they are likely to resemble one another. In bigger, more scattered or less isolated populations, languages travel, if they travel at all, on longer chains where each link is connected to a tiny fraction of all other links.

It is true, however, that the bigger languages also enjoy venues of dissemination that may be out of reach for smaller languages: writing, institutions, more extensive traveling (since bigger languages are often also trade languages). These things help, of course, but they probably do not explain the diffusion of the most important languages on their own. The differences we are talking about are enormous. The six thousand languages inventoried by *The Ethnologue* are spoken, on average, by a bit less than a million people, on a territory as big as Ireland—yet this average is swollen by a handful of very widespread languages like Mandarin, Swahili, or English. Most languages are actually spoken by much less than ten thousand speakers, on territories as big as the principality of Luxemburg (Lupyan and Dale 2010).

A well-connected merchant could correspond and converse in Swahili with hundreds or thousands of other Swahili speakers, yet this would not connect him with more than one percent of Swahiliphones. Besides, the people he would reach in that way would not resemble him very much. In contrast, a sedentary speaker of Klaron (a small Senegalese language) living in a community of a few hundred would know a larger share of Klaron speakers just by knowing his friends and neighbors. To be carried on long and narrow chains, a language such as Swahili arguably needs to fit the simplest and most general kind of cognitive constraints. Languages are communication tools. They will drift toward the least common denominator, the structures that every speaker can produce and understand. The broader a language's diffusion, the smaller that least common denominator is likely to become.

The Benefit of Moving across Scales When Looking at Culture

The effects that such studies as Lupyan and Dale's reveal are weak. They accept of many counterexamples. Most of the phenomena that have been dealt with in this chapter are like this. To see them, one needs to look at several scales of diffusion, systematically, from one-billion-strong communities to one-speaker languages. The multi-scale methods that allow us to do that are quantitative. They differ from the methods that students of culture are used to (some fields, like historical linguistics, being exceptions). They consist in asking a few simple questions to many objects, rather than many sophisticated questions to a few objects. What justifies this departure from the usual practice is the need to move across different scales.

Why this need? Because the circumstances that give birth to culture differ, depending on what scale we consider. On the smallest and most familiar scale, transmission between two individuals, the mechanisms that we see at work are those that allow traditions to be copied and memorized. These are not the engines that drive the life and death of traditions on other scales. To see those, we need to zoom out, and readjust our lens on different scales of space or time. When culture is viewed at the level of its diffusion—the only level where traditions can be seen as traditions—quantity of transmission matters more than quality.

There is not much more to be said about diffusion chains in general; they are too diverse for that. Some span centuries and continents. Others are much more humble. Between the most diffused and the most obscure (which also happen to be the most numerous) the gaps are several orders of magnitude wide. They do not fit quietly in a bell curve around a mean. The biggest traditions are not simply bigger; they occupy distinct dimensions. On such scales, cultural diffusion starts to work differently.

For a tradition to reach these scales it needs at least one of two things: a population where demography, institutions, and technologies are such that most individuals can communicate with a sizeable portion of the population (accessibility) and a capacity of its own to elicit an urge to reproduce or adopt it (attraction). In poorly accessible populations, traditions rely on their own appeal to proliferate and last. They need, if they are to travel far, to go through many individuals and at least as many transmission episodes. In so doing they form narrow and compact diffusion chains. What gets a tradition through such a chain is not the fidelity of its transmission. Neither is it the technological or institutional support that it may get. It is the most general aspects of its intrinsic appeal, the part of it that attracts vast numbers of different people. In chains that do not go as far, or that do not use as many steps, general attraction is less important.

In the next two chapters, this hypothesis will be used to solve two problems. The question of why human traditions are so numerous will be tackled in the last chapter. Before that, we will dwell on a question that once was the central problem of the social sciences: how can it be that traditions last while the populations that carry them change all the time? How does culture manage the passing of generations?

5 THE PASSING OF GENERATIONS

If humans were immortal animals existing forever—ignorant of birth, of decay, of death—the survival of traditions would be a simple matter. Efficient transmission and faithful memory would make culture last, and nothing more would be needed. Human populations, of course, are not like that. They are regularly refreshed by biological cycles. As a consequence, no tradition can last if it is not transmitted on a regular basis. The theory of diffusion chains claims that this re-transmission matters more and more as the scales of space and time that we consider become wider. When we adjust our focus to wider angles, transmission and memorization matter less than frequent transmission.

This idea will be illustrated by two mechanisms that help culture span long stretches of time. The first is well explored. It takes advantage of the fact that the more or less gradual succession of generations creates overlaps, which the oldest can exploit to reach the youngest: vertical transmission. Its importance may have been overestimated: transmission also works horizontally, inside one generation. That horizontal transmission can work is no surprise in itself, but as we can see, it reaches impressively far.

"That Constant Stream of Recruits to Mankind"
Demographic Generations Are Not Social Generations

The social sciences have been reflecting on generational renewal since they exist, as did their philosophical forebears; but the generations that modern social science cares about are not exactly biological or demographic phenomena. They are "social generations" (Mannheim 1952; Mentré 1920). These are sets of individuals defined not by some demographic characteristics, but as social units. They are composed of people who have shared some historical or cultural moment—like the trenches of World War I, or rock and roll. Their cohesion is only partly a matter of demography: it is chiefly a consequence of an event experienced together. In France, the generation of Romantic writers (a standard example of a literary generation) is not the set of Frenchmen born at the end of Napoleon's reign and who came into their twenties in the 1830s, when Victor Hugo burst on the Parisian scene with his *Hernani*. Most members of that cohort never had any experience of literary romanticism (or any kind of literary fad, for that matter). Only those whose lives were changed by the "*Hernani* battle" could be a part of the Romantic generation, and this no matter how old they were when it erupted. Social generations may overlap with demographic cohorts, but only to a point, and their relations with the demographic evolution of societies can be hard to track.

Interesting as they can be, this chapter does not focus on social generations, but on the cultural consequences of the regular renewal of human populations. That is not the easiest take on the topic of cultural generations, nor the most promising. The social sciences mostly turned their backs on it, and with good reason. Such attempts as have been made to account for the rhythm and succession of historical events, taking the pace of generational turnover as a guide, have a sad track record. Cumbersome theorizing, arbitrary mathematizing, ad hoc overfitting: critics have not been kind to generational models of social change.

First came the cyclical philosophies of history. They wanted to explain the succession of political regimes, and predict the pace of their unfolding, based on the way each generation reacts to the institutions set up by the previous one. This was antiquity's favorite philosophy of history, from Plato's *Republic* (VIII) to Polybius's theory of governments (made famous by Machiavelli). That intellectual temptation seems never to have completely disappeared, and we find an efflorescence of generational theories in the nineteenth century, some of them endorsed by writers as illustrious as Augustin Cournot, as obscure as Ottokar Lorenz or Justin Dromel. (One may find a long but entertaining review of these authors in Mentré's 1920 compendium.)

The point was always to use demographic succession as a key to determine the main scansions of history. Cournot (1872) took the natural unit of cultural change to be the century. Why? Because one hundred years coincide with three full generations, which is to say, with one complete renewal of a population. The history of astronomy according to Cournot was thus cut out in centuries. The century of geometrical astronomy starts with the birth of Copernicus and ends with the birth of Kepler (1571). Kepler's birth heralds the century of modern, empirical physics, which starts after a brief interregnum of thirty years (enough time for Galileo to rise, and for Kepler to succeed Tycho Brahé, who dies in 1601). The eighteenth century belongs to Newton; it spans the years between the publication of the *Principia* (1687) and the discovery of Uranus (1781), which opens up a new era. To each century its methods, its style, its great men.

Today the ad hoc element in such theories is all too obvious. The way in which generational models tried to compute dates for the major turning points in history is redolent of the mathematics that Jehovah's Witnesses use to predict the end times. The urge to build clear-cut boundaries out of the continuous flow of demographic change left these authors facing a choice between approximation and contrivance. The historians of the *longue durée* have been quite severe with these attempts, which the historian Marc Bloch condemned as "Pythagorean reveries" (Bloch 1952, 95; see also Nora 1992). And yet, generational theories were not entirely devoid of merit. Their authors were among the first to try to build quantitative models of cultural change, relating demography to cultural history. Their hypotheses were completely false, when testable, but at least some of them provided general and quantified predictions bearing on the interplay between biological change and cultural change. Perhaps that was an ambition worth clinging to. It was relinquished when social generations replaced demographic generations within the mainstream of social science.

Even in Cournot's time, one did not have to choose between generational theories and no theory at all, when thinking about the way demography and history influence one another. According to Auguste Comte, the speed of social change depended on the rate of succession of generations. Comte thought that in human societies, the dead outnumber the living. This raised a question: how can the living and the dead cohabit? Comte knew that the social influence of the dead was by no means direct. It had to be transmitted by previous generations to the ones that followed. The rate of replacement of human populations is usually slow, and slow in proportion to the length of individual lives. The presence of the oldest generations, which stand for the past, puts a brake on social change. As Comte explained in his *Cours de philosophie positive*:

> (...) I must note that the ordinary length of the human lifespan may have an influence on this speed [the speed of social change] that is deeper than that of any other appreciable element. As a matter of principle, we should not hide from the fact that our social progression rests essentially upon death. In other words, humanity's advance, step by step, necessarily presupposes a continuous and sufficiently fast-paced renewal of the agents who put all things into motion. Usually in the course of one human life that renewal is all but imperceptible: only when passing from one generation to the next does it become truly salient.
>
> (Comte 1864, 451–453)

Comte did not, I think, give the best possible argument in support of his simple and important idea. Why would a slow rate of generational turnover hinder social development? He thought this was because slow replacement rates made societies older. In Comte's view, age would incline societies to conservatism. The old, being the chief beneficiaries of the social order that they helped build, would put obstacles in the way of the young.

If this view is right, then the key parameter of social change is not the rate of generational succession over time, but the mean age of the population at a given time. What this factor influences is not mainly the general rate of cultural change, but the resilience of some institutions—those which benefit the old. One could imagine a population with very long average longevity, and a consequently slow rate of turnover, where there would still be no dominance of older individuals over the youngest, and no need for the population to be particularly conservative in maintaining its institutions. How is such a population possible? All we need to do is assume that generations succeed each other abruptly, in one go. David Hume suggested precisely that scenario in a thought experiment:

> Did one generation of men go off the stage at once, and another succeed, as is the case with silk worms and butterflies, the new race, if they had sense enough to choose their government, which surely is never the case with men, might voluntarily, and by general consent, establish

their own form of civil polity, without any regard to the laws or precedents which prevailed among their ancestors. But as human society is in perpetual flux, one man every hour going out of the world, another coming into it, it is necessary, in order to preserve stability in government, that the new brood should confirm themselves to the established constitution, and nearly follow the path which their father, treading in the footsteps of theirs, had marked out to them.

(Hume 1744b, 284)

For Hume, social conservatism is made necessary by the coexistence of several contemporary generations. It does not matter much whether generations were made to coexist because of the average length of people's life spans, because of the slow pace of generational turnover, or because generational turnover is gradually spread out in time, instead of occurring all at once. All that is required is the coexistence of distinct age groups. Comte's view of the issue was quite similar. His claim that societies become (and should become) more conservative as they grow older was a claim about the political effects of having certain age structures (populations with a greater or lesser proportion of elderly members). Comte's argument did not actually depend on any particular assumption concerning the speed at which populations renew themselves (his phrasing of his claim notwithstanding).

He bequeathed this vision of generational dynamics to the pioneers of social science, starting with Durkheim. His *Division of Labor in Society* (Durkheim 1893/1963) illustrated this point by showing how social innovations are better received among the urban working class, who have left their rural origins behind and are thus freed from the influence of their elders. Comte's influence on this topic also inspired psychologists like Piaget, who cited him in his analysis of marbles play (Piaget 1932). Piaget explained the conservatism of nine- and ten-year-olds on this topic by their dependence on the opinion of twelve- or thirteen-year-olds (we will meet both Piaget and marble games again before the end of this chapter).

The presence of older individuals in a population, the weight they may have, the respect they may command, are of course important consequences of generational turnover; yet there is more to it than that. Another aspect of demographic change, the rate at which populations are renewed, is quite distinct and deserves a specific treatment. This issue (not the political consequences of generational imbalances) is what this chapter is concerned with. Our topic will be the effect of the rate of generational turnover, the speed at which generations succeed each other, on cultural diffusion.

How to Link Humans Scattered across Time

As we saw in the last chapter, human populations differ in their degree of accessibility to their members. Some populations are confined to periods of time and to places so restricted that one individual may easily reach most of the rest. Others, including almost all the cultures that have lasted long enough, are much too scattered for that. The temporal aspect of that dispersion is what will interest us here. A population's degree of time dispersion is a matter of scale. The longer the stretch of time we take into account, the more scattered the population is likely to be. All else being equal, direct links are harder to establish across long stretches of time. Two things complicate this inverse relation between accessibility and time scales: the amount of time each individual spends in the population, and the degree of overlap between generations.

Let us consider, for simplicity's sake, a population that neither grows nor shrinks: departures (which can be thought of as equivalent to deaths) are constantly compensated by new arrivals (which could be births). The rate at which such a population is renewed depends on the amount of time its members stay in it. The shorter the duration of their stay, the more rapid the rate of turnover. A fast rate of turnover means it takes less time to renew the population entirely. It also makes it harder for any individual to reach others across time. Cultural diffusion should suffer in a population with such a fast rate of turnover. When one can remain for (say) fifty years in a population, then transmitting a tradition only once suffices to give it a new lease on life—a new lease of several decades. If, on the other hand, turnover is much higher (suppose the average length of stay is only five years), then transmitting a tradition does not buy it such a big amount of time—a few years instead of several decades. The higher the rate of population renewal, the harder it gets to preserve a tradition with just one or a few successful transmissions. The odds worsen for cultural stability.

That, I think, was Comte's fundamental intuition. There is no reason not to apply it to all the populations that lose and gain members with time, whatever the cause of the renewal might be. Biological change is a special case of population turnover: the case where arrivals and departures coincide with births and deaths, and populations are biological entities. Comte's principle also applies to other types of groups, providing they possess some kind of social or cultural unity: schools, corporations, cults. For such societies, departures and arrivals are not biologically caused, but socially controlled. In yet other groups, social rules follow biological trends closely enough. To enter an age group defined by an initiation ritual, for instance, one needs to be a certain age. All these groups should verify Comte's principle, since all are regularly renewed.

How Generational Overlap Makes Diffusion Easier

One thing complicates this general principle. As Hume remarked, humans are not silkworms, nor butterflies. We mate in all seasons, and we live many years. In humans, population renewal is spread out in time. As a consequence, human generations lack clear-cut boundaries. This is the main difficulty that generational philosophies of history stumbled upon, when they tried to cut up history into distinct periods, each marked by the influence of a specific generation. Generations are not born or dead on a given day. Instead, population renewal is more or less evenly spread out. Hence the failure of all these authors who tried to cut up historical periods along generational lines.

That said, demographic change is not always so even. It can be more or less smooth. In very small populations, deaths and births are not likely to be spread out evenly across time, and so the passing of generations will be marked by deep discontinuities, as we saw in the Kwaio case. Deaths, in particular, can be catastrophically concentrated. Deaths cluster by chance in small populations. In bigger ones death clusters are due to more worrying causes. All this explains why the ambition of generational philosophies of history could have seemed like a plausible one: there are indeed some discontinuities in the otherwise continuous flow of demographic change. They allow historians to identify fuzzy generations (which are no less real for being fuzzy). No one denies that discontinuities like the post-war baby boom had cultural consequences, decades later (Burguière 1994).

On the whole, however, generational change is more or less evenly spread out, and "that constant stream of recruits to mankind" (as Bossuet called it) is the best ally of cultural diffusion. François Mentré—one of the last (and most perceptive) defenders of generational theories of history—put his finger on the problem when he remarked that "the entanglement of human generations, while the greatest obstacle to their identification, is also a guarantee both of social continuity and of continuous progress" (Mentré 1920, 180). In saying so he echoed a classic view in social science (best formulated by Simmel 1898): human societies manage to persist in time thanks to the gradualness of generational turnover. Why? If demographic change were not gradual, generations would not overlap, and transmission could not occur. A slow turnover rate is good for increasing accessibility, but only if succeeding generations have some time together. Without this, a population is reduced to the condition of Hume's silkworms. Long lives and slow turnover are of no use without generational overlap. Considering all this, it would seem that traditions can only take one path across generational gaps. That path is bordered by two conditions. Stable traditions need to inhabit populations whose members remain there for a long time, and that are neither too small nor too unstable to fall prey to demographic accidents. In addition, they need to be passed on vertically, that is to say, from the old to the young.

(The term "vertical transmission" was originally borrowed from epidemiology by Cavalli-Sforza and Feldman—1981—who use it to designate transmission between parent and child. Today the meaning has been loosened, and more often refers to cross-generational transmission in general, inside or outside of kinship ties. All it takes for transmission to be vertical is a substantial age differential between participants. That meaning of the phrase is the one adopted here. Symmetrically, the phrase "horizontal transmission" is used here to refer to any case of transmission where the age differential between participants is small or negligible.)

A standard claim in the cultural evolution literature is that vertical transmission in this sense is the only way a tradition can be stabilized across long stretches of time (Cavalli-Sforza and Feldman 1981, 130–131). Boyd and Richerson's dual inheritance theory takes a different view. It minimizes the part played by parental input in cultural transmission, and takes seriously the existence of lasting horizontal traditions, like those that make up children's peer culture (Boyd and Richerson 1985, 53–55). Horizontal transmission's chief use, in this theory, is the fast diffusion of practices that serve one generation's purpose, for a short time. A typical case is adaptation to a sudden change in a population's environment. While they acknowledge that durable traditions might not need to go vertical, they do not propose a mechanism that could cause horizontal traditions to survive as long as those that go through the vertical channel.

They do share the view that transmission between generations is necessary for cultural continuity, while intuitive, is false. That a tradition's *diffusion* through time must pass from the earliest to the latest generations is a triviality; but the same is not true of its *transmission*. Diffusion through time may succeed even when the age difference between emitters and receivers is extremely small. It may never have to be transmitted to the young by the old. Its transmission just needs to be very frequent. On that condition, diffusion in the long run may depend on horizontal transmission (or rather, quasi-horizontal transmission, since there is always a need for some sources to be slightly older than their targets). As we shall see, that is often possible, and sometimes necessary—for vertical transmission has its limits.

Demographic and Social Obstacles to Transmission

An oral tradition (echoed by the sociologist Diego Gambetta—1993, 152) recounts the celebration of weddings in remote parts of the Italian countryside in the Middle Ages. The union, as the story has it, was celebrated in front of two children of the village. The children had to be as young as possible, while already of talking age. Right after the ceremony they were offered sweets, and immediately after, given a big blow on the cheek. The trick was supposed to carve the event into the children's memory. The story does not say whether this succeeded in creating a lasting record of the wedding, as a replacement for church registries. Whatever the case may be, the Italian wedding trick combined two mechanisms that are quite interesting to associate: memory and vertical transmission. By taking some of the youngest members of the population, and making the wedding very memorable for them, the villagers were ensuring that the event would stay recorded for at least the remaining lifetime of the longest-lived child (assuming they did not leave the village).

The trick needed some specific demographic conditions to work, though. As Strimling et al. (2009) show (cf. chapter 4), the faster a population's turnover, the least its traditions stand to gain by being accurately memorized. Other demographic conditions also matter besides the rate of turnover. The age gap between the children and the wedded couple needs to be as wide as possible for the trick to be interesting. Yet, in a small population, the youngest children sometimes may not be that young. There may be nothing but adolescents and adults around, simply because the population is too small a sample to include all age categories at all times—a phenomenon that we might call *demographic scarcity*.

Fortunately for the Italian villagers, they lived in a sedentary community of agriculturalists, dense enough to contain all the requisite age groups. Besides, the villagers' trick was not demanding: it merely required two young children of any gender. Finding a keeper for the memory of that wedding, someone who would talk about it when everyone else would be dead, was not difficult. Things are not that easy in some human communities. Among the Kwaio, whom we met in chapter 4, cultural diffusion needs to overcome periods of demographic scarcity. The scarcity is to a great extent artificial: it happens chiefly because strict norms regulate the passing of traditions. Most important is the sexual division of cultural transmission. Many practices transmit from women to women or from men to men, seldom crossing the gender barrier (Shennan and Steele 1999 review a series of ethnographic works providing cross-cultural evidence for such divisions). Religious taboos are especially efficient in keeping one or the other sex from learning about the rituals or beliefs of the other (Keesing 1982 about the Kwaio; Lancy 1996 for another example, in West Africa). Such rules suffice to divide in two the pool of potential receptors for a tradition. We should add on top of them the many restrictions on transmission that have to do with seniority or age groups. Some of these take the shape of explicit norms: you need to be recognized as an initiate of a certain age class, as having undergone the proper ritual. Other constraints may be more understated. Even when no taboo attaches to a practice, some categories may be kept from them simply because they are only mentioned among elders, or among young girls, or among men—with much the same results.

Note, incidentally, that social norms often work to curtail transmission rather than permit it. The issues raised by today's conflicts over intellectual property rights for indigenous cultures (mostly their pharmacological knowledge) have stimulated a fascinating current of anthropological research on norms of cultural circulation, a topic beyond this book's ambitions (but see de Vienne and Allard 2005; Déléage 2012). As Emmanuel de Vienne and Olivier Allard note, norms regulating access to chants or myths have been documented very early on in the anthropological literature (e.g., Lowie 1920, 235–243). Speaking of "property rights" would be improper, but these institutions do involve obstacles to transmission that can be lifted in exchange for goods or services.

Demographic scarcity remains a virtual problem as long as demography is generous; but it has not always been so, especially in our species' past. Estimates of the size of ancient human groups are speculative and controversial (they get all the more so as we go back in time), but orders of magnitude are not much debated. Human groups, at the time when we start to have very firm evidence of human cultures, in the Late Pleistocene, did not go beyond a few hundred (Dunbar 1993), and were quite isolated. Adam Powell and his colleagues (Powell, Shennan, and Thomas 2009) mention densities around three persons for ten thousand square kilometers (roughly the size of Michigan or Massachussets). Even in the best conditions, these small groups could have their demography disturbed by small accidents—and reality was far from the best conditions, if geneticists and archeologists are to be believed when they say that early Sapiens went through a series of demographic crises

(Hawks et al. 2000). Perhaps these only occurred episodically, but one crisis would have been enough to cut the thread of cultural diffusion. Any reasonably long-lived tradition would have had to survive a few episodes of severe demographic scarcity.

In addition to these mutually reinforcing social and demographic constraints, we should note that the competence and motivation required for learning are not equally shared. Among all the potential emitters and receivers that a tradition could have, there are some who cannot or will not learn it, and some who cannot or will not teach it. This adds to transmission scarcity, even in very big populations. One thing that is striking, when one reads about the history of pre-modern science, is the frequency of false starts, the quantity of promising discoveries that turned into dead ends for lack of transmission. Part of this impression certainly reflects our hindsight bias, but some cases of aborted transmission are genuinely baffling. Take this anecdote, told by the historian of Chinese science Joseph Needham, from a citation of the engineer and philosopher Huan Tan, who lived in the first millennium (CE).

> [Yang Xiung] made an armillary sphere himself; an old artisan once said to him: "When I was young, I was able to make such things, following the method of divisions [i.e., graduations—Needham's note] without really understanding their meaning. But afterwards I understood more and more. Now I am seventy years old, and feel that I am only beginning to understand it all, and yet soon I must die. I have a son also, who likes to learn how to make these instruments; he will repeat the years of my experience, and some day I suppose he too will understand, but by that time he too will be ready to die! How sad, and at the same time how comical, were his words!
>
> (Needham 1960, 125)

The old astronomer is not exactly refusing to transmit his knowledge, and everything indicates that his son would be happy to learn; yet he seems to despair of the possibility of passing anything on. He speaks as if this know-how, which took him decades to learn, simply cannot be communicated. The chronicler who relates his thoughts seems to share in this quiet desperation: when we die, the work of a lifetime disappears along with us, without a trace. That is just one of those ironies of life one needs to get used to.

Cultural diffusion by means of vertical transmission thus meets two obstacles: generational turnover (when too fast) and demographic scarcity (due to natural fluctuations, social norms, or ill will). Is there a way around these difficulties? Not always. They place drastic limits on the accumulation of stable traditions, and their relaxing was probably a key component in the cultural history of our species (as I will speculate in the next chapter). That said, the existence of stable traditions in small-scale populations tells us that some of them did find ways around frequent population renewals, and a way around the dearth of human material. How do they do it? By resorting to two mechanisms that we already know: reconstruction and proliferation.

Everything Your Parents Did Not Teach You about Culture

When a tradition cannot travel a great distance by hopping from the very old to the very young, it may travel just as far by multiplying the stops on its way: by being transmitted many times from the old to the slightly younger, or from the young to the even younger. That is quasi-horizontal transmission. As we shall see, children's peer culture is diffused in this way: children learn it from slightly older children. Unlike the sort of diffusion that rides the wave of vertical transmission, diffusion on the quasi-horizontal path needs a great quantity of transmission episodes to succeed. It is sustained, above all, by proliferation. If proliferation is good enough, we shall see that the horizontal path can carry traditions that are just as durable as those that put remote generations into contact.

Besides quasi-horizontal transmission, which short-cuts vertical transmission (or rather finds a way around it), other forms of diffusion use transmission inside generations. They employ it differently, though, as a complement to vertical transmission—not as a self-sufficient alternative. In chapter 2, we took a look at indirect transmission—what happens when a generation must work in complete isolation from long-dead models, to rebuild a vanished language or a religion. The distance covered by indirect transmission need not be that great. Indirect reconstruction may happen at a closer range, for instance when children repeat, rehearse, and reinvent the adult practices that happen under their eye. This type of transmission is a way of complementing vertical transmission, through collective reconstruction inside one generation. Quasi-horizontal transmission is more radical than that: it relies only on the information present inside one generation.

The first quantitative and empirical studies of cultural transmission put a great deal of stress on vertical transmission, in the strict sense the phrase had acquired in medical epidemiology: transmission from parents to children (Cavalli-Sforza et al. 1982; Hewlett and Cavalli-Sforza 1986; Ohmagari and Berkes 1997; see also Shennan and Steele 1999 for a review). These studies were based on questionnaires, asking people to specify, for a quite diverse range of cultural practices, whom they had acquired it from. In Cavalli-Sforza et al.'s pioneering study, for instance, Californians were asked about the provenance of their religious or political opinions, while Aka hunter-gatherers were asked about the know-hows required for everyday life. In general, and in spite of the great heterogeneity of the questions asked, informants in these studies overwhelmingly pointed to one of their parents.

Yet these studies did not quite manage to create a consensus. There is no disagreement about the fact that vertical transmission (along genealogical lines in particular) contributes to cultural stability everywhere. Doubters question two things, though: whether vertical transmission is similarly important in all societies (Lancy 1996; MacDonald 2007; Hewlett et al. 2011), and whether people's accounts of its importance can be taken at face value. This can be doubted when one considers some folk theories of transmission. !Kung parents (who, as parents go, seem quite unusually preoccupied with their children's education) have devised all sorts of techniques to teach their children how to walk, and all sorts of theories to explain how they acquire that skill (Lancy 1996; Konner 1976). There is, arguably, something special in the !Kung gait and bearing, something that would not exist without adult nurture; but to claim that walking is cultural through and through is a stretch. Other societies (not to mention other primate species) manage to inculcate walking to their young without fussing over it too much. Critics (e.g., Aunger 2000) fear that the notion of "transmission" that is used in questionnaire studies is full of ambiguities. It could mean one thing to researchers and another to informants.

Consider Cavalli-Sforza et al.'s 1982 study. Of all the skills that Aka hunter-gatherers claim they acquired from their parents, some seem to require communication to be passed on: knowledge of poisonous mushrooms or of healing techniques. Others, though, are bits of know-how that would certainly have been acquired without any deliberate effort at transmission: how to lull a baby to sleep or make her smile, or how to pick up fruits. And yet, the Aka would never say they learnt the skills of the latter type on their own. Their parents handed them down to them, like the rest. What claims like this amount to is not very clear: the skills in question are mastered by roughly anyone (even ten-year-olds can handle most of them), and they are displayed on an everyday basis in a society where everyone has close, daily interactions with almost everyone else.

Such remarks feed the suspicion that some cultures evaluate the parental contribution to transmission with a charitable bias. Parental influence is credited for learning processes that would have worked out without them: Pharaohs causing the Nile to flow. To recall Margaret Mead's somewhat ingenuous remark, parental education is a very special instance of communication, in that it never fails to achieve its aim. It *always* produces competent adults. Be they negligent or clumsy as can be, the parents' offspring will learn to walk, to talk, to think. Facing such claims, many students of cultural transmission smell a rat. Parenting is not magic. Perhaps, we suspect, parents are not causally responsible for everything that happens under their watch. The "nurture assumption" (Judith Harris's name for the tendency to overstate parental influence in development—Harris 1998) has been a notorious target of mainstream cognitive science, ever since Chomsky's dismissal of parental input in language learning. One may or may not agree with this reevaluation of the inborn component in human cognition, but there is another reason to doubt that parents have quite the causal importance that psychology gave them (before it took its nativist turn).

That reason is the importance given to "alloparents" in ethnographic studies of nurture across the world. Alloparents are people who contribute to the education of children without necessarily being parents, or even grown-ups: grandmothers, aunts, cousins, siblings, and other children (Hrdy 2011). Their contribution may take many forms. At first, they are closer to babysitting than to what we would call education. As children grow, though, the care provided by alloparents, both inside and outside the family circle, can involve increasingly large doses of cultural transmission.

Children may act as alloparents. Their importance as nurturers of other children is a major discovery that we owe to fieldwork researchers on socialization (Kramer 2005; Weisner and Gallimore 1977; Rogoff 1981; Lancy 1996). Children's alloparenting is more or less important, depending on the society, but in some places its impact is quite comparable to that of parental education. Barbara Rogoff's research on Mayan societies in Guatemala show us a society where five- to twelve-year-olds spend more than half of their time in the company of other children, without adult supervision (Ellis, Rogoff, and Cromer 1981). Expanding on this work, Karen Kramer shows how narrow the age gap can be between the children who do the caretaking and the ones who are taken care of. Adam Boyette's observations among the Aka show that children (four to twelve) again spend more than half their time in groups of children of both sexes and of all ages (Boyette 2011; Konner 2011, 493 makes a similar point about the Efe). May we go beyond such local observations? Yes, thanks to the *Human Relations Area Files*. In a cross-cultural analysis, Herbert Barry and Leonora Paxson (data summarized by Weisner and Gallimore 1977, see also Barry's comment on that paper) show that children are the most important caretakers and educators of young children (those who are neither babies nor considered to have reached the "age of reason," i.e., before six or seven) in three-quarters of the societies they considered.

Such is the importance of children for this task that some see it as the reason why humans have childhoods at all. The years between the last growth spurt of childhood (around six or seven) and the start of puberty (which used to be later than in today's industrial societies) are something of an evolutionary enigma. These are years of considerable cognitive and emotional maturity (Konner 2011, 277–295), and yet the reproductive potential that they represent goes wasted (so to speak). Some (like Weisner 1996) suggest the waste could be compensated by children's participation in parenting tasks (much in the same way that grandmotherhood has been claimed to be an adaptation to alloparenting). Groups of children are known to play a socializing role in all genuine hunter-gatherer cultures (Konner 2011, 489–496).

These societies where children are taken care of by other children also tend to be the ones where children are supposed to take care of themselves, where adults do not see themselves as their children's teachers. The little ones are relied upon to learn common knowledge on their own, and to perform a number of chores. As we saw in chapter 2, adults do engage in cultural transmission in those societies (their occasional denials notwithstanding). Yet we must admit that they seem to do so with considerable economies of effort. Ethnographers (e.g., Lancy 1996, 22–23, 80) are sometimes struck by the lack of conversation between parents and children: orders that are not to be discussed; no verbal help when children face a difficult task; no bantering. This cannot but encourage children to self-educate. Lancy remarks that dangerous games are a telling signature of such self-reliant nurturing. The cases that he cites are quite spectacular: Kwoma children's game of sword-swallowing; machete-juggling on Vanatinai Island (and the resulting missing fingers); scars and burns shown by Lepcha adults who got them from their toddlerhood, when no effort was made to keep them away from fires; !Kung children who were filmed toying with scorpions under their parent's blasé gaze; the daunting cliffs that Dogon adults keep away from while their children caper on them.

These are extreme examples in more than one way. Children may often stick closer to adult models, even when they learn life the hard way. There is no forced choice between imitation and reconstruction, as cultural transmission usually involves both. On all this Tarde once more had the right intuition (if we overlook his polemical interpretation of Durkheim, the target of this passage):

> Few views are more narrow-minded or further from the truth than that recently proposed by an eminent sociologist, who took it as the characteristic property of social facts that they were "*imposed from outside and by constraint.*" That is tantamount to ignoring all social ties but those between master and subject, teacher and pupil, parents and children; to dismissing free relations between equals; to closing one's eyes on the education that children freely give children. Even in schools [*collèges*], what children breathe from one another (so to speak) when they imitate their fellows, or even their professors, whose habits they *interiorize*, is far more important than what they are inculcated by force.
>
> (Tarde 1893, 62)

In other words, groups of children assist cultural diffusion in two distinct ways: one is purely horizontal, involving no one but age-peers. The other way is a mix of the vertical and horizontal pathways. The model (the teacher in Tarde's example) is drawn from the higher generation, but does not do anything (besides being passively observed). Child learners themselves take care of all that is active and effortful about transmission: they reconstruct, rehearse, and explore adult behaviors by themselves. In this form of diffusion, which may be called indirect, the diffusion chain must originate in adults, but it is inside peer groups that it proliferates in a series of repeated, robust, and redundant chains. Transmission is, as Tarde would have said, "refracted" in children's groups. Transmission may take the form of playful imitation (Corsaro and Eder 1990), or the more serious form of autonomous exploration. This mechanism makes the most of a few cues leaked from adult behavior.

Not much has yet been said here of purely horizontal transmission, as distinct from indirect diffusion. It is seldom possible to observe pure cases of it: vertical transmission is such a convenient tool that few diffusion chains completely eschew it. Should that royal pathway be blocked, though, traditions do find a way around it, and quasi-horizontal transmission can suffice to make them stable. The next section shows how this happened in the case of child-to-child transmission, and explains how horizontal transfers spawned diffusion chains spanning decades and centuries of European history.

Why Do Children Have Traditions?

In modern Europe, children (between around seven and fourteen) used to possess what is usually called a peer culture, or a folklore of childhood, to be distinguished from adult-transmitted songs and games (like nursery rhymes—traditional songs sung by adults to infants and young children). That subculture was not the one they spent most of their time in: they were too busy getting acquainted with the common cultural legacy of their society. They were also exposed to games and toys designed by adults, which became increasingly important as time went by. Today, these adult-made forms of entertainment have come to dominate children's leisure. In addition, many songs, stories, and rhymes that used to be passed on from child to child have been captured and recycled by adult educators. This might hide the fact that they belonged, for most of their history, to a corpus of traditions, vast and (mostly but not completely) forgotten, whose history defies some common-sense assumption about cultural diffusion.

That corpus mainly consists of games and rhymes. It also comprises jokes and stories; secret languages; superstitions; rituals to attract luck or to ward off bad spells. Though adults readily call "games" all the things that children do without them, there is a lot of variety in these practices, and some of them may be performed quite seriously. Some are extremely simple, so simple indeed that we cannot really know what cultural transmission contributed to their distribution. A game like cat's cradle, practiced on all continents (by children, adults, or both), is easy enough to invent, and its near-universal success need not be an effect of transmission. A series of independent discoveries suffices. For most of the traditions studied in this section, however, their complexity almost certainly rules this out.

That corpus has excited the curiosity of anthropologists, ever since the times when the discipline could hardly be distinguished from folklore (Tylor 1871; Newell 1883; Van Gennep 1935). The trend culminated in Iona and Peter Opie's compendium (Opie and Opie 1959, 1969, 1997), and subsists in many fields today, although both the methods and the material have changed. Ethnography, or provoked observation, have taken the place of folklore collection. Besides, today's researchers need to deal with the fact that children in developed countries are soaked in a commercial or educational culture of adult design. In its classic period (roughly, from Victorian times to the 1960s), this rich folkloristic tradition agreed on a simple but surprising point: the practices they studied were mostly passed on from child to child, with weak adult participation, on very large timescales.

If this is true, these traditions are mostly transmitted in a quasi-horizontal way, remaining inside one generation at each time step, and traveling from the slightly older to the slightly younger. This is equivalent to saying that they travel inside one peculiar population, a population entirely made of children (or a great majority thereof). The rate of demographic renewal of that population is determined not by the total life span of its members, but by the amount of time that they spend being children. That time span usually corresponds to the length of their stay inside the peer culture. This is what it means for a tradition to be transmitted mostly from child to child: its carriers usually stop transmitting it when they exit childhood. Every year, the oldest individuals, those who spent the longest time inside the culture (and who should thus know it best) are removed from the pool of transmitters. This happens to all human populations, but a population that consists mainly of children necessarily has a much higher rate of turnover. Every year, it loses to adulthood a cohort of members that is about as numerous as the one that a demographically complete population would lose to old age and death. But any sub-population of children is bound to be much smaller than the demographically complete population of which it is a part. As a consequence, it wins and loses members in fast-forward mode.

The theory of diffusion chains states that, in such a frequently renewed population, long-term memorization cannot help a tradition, because most of its carriers leave before they can transmit it to enough people. If it is to survive, it must proliferate: it needs to be frequently transmitted to reach every successive wave of newcomers. It also has to form long, compact, and narrow diffusion chains, since child-to-child transmission does not allow most children in a transmission chain to reach across the chain to a great number of other children. On the whole, one child does not have direct access to more than a tiny fraction of all the population that carries the peer culture (even allowing for the occasional adult relay). In other words, a high rate of population renewal means that, to the extent that a diffusion chain goes through child-to-child transmission, it must go through a large number of relays. As the Opies remarked,

> In most schools there is a wholly new generation of children every six years; and when a rhyme such as *Little fatty doctor, how's your wife?* can be shown to be more than 130 years old it may be seen that it has passed through the keeping of not less than twenty successive generations of schoolchildren, and been subjected to the same stresses that

nursery lore would meet after only 500 years of oral conveyance [...] much as if the phenomenon had been placed in a mechanical stresser to speed up the wear and tear.

(Opie and Opie 1959, 8)

No doubt some human groups have even higher turnover rates: off-shore oil-drilling platforms, migrants in some border cities, certain firms, certain political organizations; but these are exceptions to the general rule that the Opies highlight. To give a rough indication, friendship networks in today's industrial Western societies have turnover rates that are clearly lower than those in children's peer cultures (and yet, these networks are arguably more fluid than the entire population of, say, a medieval village or a hunter-gatherer band). Sociologist Gerald Mollenhorst estimates from his study of the friendships of a thousand people (2009) that we lose on average half of our friends every seven years. The remaining half consists of more stable friendships, many of which will remain after an additional seven years; some will last a lifetime. The rate of turnover in the Opies' scenario is at the very least twice faster: all the children are gone within six years.

The Opies, like other specialists of children's folklore, took the view that the repeated transmission rendered necessary by such fast population renewals made traditions vulnerable to the Wear-and-Tear Problem. Their worry echoes the claim, made popular by the imitation hypothesis, that the Wear-and-Tear Problem is a crucial ordeal that traditions must overcome at great cost. The theory of diffusion chains takes a much more relaxed view of that problem, but this in itself does not quite dissolve the enigma of children's traditions. They need to launch long, narrow, and compact transmission chains across a great number of population renewals. Such chains are by nature difficult to sustain without very frequent transmission, and so the crushing wheel of high turnover rates should be fatal, at least to some of them. How do they survive?

An answer will be given before the end of this chapter; but first, we need to take a look at the hypotheses put forward in the literature. This will be an occasion to revisit the underrated field of childhood folkloristics.

The Lost World of Children's Peer Culture

The first substantial attempt at a theory of children's peer culture came from E. B. Tylor's evolutionism. His were evolutionary views in the (now outdated) sense that he saw cultural development as unfolding around certain predetermined milestones. Childhood folklore was the final by-product of such an evolution. When a society moves up one step on the scale of progress, its elites leave behind their former culture. Rituals and magic spells fall into disuse, to be taken up by the common people. On the next move up the ladder of progress, the upper class graduate to a new cultural toolkit, and bequeath their old gear to the lower classes once again. The lower classes adopt it. What do they make of the ancient rituals they then relinquish? They leave it for children to play with. Children's peer culture is the last stop on the journey leading ancient religions to their demise; it is also our last opportunity to see them in their pristine shape (Tylor 1871, 63–86). Hence Tylor's lack of surprise when he finds in Petronius a description that applies perfectly to an English children's game of his time, up to and including the rhyme that goes with the game (that game was also documented in Opie and Opie 1969, 295–301).

For proponents of this theory, counting-out rhymes were a favorite, and probably the most written-about of all childhood traditional forms. Everyone knows one of these rhymes (*Eenie meenie miny moe; Tinker, tailor*; etc.). They serve to select a child who will be counted out of a game (or sometimes into it). One thing that fascinated specialists in these songs was the importance of meaningless strings of sounds—what Van Gennep named *mots sauvages*, "wild words," words that make no sense like *Eenie meenie* or the French *Am stram gram*. These are indeed interesting from a diffusion chains point of view (as they permit transmission beyond language boundaries), but the thing about them that enticed people like Tylor was their resemblance with some formulas used in adult rituals. The hunt was on for correspondence, genealogies, and rapprochements, a hunt fueled by a somewhat haphazard erudition and a taste for speculation. The chemist Henry Carrington Bolton's work on the topic is an illustration. He reports that, while on duty in the Pacific and attending a *kava* ceremony, one captain William Churchill heard a chant that sounded like *Eenie meenie* (Bolton 1888, 10). The rhyme, a fairly recent invention at the time, was just starting to take over the English-speaking world, which it would dominate later on (Rubin 1995, 248). The lack of a track record for the song did not stop Bolton from erecting it into a half-erased vestige of rituals more ancient than any archive. *Eenie meenie* and its family, he observed, were reminiscent of old numeration systems, in base 15 or 20, known to be preserved only in a few scattered villages (Bolton 1888, Opie and Opie 1959). The rhymes seemed to offer the cultural equivalent of the Amazonian plateau of Conan Doyle's *The Lost World*: a time capsule, preserved from the passing of time by a geological accident. A place still teeming with dinosaurs. The rhymes were windows on the deepest past.

These theories are easy to look down upon, now that their influence is a thing of the past; and it can be hard to see the alleged similarities among the children, the lower classes, and the "primitive" societies as anything else than a reflection of the condescension that was poured over all three categories. Yet the Victorians were not always wrong, as we shall see, when they claimed to identify deep continuities in childhood folklore.

Nor did that hypothesis flounder with the demise of Evolutionism. Seeing children's games as cultural vestige was a lasting legacy of Tylor's work. It is central, for instance, to Marcel Griaule's influential accounts of Dogon children's games, which he saw as an illustration of "the theory that sees most games as an end point in the evolution of obsolete social systems." The games "show us in a vivid image the fate of enormous institutions, made vulnerable by their very size: after their fall they will be discretely outlived by their humble parodies" (Griaule 1938, 1 & 15). The Victorian view found one way into contemporary social science through the work of Philippe Ariès, who, in addition to a collection of personal and controversial claims, also recycled Evolutionist ideas. His claim that "childhood becomes a conservatory for practices left over by adults" is vintage Tylor, as is the view that "children's groups are the most conservative of all human societies" (Ariès 1960, 67 & 63). Like his predecessors, Ariès remarked that many toys (like slings or miniature windmills) mimic tools that adults once used. Like them, he looked to antique Pagan rites to find the ancestors of today's games. His scenario for the evolution of European children's peer culture posits a turning point in the Renaissance. That, in his view, was the last time when children (from age three or four) and adults shared exactly the same games and practices. Indeed, there was no social dissociation between the two groups. The story of modernity is one of growing separation between them. As their subculture branched off from the rest of society, children inherited a share of what used to be a common stock of traditions, and they kept it, as it were, under wraps. The transition took time. It still was not complete in the eighteenth century, when some of the games that would later fall into the childhood repertoire continued to be shared between generations. Versailles played blind man's buff, red hands, hide-and-seek. A craze for shadow play swept Europe. The aristocracy collected dolls. Even at the start of the nineteenth century, the audience cheering for Guignol (a French version of Punch and Judy) is an adult one. Yet the transition under way was inexorable: one by one, practices that were once cross-generational became the exclusive property of one age group (Ariès 1960, 56–101). That adults could go about rolling hoops became something unthinkable. Even a game like *truth or dare* (though interesting to play in strictly adult company) quickly lapsed into children's peer culture, just like blind man's buff (Opie and Opie 1969, 265–267 & 117–120).

There are reasons to resist this Victorian picture. We should, however, distinguish two points that this literature made. One is the Victorian evolutionists' scenario that has just been sketched. As we shall see, it is very much in doubt. The other claim, is, I think, much harder to criticize. It is the view (extensively documented in the Opies' work, among others) that when cultural transmission massively involves children, that is, when it proceeds quasi-horizontally, the resulting diffusion is not less conservative than what goes on for run-of-the-mill, demographically complete cultures. In that sense, Tylor's conjecture may turn out to be half-true. Children do serve as cultural Tupperwares, as the Evolutionists claimed; but what they conserve is not a remnant of long-disappeared adult cultures. The traditions they preserve are their own.

Children's Traditions Are Not Vestigial Adult Practices

Ariès's thesis, that groups of children playing together, even childhood itself, are recent social constructions, has been refuted many times, by researchers coming from very different disciplines, and there is little need to put another nail in that coffin. Few historians deny that groups of children, identified as such and playing together, have been found wherever and whenever people have looked for them (Hanawalt 2002; Langmuir 2006; Pollock 1989). This includes children of dominated minorities and slave groups (Chudacoff 2007). The ethnographic evidence for socialization in the peer group is overwhelming. *Pace* Tylor, there is no well-documented example of a childhood game descended from a forgotten religious ritual (although present rituals may be mimicked or parodied).

What should we make of the claim that children's peer culture became progressively differentiated? Did children in modern times take up former adults' games and appropriate them? That claim is based on a selective reading of the evidence. There are, to be sure, games that followed the predicted trajectory, from adults to children. Still, for any such game one can find as many that traveled the other way, from children to adults. We also find many games that do not appear to have shifted one way or the other, and some that were common to both age groups, and remained cross-generational for centuries. There does not seem to be any precise directionality to the borrowings.

Consider the games that Rabelais had the giant Gargantua play, in his eponymous book (Rabelais 1534/1994, 58–63). At that point the giant is a child, yet he is no ordinary child (he eats cows whole and raw for breakfast), and many of the games that he plays were, had been, or would be part of the adult ludic repertoire. The list of games offered by Rabelais is a playful exercise in literary accumulation more than a scientific investigation, but it has triggered a considerable amount of research, usually on the occasion of translating or editing the book. The corpus that grew out of Rabelais's list amounts to centuries of folkloristics (amateur or professional), spanning all major European languages. This book's appendix summarizes a quantitative investigation of that corpus (or rather, the French portion of it).

Imperfect as they are, the data strongly suggest the existence of an enduring childhood peer culture in France, from the late Middle Ages to the early twentieth century. Some are cross-generational. Others (mostly games of cards or dice) are consistently described as adult from one century to the next. Most of the games that could be documented in any detail are consistently described (when their users are described at all) as children's games. For at least some of these cases, the appendix shows that the lack of mention of adult players cannot be entirely explained by the paucity of sources.

We shall meet these children's games again, but first, let us consider cross-generational games: those games that are sometimes cited as children's games, sometimes as adults' games, sometimes as both. Most of the sports mentioned in the list fall into the last category. The evolutionist view predicts that these games should get restricted to a narrower demographic niche, as time goes by. They should become children's games only or adult's games only. The evolutionist view also implies a specific direction of diffusion, from children to adults rather than the other way around. None of these claims seem to be true. Cross-generational games are not numerous enough to settle the issue, but the very fact that there are so few cross-generational games flies in the face of the evolutionist view. Had Tylor or Ariès been right, we should see every children's game turn into an adults' game as we go back in time toward the Middle Ages. Instead, we see that the games practiced by both children and adults were relatively few. Some of them, like blind man's buff or hide-and-seek, were indeed taken up by children after adults abandoned them, as Ariès had noticed. Yet they had been in children's play repertoire before adults took them up.

The story of the yo-yo is typical. An ancient toy, found everywhere, it probably had several independent inventors. Most European documents show it in the hands of children, but there was at least one period when it was very much in vogue among adults: the aftermath of the French Revolution, especially among the upper classes. The French aristocracy was hugely influential in all matters of taste, back when it was concentrated in Versailles.

When exile dispersed them all over Europe, their influence spread alongside with them. That diaspora served as the vehicle of a yo-yo epidemic. So associated was the toy with emigrated aristocrats that it went by the nickname *l'émigrette*. In the trying years of the 1790s, blue-blooded exiles found they could use a toy for stress relief. We find yo-yos in their children's hands (the Dauphin, son of the king, is an adept), and in everyone else's, too: in the hands of Parisian *élégantes* and *incroyables*, on stage with Beaumarchais's Figaro. The Prince of Wales and the Duke of Wellington have the hobby in common with Napoleon. And then, suddenly, the craze abates: yo-yos once again become a children's pastime.

Children's games are neither a recent invention nor a vestige of lost adult ways. Having laid aside the evolutionist theses, I have left untouched the most intriguing claim that this literature defended. Is it true that children's peer groups are as good a vehicle of cultural transmission as adult groups? Is it true that their traditions can be preserved as long as those of their adult counterparts? This notion is at odds with much of what we know of diffusion across generations. The folklorists seem to have gotten something wrong: either children's traditions were not as stable as they thought, or adults played an important role in transmitting them. As we shall see, though, the folklorists were right on both counts: children's traditions were their very own, and they lasted.

They Are Mostly Transmitted from Child to Child

Are children's traditions transmitted from child to child? This issue cannot be settled with certainty in each particular case. We can seldom make sure that an adult did not play some role in a game's transmission. Fortunately, we do not need to do that. What matters is the relative amount of adult participation: if it can be shown that these traditions need very little adult involvement in order to last, this is enough to make us rethink the role of vertical transmission. And the literature studying "classic" children's folklore (roughly until the 1960s) is unanimous in stating that adult contributions to the transmission of children's peer culture were minimal or nonexistent (Opie and Opie 1959; Newell 1883; Van Gennep 1935; Fine 1980). Other cultural practices travel through child-to-child transmission: language, social norms, techniques. Indeed, some have argued that the role of peer culture in their transmission is vastly underestimated (Harris 1998); but all these practices are shared between generations, and none uses peer transmission as exclusively as these do. Professional educators have endeavored to instruct children in their own traditional peer culture, but such attempts appear to be an odd quirk of modern education: these experiments were rare until recently. They did not seem to be very successful, or very necessary (Chudacoff 2007, 75; Opie and Opie 1997, 8–14). Even toy-making, a flourishing adult industry in today's rich societies, was a child's job in America (Chudacoff 2007, 83 sq.), as it continues to be for poor children worldwide. Songs undergo the strongest adult influence, but the relations between the mainstream and the playground, here again, can be complex. Skipping rhymes, for instance, adapt jingles, ads, pop songs, or nursery rhymes; but these are nearly always distorted, parodied, or fused with a preexisting traditional song. Either they fail to become traditional, or they last in a hybrid shape.

Direct testimonies concerning transmission are seldom systematically collected, but they are instructive. Jean Piaget's pioneering study of marble games around Neuchâtel (1932) tells us more about the credulity of his youngest informants than about the reality of cultural transmission. When asked about the origins and justifications of the rules of marble games (Piaget wanted to probe children's notions of normativity), young children tend to point to any kind of authority: their parents, but also God—even William Tell. Yet his older, pre-adolescent informers all say that older children passed the rules down to them, a few years back. Howard Chudacoff, a historian, studied children's diaries and adult autobiographies, mining a fair share of the material produced in the United States for the last three centuries. He found that most testimonies bearing on transmission point to other children. Very few mention adults. When David Rubin (1995) asked a hundred first-year American college students to recite *Eenie meenie miny moe* (everyone knew it), most of his informers said the last time they had uttered the rhyme was more than five years before.

I explored Iona Opie's fieldwork diary (published in 1994, but written in the 1970s) to find every testimony where a child specifies whom they picked something up from. The "something" in question could be any kind of cultural content—including things like pop music or advertisement— and not just the games and rhymes that make the canon of children's peer culture. I found thirty-six such testimonies. Five of them mention an adult, always the same: the child's father. (The point of such testimonies seems to be mostly to sing their father's praise, rather than describe his role in cultural transmission.) Seven testimonies cite the media as their source. One child heard Pink Floyd's "Another Brick in the Wall" on the radio (with its predictably popular line enjoining teachers to *leave them kids alone*). Another gives the *Sun* as the source of an urban legend (that seems too ludicrous even for *The Sun* to publish it). The media can also serve as vehicles for child-to-child transmission, like this weekly periodical collecting and spreading jokes sent by child readers. For all other testimonies (two-thirds of the total) the source cited is another child (a sibling, a friend, a cousin). When that source's source is given, it is another child (in four cases out of five). If we ignore the testimonies that deal with pop culture or recent bits of news, and consider only the traditions that have a pedigree in the folkloristic record, *all* the testimonies cite a child as the source. In saying this, they merely confirm the pattern of cultural transmission that Iona Opie observed on the playground.

They Are Children's Games, and They Look Like It

The specifically childish character of children's games is best illustrated by the practices that adults try to prevent from spreading. Not all children's traditions are innocuous: many, of course, include gratuitous risk-taking, scatology, violence, rule-breaking. Adults dominate children in a very real way (however legitimate this domination may be). The discontent that this creates makes children's peer culture look in some ways like a counter-culture (as remarked by Hirschfeld 1997, or Corsaro and Eder 1990). Some tricks resemble urban guerrilla warfare more than pranks. (The Polish rope game, for instance, consists in laying a rope or a cable across a street to make motorbikes tumble—see Opie and Opie 377–392.) Not only do adults refrain from diffusing some games, but state institutions spend a lot of money to try to contain some of them. The French school system (among others) regularly campaigns against the vogue of self-strangulation practices (French Ministry of Education, 2002).

One tradition that many adults would like their children to forget is the well-known American *cootie-lore*. It takes multiple forms. In its most sanitized version, it is a simple game of tag. Often, though, the "cooties" that get passed from child to child by touch linger on their bearer long after the game has ended. They may become the permanent possession of some unfortunate outcasts. Similar games and superstitions built around an imaginary bug, often linked to a catching game, are found in various places, under various names (Hirschfeld 1997 cites India, Madagascar, and Japan). British people of a certain age may feel a shudder when the *Tig* or the *Lurgi* get mentioned. Even in France (mostly a cootie-free land) I was told that some children in the 1980s had invented a game of "AIDS-tag." Just like the fictional miasma itself, the beliefs and practices surrounding it spread from child to child. In Sue Samuelson's study of cooties (1980), only one child out of the forty-five testimonies she collected says she heard about the practice for the first time from an adult. Some prophylactic cootie-proof rituals are so secret as to be almost impenetrable to adults. It took weeks for a British school nurse interviewed by the Opies to understand a certain talisman that children inscribed in ink on their skin (Opie and Opie 1969, 76).

Age segregation is readily seen in the nature of children's games. Let us compare adults' games and children's games in my list of games from Rabelais's *Gargantua*. Adult-specific items look every bit like our expectations of them, being mostly board games (cards, dice, tric-trac), or sports. Children-only games, though quite diverse, have some unmistakably childish features. Their toys are not imitations of grown-up tools, such as adults in many societies design to train their children for future tasks. Fun is their sole raison d'être. These toys appear simple enough to be manufactured by children themselves, as they probably were.

None of the children's games in our data involve manipulations of physical symbols where skill or strength would play no role. Thus, board games and card games are completely absent. In adults' games of symbolic manipulation (like chess, cards, or dice), physical skill is completely irrelevant to the outcome. You cannot win at chess by launching or pushing a pawn deftly across the board. In fact, the materiality of the tokens does not matter a hoot. These games could have been played on an early 1980s computer. In contrast, children's games (in my sample) are never based on abstract symbolic computation alone. They always hinge on the way players manipulate some tokens, on their skills at handling stones, nuts, pick-up sticks, other players, and so on. These games could never be played on an old-fashioned Atari: they would require a machine that allows for a much greater degree of embodiment. Both adult and children's games manipulate symbols (words, tokens, or moves) in ways that are rule-bound, but only in adults is the rule powerful enough to do away with the physical side of symbol manipulation. In children, that aspect is always what the game is about. This puts their games closer to sport than to gaming, properly speaking.

(Differences in the use of randomness are particularly striking. Most adults' games involve the use of a physical tool to generate pseudo-random symbols—dices, cards, coins, and so on. The forty-seven children's games in my sample never do so. In general, children do use pseudo-random generators in some games, but these generators are not physical, and their randomness is very much debatable. Counting-out rhymes are a case in point. It takes some skill to utter *Eenie meenie* rapidly enough, landing on each player at least once, and still end up picking the chosen one. *Eenie meenie* is not a simple counting-out device: it is fun to play on its own, in a way that heads or tails is not.)

Jean-Michel Mehl's demographic analysis of French medieval games, as seen through hundreds of official judiciary documents concerning fights or quarrels over gambling games or sports (1990, 187) shows that symbolic games (board games, chess, cards, dice) are much more common in adults than in the people that his sources call *enfants* (who are usually adolescents and young adults). My own data suggest that this was also the case with younger *enfants* across centuries. Today's children do, of course, practice games of sheer symbolic manipulation, but these are adult-designed games. They fall outside the scope of children's peer culture.

They Are at Least as Durable as Cross-Generational Traditions

The folkloristic tradition is unanimous in attributing great longevity to children's peer culture. Historians also documented contemporary rhymes that can be traced back to the times before the Black Death (Orme 2001). Others are almost as long-lived. The tongue twister *Three gray greedy geese* can be found in the notebook of a fifteenth-century *escolier*, in a Victorian compendium of rhymes, or in the mouth of a 1950s Scottish schoolgirl. The number of greedy geese changes, but little else besides. The rhyme that E. B. Tylor had tracked back to Petronius was indeed part of a large family tree, whose branches are found in the most diverse times and places (Opie and Opie 1969, 295–301). Iconographic sources leave little doubt that the catching game some call *The bear and its watcher* was played in Ancient Greece and Rome, in Brueghel's Flanders, in eighteenth-century France, in the same way that it was still practiced recently in Europe and northern Africa (Parlebas 2000).

These cases are anecdotal, though. They do not suffice to gauge the longevity of children's traditions. Two things are lacking. First, we need an adult baseline for comparison. How long can we expect similar adult practices to last? Even a very rough estimate could be instructive. Second, we need to take a broader view. An unbiased sample may be out of our reach, but we can at least try to look beyond a handful of spectacular cases of cultural survival.

Yet trying to assess the typical or average survival time of children's traditions is more than difficult. It is also slightly absurd. The last chapter explained why most oral traditions fail to spread beyond a small circle around their inventors. There is no reason that children's games should be different. The traditions that make it to distant generations should thus be rather sophisticated: most games are fun, most rhymes euphonic. If we set them side by side with the clumsy innovations that emerge from the playground (as documented, for instance, by Iona Opie's fieldwork diary), one fears that most innovations petered out before they became traditional. If this is true, then the average survival time of children's games and rhymes would be easy enough to estimate. It would be weighted down by a mass of stillborn items, and would thus tend toward zero. To consider cultural survival is to consider an exceptional minority.

If we accept to narrow our focus and concentrate on the few miraculous cases that are identified by several sources across decades or centuries, our troubles are still not over. We encounter a host of biases. The availability of sources, their relative rarity, their dispersal in time and space—all these things can distort our perspective. When sources are abundant, many games get identified, down to the most ephemeral. In times of documentation scarcity, on the other hand, only the most successful traditions can be identified—and the successful traditions also tend to be the ones that last. If documentation scarcity is prolonged, only fairly durable and successful traditions can be identified twice or more. Less durable or successful traditions, which might have been spotted had documentation been more abundant, simply drop through the holes in the net. Thus, traditions that were in vogue at times when sources were few and far between will seem to be more long-lived, on average, than traditions that were identified in times of plentiful documentation.

This may explain important discrepancies among different estimates of the longevity of children's peer culture. When I looked at the history of a hundred singing games compiled and documented by the Opies (their 1969, my estimates), I found an average survival time of 190 years. My estimate for the survival of children's games in Rabelais's *Gargantua* puts the average at 324 years. Yet the Opies date their games in ways that are often more adventurous than mine. For one thing, they consider sources outside England, and as far back as Antiquity, while my search was restricted to French sources. The key difference between the two samples is that the Opies started from a sample of games that they observed in their own days. They worked backwards from that point, building on a large corpus of sources, sources that became less abundant as they moved away from their 1969 present. My own search started from the year 1534, at a time when sources were much less abundant. Many games in Rabelais's list only appear there. No other source documents them, and I can neither date them nor know whether they were children's games or something else. The 324-year average does not take these games into account. The Opies, on the other hand, probably took into their net many games that appear only once or twice in the record, over a short time interval. My sixteenth-century sources could not detect such short-lived games.

I will go back to my study of Gargantua's games, but first, note that this problem could be partially avoided by considering the extinction rate of traditions, rather than their longevity. Few authors were patient enough to collect songs or games repeatedly, in the same places, at intervals of several years; but I found two studies that did almost that. Both concern girls' skipping rhymes in the United States—Jean Alexander's study of Maryland skipping games from 1895 to 1969 (Mergen 1975), and Leah Yoffie's study of East St. Louis from 1895 to 1944 (Yoffie 1947). The data they offer are imperfect: the places they study are not exactly the same from one observation to the next, and the populations themselves change. Skipping rhymes can fail to show up in the records because observations are not exhaustive enough, or else because the lineage of girls who knew and transmitted the rhyme has moved. All this gives us reasons to think that such studies underestimate the longevity of girls' skipping games. We can, however, still form a rough idea of extinction rates by looking at the proportion of skipping rhymes that disappear over a given time interval. In Maryland, girls appear to jettison half their rhymes every thirty years, and keep the rest. In East St. Louis, where the data are more abundant, the extinction rate is lower: 20 percent of songs disappear every fifty years. This would suggest a median lifetime between sixty years (Maryland) and 125 years (East St. Louis). Sixty years is also the average duration of the thirty-four skipping songs collected by the Opies (1997, 207–306, my estimate)—arguably an underestimate, since good records of skipping rhymes only appeared in the mid-nineteenth century. Sixty years—around ten cultural generations for a children's peer culture—is still a respectable figure. Even more so if we consider all the forms of survival that this very rough estimate fails to take into account.

My study of 103 games mentioned in Rabelais's *Gargantua*, analyzed in detail in the appendix, also has its biases, but it is the only dataset that I know of which allows the longevity of children's and adults' traditions to be compared systematically. Its main conclusion is that the children's games in my sample last much longer than their adult-only counterpart, and at least as long as their cross-generational equivalents. Part of this longevity is to be explained by a selection bias: our sources are much more likely to document games played by adults than games played by children. Adults wrote the sources, after all. As a result, the shortest-lived children's games are more likely to slip through the holes in our net. The shortest-lived adult or cross-generational games are better documented. For there to be a selection bias, though, there must be a pool of long-lived games to select from. The data show that children's peer culture does produce traditions capable of crossing centuries.

Consider the number of cultural generations that must fit into one century of a children's game's life. Suppose we put the rate of generational turnover at seven years (seven years for a complete renewal of a population of children between seven and fourteen). Suppose, further, that we take an estimate of fifty years for generational turnover in a demographically complete human population (a low estimate). When measured in population renewals, then, the longevity of children's tradition becomes daunting. Children's games in *Gargantua*'s list last for fifty cultural generations on average, while cross-generational games only reach eight generations. A North Carolina ballad or an Icelandic saga can be expected to last between three and eight population renewals (using Rubin 1995's data). Accurate memories of historical events in oral traditions are said to be even more ephemeral, even by historians who argue in favor of taking oral history seriously (Vansina 1985). In some cultures, like ancient Greece (Thomas 1990) or medieval France (Le Roy Ladurie 1975/1979, 428–431), historians do not believe that oral memories of historical events usually survive the passing of even one generation (though other types of oral traditions last longer).

Children's traditions thus face an unusually acute version of the Wear-and-Tear Problem (as the Opies had noted). They should decay much faster than other traditions. Yet they do not seem to die out any sooner than others do. The *Gargantua* data show that some children's games completely avoid this problem. Not just a handful of spectacular cases do, but dozens of them.

They Are Homogenic and Share a Common Fate

The success of children's peer culture is not only a matter of preservation. It also shows in the number of places these traditions could reach, in their homogeneity from one place to the next, from one version to another. Counting-out rhymes are a case in point. When the psychologist David Rubin, in his book on oral traditions (1995), asked students coming from all over the United States to give their version of *Eenie meenie*, almost no one departed from anyone else's rhyme by more than a syllable. Rubin found no such degree of homogeneity for the other types of material that he studied (Homeric and Balkanic epic poetry, North Carolina ballads). The folkloristic literature on counting-out rhymes also depicts a highly homogeneous corpus (even though the compilers try to showcase the most distinctive variants, and avoid mentioning simple repetitions of a rhyme).

This homogeneity is most striking when seen across linguistic boundaries. Before it became a hit in the English-speaking world, *Eenie meenie* was known on the Continent. Jean Baucomont's compendium records the following version in Western France (*i* is pronounced *ee*, *a* is *ah*, and *e*, here, is like the *u* in *sun*).

> *Ine mine mane mo*
> [Eenie meenie miny moe]
> *Cat'géningue brède to*
> Catch a nigger by the toe[1]
> *Ifisse quine letingo*
> [If he squeals, let him go]
> *Ine mine mane mo*
> [Eenie meenie miny moe]
> (Baucomont et al. 1961, 118)

That is not an isolated example. The Opies routinely mention Continental variants for their British rhymes, which sometimes spread much further than the Continent. Van Gennep (1935) gave a thorough analysis of the rhyme *Santa femina goda*, which in his time was sung all over francophone Europe, from Wallonia to Switzerland and Algeria.

Children's traditions, thus, are both remarkably stable in time and homogeneous in space. Their longevity is but one aspect of their success, a success made all the more impressive by the fact that children's peer culture does not ride on the techniques and institutions that ensure the diffusion of adult and cross-generational culture. Children's traditions are stable, if stable means ancient, widespread, and homogeneous. That said, they seem to end their course quite abruptly and be swiftly displaced. Children's peer culture is subject to catastrophic changes, in spite of the stability of the individual elements that compose it. Sudden extinctions allow new items to invade the culture in a flash. Rubin analyzes the popularity of three distinct counting-out rhymes, gauging their popularity by the number of versions of each that is cited in the folkloristic literature, as a proportion of the total number of songs cited. His data show that the rise of *Eenie meenie* was meteoric, as swift as the fall of the

---

1. This racist line is most often replaced by "Catch a tiger by the toe", but this French transliteration is based on an earlier version.

counting-out rhyme that dominated playgrounds before *Eenie meenie* (*Onery, twoery, tickery* . . .). That rhyme was even more prevalent than *Eenie meenie* would be, but it is quite forgotten today (Rubin 1995, 248).

Other analysts of children's peer traditions share this diagnostic. Brian Sutton-Smith observed, in the United States (1961) and in New Zealand (1959), that the peer culture's favor is easily gained, easily lost. Even very stable practices, like hopscotch, can see their popularity surge or decline in impressive fluctuations over a few months (Opie and Opie 1969, 8–10). Seniority in children's peer culture is no protection against oblivion, and children readily jettison traditions with a solid pedigree (Fine 1980). And yet, their traditions last. Their culture may not be a repository of outmoded adult practices, but it is a good conservatory nonetheless, and one that does not seem to need much adult intervention to preserve itself. How does an unstable society, widely scattered, constantly renewed, transmit traditions over long distances of time and space? Why do children have traditions?

Folklorists have discovered these questions and pioneered their study, but they did not answer them satisfactorily. Not much has been said in this regard since William Newell's foundational book uncovered the twin puzzle of children's peer culture: traditions that are long-lasting, yet prone to sudden collapse (Newell 1883). His answer: children possess a lasting lore because they are more conservative than adults. Their culture is also likely to change suddenly because children are more inventive than adults. Gary Fine's 1980 commentary on "Newell's paradox" essentially restates the same answer: children are die-hard conservationists, yet they are also playful innovators. If childhood were a country, tour operators would call it a harmonious blend of tradition and modernity.

Can we do better than this? There have been attempts to explain the stability of children's traditions. They fall broadly into two families. Some explain cultural preservation by the fidelity of child-to-child transmission, a fidelity that is itself due to children's natural conservatism. Others point out that children's traditions, their rhymes in particular, are extremely memorable, which is what allows them to last.

What Makes Children's Peer Culture Last?

Traditionalism Is Not What Took Children's Culture across Time

The imitation hypothesis, the view that traditions exist because they are faithfully and compulsively transmitted, is nowhere more appealing than in the case of children's traditions. One can indeed argue that cultural transmission is something children carry out with exceptional care. In many domains they are notorious sticklers. They dislike novelty in daily rituals and habits, including games and stories. Griaule's characterization of Dogon children, their "outrageous conservatism when it came to immemorial customs," seems apposite (1938, 15). Contemporary work on "overimitation" sends a similar message. Another cause of faithful transmission that specialists lay great store by is conformity, which is arguably stronger in children. They lack social autonomy, they are more dependent on others. Lastly, where games and singing games are concerned, the necessity to coordinate on the same version of the same game (which places strong constraints on some traditions, like counting-out rhymes) could be a potent conservative factor.

Let us start with this last explanation: the constraints of coordination. I do not see them as the most important source of stability in children's traditions. For one thing, the coordination of children's games should not be overestimated. Children's play, as observed by ethnographers like William Corsaro (or in Iona Opie's one ethnographic book) are not as tidy and well-ordered as they appear to be in the work of folklorists. Declaring rules arbitrarily and unilaterally is not uncommon. These games are far from the degree of organization of their adult equivalents (not to mention adult coordination in other domains). There is something anomic and ephemeral about playground interactions. Above all, though, the need to coordinate does not explain what needs explaining: the widespread diffusion and stability of children's traditions. Coordination is a problem for small groups, for a short period of time. There is no need to share the same homogeneous practice on the scale of a continent, or a century. Besides, many items in children's peer culture (riddles, for instance) require no particular coordination between participants.

Like coordination, conformity and ritualization surely play some role in stabilizing children's traditions, like they do in all societies, and possibly more strongly among children. Yet one thing should prevent us from seeing these mechanisms as the root of preservation in children's peer culture. The problem is that children constantly come up with new games or songs that will not become traditional. Only a few might spread to become permanent fixtures of the culture (as we saw, this can happen quite rapidly). The rest will not. Children have no reason not to be less faithful, conservative, or conformist when they acquire non-traditional group games. Not unless they can pick the traditional from the non-traditional—but how could they do that?

Children, who are neither folklorists nor cultural historians, do not seem capable of solving this problem; and they do not seem to care. Among the youngest of Opie's informants, some claimed to have invented traditions that were in fact much older than they were. Even the oldest, who can be trusted to inform us about a game or a song's immediate origin, have no real notion of the true longevity of the practices they have acquired. This makes it extremely difficult to take seriously the claims so often put forward in the literature:

> Besides, the old games (. . .) are recommended by the quaintness of formulas which come from the remote past, and strike the young imagination as a sort of sacred law.
> (Newell 1883, 27)

> Although no sanction hangs over those who make mistakes, it is certain that players spare no effort to avoid them, and there is something very serious about the way they recite their text. This probably has to do with the fact that this recitation is much more than a mere verbal exercise, and there is no difficulty in following (from a safe distance) A. Carrington-Bolton [sic] who thinks he can find the remnants of old ritual formulas in these texts that children recite without understanding them.
> (Griaule 1938, 16)

> No matter how uncouth schoolchildren may outwardly appear, they remain tradition's warmest friends. Like the savage, they are respecters, even venerators of custom; and in their self-contained community their basic lore and language seems scarcely to alter from generation to generation.
> (Opie 1959, 2)

> The child learns to observe a code as he goes, and though the child is nothing but instability, that code is rarely broken. The received authority of tradition is conservative. The child consents to it, but it constrains him. [. . .] It is in no one's power to change the rules received from the ancients [. . .]. Rhymes do possess, for children, the quality of a revered text, one that bestows dignity upon a game, through a kind of hallowing that gets reflected in the officiant's grave demeanor.
> (Baucomont et al. 1961)

Loving one's routine and wanting to ape one's peers is not enough to be an efficient traditionalist. One also needs to know that one has genuine traditions to preserve, and value them above personal habits, above ephemeral fads, above the parochial ways that characterize a small group. Not many people qualify, even among adult traditionalists. Children could be as conformists, as novelty-averse as possible: such attitudes do not differentiate between, on the one hand, local ways, born into a small group of children and destined to disappear with it, and on the other hand the long-standing traditions that they share with thousands of other children (past, present, future).

The abrupt fall from grace of popular counting-out rhymes shows there is no special treatment for the best-established traditions. They can be relinquished as rapidly as they had been taken up in the past, even after a reign as long and undisputed as that of *Onery twoery tickery*. Even if they wanted to, children would have no way of telling which games in the playground are ancient, which are popular beyond the playground's limits, and which are not. As adults, they will often be quite surprised to know how ancient and widespread things like "cootie lore" can be. When the game of elastics took the playgrounds of the Western world by surprise, in the 1970s, no child could have guessed that the game was a thousand times less ancient than the game or marbles. Had they known it, I doubt it would have made any difference.

Neither Does Memorability Preserve Children's Rhymes

The folklorist Arnold Van Gennep was among the first to suggest that children's rhymes are well transmitted because they are easily committed to memory. He went so far as to suggest that most counting-out rhymes were actually descendants of mnemotechnic formulas taught to schoolchildren (such as, in English, *Thirty days hath September, April, June, and November,* or *When two vowels go walking the first does the talking*). Repeated transmission, he thought, had distorted them. It had bleached the original meaning away. For instance, the following (French) rhyme

> A la Santa Femina Goda cara caci quiteau l'éguillaume principal poral
> à la tchoum principal got chau . . .
>
> (Van Gennep 1935, 707)

was, in his view, a degraded version of a list of Latin American countries and cities (in French, *Santa Fe de Bogota, Caracas et Quito, la Guyane,* etc.). He speculated further that children's peer culture would preserve most such formulas, especially those that were sung. The formulas, endlessly drilled, would have seen their (already cryptic) meaning fade away, which would explain why most counting-out rhymes consist of nonsensical strings of sounds.

David Rubin offers a considerably more refined version of this view. His book, *Memory in Oral Traditions* (1995), seeks to relate the psychology of memory to the stability of oral traditions. His studies of Homeric and Balkanic epics, North Carolina ballads, and children's counting-out rhymes are all meant to show how memorability affects cultural survival. One great advantage of this approach is that it takes full account of the importance of redundancy and repetition for transmission; but their effects on memorization are all that matters to Rubin. In his view, traditions can become stable only to the extent that they fit into efficient memorization mechanisms. A song's memorability is the key to its survival. Rubin distinguishes three techniques that reciters may use to store a rhyme, a ballad, or an epic. The first consists in attaching one's tale to standardized schemas, themes, and sequences that are familiar to the reciter and her audience; the second in tying it to salient, vivid images, and strong emotions. Last is the use of rhymes within and between words, assonances, and other poetic tricks. These do not simply make songs euphonic. They also help with its memorization, by turning certain syllables into cues that can be used to guess other syllables. Every oral tradition thus has an interest in exploiting all three forms of memorability: ready-made schemas, imagery, euphony.

Children's counting-out rhymes make heavy and sophisticated use of euphony. Rubin notes, for instance, the ubiquity of internal rhymes (such as *I like Ike*, to use Roman Jakobson's famous example). *Am stram gram, Eenie meenie*, follow that pattern (Rubin 1995: 230). The fact that magic spells like *Abracadabra* or *Hocus pocus* have a similar structure is something that gave Victorian anthropologists a lot to mull over. I can't resist quoting my personal favorite, a Yiddish children's rhyme:

> Enge-benge, stupe-stenge,
> Artse-bartse, gole shvartse,
> Eymele, reymele,
> Feygele, beygele, hop!
> (Ruth Rubin, 1952, 230)

Rubin's hypothesis further predicts that people, when asked to recite such rhymes, are more likely to introduce variations (in other words, make mistakes) in the parts of the rhyme that are least constrained by rhyme, assonance, or repetition—which is what he observes. Other predictions, based on theories of generative poetics, successfully account for many formal traits of children's rhymes. Not many cognitive theories can be applied to cultural material in such a precise, subtle, and fruitful way. Yet although Rubin's account does capture many formal aspects of counting-out rhymes, it is not clear whether he manages to explain their stability (their "folkloric stubbornness," as Van Gennep put it).

Oral traditions, Rubin predicts, should avail themselves of three mnemonic devices: not just euphony, but also imagery and schemas. For adult oral traditions, this prediction holds true. Counting-out rhymes, however, make very little use of schemas or imagery. This is odd: the three types of mnemonic tools work best in combination. Three cues are better than one, and they reinforce one another. And yet, children's rhymes fail to make use of the first two types of technique that other oral traditions employ. Ready-made formulas, easily inserted in a recitation (like the Homeric "swift-footed Achilles" or "gray-eyed Athena") are absent. Everything is sacrificed to musicality, with one word out of five being a meaningless pseudo-word (Rubin 1995, 236), while the rest makes cryptic sense at best. As Van Gennep put it, counting-out rhymes are made of *mots sauvages*. Such lack of signification erases precious cues that memory could use. As Rubin acknowledges, the accumulation of nonsense pseudo-words "would seem to be a serious flaw if stability was desired" (1995, 251).

Perhaps, though (as Rubin argues), this neglect of semantic cues just comes as an unfortunate side effect of having a very delicate system of internal rhymes. The memorability hypothesis, however, faces a stronger difficulty: Rubin finds no clear link between a rhyme's memorability (as he gauges it) and its success or stability. Euphony (rhyme schemes between or within words, assonances), or other memory-relevant parameters like length, do not seem to bear a relation with the number of distinct versions of a rhyme that one can find in dictionaries and other compilations. Rhymes that get mentioned many times, and in many different periods and places, do not differ much on these counts from others. Obscure songs seem just as euphonic and pithy as very widespread ones: the link between memorability and cultural success has not been found.

This does not mean that children's rhymes were not, during their history, under some kind of pressure to become or to stay memorable; but I doubt that memorability was the most important mechanism of their survival. The fact that children easily learn them, that adults easily recall them decades after last hearing or reciting them, may be not so much a cause of their cultural prosperity, but a consequence of it. When a rhyme is so successful that one has heard it from every corner, repetition and redundancy smooth the path of memorization. The memorability of children's tradition may not explain their survival, but their proliferation might explain their memorability. As we shall see, proliferation may explain many other things besides.

Children's Traditions Were Selected to Proliferate

What is it that so puzzled the Opies when they contemplated the longevity of children's peer culture? The source of their amazement was, I think, a form of the Wear-and-Tear Problem. Demographic turnover forces children's traditions to undergo many transmission episodes. How come they do not get distorted in the process? The natural answer to this question is to call on mechanisms that preserve transmitted information: fidelity, traditionalism, and memorization. As we saw, these explanations are inadequate. What if we had no use for preservation mechanisms?

The theory of diffusion chain suggests we forget the Wear-and-Tear Problem for one moment. Let us ask, instead: what do children's traditions get their success from? The issue of their longevity cannot be addressed if that other problem is not solved. In a frequently renewed population, every long-standing tradition must be transmitted to many children with high frequency. It must proliferate. The only things that can become traditional in the peer culture must thus be the games, jokes, or rhymes that elicit in most children an urge to disseminate them. Ethnographies testify to the existence of idiosyncratic games that never become traditional. Those that did must have been persistent, like an earworm, so as to favor frequent repetition; and they must have been catchy, so they would be frequently transmitted. In other words, they needed to be appealing.

This is true of traditions in general, but such a selection should be even more important in children's peer culture. In normal societies, traditions can rely on several means of preservation besides sheer proliferation: institutions, information storage techniques (like writing), vertical transmission between the very old and the very young. The preservative power of individual memory is also greater in a society where vertical transmission is possible between quite distant generations: staying in memory for an additional ten or twenty years makes a difference to an adult tradition's survival. Children's rhymes also stay in adult memories, but there they stay inert: adults do not usually retransmit them. Thus, in cross-generational or adult cultures, fast-multiplying cultural fashions do not necessarily carry the day—not unless they are institutionalized, stored in writing (or some other form of storage), or duly memorized. Success-fueled traditions may enjoy short vogues, but in the long run they compete against traditions that are better suited to long-term diffusion. Adults have the institutions, the old people, and the techniques that allow them to store almost anything for a very long time. As a result, their traditions can fail in the struggle for success, yet still win the struggle for survival. That is almost impossible to achieve in children's peer cultures.

One could be tempted to explain the success of children's games by the fact that children (in humans as in other species) play much more than adults do. This fact probably explains why games hold such an important place in the corpus, but does it account for all the peculiarities of diffusion among children? I doubt it. For one thing, the category of "play," vague as it may be, does not fit all of children's traditions. Some formulas are akin to rituals; they are recited in a very serious spirit. More importantly, I do not see why the importance of playtime should by itself make it easier for individual games to survive. A lot of playtime does not necessarily mean more time allotted to each individual game. It could just as well mean a greater variety of games, with the time spent on each individual game remaining unchanged. Thus, their games would be more likely to be frequently played, but also more likely to be displaced by new games. Children above age six are well past the age at which children relish repetition for the sake of it (Zohar and Felz 2001).

Thus, the importance of play in children's lives would seem to predict that their play culture should be one of great diversity and frequent change, with many games in circulation, periodically wiped away by boredom. Yet this does not seem to be the case. Children's cultural repertoires show little diversification: they are quite homogenic—remarkably so, in fact, considering the fact that they are scattered through thousands of small playground communities and also that these playground communities play their games endlessly, defying boredom, until every pastime is worn thin. The fact that children play a lot, on a restricted repertoire of tirelessly repeated games, suggests two things. The homogeneity of children's play repertoire implies that their most popular games do not face the kind of competition that adult (or cross-generational) games suffer from. The fact that they play the same games without tiring shows that these games are well designed to withstand repetitions.

There is one mechanism that could make sense of these two things. That mechanism is *selection for proliferation*. As we saw, it is not possible for all of children's innovations to become traditional: those that we can observe on large scales of space and time are a minority. They survived a drastic selection process. Practices were culled if they failed to proliferate enough to create long and compact diffusion chains: long and compact diffusion chains were the obvious result. These chains cross long distances through many different individuals, by means of very frequent transmission episodes. No other type of transmission chain can stay the distance in a fast-renewed children's population. The type of game that belongs in such a chain is one that can withstand, or better, elicit frequent repetitions. If a tradition has these qualities, then it does not matter much whether it catches on when first encountered, or whether it is easily committed to memory. Repetition and redundancy will take care of that. Few studies have asked children what makes them prefer a traditional game over another. It is interesting that the one (fairly ancient) study that I know which did, reported that the two reasons most cited by children were familiarity and repetition (questionaire in Heck 1927). Withstanding and eliciting frequent repetition is no easy thing. Children's traditions manage to do so simply because those that did not were wiped out. The crushing wheel of population turnover drove them to extinction. This would also explain why children's cultural repertoires are so homogenic.

Thus, children's traditions solve the Flop Problem and the Wear-and-Tear Problem in one go. Solve it, or rather, find the stupidest possible way around it: natural selection. If this view is correct, then the folklorists' view that children's traditions are exceptionally long-lived is still correct, but it needs to be nuanced in several ways.

First, the survival of children's games appears exceptional only if we take the Wear-and-Tear Problem too seriously. The existence of long-lived children's traditions supports a prediction of the theory of diffusion chains: given a high degree of repetition and redundancy (as certainly obtains among children playing together), the Wear-and-Tear Problem fades away. It is solved automatically, as a by-product of solving the truly hard Flop Problem. The Flop Problem itself is taken care of by natural selection.

Second, this selectionist view implies the existence of a "dark" mass of short-lived games that became traditional for some time, but not long enough to enter our records. My data on the 103 games in Rabelais's list suggest that this should be the case (as argued in the appendix). My sources, written by adults and mentioning mostly adults, tend to under-detect children's games. Looking at the number of times that a game is detected by our sources, between its first and last appearance in the record, I found that the average cross-generational game gets detected once every century. So does the average adults' game. Children's games, though, get detected twice less often, once every two hundred years. In other words, the holes in our net are twice bigger for children's games. We only catch the biggest fishes. My 103 games are a minority of the items in *Gargantua*'s list. That list must have contained games that nobody except Rabelais has documented. The fact that children's games were twice less likely to be detected when they were in circulation implies that the items of Rabelais's list that were left in the dark were, for the most part, short-lived traditions that belonged to childhood.

The most long-lived of children's traditions may not suffer from the erosion of the Wear-and-Tear Problem, as I have argued. But they should feel the pull of a fast demographic turnover in other ways. They live, so to speak, on a different clock. When a cross-generational tradition lasts for six generations, a children's tradition crosses thirty-six generations in the same time span. They live in fast-forward mode. As we saw, this need not impact their longevity, but it could have consequences on other aspects of their history: their appearance or disappearance. We saw indeed that counting-out rhymes get displaced very rapidly, belying the view of children as die-hard conservatives. No one is clinging to a rhyme like *Onery twoery tickery* in the way that Balkanic singers preserve the Homeric style of formulaic epic poetry. *Onery twoery* could be heard everywhere, yet one day it disappeared.

Generational Turnover Need Not Impair Cultural Survival

Children's peer culture illustrates what cultural transmission inside generations can achieve. Not only is diffusion possible without intergenerational transmission, it generates lasting, homogenic, and widespread practices. This implies that demographic turnover, and the accompanying aggravation of the Wear-and-Tear Problem, is no insuperable ordeal.

This goes against the grain of a certain form of cultural pessimism. On the face of it, demographic change puts traditions under stress. Vertical transmission is the only way to overcome this obstacle, and it is most successful when it is most conservative. That was the conclusion which Hume drew from his thought experiment on butterflies. This view (also defended by Arendt 1961/2006) implies a grim outlook on children's peer cultures. In Plato's *Laws*, the stranger from Athens voices his concern that children's games are bound to fall into decay for lack of faithful transmission, and asks for a law that would fixate the content of their games once and for all (*The Laws*, 797a). Children, the stranger thought, would never sustain lasting traditions unless the city forced them to. He took it that children are not naturally attached to tradition: after all, they invented and jettisoned new games all the time. In this, he was right. He concluded (wrongly) that these games could never become traditional without adult interference.

There are reasons to share in this cultural pessimism. Generational turnover is indeed a threat to cultural continuity, best averted by means of vertical transmission. We have seen, though, that this pattern admits of many exceptions. Vertical transmission is not strictly necessary to a tradition' stability, and it rarely works on its own. It often has the backup of horizontal transfers: children learn adult traditions by practicing them among themselves, with a lot of reinvention. The importance of horizontal transmission appears fully when we realize that cultural stability is more than a simple matter of faithful memorization or transmission. What makes the traditions in children's peer culture stable, for instance, is not their greater memorability. Nor is it the fidelity, or putative traditionalism, of transmission among children. What does the trick is these traditions' capacity to proliferate rapidly and ceaselessly. In a constantly refreshed population, where no child can stay for very long, a tradition has more to gain by being continually passed on to new adopters than by being faithfully retained by one individual.

That is one consequence of the theory of diffusion chains: proliferation is a key ingredient of cultural survival. Traditionalism would reduce cultural preservation to faithful transmission, or to memory. They are neither necessary nor sufficient. In the next chapter, broader consequences will be drawn from this principle. As we shall see, the richness of human culture has been attributed to the cognitive capacities that are at play in cultural transmission among humans. Transmission is often efficient in our species. It is tempting to attribute this efficiency to a faculty that would have evolved specifically to ensure the faithful passing of traditions. That explanation is not the only possible one, though: our capacities for culture may be a simple by-product of our general talent for communicating and receiving information. But the notion that natural selection built us as cultural animals has deep intellectual roots. Its seduction is not easily dissipated. In the next chapter, I will argue that this notion suffers from a fundamental difficulty: it takes the Wear-and-Tear Problem too seriously. Consequently, it sees faithful transmission and memory as the chief causes of cultural continuity, forgetting proliferation.

If we take the Flop Problem seriously (and forget about the Wear-and-Tear Problem), we need to ask about the appeal of human traditions, not about our talent in preserving them. Why do humans, of all species, possess so many catchy traditions? Such a big repertoire of appealing cultural practices would not, I will argue, have appeared overnight. A protracted building-up of our repertoires was necessary. This build-up is quite different from what students of cultural evolution refer to as "cumulative evolution," a process of gradual improvement that makes technologies more efficient. It has to do with the multiplication of appealing traditions, rather than the improvement of existing ones. It is quantitative rather than qualitative. We know that this build-up occurred at some point, since we know that human cultural repertoires are much bigger than any others. Our last chapter sketches a scenario that might explain how the build-up came about.

6 AN EVER MORE CULTURAL ANIMAL

It is high time to tackle this book's second question. Why is most of the cultural wealth of this planet concentrated in the hands of a single species? That question was kept for the last chapter for a reason: I reckoned that understanding what makes some human traditions more stable than other human traditions should be a necessary first step, before explaining why humans have so many stable traditions. At bottom, I believe these two questions to be one and the same. This implies that traditions live and die for more or less the same reasons among humans and other animals. In other words, the causes of cultural failures among humans should hold the key to the question of why non-human traditions thrive less than ours, while humans stabilize some of the things they do and say (though not all of them) into traditions.

The natural starting point, for most authors who tackle this issue, consists in noting that cultural transmission in our species routinely results in the creation or maintenance of enduring traditions. Animal social learning generally produces fewer and less complex traditions. Thus, there must be something special about the way human culture gets passed on—something that it is the scientist's job to discover. That search is not altogether forlorn. We saw in chapter 2 that human cultural transmission is indeed peculiar: it makes use of ostensive communication, a highly unusual means of information transfer. Yet researchers in quest for the uniquely human cultural transmission faculty cannot answer the deeper question—why do ideas and actions travel wider and longer among humans than anywhere else? They cannot answer this question, because they tackle it from the wrong angle. Humans, I have been arguing, are remarkably gifted for information exchange, yet we have no particular aptitude for *cultural* transmission, as opposed to the transmission of transient or local ideas and practices. The quest for a faithful and compulsive instinct, specifically selected to preserve traditions, is a misguided one. This only adds to the difficulty of our question: How could humans possess extraordinary cultures without extraordinary cultural capacities?

In this chapter we come to the juncture between two different aspects of the field of cultural evolution, what we might call (to borrow Jean Gayon's distinction) "evolution *of* culture" and "evolution *towards* culture" (Gayon 2003). The evolution of culture is what we have been studying up to now: the life of traditions, their propagation, successes, and changes. The evolution of our species *towards* culture, on the other hand, is the process that turned humans into cultural animals. Here again, I believe the two problems share common solutions. This chapter will try to show that there is much insight to be gained by looking at the appearance of human cultures as an episode of cultural history like any other. We do not have to assume that our becoming cultural followed directly upon biological changes in our species' makeup. We do not need to speculate that we developed one adaptation to culture, or one imitative faculty, which set cultural history in motion. If my impression is right, then most of the first human traditions grew and accumulated in populations that did not become more clever, more social, or better gifted at imitation in the process. To summarize this chapter's point, one could say that the evolution of our species *towards* culture was nothing but a phase in the evolution *of* our cultures.

This chapter starts with a recapitulation of three ideas, which we met in previous chapters, and which ground the claims that will be made later. The human species is characterized by our mastery of ostensive communication; traditions benefit from the exceptional conditions of cultural conservation in human societies; cultural evolution in the long run is dominated by rare but extremely durable traditions. Starting from these three cues, I will develop a theory of the accumulation process that made human repertoires much richer than all others. To do this, I will first need to discuss and refute the most popular alternative theory, the "cumulative culture" thesis. According to that thesis, complex and useful traditions can only develop through the gradual accumulation of small and infrequent improvements. As a consequence, only a species capable of extremely faithful transmission can support cumulative culture. I will explain why I doubt this view, and seize that opportunity to take issue with the imitation hypothesis one last time. I propose another scenario for human cultural accumulation. Much in my story depends on "extreme traditions," that is to say, on the cultural items that last long and diffuse widely, because they appeal to everyone. To get such traditions to arise, imitation or fidelity are useless, but invention is key. Once they appear, extreme traditions have an impetus of their own, and can survive even very harsh conditions, which means that good institutions or demography are not always necessary or sufficient to sustain rich cultures. This (admittedly sketchy) scenario does not make much room for coevolutionary dynamics between genes and culture. This leads me to wonder whether, and in what sense, we are cultural animals; I answer that we might be becoming *more* cultural with every passing century.

Three Clues for One Puzzle

Generations of scholars taught us that culture was the defining trait of human nature. Whatever is left of humanist beliefs in human exceptionality found a refuge in the culture concept. UNESCO's constitution proclaims that "the wide diffusion of culture, and the education of humanity for justice and liberty and peace are indispensable to the dignity of man and constitute a sacred duty," a principle reaffirmed in the organization's 2001 declaration on cultural diversity (UNESCO 1945, 2001). The international organization is just stating what is obvious to global elites.

Yet the traditions that we have met throughout this book told us quite a different story. Some are noble, some are precious, but many are difficult to love. As for their human carriers, they often pass their culture on without knowing that it is ancient or traditional, and without caring much whether it is so. We tend to neglect this fact, because the notion of culture is intuitively tied to high-cultural practices (religion, science, the arts) whose transmission is organized in a self-conscious fashion. They tend to be associated with conservative institutions, which tied their fate to the preservation of a venerated corpus. We saw in chapter 2, however, that much of cultural transmission is not institutionalized in this way: it can occur anywhere, at any time, from anyone, and for any reason. Everyday techniques, new words, children's rituals—these things are not preserved by their carriers as if their dignity depended on it (not always, at any rate).

We might not have come to that conclusion had we not started from a rather peculiar definition of culture. That definition was meant to cover the transmission of long-standing practices, and little else besides. Yet culture is usually taken to stand for much more than that. Culture stands for intercultural differences. It stands for social life in general. It stands for nurture. It stands for everything we value about education. Words are in the public domain, but in our definition the common use got narrowed down to something very basic: culture is everything that is traditional, in other words, everything that transmission propagates across large scales of space and time. What makes a practice traditional, thus, is a matter of scale. This abstract, quantitative characterization would not meet the needs of most students of culture in the humanities or the social sciences (and there would be no point in imposing it on them). I used that definition because it seemed most handy to study the life and death of traditions over long stretches of time. Many an important social phenomenon thus eludes our definition of culture: institutions or moral rules, for instance, may or may not be cultural in this sense.

Stretching things a bit, one could say that humans live a double life, shared between culture, as defined here, and society. Social life, a life of alliances, rivalries, friendships, and exchanges, is laced with webs of cultural transmission. The existence of these webs, their shape, their extension in space or time, need not be visible to those who pass through them—just like we ignore the trajectories that brought the coins in our pockets from other people's pockets into our own. The child who abandons a game of elastics for a game of cat's cradle does not know she is leaving a diffusion chain that is barely older than she is, to join one that spans millennia. She is now participating, in her very small way, to the stabilization of a chain much larger than her life. But did anything happen to her? Her social life went on, without skipping a beat, when she hopped from one web to another. Her parents, her play partners, her school are unchanged; yet her cultural horizon now includes millions of other human beings.

Non-human animals do not seem to spend as much time on the cultural side of life. Their social life, on the other hand, is intense: they build coalitions, they maintain hierarchies and networks of exchanges. These structures are quite ephemeral, though: chimpanzee alpha males seldom die with their crown on. Dynastic succession is hardly the rule. Behavioral innovations, too, seem to leave few traces for future generations (to judge by the simplicity and scarcity of chimpanzee culture—on which more below). The cultural side of our double life seems much less accessible to other species. Why would that be?

We have met three clues that might explain the rather special relation between our species and its cultures. Each could contribute an answer, though none is sufficient on its own.

Ostensive communication is our first clue. We saw that behavior transmission in non-human animals is usually involuntary. If and when they help a conspecific learn something, they do so by changing something in the environment of the individual they are helping, not by overtly manifesting their intention to help. Ostensive communication, humans' favorite transmission mode, rests on our capacity to recognize, in others, their intentions that target our own mental states. Bruno understands that Alice wants him (Bruno) to understand that the door is locked. This kind of communication is voluntary: Alice must *want* Bruno to understand that the door is locked. It is overt: Alice must openly make her intention known to Bruno. Ostensive communication does not work in stealth mode, unbeknownst to the emitter or the receptor. It calls for willing cooperation from all involved. Communication thus defined solves, I think, some of the problems that surround the human cultural exception, but it leaves other issues untouched. This one, for instance: how do we get from ostensive communication to stable diffusion chains? Of all the things that communication brings to our doorstep, we retain only a few, and we repeat even less. For this reason, early students of cultural transmission thought it more likely that traditions should get passed on by more conservative means, like teaching, or, above all, imitation. Yet, as we saw, traditions do pass through communication, Herder's *light, insubstantial, fugitive web*. How do they compensate for its frailties?

The theory of diffusion chains aims at explaining how we can get cultural conservation without a very faithful form of transmission. It sees transmission efficiency as the easiest and least important problem in cultural diffusion. One episode of efficient transmission is easy to get, but does not guarantee that others will follow in any way. What is transmitted may never be transmitted again, or if it gets re-transmitted, the transmission chain may peter out after a few links. What decides between aborted chains and lasting ones is cultural success: getting successful, that is, solving the Flop Problem, automatically takes care of the Wear-and-Tear Problem. Repeated transmission does not wear successful traditions out, it reinforces them. Giulio Andreotti, Italy's immutable politician, was wont to quip that "power wears out only those who don't have it." The same could be said of cultural transmission: it erodes only the traditions that are not transmitted enough.

The Flop Problems can be solved in two ways: a tradition can possess some intrinsic appeal, or it can travel in a population where demography, institutions, and storage techniques make it easier for individuals to have cultural contacts with one another. Traditions can live without one of these conditions, not without both. These extrinsic conservation conditions of culture (*conservation conditions*, for short) are our second clue.

We also saw, however, that some traditions can count on their own intrinsic appeal to become successful, without depending too much on too specific a social environment. We saw that these traditions should be relatively rare, but very important. Cultural longevity is probably, in many cases, distributed in an extreme fashion, with a privileged few getting all the success, and all the life span, so to speak. In children's peer culture, we have seen examples of extremely long-lived traditions whose success could not be accounted for entirely with conservation conditions. They thrive among groups with a weak demography, and with little in the way of technological or institutional means of preservation. Some adult traditions show a similar stubbornness. Kwaio religion, for instance, must have survived dozens of demographic bottlenecks, many more population renewals, while coping with a scarce and scattered population.

The fact that lasting traditions can be observed in a great variety of human groups shows that cultural conservation is not merely a reflection of conservation conditions. In the very same society, one may find some very long-lived traditions and some much more ephemeral, all inhabiting the same institutions, the same techniques, the same demography. The traditions that last will live long enough to come across many changes in conservation conditions, too—demographic crises, institutional collapses, technological backslidings. Such changes are likely to destroy many of the things that can make or unmake a tradition's success on a local scale. And yet, they do not unmake everything.

The traditions found at the top of the extreme distribution of longevity and success—let us call them "extreme traditions"—are our third clue. They can survive harsh conservation conditions. How? Chapter 4 suggested that they must possess some intrinsic appeal. They travel far by clinging to every possible link along the way. This means they should be of interest to anyone at all. Our study of cultural diffusion in harsh demographic settings suggests that this appeal of extreme traditions is what allows culture to make it through the passing of generations, when nothing else does.

Here, then, are our three clues: ostensive communication sets the stage for intense information exchange to occur in humans, but it can be used to transmit many things besides traditions, and it does not guarantee that *cultural* transmission will occur. *Conservation conditions* for culture have changed a lot through human history, with some very recent improvements, like writing or printing, and, arguably, less recent demographic trends that may have contributed to the constitution of rich cultural repertoires. Good conservation conditions do not explain everything, though, for we saw that *extreme traditions* can survive in harsh conditions. Their existence, like the existence of animal traditions, suggests that our species did not have to wait for conservation conditions to improve before they constituted some embryonic cultural repertoires.

To put the jigsaw puzzle together, we will start from the last piece: we begin with extreme traditions. Why are they so numerous in our species and so rare elsewhere? How did they accumulate?

What Is Cultural Accumulation?

Years of detailed research by ten primatologists, revealed in a famous *Nature* paper (Whiten et al. 1999), have uncovered, in six distinct chimpanzee populations, eighty-five ways of behaving that are thought to derive for cultural transmission. In most cases, there is no direct evidence for social transmission: their cultural character is inferred from the fact that they vary from one population to another, with no good environmental explanation to account for the variation. Some of these "traditions" could be explained away by subtle, overlooked environmental differences.

Counting, individuating, and cutting up cultural items is a tricky affair. So is disentangling cultural and environmental influences. Even so, the magnitude of cultural diversity among humans, compared to the best-documented non-human cultures, is not something that can be argued away. I just need to open my eyes to observe more traditions than an experienced primatologist observes in years of fieldwork. Over through the window I can see a city's flag, and a state's; a river, crossed by boats, bordered by docks and a highway; electric lights; passers-by and their shoes, their clothes, their umbrellas, their religious signs; the languages that they speak, and yet another language spoken on the radio. In each building, each tree, each square meter of pavement, a huge sum of know-hows is expressed. Civilizations and their cities hold great concentrations of cultural wealth, but other, stateless societies also possess cultural repertoires larger than any non-human repertoires.

The difference is huge, intuitive, and probably impossible to quantify in a very precise fashion (I doubt there would be a point in trying). It is a fuzzy distinction, which I do not mind. Others might. Scientists like their distinctions to be either quantitative (and precisely measurable) or qualitative (and clear-cut). The difference between human and non-human cultures, I think, is neither. Yet a qualitative distinction is what dominates the field: the distinction between cumulative and non-cumulative cultures. Theorists such as Tomasello (1999) or Boyd and Richerson (1995) have done much to spread the view that something fundamental separates cumulative cultures, built on faithful imitation, from non-cumulative cultures, derived from weaker forms of cultural transmission; but what exactly is cumulative culture?

"Cumulative Culture" Is an Avatar of Evolutionary Gradualism

The cumulative culture thesis holds that human cultures are different, and richer, because faithful transmission allows us to preserve useful ideas that would otherwise be lost.

> ... the single most important adaptive feature of culture is that it allows the gradual, cumulative assembly of adaptations over many generations, adaptations that no single individual could evoke on his or her own.
>
> (Boyd and Richerson 2005, 45)

> ... some human traditions change over time in ways that seem to be adaptive and, moreover, that seem to accumulate modifications made by different individuals over time in the direction of greater complexity such that a wider range of functions is encompassed—what may be called "cumulative cultural evolution" or "the ratchet effect."
>
> The process of cumulative cultural evolution requires not only creative invention but also, and just as importantly, faithful social transmission (...).
>
> (Tomasello 1999, 36, 39)

> ... while inventiveness is fairly widespread among primates, humans transmit cultural items across generations much more faithfully, and it is this faithful transmission (the ratchet) that explains why human culture accumulates modifications over time in a way that chimpanzee and other animal cultures do not.
>
> (Tennie, Call, and Tomasello 2009, 2406)

Put this way, cumulative culture seems to be nothing but the cultural diffusion of good tricks; but there is more to it than that. In these authors' view, cultural accumulation is a *gradual* progress, a progress which naturally flows from the fidelity of human imitation. The compulsive and faithful retention of small improvements is what allows human cultures to progress, one step at a time. Cumulativeness is a consequence of conservatism: human traditions improve *because* they retain any improvement brought to them.

Most debates concerning cumulative culture revolve around the question of knowing who has it. Is it a human peculiarity? On this point, cumulative culture theorists have some contradictors. Andrew Whiten and his colleague note that some ant-picking techniques are several times more efficient in certain chimpanzee communities than elsewhere (Whiten et al. 2003), which (barring huge differences in individual ingenuity) could suggest some cultural improvement. Likewise, Bernard Thierry (1997, 249–250) analyzes several chimpanzee technologies whose features seem too complex to have been devised by one single individual. Some of the best evidence for technological improvements among non-humans has been gathered by Russell Gray and his group (Hunt and Gray 2003). This important debate will not be settled here. Instead, let us consider the validity of the cumulative culture thesis itself. That claim follows the biological doctrine of gradualism quite closely.

Gradualism in biology is a thesis that depends on two assumptions. Both assumptions are true only up to a point, and they may be occasionally falsified, as we shall see, but there is a fair deal of agreement among biologists on both counts. First, adaptive change is (by and large) blind. Nature does not plan ahead: it gropes along in darkness. In other words, variations in living beings are, overall, insensitive to the future fitness of their carriers—an abundance of deleterious genetic mutations testifies to that. Second, organisms are fragile, complex things. Any change to their architecture could easily break them down—and the bigger changes are the most disruptive. In technical parlance, organisms have limited phenotypic plasticity. Together, these two assumptions imply that adaptations must accumulate gradually, which is to say by means of small improvements that occur rarely. The improvements are small because of limited plasticity, and they occur rarely, because change is blind. This may be quite wrong (I am not, here, making a point for or against the Darwinian orthodoxy), but, if gradualism makes any sense in biology, it does so because of these two assumptions: blindness, and limited plasticity.

Gradualism has many important consequences for biology; the most relevant for us is to the faithfulness of transmission. When gradualism holds, complex adaptations may only appear inside lineages where each organism preserves information in a compulsive and faithful fashion. Compulsivity is paramount here: all the information must be copied, not simply the part of it that will be relevant in the organism's lifetime. There are many tiny "good tricks" that may only serve once in ten generations, and these need to be passed on as well as the rest.

Faithfully Replicated Small Changes Cannot Explain Everything

As noted, the two assumptions that ground gradualism, blindness and limited plasticity, can sometimes prove false; both have been altogether repudiated by a few researchers. Variation can be guided to some extent, via an increase in mutation rates in certain conditions, or by having genetic changes follow upon and stabilize behavioral innovations. Phenotypic plasticity can also be substantial. What happens then? In the (implausible) case where the two assumptions were completely false, complex adaptations would arise de novo with every new generation of organisms, and there would be no need for any of the information preserved in the lineage. Biologists concur that gradualism is a more plausible scenario, although it is idealized, and sometimes wrong. Their position is not without risk. After all, new evidence on guided variation and phenotypic plasticity could turn up to show that gradualism is deeply mistaken, even as a rough idealization. Yet gradualism seems less wrong than the alternative. (Jablonka and Lamb 2005 provide a good overview of the case against gradualism in biology; paradoxically, they embrace the cumulative culture thesis with enthusiasm.)

What about human culture? There are obvious reasons to be wary of gradualism in the cultural case. The two core assumptions that ground the gradualist claim are simply too dubious here. If there is anything like insight, human inventors have it. We are not omniscient, nor fully rational, of course, but neither do we transform our traditions in a completely random fashion. Nor is there evidence that traditions are so fragile or brittle that they could not be changed: we have seen things like cars, states, religious dogmas, or marriage customs change in incredible ways without losing their primary functions and their distinctive shape. Cultural plasticity is not obviously more wrong than the alternative.

More importantly, we know that adaptive cultural change went through a brutal acceleration in the last two centuries or so (Clark 2009). The amount of energy we can use, the number of people we can feed, the diseases we can cure: all this has exploded fairly recently, after millennia of relative stagnation. Cultural gradualism does not look less wrong than the alternative—rather more. In spite of this, there have been defenders of gradualism in technological evolution, from the Victorian times to our own (Pitt Rivers 1906; Basalla 1989). Their main argument consists in pointing out the historical links between past achievements and modern inventions. Yes, they would say, the discovery of radioactivity in the twentieth century allowed us to exploit an entirely new and vastly more powerful kind of energy; but its discoverers did not build from scratch; rather, they relied on the whole legacy of physical science. This argument does not prove the point at stake, though. We all agree that there is a great deal of historical continuity in technological evolution; what gradualism entails is something different. Gradualist changes are not simply connected: they must be small, numerous, and rare. Merely noting that we stand on the shoulders of giants does not make the gradualist point—the gradualist point being that we stand on the shoulders of dwarves. Many, many dwarves.

Extreme gradualism could turn out to be the least implausible option in some cases of technological evolution, but assuming it to be true across the board would be risky, to say the least. Even biologists sometimes get their gradualist assumptions wrong. If the issue of biological gradualism is a can of worms, then its cultural equivalent is a basket of jumping spiders. One would need to write off all the evidence for abrupt, disruptive, and useful cultural innovations, along with the fact that cultural conservation does not automatically lead to an accumulation of good tricks.

Traditions Often Endure without Improving . . .

Cultural stability is compatible with complete stagnation. Well-documented children's games and rhymes do not change much between the time we first observe them and the time they become extinct (typically centuries later). No one thought of describing their history as a gradual increase in complexity or sophistication: what sophistication they possess was present from the start. This is not, of course, valid for children's peer culture only. Many students of cultural history over the long run object to narratives of gradual progress. Here, for instance, is the archeologist Steven Mithen on the first human lithic traditions:

> Tomasello et al. (1993, 508) are simply wrong to invoke a "gradual increase in complexity" of "hammer-like tools" during prehistory, as are Boyd and Richerson (1995, 80) when they claim that gradual change is documented in the archeological record. Such cumulative change is only a feature of the most recent prehistory, that after 50,000 years ago, after early humans with fully modern brain size and evident powers of imitation had been present for at least one million years.
>
> (Mithen 1999, 398)

To this kind of argument, proponents of cumulative culture can reply that simply keeping lithic techniques in use was, in and of itself, a kind of accumulation. After all, it allowed humans to gain the benefit of good tricks, which they could probably not have retrieved by themselves without the benefit of transmission. This is accumulation in a much weaker sense, though; in fact it is nothing else or more than cultural transmission. That, indeed, is what cumulative culture seems sometimes to boil down to: the simple fact that human cultures are preservative. They do not allow good ideas to go to waste. This is the view of cultural progress that Tarde offered in his *Laws of Imitation*:

> (. . .) among animals (. . .) imitation is effected in a pretty inexact manner (. . .). Because of this animal societies stand still; for although some ingenious idea might gleam through the brain of a crow or bison, it would, according to hypothesis, die with it and be necessarily lost to the community. With animals it is primarily and pre-eminently muscle which imitates muscle; with us, it is primarily and pre-eminently nerve which imitates nerve and brain which imitates brain. This is the chief contrast through which we may explain the superiority of human societies. In them no good idea is lost, and every exceptional thinker lives on in the posterity which he raises to his own level.
> (Tarde 1893/1903, 206)

Tarde slightly overstated his point: not all ideas survive in human cultures, and even some "exceptional thinkers" fail to grow roots (remember the old Chinese clock-builder that we came across in chapter 5). Still, he was obviously right in stating that, thanks to transmission, good ideas manage the passing of generations. What he could not know, though, is that good ideas survive in other species as well. Such survival should not be construed as a special property of some cultures: survival, made possible by transmission, is part of the definition of culture. All cultures are "cumulative" in the very weak sense that they are made of transmitted traditions. What we want to know is whether traditions improve with time, and whether these improvements are only made possible by faithful transmission, as opposed to human ingenuity.

. . . and Cultural Progress May Do without Conservation

The cumulative culture thesis rests on the assumption that good ideas do not last, or accumulate, unless they are faithfully transmitted. When we find that a culture has traditions too complex to have been invented by one individual, we must conclude that the individual in question copied the complexity from some external source. If individuals in that culture can copy complex things, it seems to follow that they are particularly gifted imitators. This reasoning, though not absurd, fails to consider two plausible options. First, cultural complexity may arise because individuals have a large pool of smart ideas to choose and copy from, not because they have become better at copying those. Second, the complexity of individual behavior may not consist in copies of others' good ideas, but in combinations, or transformations. We saw in chapter 4 that transmission fidelity was not a crucial parameter in cultural preservation. The same view could apply to cultural improvements: they can still occur when cultural transmission is selective and transformative. In fact, selectivity and transformation help traditions become more functional. Traditions improve in the same way that they diffuse: not by being faithfully preserved, but by being passed around a lot, and often reconstructed.

An ingenious transmission experiment shows how this may occur. Christine Caldwell and Alisa Millen (2009) asked several series of subjects to join a transmission chain, where each link tries to build a paper plane that flies as far as possible (variant: a spaghetti tower as high as possible). Every link is given the possibility to observe the previous link in the chain (who can also give advice). Subjects' performances can be quantified (higher towers, longer-ranging planes) and they increase a lot between the two ends of the chains (on average, they get twice better). There is progress, thus, in these chains; but is it because each link copies the good tricks left by the previous link? Is it because imitation allows functional forms to be preserved?

No. There is surprisingly little imitation between the links in the chain. External observers find scarcely more resemblance between two paper planes (or two spaghetti towers) when they are taken from the same chains than when taken from two different chains. In the planes chains (but not the tower chains), there is a tendency for subjects to copy their immediate predecessor: planes on neighboring links resemble each other more than planes from different chains. The resemblance fades rapidly as links get distant, though. (This won't come as a surprise to readers of chapter 4: sequential chains like this one do not maintain information on long distances: the Wear-and-Tear Problem gets at them, even when transmission is faithful.)

Although the participant's fidelity to their predecessors is not exceptional, the design of paper planes and spaghetti towers gradually grows more clever and efficient; is it because good ideas are preserved? Here again, not particularly. Good tricks get lost by the dozens, with many subjects choosing to jettison a smart innovation. This shows in the frequent regressions in performances that can be observed as the chain rolls along. Not every efficiency gain is caught by the "ratchet effect." This example may be a bit artificial, but the basic point that it underscores is simple enough: there is no logical reason to think that a tradition's improvement should only depend on the fidelity of its transmission. These arguments do not make the cumulative culture thesis wrong: it could still be the case that human techniques accumulate good design features because they are well preserved. What they do suggest is that cultural progress is also driven by other dynamics—transformative ones. Where the cumulative culture thesis errs is when it implies that progress requires faithful imitation. That this implication seems obvious just illustrates how entrenched the imitation hypothesis has become: we tend to take it for granted that all good things in cultural evolution have their roots in faithful and compulsive transmission.

The Growing Number of Traditions Is What Matters

One last reason to be wary of the cumulative culture thesis is that it draws our attention away from the feature of our cultural history that most needs explaining: the fact that human cultural repertoires are much richer than others. Proponents of cumulative culture are interested in a qualitative change—the growing efficiency of some tools. The word *cumulative* can induce a degree of confusion here, since the things that accumulate, according to the thesis, are not traditions, but improvements on existing traditions. Cumulative traditions become more functional or complex with time, not necessarily more numerous. Because of this focus on improvements, cumulative culture draws excessive attention to techniques, leaving aside traditions for which progress or efficiency are hard to measure: linguistic, artistic, or ritual culture. Above all, it puts all the weight of human exceptionality on a qualitative phenomenon, on a process that occurs to some traditions but not all, the gradual improvement of functional features. The quantitative side of human exceptionality, the fact that we have so much more culture than other species, is shoved aside.

It thus seems that the word *accumulation* would be better employed to refer to this quantitative side of the issue. At one point during our evolution, the human species came to possess an increasingly large stock of traditions, quantitatively if not qualitatively different from the cultures of other species. That process is what needs explaining—the growing sophistication of some techniques is secondary. So, how did we get to possess so many traditions?

This book started from the assumption that most transmitted information is not transmitted back again. There is, in other words, no human compulsion to copy every action we see, or repeat everything we hear. (Just trying to imagine a world where this would be the case suffices to make the point.) Some things reach a greater degree of diffusion and start transmission chains, but here again, most transmission chains peter out after a few steps. A small minority of diffusion chains takes over. As a consequence, any reasonably important cultural repertoire presupposes the existence of a vastly larger corpus—one made of extinct ideas and practices. Accumulating many traditions means accumulating even more failed traditions.

This we might call the "Shadok Rocket Principle." Due to a puzzling cultural injustice, *Les Shadoks*, a delightful 1970s French series of animated pictures, has not yet made it to the global mainstream. It does not fit any genre (absurdist space opera with a Dadaïst touch, perhaps.) The Shadoks, an alien species seeking to invade Earth, have decided to build and launch a space rocket. The Shadoks' only problem is their sheer incompetence. Their rocket science is abysmal. Their chances of getting a rocket into space are less than one in a million. Still, the ever confident Shadoks decide to take that one in a million chance. One million failed launchings later, the Shadok engineers are elated:

> The situation was quite satisfactory. The trial rocket launches continued to *fail very well*. (. . .) For such was the first basic principle of Shadok logic: only by continually trying things out does one eventually achieve one's goals. In other words, *the more you fail, the most likely you are to succeed*.
>
> (Rouxel 1994)

The sophistry hinges on the ambiguity of the conclusion. If the Shadoks try a million rocket launches, this does not, of course, make them more likely to get *the next* launching right. Still, it does increase the odds that they will get *one* rocket into space. We can generalize: if the galactically dumb Shadoks ever manage to launch a rocket, they will have failed a vast number of launches.

In the cultural case, we need to consider two types of failed rocket launches. There are simple information exchanges where information is simply not re-transmitted, and then there are diffusion chains that do not go very far. In a sense, cultural accumulation depends on these stifled chains, on these innovations that were never taken up. I say "in a sense" only, because I am not claiming that stable traditions arise by chance alone. They did not appear simply because, when one says or does anything at all, one has a small chance of launching a wide-ranging diffusion chain. Not all candidates for cultural diffusion are equal. We saw, when we studied cultural selection, that it was not neutral. Unappealing traditions are less likely to stabilize—this becomes more true when time and space scales are enlarged, or when institutional and demographic conditions are less than optimal. The formation of cultural repertoires is not a by-product of random information exchanges: what is being innovated, what is being passed on is polished by human minds, which make it more appealing to other human minds.

Now we can rephrase the question of cultural accumulation in light of the Shadok Rocket Principle. Our question is no longer: *Why are human traditions so numerous?* It becomes: *Why are so many innovations put in common in human populations?* That, I think, is because there is something extraordinary about information exchange in our species—what might be called the human public domain.

The Opening Up of the Human Public Domain

Human Populations Became Increasingly Hospitable to Culture . . .

The public domain that enables cultural transmission is the set of all ideas and practices that are accessible in a given population at a given time. Its scope depends on a myriad of different factors, some of which have already been presented: institutions, information storage techniques, demography, sociability. Institutions and information storage techniques have no clear animal equivalent. Demography and sociability, I have argued, are more favorable to cultural accumulation in our species than among our cousins.

Students of cultural transmission expect big populations to possess important repertoires for two basic reasons: innovation should be more frequent and retention should be easier (Shennan 2001; Powell, Shennan, and Thomas 2009). Why more innovation? Because innovators are more numerous and (if density follows demography) more likely to come into contact with others. Why better conservation? Because the passing of generations is smoother in big populations. In small populations, turnover tends to create bottlenecks: teachers or pupils become scarce. Such demographic scarcity is typically compounded by institutional or ritual constraints: traditions that can only travel within specific subpopulations, from men to men, initiates to initiates, and so on. These traditions are vulnerable to all the accidents that may befall a small community.

All else being equal, there is evidence that small human populations (provided they are isolated enough) tend to possess smaller technological repertoires (Kline and Boyd 2010). Human populations do not seem to be special in this respect. In bird species where each individual knows a number of songs, the size of these individual repertoires is observed to shrink in insular or quasi-insular populations (Baker, Baker, and Baker 2001). Among humans, the links between depopulation and cultural devolution are well explored, most notably by Henrich (2004), in a paper tackling the venerable question of the "disappearance of useful arts" in Melanesia (as raised by W. H. R. Rivers, 1912). Henrich argues that tradition preservation cannot be guaranteed under certain population thresholds, even for the most useful techniques. Depopulation also means that losses are less likely to be compensated by innovations. Even the critics of this argument (e.g., Read 2006) agree that small populations must see fewer useful innovations, and are more vulnerable to chance losses (a cultural equivalent of the biological phenomenon of adaptation loss through drift).

Cultural transmission, we saw in chapter 2, is social only in the minimal sense that one can't transmit something on one's own. This does not make it a particularly cooperative activity. In many species indeed, transmission can happen by mere eavesdropping. Human communication is different: it is voluntary. Its voluntariness is, first of all, a logical necessity, since ostensive communication cannot work if the emitter does not openly intend to communicate. Just saying this, though, does not do justice to the amounts of effort that go into information exchange in our species. As is well known, human learning (cultural or otherwise) is supported at great costs by the surrounding society. In fact, it is not just learning processes that are supported in that way. Human growth is far too slow and expensive to sustain itself without the assistance of previous generations (Hrdy 2011). In hunter-gatherer populations where food transfers have been extensively studied, it has been established that young humans only reach their peak hunting or gathering capacities by their mid-thirties (Kaplan, Lancaster, and Robson 2003). Mastering these skills takes years of learning, but reaps big rewards, since it allows the exploitation of better sources of food, in a great variety of environments. The share of difficult-to-process foods, such as hunted meat, seashells, roots, seeds, or nuts (as opposed to fruits or grass) is ten times more important among human hunter-gatherers than among chimpanzees (still according to Kaplan et al.).

"Education" is too strong, too specific a word for this kind of support, which need not involve any information exchange at all. Better call it "assisted development." Ours is not the only species that engages in it. It is common for parents to spend resources and energy to buy their children a more or less extended time of dependence. Humans are on the far end of that continuum: they are more intensively engaged in this kind of investment, and they get bigger gains from it. Several traits of human biology are touted to have evolved as adaptations to this slow life history. This has been said, for instance, about our long childhoods (as seen in chapter 2); about our grandmothers (who live long past menopause and provide crucial assistance to their grandchildren—Hawkes, O'Connell, and Blurton-Jones 1997); even about our digestive system (suitable for assimilating the sort of protein-rich, fiber-poor fare that complex techniques allow us to get and eat).

The extent of parental (and alloparental) involvement in assisting the young is certainly extraordinary among humans, and of great consequence, too. Yet it is still only a difference in degree. Other species invest in a long period of immaturity, allowing complex, adapted behaviors to develop. They just pay the tuition fees for an education at the school of life, but will not be the ones doing the teaching. The type of learning that assisted development permits can be individual rather than social. All parents need to provide is protection and food; they need not involve themselves directly in the rest. Assisted development can thus evolve in the absence of voluntary transmission. The period of dependent immaturity is then used for individual learning, playing with age peers, exploring the environment, and otherwise using the many tools for non-social learning that exist everywhere. Social learning may well happen, taking the form of tolerated spying or information scrounging; but with little voluntary transmission (judging by the rarity of examples found by Caro and Hauser 1992) and no ostensive communication.

Long periods of assisted development and learning are thus already beneficial enough without cultural transmission. We know that our ancestors, like today's apes, raised and assisted dependent juveniles long before they had ostensive communication—indeed, before they were humans. The juveniles simply developed a flexible set of learned, adapted behaviors without direct social intervention. In a way, then, human investment in assisted development is nothing fundamentally different, just more (much more) of the same; but there is a whole new dimension to it, too. Our species did not simply increase its investment in long stretches of assisted development. We invest differently. The ethnographic literature shows no example of a society where people do not intervene voluntarily in children's learning (the alleged counterexamples were reviewed in chapter 2). Merely voluntary transmission is common, but ostensive communication (information exchange relying on the recognition of the communicator's manifest intention) is crucial everywhere. The helping hand of conspecifics remains active throughout our lifetime. This participation makes no miracle: individual learning remains necessary to acquire skills fully. (Otherwise there would be no need to spend decades mastering hunting or gathering techniques—they would simply be uploaded from one brain to another.) There is still a part requiring painstaking individual learning. For the rest, ostensive communication is helpful.

Just like our species is said to have acquired adaptations around assisted development, it has been argued that human cognition has built-in features that make ostensive communication easier for us. The anatomy of human eyes, for instance, makes gaze following very easy, and there is evidence that humans rely on eye cues to track others' attention (Hood, Willen, and Driver 1998; Tomasello et al. 2007). The combination of a dark iris and cornea over an exceptionally bright sclera is of help here (Kobayashi and Kohshima 1997). The psychologists György Gergely and Gergely Csibra (whose views on cultural transmission will be discussed later) have extensively documented the various cues (gazing, "motherese" speech, pointing gestures) that allow human infants to grasp ostensive communication. Some of these cues can be handled by newborns a few days old (Farroni et al. 2002).

Humans, thus, go beyond mere assisted development: they engage in cooperative learning on a massive scale. This, however, is but one side of human cooperation. Other aspects of human sociability also matter for cultural transmission. Peaceful coexistence with non-kin is one. Among other primates (with a few exceptions, all rather remote from us on the tree of life) parents assist their children, but their support does not extend much further. It does not extend outside the immediate circle of kinship. Even inside that circle, siblings, nephews, grandchildren, affines, and so on are seldom assisted with food. In contrast, young humans receive substantial help from quite an extended family circle (obviously with variations from one society to the next, as documented in Hrdy 2009). Helping children is one of those many tasks for which unrelated or distantly related humans join forces. The reasons for this pattern of cooperation have been a matter for considerable speculation. Here, I will just look at its consequences for the question at hand.

One of the factors that keep cultural repertoires small among other apes is a scarcity of peaceful contacts: that is what is suggested by research from Carel van Schaik and his colleagues (van Schaik and Pradhan 2003a; van Schaik et al. 2003b), who compared various populations of chimpanzees and orangutans with more or less rich cultural repertoires. The best predictor of such cultural wealth, from one population to another, is the frequency of peaceful social interactions (excluding mother-child interactions). "Tolerant proximity" is needed for apes to be able to observe and learn gestures from someone other than their mother. Tolerant proximity is in limited supply among great apes, either for lack of proximity (in orangutans) or for lack of tolerance (in chimpanzees). Yet it is a crucial condition of cultural transmission: innovations need to be made public, preferably with non-kin, if they are to be learnt.

The simple observation of a conspecific using a tool may not be such an easy thing among great apes. Social relations need to be reestablished, negotiated, or mended continuously, in more or less peaceful ways ranging from grooming to fighting. This makes chimpanzee social life a permanent mental investment. Frans de Waal's famous book on *Chimpanzee Politics* (de Waal 1982) illustrates the complexity of primate social networks, the amount of attention and cognitive efforts that one needs to invest to stay in the game. This atmosphere of contentiousness does not simply restrict the range of peaceful interactions that could be used for social learning; it also takes away mental resources that could have gone to culture. It matters little whether an animal possesses capacities for imitation (as great apes certainly do), when social life keeps a lid on cultural life.

There is little doubt that human sociability provides a better context for information exchange. Social life does weigh on our minds like it preoccupies other apes, but cooperation does not need to be constantly renegotiated and social ranks are not up for grabs at any moment. This is in no small part thanks to increases in cooperation, starting inside the family nucleus, with cooperative breeding or food sharing, and sometimes extending to anonymous strangers (Tomasello 2008, 174–190, reviews the comparative evidence). Not only do we often tolerate the presence of non-kin (a feat in itself), we are ready to help them, with information among other things—and to use ostensive communication for it. This stands in marked contrast with the way other species deal with transmission among non-kin. It is seldom voluntary, and closer to tolerated spying than to teaching.

. . . But Hospitable Populations Are No Guarantee of Cultural Progress

Allow me to summarize. A lot of information is shared in human societies, thanks to human demography and sociability—the latter especially, which is marked by cooperative learning and the public use of knowledge. The broadening of the human public domain during our species' evolution laid down the condition for cultural accumulation, the enlargement of human cultural repertoire (not the gradual sophistication of a few techniques). That being said, how did cultural accumulation occur? I can see two possible ways to answer this question. A larger public domain is, first of all, something that allows more new ideas to be shared, more innovations to be put in common (with some of them becoming traditional in the end). Second, a large public domain provides more possibilities to share what traditions already exist, thus lengthening their survival. Which of these two aspects of accumulation mattered the most: the innovations that were shared in greater numbers, or the traditions whose conservation improved? The answer, of course, would probably turn out to be "a little bit of both"; and, since I will not try to quantify the respective importance of innovation and conservation in the first stages of human cultural accumulation, I should perhaps leave it at that. Yet I believe there are reasons to expect one cause to be much more important than the other.

If conservation conditions were the main force driving cultural accumulation, then we should expect cultural repertoires to grow as the conditions of accessibility get better, and shrink when they deteriorate. In other words, stable traditions should not be able to endure poor conservation conditions, with technologies, demography, or institutions too weak to sustain them. Once these felicitous conditions disappear, it should be over for the traditions that thrived in these contexts. Is that what we observe?

In chapter 1, I argued that cultural transmission has no inertia: transmitted things, in general, have no inner tendency to be transmitted anew. This is because human imitation is not compulsive: there is no pull to reproduce anything and everything. That being said, I do think that some traditions have been selected to elicit their own reproduction. Of these we could say that they do possess a sort of inertia. "Extreme" traditions seem to last much longer than others, even when institutional, demographic, or technological conditions are harsh. These are traditions that painlessly get across demographic bottlenecks or frequent waves of population renewal. Thus, conservation conditions constrain cultural diffusion only up to a point: accumulation may occur in spite of them, with extreme traditions. What would accumulation look like if it were driven by these traditions?

The Extreme Accumulation Hypothesis

Accumulation, in that scenario, would be driven by the appearance of attractive traditions, the type that appeal to almost everyone and can survive in the harshest conditions. It would take the form of a slow piling up of very resilient cultural practices. This accumulation would start even before the conditions of cultural conservation (demography, technology, institutions) become favorable, and it would keep happening even in times when these conditions get unfavorable. The resilience of extreme traditions also means that accumulation would not rewind, in spite of the ups and downs of conservation conditions. This type of accumulation would be more sustainable in the long run. It might also be slower, at first, than an accumulation driven by conservation conditions. Extreme traditions are rare by definition. To get one, a huge quantity of Shadok-rocket-style traditions must be launched, and must fail. This is what it means for accumulation to be driven by the quantity of shared innovations, rather than conservation conditions: the factor that limits accumulation is the number of good ideas that get put in common, not the ability to keep them in circulation. The only way to build up a repertoire of extreme traditions is to try out many innovations—to share a lot of information. Conservation conditions do help with that, but the process of accumulation need not stop when these conditions get bad. Besides, cultural repertoires may not explode immediately with an improvement in conservation conditions. Let us call this the *"extreme accumulation" hypothesis*: cultural repertoire build up slowly and dwindle just as gradually, and a kernel of very resilient traditions drives that process.

What would cultural repertoires look like in the first stages of accumulation, or in the last stages of cultural extinction? If the extreme accumulation hypothesis is correct, they should consist of a small handful of very durable traditions, surrounded by practices that are hardly traditional at all. Nonhuman cultures today may give us a glimpse of what culture looks like, when sociability and demography are not sufficiently favorable for accumulation to get started. As Bernard Thierry (1994) noted, ape cultures combine practices whose cultural status is very much open to doubt, with a hard core of long-lasting traditions. When this hard core can be observed over the long run, either with archeological methods (Mercader, Panger, and Boesch 2002) or by means of prolonged fieldwork (as has been done on Koshima island since the 1950s), it shows surprising longevity. Even socially transmitted bird songs, which we have been able to record for a few decades only, are quite durable, especially considering the short lives of their bird carriers (Trainer 1983). The fact that stable traditions can survive in populations where information transfers are limited, social contacts can be hard to provoke, and demography has ups and downs—that fact signals the presence of extreme traditions.

Things would be very different, presumably, if cultural evolution were not extreme—in other words, if the conditions of conservation of culture alone drove the accumulation of traditions. If that were the case, then the cultural wealth of great apes or birds would directly depend on their capacity to transmit and preserve their traditions. Good conservation capacities would mean a large number of durable traditions. Mediocre conservation capacities would imply a small number of fragile traditions. What they seem to have instead is a few items, but durable ones.

The extreme accumulation hypothesis also acquires some plausibility from Rivers's famous case of the "disappearance of useful arts," in Melanesia and Tasmania. If our hypothesis is right, cultural repertoires should go away with a long whimper, not with a bang. The resilience of extreme traditions should keep carrying human cultures across time, long after conservation conditions cease to be optimal. Cut out from the mainland by rising sea levels, and reduced to the smallest numbers, the Tasmanians seem to have stopped replacing lost innovations with new ones. Yet it took them many centuries to lose the techniques they had invented before that, and which they had (seemingly) become incapable of developing. Bone working, for instance, is only forgotten after five millennia. Several thousand years is also what it takes for fishing (as observed through the share of fish in the diet) to decline (estimates in Henrich 2004). Some even argue that the Tasmanians only "lost" techniques that had been made redundant by environmental changes (Read 2006).

Such a scenario would, I think, be less probable if the size of a population's cultural repertoire, at any one time, depended only on the local conditions of cultural conservation such as they are at that time. Extreme accumulation, on the other hand, accounts for the inertia that can be observed: the possibility of conserving any given tradition, here and now, does not matter so much, because different traditions can react in multiple ways to the same conditions of conservation. If, at some point in its past (and that point can be quite remote) the culture produced resilient traditions, a repertoire can preserve this hard core for quite a long time. That hypothesis could explain how some cultural repertoires can be both small and durable, and why cultural repertoires disappear gradually (unless their decline is precipitated by a population's physical extinction).

One notable trait of extreme accumulation is that, compared to changes in conservation conditions, it is unlikely to be reset or to fall back to previous levels. Extreme traditions die hard. Their presence somehow acts like the "ratchet effect" of theoreticians of cumulative culture. Only here, what the "ratchet effect" preserves is not smart twists on existing techniques, but whole cultural repertoires. In any case, the inertia of extreme accumulation means that the counters of cultural history are seldom set back to zero. This, of course, is a good way to get cultural repertoires to grow. This ratcheting property of extreme accumulation suggests a possible (and quite sketchy) answer to our question: why is the cultural wealth of the planet mostly found in human populations? More precisely, it suggests a way to account for the apparent fact that, once a certain threshold of accessibility and sociability is reached, the populations above that threshold are able to accumulate vast cultural repertoires, while repertoires in other populations remain small.

Here is how it might work. Traditions can only accumulate if new traditions appear more often than they disappear (for even extreme traditions eventually collapse). Thus, accumulation gets into motion only when many innovative ideas are put in common, increasing the odds of chancing upon a resilient tradition. Below this innovation/disappearance threshold, cultural repertoires cannot grow significantly, though a small hard core of extreme traditions can persist. If the threshold is crossed, however, the cumulative growth of the lucky repertoires would set them apart from others, the inequality becoming greater and less reversible with time. A deep divide between the most cultural species and the rest would result. Thus, a widening of the human public domain, taking it above the accumulation threshold, could have triggered the slow but inexorable growth of our cultural repertoires. Yet if that hypothesis is right, the process of accumulation would have taken time. It would not have followed immediately upon the emergence of human sociability. On the contrary, it would have been an episode of cultural history, quite independent of any change in the cognitive, emotional, or genetic makeup of the species.

The extreme accumulation hypothesis thus leaves open the possibility that humans could have lived socially, emotionally, and cognitively normal lives long before they became the most cultural species on earth. This view goes against the grain of a lot of theorizing, ancient and modern, about the relation between humans and their traditions. We value our culture so much that it would seem demeaning to grant it anything else than the lead part in the play. Besides, the view that human culture made human beings what they are flatters our sense of agency: we love to believe that our species was fashioned by its own traditions, in a dialectical relationship.

The picture painted by the extreme accumulation hypothesis is less emotionally comforting, perhaps, but I see it as plausible nonetheless. If this view is right, then modern human populations happen to live at a time when cultural repertoires are extremely important, thanks to the millennia of accumulation behind us. That you and I find ourselves living at such a time, rather than at the start of the cumulative process, is a historical contingency. It does not mean we have any special talent for cultural transmission that people or animals with access to smaller repertoires would lack. The next section develops the implications of this idea: the growth of large cultural repertoires is something that happened to many, but not all human beings, at some point in their history. It is not some basic trait of the species, like being a bipedal or a breathing animal. We can imagine humans without culture.

What Kind of Cultural Animal Are We?

This way of seeing does without two cumbersome hypotheses. The first hypothesis is a variant of the imitation hypothesis: it states that humans have a specific knack for the transmission of traditions. The second hypothesis states that evolution has turned us into cultural animals: in other words, some human traits are adaptations to the existence of culture.

The two hypotheses can be combined into the following scenario: at one point in their evolution, human beings developed cognitive capacities allowing them to imitate their conspecifics with unusually high fidelity and precision. These new skills of imitation enabled cumulative culture to appear and to grow ("cumulative culture," here, is taken in the standard sense: techniques that become more refined with time). Accumulation produced ever more complex and ever more useful traditions, and mastering culture became as indispensable to survival as any other talent. Thus, capacities for faithful imitation were under a natural selection pressure. Other talents that contribute to faithful cultural transmission may also have evolved because of their contribution to cultural transmission (language is often cited here). If this scenario is accurate, then ours is a doubly cultural species: because our social learning skills were originally fit for transmitting cultural traditions with fidelity and precision; and because natural selection has strengthened this gift, making human social learning better adapted to culture. It is common nowadays to remark that human physiology has adapted to various features of our environment that have been influenced by culture (the availability of milk, for instance). The above scenario goes much further: humans (their social learning skills most particularly) are adapted to culture per se. We are quite specifically wired to transmit traditions—that is, to transmit and receive, not just any kind of information, but the kind that creates chains of cumulative culture.

We are now, I think, well equipped to see the gaps in this scenario. It makes a muddle of three things that ought to be distinguished: the transmission, the diffusion, and the accumulation of traditions. Faithful transmission is not diffusion, nor does it guarantee that diffusion will occur. Traditions can travel far and wide even when transmission is quite imperfect, and faithful transmission may well take place only once, leaving no lasting tradition behind. Transmission is easy, diffusion is hard. Thus, the hypothetical emergence of highly accurate imitation skills would not by itself ensure the birth of big, complex cultural repertoires. Moreover, simple diffusion with conservation does not necessarily make traditions more complex or more useful. Preservation without progress is common. Even supposing that human beings did evolve a capacity for faithful, precise, and compulsive imitation (the way the imitation hypothesis sees it), I do not quite see what cultural benefits this would have brought. Cultural diffusion could hardly have been made easier, while improving upon existing traditions (which often implies changing them) would have become harder.

Yet nothing forbids us from speculating that humans possess dedicated mental faculties that evolved to deal specifically with lasting, widespread traditions (as opposed to any and all pieces of socially transmitted information). Let us see what could back such a view. (We will be treading on speculative ground, so remember that nothing in the rest of the book depends on the falsity—or truth—of that view).

We Need Not Believe that We Are Wired for Culture . . .

The imitation hypothesis, the view that sees the origins of human culture in a special psychological capacity for preserving and copying traditions, had a hold on the social sciences long before the field of cultural evolution existed. Here again, Herder wrote the blueprint for much later theorizing:

> All education must spring from imitation and exercise, by means of which the model passes into the copy; and how can this be more aptly expressed than by the term tradition? But the imitator must have powers to receive what is communicated or communicable, and convert it into his own nature, as the food by means of which he lives. Accordingly, what and how much he receives, whence he derives it, and how he uses, applies it, and makes it his own, must depend on his own receptive powers.
>
> (Herder 1791/2010, 409–410)

It is still popular (dominant, even) among specialists of cultural evolution today, be they philosophers, psychologists, anthropologists, or biologists.

> High-volume, high-fidelity cultural learning depends on (...) specific perceptual and cognitive adaptations, probably of the source as well as the sink.
> (Sterelny 2012, 13)

> [Human] processes of social learning are especially powerful forms of social learning because they constitute (...) especially faithful forms of cultural transmission (creating an especially powerful cultural ratchet) (...) human beings evolved a new form of social cognition, which enabled some new form of social learning, which enabled some new processes of sociogenesis and cumulative cultural evolution. This scenario (...) posits one and only one biological adaptation.
> (Tomasello 1999, 6–7)

> Cumulative cultural change seems to require some special, derived, probably psychological capacity.
> (Boyd and Richerson 1995, 78)

> Cultural transmission mechanisms, with their different degrees of conservativeness, determine the stability of cultural traits.
> (Guglielmino et al. 1995, 7589)

> (...) pedagogy has played an essential role in securing the faithful transmission of skills across generations, and should be regarded as the central mechanism through which long-term and stable material culture traditions are propagated and maintained.
> (Tehrani and Riede 2008, 316)

These quotes posit a *specific* mechanism that would underpin the transmission of traditions among humans (there may be disagreements about the mechanism's nature). Some of these authors go further and embrace the Imitation Hypothesis: faithful transmission mechanisms account for the rise and the stability of human cultures (e.g., "high-fidelity cultural learning depends on ... specific perceptual and cognitive adaptations"). If the arguments presented in this book are on the right track, then these two ideas can be done without. Transmission fidelity is not central to cultural diffusion, and there is no reason to think that traditions travel on some kind of informational superhighway set apart for them. One can have a coherent and plausible theory of cultural transmission where traditions go through the same channels as any other bit of socially transmitted information. (Indeed, many people do not make any difference between the social and the cultural, a view examined below.) The usual channels, to be specific, are involuntary, voluntary, and ostensive transmission, always accompanied by a modicum of reconstruction. These channels need neither be particularly faithful nor specifically adapted (functionally or evolutionarily) to culture per se.

Some of the quotes just presented hint at another popular hypothesis: that natural selection turned us into cultural animals. That thesis exists in different guises. Some versions are quite plausible: for instance, it is plausible that we recently evolved adaptations to an environment that contained traditional technologies, like farming. But we might also be adapted to culture in a stronger and more interesting sense. Some of the traits that enable humans to acquire traditions might exist because the benefits that their carriers derived from culture meant that natural selection stabilized these traits.

The fitness benefits of (at least some) cultural practices cannot be denied or quibbled over: the great pre-Neolithic human migrations, which led the species to take over a vast share of the planet's dry land, would probably not have been possible without a large stock of culturally transmitted techniques. Culture (whatever perils it might have in store for us) drove one of the most rapid and (so far) successful biological invasions in natural history.

Learning traditions would have been beneficial to individuals, in a more immediate way, long before that. Today's chimpanzee traditions are mostly technical fixes to common problems of direct import for survival. If a chimpanzee developed some heritable predisposition to acquire these things more efficiently, that trait would, other things being equal, be under selection, like any other adaptive trait. The presence of a few useful traditions could suffice for that, and we can be sure that human technological repertoires have been comparable to chimpanzee ones at least since *Homo erectus*. Selection would then stabilize the new adaptations, giving rise to populations where traditions would be more readily picked up than they would be elsewhere. This would not necessarily push traditions to become more numerous or more sophisticated: I have argued that a lot of not-yet-cultural information needs to be shared for traditions to multiply, and that faithful preservation by itself usually fails to make cultural practices more sophisticated or useful. Yet it would be the beginning of a coevolutionary process: natural selection on human cognitive capacities would stabilize traditions, and the availability of traditions would strengthen the selection pressures favoring minds capable of learning them.

Social scientists do not usually look kindly on stories of biological adaptation, but this one is an exception. One can see why. It provides a nice recasting, in naturalistic terms, of the old humanist creed: man makes himself, through culture. Even Clifford Geertz devoted some pages of his *Interpretation of Cultures* to an explanation of how culture fashioned the human species through biological evolution (Geertz 1973, 55–83). Today's students of cultural evolution do not ask themselves whether this scenario occurred, they ask why it failed to occur in other species (Boyd and Richerson, 1995, being a classic answer to this question). These two quotes are, I think, quite representative:

> Culture itself is an adaptation—i.e., the psychological mechanisms that permit social learning and cultural transmission are the products of natural selection. The reason culture came to be selected for is that by acquiring psychological mechanisms for culture, humans became able to acquire adaptive behavior much more quickly and reliably than they had before.
>
> (Driscoll 2008, 102)

> Most social scientists would agree that the capacity for human culture was probably fashioned by natural selection.
>
> (Rogers 1988, 819)

Are humans adapted to culture? It all depends, of course, on what one puts behind the word "culture." Quite possibly, what these authors have in mind is simply communication and the sort of social life that it makes possible—a broad notion of culture, quite different from the one that is developed in the field of cultural evolution (and here). I have no problems with the view that evolution shaped human minds so that they were adapted to, say, ostensive communication. Communication in our species does depend on a set of very specific adaptations, from the color of the eye's sclera to our capacity for mind-reading. There is a good case to be made for the view that one of the things that caused natural selection to maintain these traits is their contribution to communication, and to cooperative learning more generally. Yet the slogan *Culture is an adaptation* (Richerson and Boyd 2005, 99 sq.; Henrich and McElreath 2007, 556) points to another, more specific thesis that is worth discussing. Natural selection could have favored cognitive traits that allow us to acquire precisely the bits of socially transmitted information that form part of lasting traditions, shared by a whole society.

In other words, human cultural repertoires could have been a part of the selection pressure that led to the evolution of cooperative learning. Investing in assisted learning and in communication is likely to be more beneficial when useful traditions are in circulation. Through culture, cooperative learning could have created some of the conditions of its own evolution. We could, then, consider human sociability as an adaptation to culture, among other things. Other scenarios could probably be thought of that would lead to the same conclusion. Why not indulge them? I cannot rule them out, and will not try to. I would simply highlight the fact that many other equally plausible explanations exist to account for the emergence of our social nature, without granting cultural traditions a major role to play in these early stages.

We get the first clear clues that some human populations practiced cooperative learning from the times of *Homo erectus* at least: these humans reared children whose calories-hungry bodies and brains were beyond the power of a single individual to feed, and they produced them at a high frequency, thus making human offspring much more expensive than the young of other apes (Kaplan, Lancaster, and Robson 2003; Hrdy 2009). At that time, though, their cultural repertoires also seemed to be much less well-furnished than those that would appear later: no funerals, few or no images, a limited range of stone-knapping techniques, and foraging techniques that were not nearly as elaborate as they would later become. Consistent with the extreme accumulation hypothesis, a small number of highly resilient traditions (like stone-knapping techniques) coincided with a paucity of traditions in domains, like art or ritual, which would flourish later. In a rarefied cultural environment, cooperative learning would still have been extremely useful, but most of it would have served to acquire locally relevant information—the kind of information (concerning, for instance, the location of a shelter, or a source of food) that does not warrant building a far-reaching, long-standing tradition around it.

Such information could have been sufficient to make cooperative learning useful enough to nudge the evolution of specific adaptations. The extreme accumulation hypothesis, along with what little data we have on the earliest human cultures, suggests that long-standing traditions, at that stage, would have existed in small numbers. They would certainly have been a valuable part of the stock of public information that drove this process—I do not wish to say that culture (or what stood for it at that stage) had no influence whatsoever; only that it need not be central to the evolution of cooperative learning.

Cooperation among non-kin is one facet of human sociability that would have been possible without culture. It is not rare in other species, even those that are only very weakly cultural, or not at all: we encounter it among bacteria, in organisms of different species that practice mutualistic cooperation, and between unrelated individuals of various species, from meerkats to deer (Clutton-Brock 2002). Its evolution, though not unproblematic, is something the standard toolkit of evolutionary biology is well-equipped to deal with (West, Griffin, and Gardner 2007a, 2007b; West, El Mouden, and Gardner 2011; Clutton-Brock 2002). Scientific parsimony asks us to try out the tools of that toolbox on the question of how human cooperation evolved, before we try something else. One part of the toolbox that has been put to great use concerns cooperative breeding, a form of cooperation among non-kin that is distinctly more developed in humans than in other apes, but also exists in many other species. Cooperative breeding is a plausible precursor for more general forms of cooperation, because it seems to be present in all the other species known to practice extensive cooperation among non-kin—social insects, meerkats, and so on. (Clutton-Brock 2002). We do not know everything about its evolution, but enough to warrant some trust in our standard toolbox: plausible scenarios have been developed that link the evolution of human cooperative breeding with the rise of generalized cooperation beyond the narrow circle of the nuclear family (see, for instance, Chapais 2010; Hrdy 2009). In most of the works I have mentioned, culture (understood as a collection of long-standing traditions) is not a driving force. Likewise, many a plausible evolutionary account for the origins of communication gives no central role of culture (Origgi and Sperber 2000; Dunbar 1993).

. . . or that Communication Is Designed for Cultural Transmission

Chapter 2 used, among other things, the work of the developmental psychologists Gergely Csibra and György Gergely on the innate bases of our communication abilities. I share with them the view that ostensive communication is paramount in humans. As I just argued, one does not need to assume that its contribution to cultural transmission played an important part in its evolution. It has many other frequent and important uses. Csibra and Gergely dispute this claim, and they have developed an ambitious research program to show that human communication is biased in ways that make it easier for us to treat cultural information (Csibra and Gergely 2009).

Their main piece of evidence is something they call the "genericity bias." Some of their experimental data, obtained with preverbal infants who are shown acts of non-verbal ostensive communication (mostly pointing actions) show a tendency for generic interpretations to prevail over particularistic ones, in some contexts. If, for instance, someone points at an ashtray or at a blackbird in an ostensive way, a genericity bias would mean we tend to pay attention to the traits that this individual ashtray or blackbird shares with other tokens of the same kind, rather than the traits that characterize it individually (such as the blackbird's age, the ashtray's color, its location, and so on). This Csibra and Gergely take as a sign that communication's primary function is for sharing information that applies to kinds as opposed to individuals. They are quick to link this with the fact that important bits of cultural knowledge are generic in just that way: a lot of technological or scientific material is indifferent to the individual circumstances of, say, electrons, blackbirds, or combustion engines. Thus the genericity bias would be a vestige of the primary function of communication. It is, so to speak, a giveaway of its origins, which according to Csibra and Gergely have to do with the teaching of useful techniques.

This evocative proposal raises more questions than it settles, though. For one thing, Csibra and Gergely accept that cultural information is not at all the same thing as generic information: the story of the crucifixion is just as cultural as the periodic table of elements. Besides, they do not deny that ostensive communication serves most often to transmit locally relevant information, not cultural knowledge. In other words, our capacities for communication would have evolved in a world where every sort of information was being exchanged: cultural and generic, cultural but not generic, generic but not cultural, neither generic nor cultural. What role would the genericity bias play in this context? Its most obvious effect would be to cause mistakes in interpretation. Even when mothers talk with their babies (babies who lack most of adults' cultural knowledge and thus need to be taught more than others), generic communication is not the most frequent type of communication (according to the data collected by Gelman et al. 2008). In other settings, it is probably even less prevalent: the main bulk of information exchanged in human communication is not generic. If we mistook even a tiny proportion of it for generic information, efficient communication among humans would suffer. How this bias would help us acquire cultural information is far from obvious. All it would do is lead us to misunderstand some locally relevant messages, pointlessly believing them to be generic. The drawbacks of this bias are evident, its advantages obscure.

A more charitable interpretation of Csibra and Gergely's thesis is that the genericity bias does not occasion any mistakes—in fact, it is not a "bias" at all. It is simply a capacity to grasp and process generic messages, if and when that is what the messenger intends us to understand. Such an ability, though, is simply what we expect from a well-functioning capacity for ostensive communication. It does not tell us much about its origins, and does not support the view that communication evolved specifically to support culture. I believe that hypothesis (communication as an adaptation to culture) to be superfluous. "Superfluous" does not mean "wrong," but the view that human cognition is biologically adapted to culture per se is a piece of adaptationist speculation that we might do without.

To see how dispensable it is, let us imagine what things would be like if the conjecture were true. Suppose we identify cognitive capacities for imitation or communication that are much better at handling traditional information than at handling other kinds of information. This is not unthinkable: many traditions, after all, differ from the give and take of transmitted information because they are much more widely distributed. Let us suppose we do notice these patterns. Suppose, also, that we switch on a special learning mode when dealing with such information. Lastly, assume we can even prove (thanks to some future progress of natural history) that this special learning mode evolved because it increased the fitness of those who possessed it, allowing them to master useful bits of cultural knowledge more easily. This is much more than we can hope ever to find evidence for; what would it tell us about the origins of human cultures?

A lot certainly, but not everything. The cultural wealth of human beings is not a straightforward product of our ability to communicate, or of our cooperative and communicative nature. Neither gave birth to modern cultural repertoires overnight, if the extreme accumulation hypothesis is right (and probably also in many cases where it is not). Presumably, not all species of the Homo genus, not all early human populations fully saw the result of the cumulative process. The extreme accumulation hypothesis suggests that human societies started their cultural history with little cultural baggage, apart from a few resilient traditions. Some populations may not have been demographically robust enough to accumulate more. The outstandingly cultural character of today's humans, then, would not be a characteristic of the species, but a historical event that happened to many populations. If a simplistic slogan may be offered here, one could say that humans are not particularly cultural animals; it is human populations that have become extremely cultural.

A Species Taken in a Cultural Avalanche

Extreme accumulation, to recall, means that cultural evolution is transformed by traditions that appear rarely but may last a long while (no upper limit to their longevity can be determined in advance). In populations where little information gets shared, such traditions do appear, but not frequently enough to accumulate in the long run—in other words, their rate of appearance is not much higher than their rate of extinction. What tips the balance is a widening of the public domain: the possibility to share more innovations, more information, some of which may eventually give rise to lasting traditions. In humans, both cognitive changes (the emergence of ostensive communication) and social or demographic changes (the changes brought about by cooperative breeding and the changes that cascaded from its evolution) opened up the public domain.

The extreme, die-hard nature of successful traditions means that such enlargements of the public domain accelerate cultural accumulation in a way that is difficult to reverse. Two key parameters that constrain the size of the public domain are population size and the possibility of peaceful, cooperative interactions. Both these things have exploded in the evolutionary history of our species. In the case of populations sizes at least, there was not just one explosion: there were several, some of them quite recent. If the extreme accumulation hypothesis is on the right track, then each explosion should translate into an acceleration of the cumulative process. Each should make us more cultural than we used to be.

This idea is at odds with our intuitive understanding of what it means to be cultural, which is essentialist and not quantitative—a species either "has culture," or lacks it. If we take seriously the notion of culture as diffusion that was developed in chapter 1, though, nothing there tells us that the importance of culture in our lives cannot vary. The extreme accumulation of culture need not have any a priori limits, or if it does have limits, we may not have reached them yet. To try to assess the importance of culture in human lives at any point in time may seem like a mad endeavor (and I am not claiming we could measure it with any precision), but I think there is a fact of the matter: human life can be more or less cultural. We can attend to widely diffused ideas and behaviors, as opposed to pieces of information that are only locally relevant. It makes sense to assume, for instance, that the rise of information storage technologies allows cultural transmission to get across wider distances (in space and time) than it did before. In that sense, the transmission chains that we inhabit are, arguably, reaching further and wider than they used to. This, according to the quantitative view of culture adopted here, means that we may be in the process of becoming ever more cultural animals.

That idea is ancient enough, having been proposed by the early students of cross-generational transmission whom we met in chapter 5. Comte wrote (with his usual gloomy seriousness) that the dead were weighing on the living, a weight that was getting heavier with each passing generation. The weight in question was, of course, not that of dead souls: it was the burden of traditions left behind by previous generations. That Comtean view was widely propagated to other students of generational dynamics—to positivists like John Stuart Mill (as we shall see shortly), but also to some of Comte's opponents, like Gabriel Tarde. François Mentré (who wrote the essay on cultural generations discussed in chapter 5) summarized Comte's intuition by comparing the influence of past generations to an avalanche: each step in its progression makes it heavier and stronger.

The extreme accumulation hypothesis offers a way to make sense of this intuition. Any cumulative change allows a past process to have a present casual weight that is proportional to its past duration. The longer a cumulative process has been going on, the more impressive its results. I am not, however, defending each and every aspect of Comte's thesis. For instance, I am not trying to frame cultural accumulation as a progress (or a decadence) in any ethically relevant sense. Another point of departure with Comte concerns the relations between culture and human nature. The positivists thought that, as the weight of tradition increased, along with the pressure that the dead brought to bear upon the living, our pre-cultural instincts would retreat. That claim seems fairly obvious at first blush: if the influence of things cultural increases, non-cultural influence would seem to decrease in proportion. Mill put it quite clearly:

> M. Comte alone, among the new historical school, has seen the necessity of thus connecting all our generalizations from history with the laws of human nature. But (. . .) I do not think any one will contend that it would have been possible, setting out from the principles of human nature and from the general circumstances of the position of our species, to determine *a priori* the order in which human development must take place, and to predict, consequently, the general facts of history up to the present time. After the first few terms of the series, the influence exercised, over each generation by the generations which preceded it, becomes, (as is

well observed by the writer last referred to [Comte]) more and more preponderant over all other influences; until at length what we now are and do, is in a very small degree the result of the universal circumstances of the human race, or even of our own circumstances acting through the original qualities of our species, but mainly of the qualities produced in us by the whole previous history of humanity.

(Mill 1843, 633)

If we look closer, though, Mill's reasoning is based on one questionable premise: cultural and non-cultural factors compete to influence human thoughts and actions in a way that would be mutually exclusive—like a zero-sum game. There would be, on one side, the motivations and capacities universal to the species, modulated by each individual's singular environment and history—and culture on the other side. Whatever hold culture takes on our mind would make non-cultural mechanisms lose traction in exact proportion to the influence gained by culture, like a war of occupation where the two armies lose or gain territory. Mill's vision chimes well with the view (made popular by centuries of humanism) that humans are animals that have been stripped from their nature, their instincts lost, their behavior dictated by culture rather than heredity.

The Growing Weight of Traditions Does Not Erase Human Nature

There are less simplistic angles from which to look at the way traditions interact with everything else. Cultural factors interact with less cultural ones, they do not simply supersede them. Traditions would not necessarily weaken the tendencies that preexisted them—quite the contrary. The theory of diffusion chains says that the traditions that managed to accumulate in the long run succeeded because they appealed to the most generic, species-universal kind of appeal. Those that traveled on the strength of local idiosyncrasies, specific to some people or some societies, would not have made it that far. If so, we would expect successful traditions to fit the most common human preferences, not counteract them. What Mill calls "the universal circumstances of the human race" and "the original qualities of our species" would have been magnified, not erased. Let us consider two examples where cultural traditions work to strengthen psychological biases derived from the human biological legacy.

Most humans are endowed with a cognitive capacity to recognize faces rapidly, without conscious choice, with subtly tuned visual skills that many think are specific to faces. These neural mechanisms are rather uniform from one individual to the next, and their development, though influenced by the environment, is so narrowly canalized that the word "innate" is not farfetched: newborns recognize face-like schematic forms (McKone, Crookes, and Kanwisher 2009). Face recognition, then, is a good candidate to count as one of "the original qualities of our species." Many visual art traditions exploit our ability to grasp a face-like shape, or imagine one, from the slightest cues— as little as a few strokes (Sperber 1996). Artists sometimes produce æsthetic effects by disrupting those perceptual expectations (e.g., by interchanging the eyes and mouth), but such experiments are rare. Overall, portraits, caricatures, masks, and makeup do respect the basic parameters of face contours, contrasts, and proportions. By so doing these traditions reinforce the mechanisms that they exploit: they train our face recognition skills on a larger, more diverse array of shapes than would have been available otherwise. Before the visual arts developed, human populations (which were presumably small) were not the best training ground for face recognition capacities: a handful of faces, with little variety. The sample of eyelids and noses that one learnt to recognize eyelids and noses from was narrow, marked by local morphological peculiarities. The visual arts increased the range of our experience of faces, and its vividness, too.

One taste that is clearly universal and innate is our craving for salt, which we share with other mammals (Duncan 1962; Birch 1999). Requiring some salt in one's food is quite a general proclivity, but of course the intensity of the craving varies a lot, depending on each person's environment and history. Habituation effects, in particular, are strong: the more salt we get, the more we like it. Salt cravings abate considerably if we just reduce the amount of salt in our food. Habituation effects mean that salt consumption should vary a lot from one place to the next, even after discounting environmental causes. We know that our ancestor must have craved salt, but the savor of it would have been very different to them. It would have been undistinguishable from the taste of blood, or that of minerals in water. Refined salt, a fairly recent cultural innovation, exploits a basic preference that it also increases and transforms. The taste of salt is, for us, a thing better defined and more specific than it would have been if we had known it only through a few hybrid flavors. More importantly, habituation strengthened our craving for it. The craving itself has changed: we have fine-grained expectations about the salt content of our food, which we can adjust with chemical precision. Our craving is solicited and strengthened every day, in a way it never was in our ancestors.

Evolutionary psychologists are used to saying (it is almost a cliché of the discipline) that industrial junk food exploits an innate preference, inherited from our evolutionary past, for fatty, salty, sugary food. Why these flavors in particular? In mankind's pre-Neolithic environment, these represented rare and valuable nutrients, so rare indeed that the thing to do, when one encountered them, was to make provisions for hard times. This innate preference, the story goes, was adapted to a Pleistocene environment but proves disastrous in today's settings: we are Pleistocene women and men trapped in a world of sodas and popcorn (Symons 1992). This story is plausible, perhaps true, but it also misses what is most important. The food industry did not simply exploit the preferences we inherited from our ancestors. In a way, it created these preferences. Our taste for salt is not some dead-weight vestige from an ancestral past. It is much stronger than it ever was. Our sugar-hungry, fat-hungry, salt-hungry psychology is not that of a Pleistocene man—it is a caricature of a Pleistocene man. In this case culture brings us, if anything, closer to ancestral type. If the phrase made any sense we could say that it made us more natural, not less. I mean that, because of such inventions as portraits or refined salt, psychological traits that were common to the species, but subtle and blurred by local circumstances, came out more clearly.

Culture should have that effect, in general, because the traditions that stand the test of diffusion must address a simplified caricature of the human mind. They rely on the most stereotypical aspects of human cognition, which they are designed to capture, even to underline. Failing that, a tradition will be nipped in the bud when societies or generations change. But, surely locally relevant traditions may survive and thrive? Yes, for a time, in their local niche. They will not, though, be the ones that drive cultural accumulation. The hard core of our repertoires, what lasts when nothing else does, is made of die-hard traditions that appeal more or less to everyone. These can withstand the transmission steps and the changes of context that long and narrow transmission chains must go through. These chains, which bridge long distances by going through a large number of relays, none of them well-connected enough to command the whole chain, are the most plausible link connecting us with our deeper cultural past. When such chains can be observed to work, they teach us a lot about the human mind in general. Think of the population of American students tested in an average psychological experiment: so few people, so uniform, so similar from one experiment to the other. Now consider all the individuals feeding a long and narrow cultural transmission chain: so many people, from so many times and places, from so many stages of life and situations—such a representative sample of mankind. Cultural material that has been filtered through such a variety of mental sieves should bear the mark of general structures of the human mind.

A Cultural Animal by Accident

It is an obvious fact that humans are cultural animals. Yet that obvious fact may well not be a necessary one. I do not deny that human sociability predisposes us to accumulate traditions. Accumulation, though, is a historical process. It may have failed to happen. It must have hit a few dead ends, a few false starts. It would have unfolded rather slowly. Before accumulation gained traction, the social background that eventually made culture possible must have been there already—or at least, I have argued, a large part of it. I believe, in other words, that we lived and felt, for the most part, like humans, before history made us cultural.

Humans are "beyond instinct," "cultural by essence," "programmed to be taught," "made-not-born"... We are used to the ready-made slogans of humanism. They have been drilled successfully into the average educated brain (at least in the place where I was educated, France). The twofold magic of habit and authority keeps us from standing back and seeing them as actual propositions with truth conditions. What would we be like if we were truly "cultural by essence"?

Species do not have essences, at least not in up-to-date biology handbooks. They do have an evolutionary history, though. As they evolved, a species' members got equipped with characteristic adaptations that were passed on. Bats can sonar-hunt at night, and some bacteria can bathe in radioactive fire. Are humans adapted to cultural transmission in a similar way? Are traditions our "niche"? I have argued that such an adaptation would not change so many things. In the view developed here, the best way to accumulate numerous, lasting traditions is to communicate abundantly and exchange a lot of information. This condition can be thought of as a public domain, a common stock of ideas and behaviors. Yet the public domain does not by itself ensure cultural diffusion: it could turn out to be a seedbed of arrested traditions. That need not always be a problem: even when only a tiny proportion of shared ideas become traditional, a large enough public domain will not fail to give birth to at least a few traditions. When the public domain reaches a certain size, accumulation can gather steam. Once it gets over that threshold there is no telling how far it will go. This scenario only assumes a public domain that is capable of substantial growth, but it says nothing about the human capacity to preserve traditions as such. What Herder called man's *receptive powers* do not figure in this story—or if they do, they enable us to receive and process any message, traditional or not. I am proposing that human societies have the cultural wealth that they have because of the quantity of things that are shared there, some of which may prove appealing enough to endure. The only biological gifts we need for this are those that make us good at communicating and cooperating—and these are considerable. We do not need any particular talent for cultural transmission. Culture is not of the human essence. It is, in the context of human sociability, an accident that was quite likely to occur.

*

This book started by thinking on the consequences of a well-to-do education and I'll end it on the same note. The writer Quentin Crisp liked to cite a witticism that he attributed to Saki (but the actual Saki quote is quite different, and rather longer—Saki, 2012). Clovis, Saki's recurrent protagonist, is talking morality with an aristocrat.

> "When I was young," said Clovis, "my mother taught me the difference between good and evil—only I've forgotten it."
>
> "You've forgotten the difference between good and evil?" gasped the princess.
>
> "Well, she taught me three ways of cooking lobster. You can't remember everything."
>
> (Crisp 1987, 70)

If he had read this book, and put a lid on his sense of wit, Clovis might have added that culture gets transmitted piecemeal, not as a block, and parts of it survived the long run of things because of their intrinsic appeal. We tend to associate traditions with fidelity or conservation, but it is a series of selective choices, applied to any and all traditions from moral norms to cooking recipes, that made Clovis—that made us all—into cultural animals.

APPENDIX

CENTURIES OF FUN: THE FATE OF 103 GAMES FROM RABELAIS'S *GARGANTUA*

The treatment of children's peer cultures in chapter 5 makes two claims. First, the traditions studied by European folklorists, for a stretch of time encompassing the Renaissance and modern times, were part of children's very own peer culture. They were not antique rituals left over from an adult past. Second, children's peer culture is capable of sustaining traditions whose longevity is more than comparable with that of adult traditions. This appendix is meant to substantiate these two claims with quantitative data, using a corpus of 103 games documented in France from the Middle Ages to the early decades of the twentieth century.

Some historians have voiced doubts that children's peer culture was their own from the start. They suggested instead that a progressive differentiation took place in the Renaissance: games and pastimes that used to be shared by all generations were gradually devolved to children (themselves mooted to be a novel sociological category). The record indeed offers several examples of games (like blind man's buff, or yo-yos) that attracted a substantial adult following before they became restricted to children. The focus on children that characterizes the folkloristics literature reviewed in chapter 5 may mask this fact. The longevity of children's peer culture can also be doubted, since no systematic, quantitative work (that I know of) has addressed that issue, and the existing literature is prone to focus on a few spectacular examples that may not be representative, or even quite specific to children. More importantly, the longevity of children's games is never assessed against an adult baseline, making comparative claims rather shaky. A systematic, quantitative survey that does not exclude adults, and that documents a large sample of games, studying them all on the same timescale, using the same sources, can help clear this issue.

RABELAIS'S LIST OF GAMES IN *GARGANTUA*

For this, we need a corpus of games that contains a substantial number of adults' games and children's games; games that can be easily followed through a long period of time;

games that would not have been selected by today's authors, with their inevitable presentist biases. Rabelais's list of games in *Gargantua* (1994, 58–63, first two editions between 1533 and 1535, major revision in 1542) is appropriate on all three counts. Furthermore, it has been extensively explored and documented by all major editors of Rabelais's work, as well as many specialists, in each century that passed since the publication of the best-selling novel. The list is playful, sometimes whimsical. Not every item refers to a game. Yet it is without a doubt an early masterpiece of folkloristic investigation, one that all subsequent researchers marveled at. Though not the first list of children's games (there were several in other literary traditions, and some in the French traditions during the Middle Ages, which were used here), it was by far the most comprehensive in its time. Most of the games studied here got their very first mention in our records from Rabelais's list.

A detailed inventory of all the 217 games in Rabelais's list is available online at [http://sites.google.com/site/sitedoliviermorin/morin-rabelais-online-material.pdf]. That document provides an entry for every game, those that were included in this study, and those that were not. For excluded games the reasons for exclusion are given. For each of the 103 games that I included in this study, its dates of first and last appearance in my sources are given, along with a list of all the sources that document the demography of its players, a discussion of any ambiguities concerning its identification, and a very short description. For the games included in the study, dates of first and last mention in our sources are given, with sources; reference is given to all the sources that give information about the demographic categories playing the game.

In order to date the games, and determine who their players were, sources were explored in a systematic way. This meant identifying the games named in Rabelais's list with games named by other sources. Rabelais's list, unfortunately, does not describe any game in any detail (although he depicted some of them in the rest of his work). He only left us with names (albeit characteristic and recognizable names). Not being a specialist, I adopted a conservative attitude, sticking to expert opinion whenever possible, and jettisoning games when the sources showed too much disagreement. In a minority of cases, personal choices had to be made (all described in the online document). Individuation was a recurring problem: what makes a game *one* game rather than a family of games, or a component in another game, is not always clear. Some sources will say that item X refers to a move in card game Y, while others insist that X and Y are one and the same thing, and others claim that X is actually an umbrella term for a family of card games that includes Y. Game ontology (so to speak) is a tangled business. To say that there is no established taxonomy is to understate the problem. Such disagreements were solved by following the clear majority of sources (when there was such a majority). Otherwise the game was discarded. Still, it is clear that in some cases we may be measuring not the fate of two distinct games, but two aspects of one ludic practice. In other cases, there is simply no fact of the matter, and any limit that a definition could trace is bound to be arbitrary.

There are other reasons to believe we are not dealing with independent data points here. In a sense, all these games were involved in the same cultural history. They had to share some causes of successes and some vicissitudes. Thus the number of independent observations that our estimates rely upon is smaller than it appears to be. Consequently, I chose to keep the statistical analysis as descriptive as possible, focusing on two basic historical issues: did a long-standing, specifically children-based play tradition exist in modern France, and did children sustain their traditions as well as other demographic groups did?

SCOPE AND LIMITS OF THE SEARCH

My main entry points into the literature were three editions of *Gargantua* by Le Duchat (1711), Esmangart and Johanneau (1823) and Lefranc et al. (1912), as well as the two comprehensive essays by Psichari (1908) and Sainéan (1922, 278–291). To a large extent, this work is parasitic upon theirs, even though their claims were systematically checked (whether they agreed with one another or not). Each of the sources cited by one of these primary references was checked to document the demographic context of the game being mentioned. The richest sources were also searched systematically, to find as many other games from Rabelais's list as possible. All the dictionaries and encyclopedias cited in the online material were searched in this way. An online database of European games (jocari.be), was also systematically checked, and was quite useful to verify references. Likewise, Jean-Jacques Mehl's glossary of French traditional games (Mehl 1990, 475–490) was precious, as was the rest of his classic book. The full list of references is to be found in the online material.

The only sources that were used to date a game (or document its demography) were the ones that appeared to provide a direct and independent testimony for the existence of a game. Editors citing other editors; material left over from previous editions of a dictionary or encyclopedia: these were not considered independent testimonies. The search was restricted to sources written in French and Latin (though it included bilingual dictionaries in other languages). Games are hard enough to identify from one century to the next, without having to juggle between several translations of a game's name. Names are not our only cue, but they do constitute one of our main tracers, along with game descriptions. Good iconographic sources are quite rare. Iconographic evidence, absent corroborating verbal material, was not considered sufficient and was not included. Obviously, all these decisions restrict the scope of the search. In some cases, this results in drastic underestimates for the age of certain games: cup-and-ball, chess, hide-and-seek, or marbles are (of course) much older than the data imply. This bias, which affects all three categories of games (cross-generational, children's, and adults'), is a price to pay for a systematic study of a hundred games in a standardized, linguistically homogenic corpus of sources.

For each game, I went back to the relevant sources to determine what it said about the players. Sources were counted as bearing no demographic information if they did not explicitly claim the game to be a children's or an adult's game, or if they did not give a description of the game being played by adults (playing together) or children (playing together). Ambiguous references (to people who could be adolescents, young adults, or children) were not used to determine a game's demography. These sources could still be used to date the game. The Gargantuan list was treated as such a source: it carries no demographic information. Gargantua is still a child in chapter 22, but what he is, above all, is a super-human monster. Besides, all specialists agree that the list of his games contains many adults' games.

The extension of words referring to children in medieval sources is often ambiguous. Looking at the *lettres de rémission*, Mehl (1990, 185) claims that the word *enfant* refers to adolescents and young adults (from 15 to 20 years old), proper children (before 15) being called *jeunes enfants*. However, he acknowledges that this is not systematically true. For such sources, we were careful not to take that word in itself as indicating that the game was a children's game.

Exclusion criteria. Most items in Rabelais's list were excluded from the study (114 items). The most common criterion for exclusion is simply a complete lack of information: many games in Rabelais' list have resisted all attempts at identifying them, except in the most speculative ways. Others are found elsewhere referred to by their name, but with such an absence of context that we have no idea what they were about: we do not even know whether they were board games, outdoor games, etc. For yet other games, the sources disagree with each other too much to allow me to choose one interpretation over others. (Disagreement was considered "excessive" when more than two substantial and contradictory solutions were present, or when sources were evenly split between solutions.) 60 items were excluded for these reasons. Many items on the list do not refer to games, strictly speaking, but to components of games already included in the list: moves or figures at cards, general ways of playing (reversing the rules or adding constraints), and so on (11 exclusions). 9 items were excluded because they did not refer to a game, even broadly construed (in keeping with the folkloristic tradition, I counted the occasional formulas, pastimes, singing games, as games). A few items were fused with other items in the list, when the sources unanimously considered them to refer to the same game (5 exclusions). Finally, games were discarded when they provided no demographic information whatsoever about their players (12 exclusions). Exclusion was usually determined by more than one criterion.

Sources. Around 100 distinct sources were consulted (listed in the online material), with no author providing more than 10 percent of the total amount of references used to document the games. A lot of information about the games comes from Rabelais' editors, followed by dictionaries and encyclopedias. Poetry, novels, and drama provide the third most important family of sources. The sources vary considerably in their attention to children, as we shall see.

ADULTS AND CHILDREN: TWO CULTURES OF PLAY

A look at the overall distribution of references to children's and adult play would seem to support the view that *Gargantua*'s games underwent a shift in the Renaissance, starting as multi-generational games, then becoming gradually restricted to children. Looking at the sources that provide demographic information, 80 percent of medieval references (up to the year 1500) mention adults, while only 20 percent mention children. These proportions are reversed for nineteenth- and twentieth-century sources (80 percent refer to children). In the three centuries in between, references mentioning children are stable, at around 35 percent. This would seem to vindicate the claims of theorists like Ariès (in *Centuries of Childhood*—1960). That impression would be misleading, though. Most of the rise in children's play reflects biases in the sources.

Demographic biases in the sources. Medieval references mainly come from three sources: Du Cange's franco-latin *Glossarium,* Godefroy's *Lexicon* of Old French, and Froissart's poetry (which includes a list of "games played by children under twelve" in *L'espinette amoureuse).* While Froissart's work mentions adults' games and children's games roughly in equal parts, the other two types of sources are clearly adult-biased. They are based on archives of legal disputes, most importantly the *lettres de rémission* ("letters of forgiveness") issued in the name of the king to pardon various crimes and misdemeanors. Mehl (1990, 180–226) explores in great detail the demographic biases that affect the *lettres de rémission,* which rarely concern anyone but adults. These letters figure all sorts of gruesome accidents that wounded, maimed, or killed adult sportsmen. Games of *soule* gone awry abound. So do gambling fights. (We can be reasonably sure that children sometimes "played for keeps," just like adult gamblers, but they are unlikely to have played for cash, or at least not with the sort of sum that would attract legal scrutiny). This bias can be explained in various ways: by better preservation for administrative documents, by greater attention given to adults' games at that time, and so on. In spite of this, all three sources occasionally describe children (with their age specified in years) playing, together, at some game that would end up in Rabelais's list.

The Gargantuan list is one sign of a surge of interest for children's peer culture, which began in the sixteenth century. Rabelais's place in this movement is hard to overstate: his list inaugurated the study of children's peer culture not just in France, but in the many countries where his books were translated— the translation being an occasion to inquire about the list, and to augment it with local games. Rabelais was not alone, though: other compendia of children's games appear in France during that century (e.g., Guillaume Le Blé's

1587 compilation). That attention to children's peer cultures increased in subsequent centuries is obvious from a simple look at the titles in the reference list (online material), especially for the last two centuries of our period. Rabelais's editors by that time had integrated the new science of childhood folklore, in full bloom at the end of the nineteenth century.

When we do not lump references together, but consider the material one game at a time, the continuity and exclusivity of children's and adult play culture becomes apparent. Of the 103 games included in the study, 32 are only documented as being played by adults, and 47 are exclusively played by children. Only 24 are provably cross-generational. The rarity of cross-generational games is, however, exaggerated by a simple statistical bias. To identify a cross-generational game, two references with demographic information are needed. The more numerous the references, the easier it is to identify cross-generational games. Here, I assign a game to the "children's games" or "adults' games" categories if all my sources describe them as children's or adults' games. This method clearly misidentifies some games that would turn out to be cross-generational if we had more information: they just appear to be age-segregated because they are not well documented enough. Not all putative children-only or adult-only games are what they seem, then, and the true number of cross-generational games must thus be higher than 24.

How much of the age segregation in the data can we explain in this way? Certainly not all of it. Table A.1 compares the actual number of age-segregated games with what it would be if age segregation were entirely a statistical illusion. The simulated

Table A.1 Age Segregation in Gargantua's Games.[a]

Sources	Age-segregated games		Cross-generational games	Occurrence of age-segregated games	
	Adults	Children		Chance probability	Actual proportion
2	8	10	2	66%	90%
3	7	3	6	50%	62%
4	6	5	4	40%	73%
5	1	2	5	33%	37%
6	1	1	3	29%	20%
7	2	1	1	25%	75%
8	1	2	1	22%	50%
9+	1	1	2	<20%	50%

[a] This table shows all the games whose demography is documented by at least two sources.

percentages in the penultimate column assume all games to be cross-generational. Under this assumption, some poorly documented games will appear segregated, because of a lack of data. The last column shows the actual prevalence of age-segregated games. It is almost systematically higher than its simulated value. In other words, some adult and children's games may indeed be cross-generational games in disguise, but the existence of an important degree of age segregation in modern France is not a statistical artifact.

What about the claim that modern children's games were cross-generational in the past, before a shift occurred in the Renaissance? That hypothesis would suggest that segregation, while real, is a recent phenomenon. It also implies that our childhood games would turn out to be cross-generational, if only our data covered a wider time span. None of this seems true. First, segregation does not seem recent. It is not less likely for the games that went extinct before 1600 (12 in 13 are segregated) or before 1700 (18 in 22). Second, our documentation on children's games is certainly patchier than it is for other games, but the time range that it covers is equal or superior to that of cross-generational games (keeping the quantity of demographic information constant). This is what Table A.2 shows. Suppose that children's games were a recent innovation, having become childhood-specific in the recent past. Then, we would expect that many games appear to be child-specific only because the adult part of their history is underdocumented. That is not the case. Demographic information for (putative) children's games is not particularly clustered in time. This suggests the use of these games by children was not a transient phase in a cross-generational cycle.

Table A.2 Range of Time Covered by the Sources: Children's Games and Cross-Generational Games Compared.[a]

Sources	Children's games		Cross-generational games	
	n	Average time (in years) covered by the two most distant sources	n	Average time (in years) covered by the two most distant sources
2	10	164	8	134
3	3	124	7	107
4	5	232	6	132
5	2	440	1	100
6	1	460	1	50
7	1	300	2	192
8	2	445	1	95
9+	1	530	1	290

[a] Only the sources containing demographic information are included.

To summarize, there is no denying that some children's games appear to be children's games just because we lack information to keep track of who played them. Yet this point cannot be used to explain away the demographic segregation of games. Even among our best-documented items, we find games that are both enduring and specific to children playing together.

DETECTION BIASES AND SELECTION BIASES

Until now, I have been taking my longevity measurements at face value. That, of course, is a mistake. Our data do not give us direct evidence of the games' life span—not unless we systematically turn absence of evidence into evidence of absence. We need to worry about three categories of missing data points.

(1) *Underdetected longevity.* Our measures of any game's life span obviously underestimate its true longevity, since any game must have existed, unrecorded, before and after its first and last identification. The duration of this before-and-after "dark" period may differ depending on which of our three categories of games we consider (children, adult, or both). Some categories may be particularly sensitive to the underdetected longevity bias.

(2) *Missing games (Selection bias).* The need to document a game's life span and its demography implies that the games we observe are better documented, and thus, probably longer-lived than the average game. This selection bias is highest for cross-generational games, because the best-documented games are also the most likely to be detected as cross-generational. This selection bias is also likely to exaggerate the average longevity of underdetected games, since our nets catch only the games that lasted long enough to be detected.

(3) *Missing demographic information.* As we saw, some adult and children's games on our list—but not all of them—are likely to be cross-generational games in disguise. The probability of adult involvement in their transmission decreases when the number of testimonies describing it as exclusive to children increases, but we can never be completely sure that a given game is segregated.

The importance of the first source of bias—the lack of traces for the earliest and latest stretches of a game's lifespan—can be assessed to a certain extent. For each game in the three categories (putative children's games, putative adults' games, and cross-generational games), I looked at the ratio of its (estimated) longevity on the number of references that documented it (after its first appearance and before its last). This ratio gives us the average number of years that it takes for the game to be detected while it is in use. (I assume that each game is continuously in existence during its recorded lifetime, without gaps.) This ratio (i.e., the number of detections related to the amount of time in use) represents a rough estimate of the probability that a game will be detected by our sources, if it is there to be detected. This measure indicates a clear bias *against* children's games. Adult and cross-generational games will both, on average, get detected once in every century of their recorded existence (once every 98 or 96 years respectively). Children's games take twice that time to get detected (once every 196 years on average). The figure is the same for the games that we start observing before 1534 (i.e., before the first edition of *Gargantua*) and for those that get their first mention only in Rabelais. This measure does not consider the games that *never* get detected between their first and last appearance, but these games are also instructive. A quarter of children's games (13 in 47) never got detected between their first and last appearance, while only two adults' games out of 32 escaped detection altogether. Thus, children's games are much less likely to get recorded by our sources during the time that they are around to be observed: once every two centuries, instead of twice. This is not surprising. Adults, after all, wrote our sources. Adult writers dwelt on adult matters, or at least they did before folkloristics took off in the nineteenth century. This underdetection has two consequences, which are somewhat conflicting.

On the one hand, children's games in our sample are probably much longer-lived than they appear to be (a bias that is much stronger for children's games than for the rest). This would make our estimates for the longevity of adults' games more accurate, but it would make children's games seem less ancient and long-lived than they really were. On the other hand, underdetection may also result in a selection bias. Children's games need a longer life span to get detected, and to get included in our sample. As a result, short-lived children's games are less likely to enter our sample than short-lived adult or cross-generational games. Most of Gargantua's 217 games did not last long enough to be documented, and were not included in this study. Underdetection means that, if we could know about these "dark" games, we would probably find that "dark" games are less long-lived than the games we can observe. We would also find that most of these "dark" games are children's games.

To summarize, Gargantua's games appear more long-lived than they really were, because we are seeing only the top of the pile. This illusion is more pronounced for children's games, as a group, because the holes in our network of sources are much wider when it comes to catching children's games. It only catches the biggest fishes. Yet the same bias that inflates longevity for children's games as a group makes us underestimate the individual longevity of the individual children's games that we observe. In other words, the fishes in the nest are bigger than the fishes in the sea, but each fish in the net is probably bigger than it seems to be.

THE LONGEVITY OF CHILDREN'S GAMES

Some games that I count as children's or adults' games are probably just undetected cross-generational games. The risk is greatest for poorly documented games. The more documented a game is, the easier it is to know that it was cross-generational. Less documented games will misleadingly fall into the "children" and "adult" categories. These poorly documented games, which cannot be included in the cross-generational group, also happen to be short-lived. There is an unsurprising correlation between the number of references that a game gets, and its longevity (Spearman's rho > 0.4, n = 103). Thus, a bias inflates the longevity of cross-generational games (as a group), and it underestimates the longevity of the other two groups.

Correcting for this bias seems simple. All we need to do is keep the amount of documentation for each game equal. Compare, in other words, well-documented children's games with equally well-documented games from the other two categories.

Yet this solution introduces a new bias, due to the underdetection of children's games. Since these games are detected twice more rarely, it takes longer for them to be detected a given number of times, than for an adult or cross-generational game to get the same number of detections. When the amount of documentation is kept equal, this bias will make children's games appear very long-lived, because we will only be looking at the top of the pile. This leaves us with several imperfect ways of assessing the longevity of children's games, depending on whether or not we control for the amount of documentation. While each comes with its own biases, the answers tend to point in the same direction.

First comparison: children's games compared with cross-generational games. The cross-generational games appear to survive longer, on average, than putative children's games (Table A.3). However, this difference is entirely due to the least documented of children's games, the ones most likely to be cross-generational games in disguise. The difference between children's games and cross-generational games becomes negligible when we consider only the best-documented games on each side (i.e., excluding games documented by only two or three sources). If we split the data according to the number of sources available to document each game, children's games are longer-lived in most row-wise comparisons. Part of this longer life span, though, is probably an illusion due to the underdetection of children's games.

Second comparison: children's games vs. the rest. I now compare children's peer culture with all the other games in our sample, including both proven cross-generational games and putative adults' games. These two sorts of game benefited from excellent demographic conditions, compared to children's peer culture. Life expectancy at birth was poor in modern France, as far as we know (the first complete datasets are from the eighteenth century—Blayo 1975). Yet, in eighteenth-century Europe, just like in the developing world today, high infant mortality and overall poor life expectancy did not prevent some people from reaching a respectable age, with most 15-year-olds being likely to reach the age of sixty (Kannisto, Nieminen, and Turpeinen 1999). All the adult references used in this study refer to grown men, as opposed to adolescents (most references to *escoliers*—students—or *pages* were excluded as demographically ambiguous, as well as some medieval references to *enfants*). There would thus be a considerable scope for vertical transmission both among adults and between adults and children—much wider, at any rate, than the six-to-fourteen window characteristic of children's peer culture. In spite of this, the data show children's games in our sample to be as long-lived as others (324 years vs. 317), even though they are not as well documented. They even seem to be longer-lived when the number of sources per game is taken into account, beating other games on every row-wise comparison but two (Table A.4).

Third comparison: children's games vs. adults' games. Documentation biases are less severe when we compare children's games with adults' games. Children's games, being less likely to be detected by our sources, are naturally less documented than adults' games (four sources per game on average, vs. five sources for adults' games), but only slightly so. In spite of this small disadvantage, children's games last much longer—seventy years longer on average—than adults' games (324 years vs. 254 years on average). Figure A.1 shows a timeline of all the adult and children's games from the late thirteenth century to the early decades of the twentieth century.

Table A.3 Mean Longevity: Children's Games Compared with Cross-Generational Games.[a]

Sources	Children		Cross-generational	
	n	Mean longevity	n	Mean longevity
2	13	231	0	/
3	16	289	1	71
4	4	396	1	374
5	2	364	7	344
6	5	437	6	370
7	2	401	2	622
8	1	374	2	571
9	1	443	3	424
10 +	3	502	2	443
Total	47	324	24	401
Total (Games with > 3 sources)	18	424	23	415

[a] The "Sources" column considers all the sources, including those that do not provide demographic information.

Table A.4 Mean Longevity: Children's Games Compared with Cross-Generational and Adult Games.[a]

Sources	Children n	Mean longevity	Adult & Cross-generational n	Mean longevity
2	13	**231**	2	62
3	16	**289**	5	172
4	4	**396**	6	298
5	2	**364**	15	302
6	5	**437**	12	344
7	2	401	4	**451**
8	1	374	3	**416**
9	1	**443**	6	344
10 +	3	**502**	3	401
Total	47	324	56	317

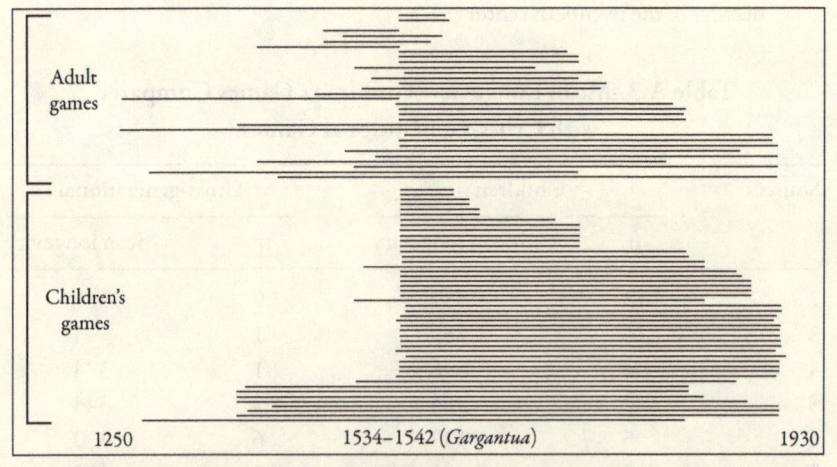

FIGURE A.1 A timeline of the 79 children's and adults' games mentioned in Rabelais's *Gargantua*. Each gray line represents a game's estimated life span, as given by the sources. Games are arranged by longevity within each group. One recognizes the period between 1534 and 1542—corresponding to the three editions of *Gargantua*—as the time when many games in our sample were first documented.

LASTING TRADITIONS, SPECIFIC TO CHILDHOOD

The data, imperfect as they may be, seem to warrant three conclusions.

(1) *Children's traditional games are neither a recent phenomenon nor an illusion.* Play segregation between children and adults is ancient, and cannot be explained away

by the limitations of our sources. Some of Gargantua's games were played by children long before Rabelais lived to document them, and continued to be played by groups of children, exclusively, for as long as our records can reach. As argued in chapter 5, these games lack some key features of adults' games, like the presence of purely symbolic manipulations. We cannot, of course, be certain that no adult ever played a part in their transmission—but that is not the point: the point is that their diffusion mostly relied on horizontal transmission, which should have weakened them.

(2) *The most long-lived of children's games do at least just as well as adult or cross-generational games, and arguably better.* Our measures of the longevity of children's games, in spite of the biases they may contain, are coherent with this view. This may result in part from a selection bias: these games being underdocumented, our sources will turn up only the most important and long-lived ones, leaving others in darkness. Controlling the amount of documentation per game may exacerbate this bias. This confounding factor does not change the truly significant phenomenon. Even if we are biased to look at the top of the pile, the very fact that the top of the pile is not empty is amazing. There should be a stringent upper limit on the longevity of children's peer culture. To the extent that they rely on quasi-horizontal transmission, children's traditions must be more frequently destabilized by generational turnover. They are walking, as it were, a demographic treadmill that should make them live much faster, and die sooner as a result. Their age should be counted in dog years, so to speak. This should never allow them to last as long as the traditions traveling down a more comfortable, vertical road. Yet the data show this peculiar mode of transmission does not seem to hurt them. The folklorists were right.

(3) *Adults' games do markedly worse than children's games.* Adults' games are surprisingly short-lived, compared to both children's games and cross-generational games. The difference with children's games is rather strong, and it cannot be entirely accounted for by detection and selection biases. One possible cause for the ephemeral quality of adults' games could be that the grain of description is finer for them. Our list includes, for instance, 15 games of cards. One can imagine how these 15 games could have been classified as only one game, had they been described by less informed or less careful observers. A coarser or finer grain of individuation could confound our observations. One reason to not worry too much about this problem is that children's games are also classified in much detail. Our list details, for instance, half a dozen games of tag (each lasting more than 300 years). The longevity differential, besides, is not specific to a particular category of games. Board games and gambling games (involving dices, cards, backgammon tables, etc.) are short-lived (218 years on average), but the other adults' games still lag behind children's games (with 308 years of survival on average).

The ephemeral quality of board games, incidentally, is a puzzle. These games, after all, are inscribed in very elaborate and durable artifacts. Most games in our sample are not: children's toys (windmills, nuts, balls) are mostly improvised, transient, disposable. Other adult or cross-generational games either involve everyday objects (knives, keys, coins, etc.) or general-purpose instruments (balls or rackets). What is more, rules for board games have been commented on and codified in writing long before most popular sports were recorded in any detail. Perhaps this last point holds the key to the puzzle: the ease of recording complex rules that writing affords may also permit greater invention and more complex variations, while non-written games need to be transmitted more conservatively.

Even then, the extinction of so many popular adults' games in France, in the modern period, remains surprising given their past success. Some, like the Italian *morra* (a cousin of *rock-paper-scissors*), are still alive in other countries. I doubt such extinctions can be blamed on a general crisis of adults' games in the sixteenth to eighteenth centuries. True, Christianity (both Protestant and Catholic) tried to limit gambling. But the Church and the State had always been fighting gamblers (for an account of this repression, in France, from 1200 to 1534, see Mehl 1990, chapter 16). The modern period shows no great improvement in that fight. Versailles was notorious for its gaming excesses. (Versailles was, admittedly, an outlier, but still one of the best documented social settings of the time.) Like other European countries, France went through an "industrious revolution"—a general increase in the time spent working on money-earning tasks (de Vries 2008). However, the proponents of that hypothesis insist that the revolution was actually led by women and children. It occurred at the level of households (de Vries 2008, chapter 3). If the rise of modern industriousness in the "long seventeenth century" interfered with the survival of traditional games (which it arguably did), the pressure would have been at least equally spread between cross-generational games, children's games, and adults' games.

Rabelais's list contains a substantial number of long-lived games that are consistently recorded throughout time as played by children. There is no upper limit to their longevity when compared to that of cross-generational games or adults' games: the most long-lived and well-documented children's games do better than their adult counterpart, and as well as their cross-generational equivalent. What is more, children's games appear to be victims of an underdetection bias: our measures underestimate their life span more than they do for other categories of games. On the flip side, underdetection probably means that many short-lived children's games in Rabelais's list eluded our search, for lack of documentation. These data confirm the hunch of generations of folklorists: as far as their longer-lived traditions are concerned, children's peer culture is on a par with other environments of cultural transmission. The endless wear-and-tear induced by rapid demographic turnover in children's groups does not do any harm to their most stable traditions.

BIBLIOGRAPHY

Abu-Lughod, Lila. 1991. "Writing against Culture." In *Recapturing Anthropology*, edited by R. G. Fox, 137–62. Santa Fe: School of American Research.
Allen, Jenny, Mason Weinrich, Will Hoppitt, and Luke Rendell. 2013. "Network-Based Diffusion Analysis Reveals Cultural Transmission of Lobtail Feeding in Humpback Whales." *Science* 340 (6131): 485–88.
Allport, Gordon W., and Leo Postman. 1947. *The Psychology of Rumor*. Oxford: Henry Holt.
Amos, Clinton, Gary Holmes, and David Strutton. 2008. "Exploring the Relationship between Celebrity Endorser Effects and Advertising Effectiveness: A Quantitative Synthesis of Effect Size." *International Journal of Advertising* 27 (2): 209–34.
Aral, Sinan, Lev Muchnik, and Arun Sundarajan. 2009. "Distinguishing Influence-Based Contagion from Homophily-Driven Diffusion in Dynamic Networks." *Proceedings of the National Academy of Sciences* 106 (51): 21554–49.
Arendt, Hannah. 2006 (1961). *Between Past and Future*. Translated by Jerome Kohn. Revised edition. New York: Penguin Classics.
Aristotle. 1997. *Poetics*. Edited and translated by M. Heath. New York: Penguin Classics.
Ariès, Philippe. 1960. *L'enfant et la vie familiale sous l'ancien régime*. Translated in English by R. Howlick as *Centuries of Childhood*, London: Pimlico, 1996. Page Numbers Refer to the French Version. Paris: Plon.
Asch, Solomon. 1955. "Opinions and Social Pressure." *Scientific American* 193: 31–35.
Atran, Scott. 2001. "The Trouble with Memes: Inference versus Imitation in Cultural Creation." *Human Nature* 124: 351–81.
———. 2003a. "Genesis of Suicide Terrorism." *Science* 299: 1534–39.
———. 2003b. "Théorie cognitive de la culture. Une alternative évolutionniste à la sociobiologie et à la sélection collective." *L'Homme* 166: 107–44.
Atran, Scott, and Dan Sperber. 1991. "Learning without Teaching: Its Place in Culture." *Human Development* 4: 39–55.

Aunger, Robert. 1999. "Against Idealism/Contra Consensus." *Current Anthropology* 40: 93–115.

———. 2000. "The Life History of Culture Learning in a Face-to-Face Society." *Ethos* 28: 1–38.

———. 2002. *The Electric Meme: A New Theory of How We Think*. New York: The Free Press.

Axsom, Dany, Susan M. Yates, and Shelly Chaiken. 1987. "Audience Response as a Heuristic Cue in Persuasion." *Journal of Personality and Social Psychology* 53: 30–40.

Baillargeon, Renée, Rose M. Scott, and Zijing He. 2010. "False-Belief Understanding in Infants." *Trends in Cognitive Sciences* 14 (3): 110–18.

Bakeman, Roger, Lauren B. Adamson, Melvin Konner, and Ronald G. Barr. 1990. "!Kung Infancy: The Social Context of Object Exploration." *Child Development* 61(3): 794–809.

Baker, M. C., T. M. Howard, and P. W. Sweet. 2000. "Microgeographic Variation and Sharing of the Gargle Vocalization and Its Component Syllables in Black-Capped Chickadee (Aves, Paridae, Poecile Atricapillus) Populations." *Ethology* 106: 819–38.

Baker, Myron C., Esther M. Baker, and Merrill S. A. Baker. 2001. "Island and Island-Like Effects on Vocal Repertoire of Singing Honeyeaters." *Animal Behaviour* 62: 767–74.

Baker, Myron C., and D. Gammon. 2008. "Vocal Memes in Natural Populations of Chickadees: Why Do Some Memes Persist and Others Go Extinct?" *Animal Behaviour* 75: 279–89.

Baller, Robert D., and Kelly K. Richardson. 2002. "Social Integration, Imitation, and the Geographic Patterning of Suicide." *American Sociological Review* 67 (6): 873–88.

Bandura, Albert. 1963. "The Role of Imitation in Personality Development." *The Journal of Nursery Education* 18 (3): 1–9.

Bangerter, A. 2000. "Transformation between Scientific and Social Representations of Conception." *British Journal of Social Psychology* 39: 521–35.

Baron, James N., and Peter C. Reiss. 1985. "Same Time, Next Year: Aggregate Analyses of the Mass Media and Violent Behavior." *American Sociological Review* 50: 347–63.

Baron, R., J. Vandello, and B. Brunsman. 1996. "The Forgotten Variable in Conformity Research: Impact of Task Importance on Social Influence." *Journal of Personality and Social Psychology* 71 (5): 915–27.

Barth, Fredrik. 1969. "Pathan Identity and Its Maintenance." In *Ethnic Groups and Boundaries*, 130–50. Oslo: Little Brown and Co.

———. 1975. *Ritual and Knowledge among the Baktaman of New Guinea*. New Haven: Yale University Press.

———. 1987. *Cosmologies in the Making: A Generative Approach to Cultural Variation in New Guinea*. Cambridge, Mass.: Cambridge University Press.

Bartlett, Frederic. 1932. *Remembering: A Study in Experimental and Social Psychology*. Cambridge, Mass.: Cambridge University Press.

Basalla, George. 1989. *The Evolution of Technology*. Cambridge, Mass.: Cambridge University Press.

Baucomont, Jean, François Guibat, Tante Lucie, Rolland Pinon, and Philippe Soupault. 1961. *Les comptines de langue française*. Paris: Seghers.

Baum, William, Peter Richerson, Charles Efferson, and Brian Paciotti. 2004. "Cultural Evolution in Laboratory Microsocieties Including Traditions of Rule Giving and Rule Following." *Evolution and Human Behavior* 25: 305–26.

Bell, Adrian V., Peter J. Richerson, and Richard McElreath. 2009. "Culture Rather than Genes Provides Greater Scope for the Evolution of Large-Scale Human Prosociality." *Proceedings of the National Academy of Sciences* 106 (42): 17671–74.

Bentley, R. A., C. P. Lipo, H. A. Herzog, and M. W. Hahn. 2007. "Regular Rates of Popular Culture Change Reflect Random Copying." *Evolution and Human Behavior* 28: 151–58.

Berger, Jonah, and Gaël Le Mens. 2009. "How Adoption Speed Affects the Abandonment of Cultural Tastes." *Proceedings of the National Academy of Sciences* 106 (20): 8146–50.

Berliner, David. 2010. "L'anthropologie et la question de la transmission." *Terrain*, 55: 4–19.

Bicchieri, Cristina. 2006. *The Grammar of Society: The Nature and Origins of Social Norms*. Cambridge, Mass.: Cambridge University Press.

Bicchieri, Cristina, and Yoshikata Fukui. 1999. "The Great Illusion: Ignorance, Informational Cascades and the Persistence of Unpopular Norms." In *Experience, Reality and Scientific Explanation*, edited by M. C. Galavotti and A. Pagnini, 89–121. The Western Ontario Series in Philosophy of Science. New York: Kluwer Academic Publishers.

Bikhchandani, Sushil, David Hirshleifer, and Ivo Welsh. 1998. "Learning from the Behavior of Others: Conformity, Fads and Informational Cascades." *The Journal of Economic Perspectives* 12 (3): 151–70.

Birch, Leann L. 1999. "Development of Food Preferences." *Annual Review of Nutrition* 19: 41–62.

Blackmore, Susan. 1999. "Imitation and the Definition of a Meme." *Journal of Memetics—Evolutionary Models of Information Transmission* 2.

Blayo, Yves. 1975. "La mortalité en France de 1740 à 1829." *Population (French Edition)* 30: 123.

Bloch, Marc. 1952. *Apologie pour l'Histoire ou: Le métier d'historien*. Paris: Armand Collin.

Bloch, Maurice. 1997. *How We Think They Think: Anthropological Approaches to Cognition, Memory, and Literacy*. Boulder, Colo.: Westview Press.

———. 2011. *Anthropology and the Cognitive Challenge*. Cambridge, Mass.: Cambridge University Press.

Boesch, Christopher. 1991. "Teaching among Wild Chimpanzees." *Animal Behaviour* 41: 530–32.

―――. 1993. "Towards a New Image of Culture in Wild Chimpanzees?" *Behavioral and Brain Sciences* 16(3): 514–15.

Boesch-Akerman, Hedwige, and Christopher Boesch. 1993. "Tool Use in Wild Chimpanzees: New Light from Dark Forests." *Current Directions in Psychological Science* 2: 18–21.

Bourdieu, Pierre. 1977. *Outline of a Theory of Practice*. Translated by Richard Nice. Cambridge, Mass.: Cambridge University Press.

Boyd, Robert, and Peter J. Richerson. 1985. *Culture and the Evolutionary Process*. Chicago: The University of Chicago Press.

―――. 1995. "Why Culture Is Common, but Cultural Evolution Is Rare." *Proceedings of the British Academy* 88: 73–93.

―――. 2009. "Voting with Your Feet: Payoff Biased Migration and the Evolution of Group Beneficial Behavior." *Journal of Theoretical Biology* 257 (2): 331–39.

Boyd, Robert, Peter J. Richerson, and Joseph Henrich. 2011. "The Cultural Niche: Why Social Learning Is Essential for Human Adaptation." *Proceedings of the National Academy of Sciences of the United States of America* 108 (Suppl. 2): 10918–25.

Boyer, Pascal. 1990. *Tradition as Truth and Communication: A Cognitive Description of Traditional Discourse*. Cambridge, Mass.: Cambridge University Press.

―――. 1994. "Cognitive Constraints on Cultural Representations: Natural Ontologies and Religious Ideas." In *Mapping the Mind: Domain-Specificity in Cognition and Culture*, edited by L. A. Hirschfeld and S. Gelman, 391–411. Cambridge, Mass.: Cambridge University Press.

―――. 2001. *Religion Explained: The Evolutionary Origins of Religious Thought*. New York: Basic Books.

Boyer, Pascal, and Charles Ramble. 2001. "Cognitive Templates for Religious Concepts: Cross-Cultural Evidence for Recall of Counter-Intuitive Representations." *Cognitive Science* 25 (4): 535–64.

Boyette, Adam. 2011. "Middle Childhood among Aka Forest Foragers of the Central African Republic: A Comparative Perspective." Unpublished ms., retrieved from http://anthro.vancouver.wsu.edu/media/PDF/boyette_hn_draft_6-09.pdf.

Brumann, Christoph. 1999. "Writing for Culture." *Current Anthropology* 40 (S1): 1–25.

Brunton, Ron. 1980. "Misconstrued Order in Melanesian Religions." *Man* 15 (1): 112–28.

―――. 1989. "The Cultural Instability of Egalitarian Societies." *Man* 24 (4): 673–81.

Bryan, James. 1971. "Model Affect and Children's Imitative Altruism." *Child Development* 42 (6): 2061–65.

Bryan, James, and Mary Ann Test. 1967. "Models and Helping: Naturalistic Studies in Helping Behavior." *Journal of Personality and Social Psychology* 6 (4): 400–407.

Bryan, James, and D Walbeck. 1970. "Practicing and Preaching Generosity: Children's Actions and Reactions." *Child Development* 41: 329–53.

Burguière, André. 1994. "Les rapports entre générations: un problème pour l'historien." *Communications* 59: 15–27.

Buttelmann, David, Malinda Carpenter, Josep Call, and Michael Tomasello. 2007. "Enculturated Chimpanzees Imitate Rationally." *Developmental Science* 10 (4): F31–38.

Bybee, Joan. 2010. *Language, Usage and Cognition*. Cambridge, Mass.: Cambridge University Press.

Caldwell, Christine, and Alisa Millen. 2008. "Experimental Models for Testing Hypotheses about Cumulative Cultural Evolution." *Evolution and Human Behavior* 29: 165–71.

———. 2009. "Social Learning Mechanisms and Cumulative Cultural Evolution—Is Imitation Necessary?" *Psychological Science* 20 (12): 1478–83.

Carassa, Antonella, and Marco Colombetti. 2009. "Joint Meaning." *Journal of Pragmatics* 41 (9): 1837–54.

Caro, T. M., and Marc D. Hauser. 1992. "Is There Teaching in Non-Human Animals?" *The Quarterly Review of Biology* 67(2): 151–74.

Cavalli-Sforza, Luigi-Luca, and Marcus Feldman. 1981. *Cultural Transmission and Evolution: A Quantitative Approach*. Princeton: Princeton University Press.

Cavalli-Sforza, Luigi Luca, Marcus W. ldman, K. H. Chen, and S. M. Dombusch. 1982. "Theory and Observation in Cultural Transmission." *Science* 218 (1).

Chapais, Bernard. 2010. *Primeval Kinship: How Pair-Bonding Gave Birth to Human Society*. Cambridge, Mass.: Harvard University Press.

Chartier, Roger. 1982. "Stratégies éditoriales et lectures populaires, 1530–1660." In *Histoire de l'édition française, 1: Le livre conquérant, du Moyen Âge au milieu du XVIIe siècle*, edited by R. Chartier, 585–603. Paris: Promodis.

Chomsky, Noam. 1980. *Rules and Representations*. Oxford: Blackwell.

Christakis, Nicholas, and James H. Fowler. 2007. "The Spread of Obesity in a Large Social Network over 32 Years." *New England Journal of Medicine* 357: 370–79.

———. 2009. *Connected: The Surprising Power of Our Social Networks and How They Shape Our Lives*. London: Little Brown and Co.

Chudacoff, Howard P. 2007. *Children at Play: An American History*. New York: New York University Press.

Claidière, Nicolas, and Dan Sperber. 2010. "Imitation Explains the Propagation, Not the Stability of Animal Culture." *Proceedings of the Royal Society B.*, 277, 651–59.

Clark, Gregory. 2009. *A Farewell to Alms: A Brief Economic History of the World*. Princeton: Princeton University Press.

Clauset, Aaron, Cosma Shalizi, and Mark E. Newman. 2009. "Power-Law Distributions in Empirical Data." SIAM Rev., 51 (4), 661–703.

Clutton-Brock, Tim. 2002. "Kin Selection and Mutualism in Cooperative Vertebrates." *Science* 296 (5565): 69–72.

Coleman, James S., Elihu Katz, and Herbert Menzel. 1957. "The Diffusion of an Innovation among Physicians." *Sociometry* 20: 253–70.

Comte, Auguste. 1864. *Cours de philosophie positive*. 2e ed. Vol. IV. Paris: J. Baillère et fils.

Conway, Lucian Gideon, and Mark Schaller. 2003. "How Communication Shapes Culture." In *Social Communication*, edited by K. Fiedler, 107–27. New York: Psychology Press.

———. 2005. "When Authorities' Commands Backfire: Attributions about Consensus and Effects on Deviant Decision-Making." *Journal of Personality and Social Psychology* 89 (3): 311–26.

Corsaro, William A., and David Eder. 1990. "Children's Peer Cultures." *Annual Review of Sociology* 16: 197–220.

Coultas, Julie C. 2004. "When in Rome . . . An Evolutionary Perspective on Conformity." *Group Processes and Intergroup Relations* 7 (4): 317–31.

Cournot, Antoine Augustin. 1872. *Considérations sur la marche des idées et des évènements dans les temps modernes*. Vol. 1. Paris: Hachette.

Crisp, Quentin. 1987. "Antihero." *Spin* 3(1): 70.

Csibra, Gergely. 2007. "Teachers in the Wild." *Trends in Cognitive Sciences* 11: 95–96.

Csibra, Gergely, and György Gergely. 2009. "Natural Pedagogy." *Trends in Cognitive Sciences* 11: 95–96.

Dana, Jason, Roberto A. Weber, and Jason Xi Kuang. "Exploiting Moral Wiggle Room: Experiments Demonstrating an Illusory Preference for Fairness." *Economic Theory* 33, no. 1 (September 23, 2006): 67–80.

Danchin, Étienne, Luc-Alain Giraldeau, Thomas J. Valone, and Richard H. Wagner. 2004. "Public Information: From Nosy Neighbors to Cultural Evolution." *Science* 305: 487–91.

D'Andrade, Roy G. 1987. "Modal responses and cultural expertise". *American Behavioral Scientist*, 31(2), 194–202.

Dawkins, Richard. 1976. *The Selfish Gene*. Oxford: Oxford University Press.

Déléage, Pierre. 2012. "Transmission et stabilisation des chants rituels." *L'Homme* 203–204: 103–37.

Dennett, Daniel C. 1995. *Darwin's Dangerous Idea: Evolution and the Meaning of Life*. New York: Simon and Schuster.

Descombes, Vincent. 1998. "L'identification des idées." *Revue Philosophique de Louvain* 96 (1): 86–118.

Deutscher, Guy. 2009. "'Overall Complexity': A Wild Goose Chase?" In *Language Complexity as an Evolving Variable*, edited by G. Sampson, P. Trudgill and P. Turchin, 243–51. New York: Oxford University Press.

De Vienne, Emmanuel, and Olivier Allard. 2005. "Pour une poignée de dollars ? Transmission et patrimonialisation de la culture chez les Trumai du Brésil central." *Cahiers Des Amériques Latines* 48–49: 127–45.

de Vries, Jan. 2008. *The Industrious Revolution*. Cambridge, Mass.: Cambridge University Press.

De Waal, Frans. 1982. *Chimpanzee Politics: Power and Sex among Apes*. Baltimore, Md.: The Johns Hopkins University Press.

Dijksterhuis, A., and J. Bargh. 2001. "The Perception-Behavior Expressway: Automatic Effects of Social Perception on Social Behavior." *Advances in Experimental Social Psychology* 33: 1–40.

Doris, John, and Alexandra Plakias. 2007. "How to Argue About Disagreement: Evaluative Diversity and Moral Realism." In *Moral Psychology, Vol. 2: The Cognitive Science of Morality*, edited by W. Sinnott-Armstrong, 303–32. Cambridge: MIT Press.

Driscoll, Catherine. 2008. "The Problem of Adaptive Cultural Choice in Cultural Evolution." *Biology and Philosophy* 23: 101–13.

Dunbar, Robin. 1993. "Coevolution of Neocortical Size, Group Size and Language in Humans." *Behavioral and Brain Sciences* 16 (4): 681–735.

Duncan, C. J. 1962. "Salt Preferences of Birds and Mammals." *Physiological Zoology* 35 (2): 120–32.

Durkheim, Émile. 1893 (1963). *The Division of Labor in Society*. Translated by G. Simpson. Glencoe, Ill.: The Free Press.

———. 1897 (1952). *Suicide: A Study in Sociology*. Translated by G. Simpson. London: Routledge.

Ebbinghaus, Hermann. 1885. *Memory: A Contribution to Experimental Psychology*. New York: Dover.

Efferson, Charles, R. Lalive, Peter J. Richerson, Richard McElreath, and Mark Lubell. 2008. "Conformists and Mavericks: The Empirics of Frequency-Dependent Cultural Transmission." *Evolution and Human Behavior* 29: 56–64.

Efferson, Charles, Peter Richerson, Richard McElreath, Mark Lubell, Ed Edsten, Timothy Waring, Brian Paciotti, and William Baum. 2007. "Learning, Productivity, and Noise: An Experimental Study of Cultural Transmission on the Bolivian Altiplano." *Evolution and Human Behavior* 28: 11–17.

Elias, Norbert. 1939. *The Civilizing Process, Vol. I: The History of Manners*. Oxford: Blackwell.

Ellis, Shari, Barbara Rogoff, and Cindy C. Cromer. 1981. "Age Segregation in Children's Social Interactions." *Developmental Psychology* 17 (4): 399–407.

Enquist, Magnus, Pontus Strimling, Kimmo Erikson, Kevin Laland, and Jonas Sjostrand. 2010. "One Cultural Parent Makes No Culture." *Animal Behaviour* 29: 1353–62.

Eriksson, Kimmo, and Julie C. Coultas. 2012. "The Advantage of Multiple Cultural Parents in the Cultural Transmission of Stories." *Evolution and Human Behavior* 33 (4): 251–59.

Farroni, Teresa, Gergely Csibra, Francesca Simion, and Mark H. Johnson. 2002. "Eye Contact Detection in Humans from Birth." *Proceedings of the National Academy of Sciences* 99 (14): 9602–605.

Fehr, Ernst, and Urs Fischbacher. 2003. "The Nature of Human Altruism." *Nature* 425: 784–91.

Ferrari, Pier F., Elisabetta Visalberghi, Annika Paukner, L. Fogassi, and A. Ruggiero. 2006. "Neonatal Imitation in Rhesus Macaques." *PLoS ONE* 4 (9): e302.

Fessler, Daniel M.T., and Carlos Navarrete. 2003. "Meat Is Good to Taboo—Dietary Proscriptions as a Product of the Interaction of Psychological Mechanisms and Social Processes." *Journal of Cognition and Culture* 3 (1): 1–40.

Ficken, Millicent Sigler, and James W. Popp. 1995. "Long-Term Persistence of a Culturally Transmitted Vocalization of the Black-Capped Chickadee." *Animal Behaviour* 50: 683–93.

Ficken, Millicent Sigler, and Charles Weise. 1984. "A Complex Call of the Black-Capped Chickadee (*Parus Atricapillus*), 1: Microgeographic Variation." *The Auk* 101 (2): 349–60.

Fine, Gary Allan. 1980. "Children and Their Culture: Exploring Newell's Paradox." *Western Folklore*, 170–83.

Fisher, James, and Robert A. Hinde. 1949. "The Opening of Milk Bottles by Birds." *British Birds* 42: 347–57.

Fiske, Alan P. 1996. "Learning a Culture the Way Informants Do: Observing, Imitating and Participating." (unpublished ms.)

Franks, Bradley. 2011. *Culture and Cognition: Evolutionary Perspectives*. Houndmills, Basingstoke, Hampshire: Palgrave Macmillan.

Gambetta, Diego. 1993. *The Sicilian Mafia: The Business of Private Protection*. Cambridge, Mass.: Harvard University Press.

———. 2005. *Making Sense of Suicide Missions*. New York: Oxford University Press.

Gayon, Jean. 2003. "Évolution culturelle: Le spectre des possibles." In *Gènes et culture*, edited by J.-P. Changeux, 57–72. Paris: Odile Jacob.

Geertz, Clifford. 1973. *The Interpretation of Cultures: Selected Essays*. New York: Fontana Press.

Gelman, Susan A., Peggy J. Goetz, Barbara W. Sarnecka, and Jonathan Flukes. 2008. "Generic Language in Parent-Child Conversations." *Language Learning and Development: The Official Journal of the Society for Language Development* 4 (1): 1–31.

Gergely, György, Harold Bekkering, and Ildikó Király. 2002. "Rational Imitation in Preverbal Infants." *Nature* 415: 755.

Gigerenzer, Gerd, and Daniel G. Goldstein. "Reasoning the Fast and Frugal Way: Models of Bounded Rationality." *Psychological Review* 103, no. 4 (1996): 650–69.

Gintis, Herbert. 2003. "The Hitchhiker's Guide to Altruism: Gene-Culture Coevolution, and the Internalization of Norms." *Journal of Theoretical Biology*, 220 (4): 407–18.

Gintis, Herbert, Samuel Bowles, Robert Boyd, and Ernst Fehr. 2003. "Explaining Altruistic Behavior in Humans." *Evolution and Human Behavior* 24: 153–72.

Gladwell, Malcolm. 2000. *The Tipping Point*. Boston: Little Brown and Co.

Glassie, Henry. 1995. "Tradition." *Journal of American Folklore* 108 (430): 395–412.

Goldgar, Anne. 2007. *Tulipmania: Money, Honor and Knowledge in the Dutch Golden Age*. Chicago: University of Chicago Press.

Goody, Jack. 1977. *The Domestication of the Savage Mind*. New York: Cambridge University Press.

Gosselin, Gabriel. 1975. "Tradition et traditionalisme." *Revue Française de Sociologie* 16: 215–27.

Greenfield, Patricia. 2005. *Weaving Generations Together: Evolving Creativity in the Maya of Chiapas*. Santa Fe: School of American Research.

Griaule, Marcel. 1938. *Jeux Dogons*. Paris: Institut d'ethnologie.

Grice, Paul. 1957. "Meaning." *Philosophical Review* 66 (3): 377–88.

Griffiths, Thomas L., Stephan Lewandowsky, and Michael L. Kalish. 2013. "The Effects of Cultural Transmission Are Modulated by the Amount of Information Transmitted." *Cognitive Science* 37 (5): 953–67.

Guglielmino, Carmela R., Carla Viganotti, Barry S. Hewlett, and Luigi-Luca Cavalli-Sforza. 1995. "Cultural Variation in Africa: Role of Mechanisms of Transmission and Adaptation." *Proceedings of the National Academy of Sciences* 92: 7585–89.

Gurven, Michael, Arianna Zanolini, and Eric Schniter. 2008. "Culture Sometimes Matters: Intra-Cultural Variation in Pro-Social Behavior among Tsimane Amerindians." *Journal of Economic Behavior & Organization* 67 (3–4): 587–607.

Hahn, Matthew W., and Alexander Bentley. 2003. "Drift as a Mechanism for Cultural Change: An Example from Baby Names." *Proceedings of the Royal Society B* 270: S120–23.

Haidt, Jonathan, Fredrik Bjorklund, and Scott Murphy. 2000. "Moral Dumbfounding: When Intuition Finds No Reason." (unpublished ms.)

Halbwachs, Maurice. 1992 (1925). *On Collective Memory*. Edited, translated, and with an introduction by L. A. Coser. Chicago: University of Chicago Press.

Hall, K. R. L. 1951. "The Effect of Names and Titles upon the Serial Reproduction of Pictorial and Verbal Material." *British Journal of Social Psychology* 41: 109–21.

Hanawalt, Barbara. 2002. "Medievalists and the Study of Childhood." *Speculum* 77 (2): 440–60.

Harris, Judith Rich. 1998. *The Nurture Assumption: Why Children Turn out the Way They Do*. New York: The Free Press.

Harrison, Lawrence E., and Samuel P. Huntington. 2000. *Culture Matters: How Values Shape Human Progress*. New York: Basic Books.

Hawkes, Kristen, James F. O'Connell, and Nicholas G. Blurton-Jones. 1997. "Hazda Women's Time Allocation, Offspring Provisioning, and the Evolution of Long Postmenopausal Life Spans." *Current Anthropology* 38 (4): 551–77.

Hawks, John, Keith Hunley, Sang-Hee Lee, and Milford Wolpoff. 2000. "Population Bottlenecks and Pleistocene Human Evolution." *Molecular Biology and Evolution* 17: 2–22.

Hawton, K., Louise Harris, Sue Simkin, Edmund Juszczak, Louis Applebby, Ros McDonnell, Tim Amos, and Katy Kiernan. 2000. "Effect of Death of Diana, Princess of Wales, on Suicide and Deliberate Self-Harm." *The British Journal of Psychiatry* 177: 463–66.

Heath, Chip, Chris Bell, and Emily Sternberg. 2001. "Emotional Selection in Memes: The Case of Urban Legends." *Journal of Personality and Social Psychology* 81 (6): 1028–41.

Heck, Jean Olive. 1927. "Poetry and Folk Criticism, as Illustrated by Cincinnati Children in Their Singing Games and in Their Thoughts about These Games." *Journal of American Folklore* 155: 1–77.

Henrich, Joseph. 2001. "Cultural Transmission and the Diffusion of Innovations: Adoption Dynamics Indicate That Biased Transmission Is the Predominate Force in Behavioral Change." *American Anthropologist* 103 (4): 992–1013.

———. 2004. "Demography and Cultural Evolution: Why Adaptive Cultural Processes Produced Maladaptive Losses in Tasmania." *American Antiquity* 69 (2): 197–214.

Henrich, Joseph, and Robert Boyd. 2001. "Why People Punish Defectors: Weak Conformist Transmission Can Stabilize Costly Enforcement of Norms in Cooperative Dilemmas." *Journal of Theoretical Biology* 208: 79–89.

Henrich, Joseph, Robert Boyd, Samuel Bowles, Colin Camerer, Ernst Fehr, Herbert Gintis, Richard McElreath, et al. 2005. "Economic Man in Cross-Cultural Perspective: Behavioral Experiments in 15 Small-Scale Societies." *Behavioral and Brain Sciences* 28: 795–855.

Henrich, Joseph, and Francisco J. Gil-White. 2001. "The Evolution of Prestige: Freely Conferred Deference as a Mechanism for Enhancing the Benefits of Cultural Transmission." *Evolution and Human Behavior* 22 (3): 165–96.

Henrich, Joseph, and Natalie Henrich. 2010. "The Evolution of Cultural Adaptations: Fijian Food Taboos Protect against Dangerous Marine Toxins." *Proceedings of the Royal Society B*, 277(1701): 3715–24.

Henrich, Joseph, and Richard McElreath. 2007. "Dual Inheritance Theory: The Evolution of Human Cultural Capacities and Cultural Evolution." In *Oxford Handbook of Evolutionary Psychology*, edited by R. Dunbar and L. Barrett, 555–70. New York: Oxford University Press.

Henrich, Nathalie, and Joseph Henrich. 2007. *Why Humans Cooperate*. Cambridge, Mass.: Oxford University Press.

Herder, Johann Gottfried. 1791 (2010). *Outlines of a Philosophy of the History of Man*. Translated by T. O. Churchill. New York: Bergman Publishers.

Hewlett, Barry, and L. L. Cavalli-Sforza. 1986. "Cultural Transmission among Aka Pygmies." *American Anthropologist* 88: 922–34.

Hewlett, Barry, Hillary Fouts, Adam Boyette, and Bonnie Hewlett. 2011. "Social Learning among Congo Basin Hunter Gatherers." *Proceedings of the Royal Society B* 366: 1168–78.

Heyes, Cecilia. 1993. "Imitation, Culture and Cognition." *Animal Behaviour* 46: 999–1010.

Heyes, Cecilia M., and Chris D. Frith. 2014. "The Cultural Evolution of Mind Reading." *Science* 344 (6190): 1346–47.
Higham, T. M. 1951. "The Experimental Study of the Transmission of Rumour." *British Journal of Psychology* 42: 42–55.
Hill, Kim, and Keith Kintigh. 2009. "Can Anthropologists Distinguish Good and Poor Hunters? Implications for Hunting Hypotheses, Sharing Conventions, and Cultural Transmission." *Current Anthropology* 49 (5): 927–34.
Hirschfeld, Lawrence. 1997. "Why Don't Anthropologists Like Children?" *American Anthropologist* 1042: 611–27.
Hobsbawm, Eric, and Terence Ranger. 1992. *The Invention of Tradition*. Cambridge, Mass.: Cambridge University Press.
Hocart, Arthur Maurice. 1927. "Are Savages Custom-Bound?" *Man* 27: 220–21.
Holden, Clare, and Ruth Mace. 2009. "Phylogenetic Analysis of the Evolution of Lactose Digestion in Adults." *Human Biology* 81 (5–6): 597–619.
Hood, Bruce M., J. Douglas Willen, and Jon Driver. 1998. "Adult's Eyes Trigger Shift of Visual Attention in Newborn Infants." *Psychological Science* 9 (2): 131–34.
Hoppitt, W., G. Brown, R. Kendal, L. Rendell, A. Thornton, M. Webster, and K. Laland. 2008. "Lessons from Animal Teaching." *Trends in Ecology and Evolution* 23 (9): 486–93.
Hrdy, Sarah B. 2009. *Mothers and Others: The Evolutionary Origins of Mutual Understanding*. Cambridge, Mass.: Belknap Press of Harvard University Press.
Hume, David. 1744a (1998). "Of the Rise of the Arts and Sciences." In *Selected Essays*, 56–77. New York: Oxford University Press.
———. 1744b (1998). "Of the Original Contract." In *Selected Essays*, 274–92. New York: Oxford University Press.
Hunt, Gavin, and Russell Gray. 2003. "Diversification and Cumulative Evolution in New Caledonian Crow Tool Manufacture." *Proceedings of the Royal Society B: Biological Sciences* 270: 867–74.
Inspection générale de l'éducation nationale. 2002. *Éléments d'information sur le jeu du foulard: Rapport à monsieur le ministre de l'éducation nationale*. Paris: Ministère de la jeunesse et de l'éducation nationale.
Jablonka, Eva, and Marion Lamb. 2005. *Evolution in Four Dimensions: Genetic, Epigenetic, Behavioral and Symbolic Variation in the History of Life*. Boston: MIT Press.
Jacobs, Robert C., and Donald T. Campbell. 1961. "The Perpetuation of an Arbitrary Tradition through Several Generations of a Laboratory Microculture." *Journal of Abnormal Social Psychology* 62: 649–58.
James, Clive. 1978. "Brezhnev: A State of Boredom." *New Statesman*, 27: 154.
Jones, Eric L. 2004. *Cultures Merging: A Historical and Economic Critique of Culture*. Princeton: Princeton University Press.
Kalish, Michael, Thomas L. Griffiths, and Stephan Lewandowsky. 2007. "Iterated Learning: Intergenerational Knowledge Transmission Reveals Inductive Biases." *Psychonomic Bulletin & Review* 14 (2): 288–94.

Kannisto, Väinö, Mauri Nieminen, and Oiva Turpeinen. 1999. "Finnish Life Tables since 1751." *Demographic Research* 1(1).

Kaplan, Hillard, Jane Lancaster, and Arthur Robson. 2003. "Embodied Capital and the Evolutionary Economics of the Human Life Span." *Population and Development Review* 29: 152–82.

Karsenti, Bruno. 1993. "Présentation" to Gabriel Tarde's *Lois de l'imitation*, pp. I—XXVI. Paris: Kimé.

Kashima, Yoshihisha. 2000. "Maintaining Cultural Stereotypes in the Serial Reproduction of Narratives." *Personality and Social Psychology Bulletin* 26: 594.

Katz, Elihu, and Paul F. Lazarsfeld. 1955. *Personal Influence: The Part Played by People in the Flow of Mass Communication.* Glencoe, Illinois: The Free Press.

Keesing, Roger. 1982. *Kwaio Religion: The Living and the Dead in a Solomon Islands Society.* New York: Columbia University Press.

Király, Ildikó, Gergely Csibra, and György Gergely. 2013. "Beyond Rational Imitation: Learning Arbitrary Means Actions from Communicative Demonstrations." *Journal of Experimental Child Psychology* 116 (2): 471–86.

Klein, Daniel B., and John Majewski. 1994. "Plank Road Fever in Antebellum America: New York State Origins." *New York History*, 65: 39–65.

Kline, Michelle, and Robert Boyd. 2010. "Population Size Predicts Technological Complexity in Oceania." *Proceedings of the Royal Society B* 277 (1693): 2559–64.

Kobayashi, H., and S. Kohshima. 1997. "Unique Morphology of the Human Eye." *Nature* 387: 767–68.

Köhler, Wolfgang. 1947. *Gestalt Psychology*. 2e. New York: Liveright.

Konner, Melvin. 1976. "Maternal Care, Infant Behaviour, and Development among the !Kung." In *Kalahari Hunter-Gatherers: Studies of the !Kung San and Their Neighbors*, edited by R. B. Lee and I. DeVore, 218–45. Cambridge, Mass.: Harvard University Press.

———. 2011. *The Evolution of Childhood: Relationships, Emotion, Mind*. Cambridge, Mass.; London: Belknap Press.

Kramer, Karen L. 2005. "Children's Help and the Pace of Reproduction: Cooperative Breeding in Humans." *Evolutionary Anthropology* 14: 224–37.

Kroch, Anthony S. 1978. "Toward a Theory of Social Dialect Variation." *Language in Society* 7: 17–36.

Kroeber, Alfred L. 1931. "Historical Reconstruction of Culture Growths and Organic Evolution." *American Anthropologist* 33: 149–56.

———. 1940. "Stimulus Diffusion." *American Anthropologist* 42 (1): 1–20.

Krutzen, Michael, Janet Mann, Michael R. Heithaus, Richard C. Connor, Lars Bedjer, and William B. Sherwin. 2005. "Cultural Transmission of Tool Use in Bottlenose Dolphins." *Proceedings of the National Academy of Sciences* 102 (205): 8939–43.

Kummer, Hans, and Jane Goodall. 1985. "Conditions of Innovative Behavior in Primates." *Philosophical Transactions of the Royal Society B* 308: 203–14.

Kuran, Timur, and Cass Sunstein. 1999. "Availability Cascades and Risk Regulation." *Stanford Law Review* 51 (4): 683–768.
Kurke, Lance E., Karl E. Weick, and Elizabeth C. Ravlin. 1989. "Can Information Loss Be Reversed? Evidence for Serial Reconstruction." *Communication Research* 16 (1): 3–24.
Labov, William. 1980. "The Social Origins of Sound Change." In *Locating Language in Time and Space*, edited by W. Labov, 251–65. New York: Academic Press.
Laland, Kevin N. 2002. "Imitation, Social Learning and Preparedness as Mechanisms of Bounded Rationality." In *Bounded Rationality: The Adaptive Toolbox*, edited by G. Gigerenzer and R. Selten, 233–47. Cambridge, Mass.: MIT Press.
Laland, Kevin N., John Odling-Smee, and Sean Myles. 2010. "How Culture Shaped the Human Genome: Bringing Genetics and the Human Sciences Together." *Nature Reviews Genetics* 11: 137–49.
Lamba, Shakti, and Ruth Mace. 2011. "Demography and Ecology Drive Variation in Cooperation across Human Populations." *Proceedings of the National Academy of Sciences* 108 (35): 14426–30.
———. 2012. "Reply to Henrich et al.: Behavioral Variation Needs to Be Quantified at Multiple Levels." *Proceedings of the National Academy of Sciences* 109 (2): E34–E34.
Lancy, David F. 1996. *Playing on the Mother-Ground: Cultural Routines for Children's Development*. New York: Guilford Press.
Langmuir, Erika. 2006. *Imagining Childhood*. New Haven, Conn.: Yale University Press.
Le Roy Ladurie, Emmanuel. 1979. *Montaillou: The Promised Land of Error*. Translated by Barbara Bray. New York: Vintage.
Leach, Edmund. 1954. *Political Systems of Highland Burma: A Study of Kachin Social Structure*. London: Berg.
Levinson, Stephen. 2000. *Pragmatics*. Cambridge, Mass.: Cambridge University Press.
Lieberson, Stanley. 2000. *A Matter of Taste: How Names, Fashions, and Culture Change*. New Haven, Conn.: Yale University Press.
Lillard, A. 1998. "Ethnopsychologies: Cultural Variations in Theories of Mind." *Psychological Bulletin* 123 (1): 3–32.
Lord, Albert B. 1960. *The Singer of Tales*. Cambridge, Mass.: Harvard University Press.
Lowie, Robert Harry. 1920. *Primitive Society*. New York: Bonie and Liveright.
Lupyan, Gary, and Rick Dale. 2010. "Language Structure Is Partly Determined by Social Structure." *PLoS One* 5 (1): e8559.
Lyman, R. Lee, and Michael J. O'Brien. 2003. "Cultural Traits: Units of Analysis in Early Twentieth-Century Anthropology." *Journal of Anthropological Research* 59 (2): 225–50.
Lyons, Russell. 2011. "The Spread of Evidence-Poor Medicine via Flawed Social-Network Analysis." *Statistics, Politics, and Policy* 2 (1).

Lyons, Derek E., Diana H. Damrosch, Jennifer K. Lin, Deanna M. Macris, and Frank C. Keil. 2011. "The Scope and Limits of Overimitation in the Transmission of Artefact Culture." *Philosophical Transactions of the Royal Society B* 366 (1567): 1158–67.

MacDonald, Katharine. 2007. "Cross-Cultural Comparison of Learning in Human Hunting." *Human Nature* 18: 386–402.

Machery, Edouard, Ron Mallon, Shaun Nichols, and Stephen Stich. 2004. "Semantics, Cross-Cultural Style." *Cognition* 92: B1–12.

MacIntyre, Alasdair. 1989. *Whose Justice? Which Rationality?*. Notre Dame, Ind.: University of Notre Dame Press.

Mackay, Charles. 1841. *Extraordinary Popular Delusions and the Madness of Crowds.* Three Rivers, Calif.: Three Rivers Press.

Mackie, D. M., L. T. Worth, and A. G. Asuncion. 1990. "Processing of Persuasive in-Group Messages." *Journal of Personality and Social Psychology* 58: 812–22.

Mameli, Mateo. 2008. "Understanding Culture: A Commentary on Richerson and Boyd's Not by Genes Alone." *Biology and Philosophy* 23: 269–81.

Mannheim, Karl. 1952. "The Problem of Generations." In *Essays on the Sociology of Knowledge*, edited by P. Kecskemeti, 276–322. London: Routledge.

Marino, L. et al. 2007. "Cetaceans Have Complex Brains for Complex Cognition." PLoS Biology 5: e139.

Mauss, Marcel. 1931. "La cohésion sociale dans les sociétés polysegmentaires." *Bulletin de L'institut Français de Sociologie* 1: 49–68.

———. 1934 (1950). *Sociologie et Anthropologie*. Paris: Presses Universitaires de France.

McElreath, Richard, Adrian V. Bell, Charles Efferson, Mark Lubell, Peter J. Richerson, and Timothy Waring. 2008. "Beyond Existence and Aiming Outside the Laboratory: Estimating Frequency-Dependent and Pay-Off-Biased Social Learning Strategies." *Philosophical Transactions of the Royal Society B* 363 (1509): 3515–28.

McElreath, Richard, Mark Lubell, Peter J. Richerson, Timothy M. Waring, William Baum, Edward Edsten, Charles Efferson, and Brian Paciotti. 2005. "Applying Evolutionary Models to the Laboratory Study of Social Learning." *Evolution and Human Behavior* 26 (6): 483–508.

McKone, Elinor, Kate Crookes, and Nancy Kanwisher. 2009. "The Cognitive and Neural Development of Face Recognition in Humans." In *Handbook of Neuroscience for the Behavioral Sciences*, edited by J. T. Cacioppo and G. G. Berntson, 467–82. Hoboken, N.J.: J. Wiley and Sons.

Mead, Margaret. 1930. *Growing Up in New Guinea: A Comparative Study of Primitive Education*. New York: William Morrow.

———. 1940. "Social Change and Cultural Surrogates." *Journal of Educational Sociology* 14 (2): 92–109.

Mehl, Jean-Michel. 1990. *Les jeux au royaume de France, du XIIIe au début du XVIe siècle*. Paris: Arthème Fayard.

Meltzoff, Andrew. 1988. "Infant Imitation after a 1-Week Delay: Long-Term Memory for Novel Acts and Multiple Stimuli." *Developmental Psychology* 24: 470–76.

———. 1995. "Understanding the Intentions of Others: Re-Enactment of Intentions by 18-Months-Old Children." *Developmental Psychology* 31 (5): 838–50.
Mentré, François. 1920. *Les générations sociales*. Paris: Brossard.
Mercader, Julio, Melissa Panger, and Christopher Boesch. 2002. "Excavation of a Chimpanzee Stone Tool Site in the African Rainforest." *Science* 5572: 1452–55.
Mergen, Bernard. 1975. "The Discovery of Children's Play." *American Quarterly* 27 (4): 399–420.
Merton, Robert K. 1968. "Social Theory and Social Structure." Glencore, Ill.: The Free Press.
Mesoudi, Alex. 2009. "The Cultural Dynamics of Copycat Suicide." *PLoS ONE* 4 (9): e7252.
Mesoudi, Alex, and Andrew Whiten. 2004. "The Hierarchical Transformation of Event Knowledge in Human Cultural Transmission." *Journal of Cognition and Culture* 4: 1–24.
———. 2008. "The Multiple Roles of Cultural Transmission Experiments in Understanding Human Cultural Evolution." *Philosophical Transactions of the Royal Society B* 363: 3489–501.
Mesoudi, Alex, Andrew Whiten, and Robin Dunbar. 2006. "A Bias for Social Information in Human Cultural Transmission." *British Journal of Psychology* 97 (3): 405–23.
Mesoudi, Alex, Andrew Whiten, and Kevin N. Laland. 2006. "Towards a Unified Science of Cultural Evolution." *Behavioral and Brain Sciences* 29: 329–83.
Milgram, Stanley, Leonard Bickman, and Lawrence Berkowitz. 1969. "Note on the Drawing Power of Crowds of Different Size." *Journal of Personality and Social Psychology* 13: 79–82.
Mill, John Stuart. 1843. *A System of Logic, Ratiocinative and Inductive*. Gutenberg Project ebook.
Mithen, Steven. 1999. "Imitation and Cultural Change: A View from the Stone Age, with Specific Reference to the Manufacture of Handaxes." In *Mammalian Social Learning: Comparative and Ecological Perspectives*, edited by H. Box and K. Gibson, 389–99. Cambridge, Mass.: Cambridge University Press.
Miyamoto, Yuri, Richard E. Nisbett, and Takahiko Matsuda. 2006. "Culture and the Physical Environment—Holistic versus Analytic Perceptual Affordances." *Psychological Science* 17 (2): 113–19.
Moll, Henrike, and Michael Tomasello. 2007. "Cooperation and Human Cognition: The Vygotskian Intelligence Hypothesis". *Philosophical Transactions of the Royal Society B* 362 (1480): 639–48.
Mollenhorst, G. 2009. "Networks in Contexts: How Meeting Opportunities Affect Personal Relationships." Utrecht: Université d'Utrecht.
Moore, Richard. 2014. " Enacting and Understanding Communicative Intent." (unpublished ms.)
Moretti, Franco. 1998. *Atlas of the European Novel 1800–1900*. New York: Verso.
———. 2000. "The Slaughterhouse of Literature." *Modern Language Quarterly* 61: 207–28.

Morin, Olivier. 2010. "Pourquoi les enfants ont-ils des traditions?" *Terrain: Revue d'ethnologie de l'Europe* 55: 20–39.

———. 2014. "Is Cooperation a Maladaptive by-Product of Social Learning? The Docility Hypothesis Reconsidered." *Biological Theory* 9 (3): 286–95.

Saki (HH Munro). 2012. "Clovis on Parental Responsibilities." In *The Complete Short Stories*. London: Penguin Classics.

Nadel, Jacqueline. 1986. *Imitation et communication entre jeunes enfants*. Paris: Presses Universitaires de France.

Needham, Joseph. 1960. *Heavenly Clockwork*. Cambridge, England: Cambridge University Press.

Nettle, Daniel. 1999. *Linguistic Diversity*. New York: Oxford University Press.

Nettle, Daniel, Agathe Colléony, and Maria Cockerill. 2011. "Variation in Cooperative Behaviour within a Single City." *PLoS ONE* 6 (10): e26922.

Newell, William A. 1883. *Games and Songs of American Children*. New York: Dover.

Nichols, Shaun. 2002. "On the Genealogy of Norms: A Case for the Role of Emotion in Cultural Evolution." *Philosophy of Science* 69: 234–55.

Nisbett, Richard E. 2003. *The Geography of Thought: How Asians and Westerners Think Differently . . . and Why*. New York: The Free Press.

Nisbett, Richard E., and Dov Cohen. 1996. "*Ifs* and *Thens* in Cultural Psychology." In *The Automaticity of Everyday Life*, edited by J. Bargh and R. S. Wyer, 121–31. Mahwah, N.J.: Westview Press.

Nora, Pierre. 1992. "La génération." In *Les lieux de mémoire III: Les France, vol. 1. Conflits et partages*, edited by P. Nora, 275–301. Paris: Gallimard.

Norenzayan, Ara, Scott Atran, Jason Faulkner, and Mark Schaller. 2006. "Memory and Mystery: The Cultural Selection of Minimally Counterintuitive Narratives." *Cognitive Science* 30 (3): 531–53.

Northway, M. L. "The Influence of Age and Social Group on Children's Remembering." *British Journal of Social Psychology* 27 (1936): 11–29.

Ohmagari, Kayo, and Fikret Berkes. 1997. "Transmission of Indigenous Knowledge and Bush Skills among the Western James Bay Cree Women of Subarctic Canada." *Human Ecology* 25 (2): 197–222.

Opie, Iona. 1994. *The People in the Playground*. New York: Oxford University Press.

Opie, Iona, and Peter Opie. 1959. *The Lore and Language of Schoolchildren*. New York: Oxford University Press.

———. 1969. *Children's Games in Streets and Playground*. New York: Oxford University Press.

———. 1997. *Children's Games with Things*. New York: Oxford University Press.

Origgi, Gloria, and Dan Sperber. 2000. "Evolution, Communication and the Proper Function of Language." In *Evolution and the Human Mind*, edited by P. Carruthers and A. Chamberlain, 140–69. Cambridge, Mass.: Cambridge University Press.

Orme, Nicholas. 2001. *Medieval Children*. New Haven, Conn.: Yale University Press.

Ormerod, Paul. 2006. *Why Most Things Fail: Evolution, Extinction and Economics*. New York: Pantheon.

Ostler, Nicholas. 2005. *Empire of the Word: A Language History of the World*. London: Harper and Collins.
Pagel, Mark, Quentin Atkinson, and A. Meade. "Frequency of Word-Use Predicts Rates of Lexical Evolution throughout Indo-European History." *Science* 449 (2007): 717–21.
Parlebas, Pierre. 2000. "Les jeux transculturels." *Vers l'éducation nouvelle* 494: 8–15.
Petroski, Henry. 1989. *The Pencil, a History of Design and Circumstance*. London: Faber and Faber.
Petty, Richard E., J. T. Cacciopo, and R. Goldman. 1981. "Personal Involvement as a Determinant of Argument-Based Persuasion." *Journal of Personality and Social Psychology* 41: 847–55.
Petty, Richard E., and Duane T. Wegener. 1998. "Attitude Change: Multiple Roles for Persuasion Variables." In *The Handbook of Social Psychology*, edited by D. Gilbert, S. Fiske, and G. Lindzey, 323–90. Columbus, Ohio: McGraw-Hill.
Phillips, David P. 1974. "The Influence of Suggestion on Suicide: Substantive and Theoretical Implications of the Werther Effect." *American Sociological Review* 39 (3): 340–54.
Piaget, Jean. 1932. *Le jugement moral chez l'enfant*. Paris: Presses Universitaires de France.
Pitt Rivers, Augustus Henry Lane-Fox. 1906. *The Evolution of Culture, and Other Essays*. Edited by J. L. Myres and H. Balfour. Oxford: Clarendon Press.
Pollock, Linda. 1989. *Forgotten Children: Parent-Child Relations from 1500 to 1900*. Cambridge, England: Cambridge University Press.
Pouillon, Jean. 1991. "Tradition." In *Dictionnaire de L'anthropologie*, edited by P. Bonte and M. Izard, 710–12. Paris: Presses Universitaires de France.
Powell, Adam, Stephen Shennan, and Mark Thomas. 2009. "Late Pleistocene Demography and the Appearance of Modern Human Behaviour." *Science* 324: 1298–301.
Proust, Marcel. 1921 (1982). *Remembrance of Things Past: Volume II—The Guermantes Way & Cities of the Plain*. Translated by C. K. Scott Moncrieff and Terence Kilmartin. New York: Vintage.
———. 1922 (2000). *In Search of Lost Time: Volume IV—Sodom and Gomorrah*. Translated by C. K. Scott Moncrieff and Terence Kilmartin. New York: Random House Publishing Group.
Psichari, Michel. 1908. "Les jeux de Gargantua." *Revue des études rabelaisiennes* 6–7: 1–37, 124–81, 49–64.
Quinn, Naomi. 2006. "The Self." *Anthropological Theory* 6: 362–84.
Rabelais, François. 1711. *Œuvres de Maître François Rabelais*, vol. 1. Edited by J. Le Duchat. Amsterdam: Henri Bordesius.
———. 1823. *Œuvres de Rabelais, vol. 1*. Edited by M. Esmangart and E. Johanneau. Paris: Dalibon.
———. 1912. *Œuvres*, vol. 1. Edited by A. Lefranc. Paris: H. et E. Champion.
———. 1994. *Œuvres Complètes*. Edited by M. Huchon. Paris: Gallimard.

Radcliffe-Brown, A. R. 1949. "White's View of a Science of Culture." *American Anthropologist* 51 (3): 503–12.
———. 1952. *Structure and Function in Primitive Society*. Glencore, Ill.: The Free Press.
Range, Friederike, Zsófia Virány, and Ludwig Huber. 2007. "Selective Imitation in Domestic Dogs." *Current Biology* 17: 868–72.
Read, Dwight. 2006. "Tasmanian Knowledge and Skill: Maladaptive Imitation or Adequate Technology?" *American Antiquity* 71 (1): 164–84.
Reali, Florencia, and Thomas L. Griffiths. 2010. "Words as Alleles: Connecting Language Evolution with Bayesian Learners to Models of Genetic Drift." *Proceedings of the Royal Society B* 277 (1680): 429–36.
Reber, R., P. Winkielman, and N. Schwarz. 1998. "Effects of Perceptual Fluency on Affective Judgments." *Psychological Science* 9: 45–48.
Reyes-Garcia, Victoria, Jose-Luis Molina, James Broesch, Laura Calvet, Tomas Huanca, Judith Saus, Susan Tanner, William Leonard, and Thomas McDade. 2008. "Do the Aged and Knowledgeable Men Enjoy More Prestige? A Test of Predictions from the Prestige-Biased Model of Cultural Transmission." *Evolution and Human Behavior*, 29 (4): 275–81.
Rhine, Ramon J., and Laurence J. Severance. 1970. "Ego-Involvement, Discrepancy, Source-Credibility and Attitude Change." *Journal of Personality and Social Psychology* 16: 175–90.
Richerson, Peter J., and Robert Boyd. 2005. *Not by Genes Alone*. Chicago: The University of Chicago Press.
Rivers, William H. R. 1912. "The Disappearance of Useful Arts." *Reports of the British Association for the Advancement of Science*, 82: 598–99.
Rogers, Alan R. 1988. "Does Biology Constrain Culture?" *American Anthropologist* 90 (4): 819–31.
Rogers, Everett. 1995. *The Diffusion of Innovations*. Glencore, Ill.: The Free Press.
Rogoff, Barbara. 1981. "Adults and Peers as Agents of Socialization: A Highland Guatemalan Profile." *Ethos* 9 (1): 18–36.
Rogoff, Barbara, M. J. Sellers, S. Pirotta, N. Fox, and S. H. White. 1975. "Age of Assignment of Roles and Responsibilities to Children: A Cross-Cultural Survey." *Human Development* 18: 353–69.
Rouxel, Jacques. 1994. *Les Shadoks*. Paris: Circonflexe.
Rozin, Paul, and April Fallon. 1987. "A Perspective on Disgust." *Psychological Review* 94 (1): 23–41.
Rubin, David. 1995. *Memory in Oral Traditions: The Cognitive Psychology of Epics, Ballads and Counting-Out Rhymes*. New York: Oxford University Press.
Rubin, Ruth. "Nineteenth-Century Yiddish Folksongs of Children in Eastern Europe." *Journal of American Folklore* 65, no. 257 (1952): 227–54.
Rushton, J. P., A. C. Campbell. 1977. "Modelling, Vicarious Reinforcement and Extraversion on Blood Donation in Adults: Immediate and Long-Term Effects." *European Journal of Social Psychology* 7: 297–306.

Sainean, Lazare.1922. *La langue de Rabelais, vol. I*. Paris: E. de Boccard.

Salganik, Matthew J., Peter Sheridan Dodds, and Duncan J. Watts. 2006. "Experimental Study of Inequality and Unpredictability in an Artificial Cultural Market." *Science* 311: 854–56.

Salganik, Matthew J., and Duncan J. Watts. 2009. "Web-Based Experiments for the Study of Collective Dynamics in Cultural Markets." *Topics in Cognitive Science* 1: 439–68.

Sampson, Geoffrey. 2009. "A Linguistic Axiom Challenged." In *Language Complexity as an Evolving Variable*, edited by G. Sampson, D. Gil, and P. Trudgill, 1–18. New York: Oxford University Press.

Samuelson, Susan. 1980. "The Cooties Complex." *Western Folklore* 363: 198–210.

Schönpflug, Ute. 2009. "Introduction to Cultural Transmission." In *Cultural Transmission: Psychological, Developmental and Methodological Aspects*, edited by U. Schönpflug, 1–8. Cambridge, Mass.: Cambridge University Press.

Scott-Phillips, Thom. 2014. *Speaking Our Minds: Why Human Communication Is Different, and How Language Evolved to Make It Special*. New York: Palgrave Macmillan.

Severi, Carlo. 2007. *Le principe de la chimère*. Paris: Æsthetica.

Shennan, Stephen. 2001. "Demography and Cultural Innovation: A Model and Its Implications for the Emergence of Modern Human Culture." *Cambridge Archaeological Journal* 11 (1): 5–16.

Shennan, Stephen, and James Steele. 1999. "Cultural Learning in Hominids: A Behavioural Ecological Approach." In H. R. Box and K. Gibson (eds.), *Mammalian Social Learning: Comparative and Ecological Perspectives*, 367–88. Cambridge, Mass.: Cambridge University Press.

Sherry, D. F., and B. G. Galef. 1990. "Social Learning without Imitation: More about Milk Bottle Opening by Birds." *Animal Behaviour* 40 (5): 987–89.

Shils, Edward. 1971. "Tradition." *Comparative Studies in Society and History* 13 (2): 122–59.

Shweder, Richard A. 1979. "Rethinking Culture and Personality Theory Part I: A Critical Examination of Two Classical Postulates." *Ethos* 7 (3): 255–78.

Simmel, Georg. 1898. "The Persistence of Social Groups." *The American Journal of Sociology* 3 (5): 662–98.

Simon, Herbert. 1955. "On a Class of Skew Distribution Functions." *Biometrika* 42 (3–4): 425–40.

———. 1990. "A Mechanism for Social Selection and Successful Altruism." *Science* 250: 1665–68.

Slobin, Dan. 1968. "Antonymic Phonetic Symbolism in Three Natural Languages." *Journal of Personality and Social Psychology* 10 (3): 301–305.

Small, Michael, David Walker, and Chi Kong Tse. 2007. "Scale-Free Distribution of Avian Influenza Outbreaks." *Physical Review Letters* 99 (188702): 1–4.

Sober, Eliott, and David Sloane Wilson. 1999. *Unto Others: The Evolution and Psychology of Unselfish Behavior*. Cambridge, Mass.: Harvard University Press.

Southgate, Victoria, Coralie Chevallier, and Gergely Csibra. 2009. "Sensitivity to Communicative Relevance Tells Young Children What to Imitate." *Developmental Science* 12 (6): 1013–19.

Sperber, Dan. 1996. *Explaining Culture: A Naturalistic Approach*. Oxford: Blackwell.

———. 1998. "Réponse à Gérard Lenclud." *Communications* 66 (1): 185–92.

———. 1999. "An Objection to the Memetic Approach to Culture." In *Darwinizing Culture: The Status of Memetics as a Science*, edited by R. Aunger, 163–73. New York: Oxford University Press.

———. 2000. "Metarepresentations in an Evolutionary Perspective." In *Metarepresentations: A Multidisciplinary Perspective*, edited by D. Sperber, 117–37. New York: Oxford University Press.

Sperber, Dan, and Lawrence A. Hirschfeld. 2004. "The Cognitive Foundations of Cultural Stability and Diversity." *Trends in Cognitive Sciences* 8 (1): 40–46.

Sperber, Dan, and Deirdre Wilson. 1995. *Relevance: Communication and Cognition*. 2e édition. Oxford: Blackwell.

Spiro, Melford. 1993. "Is the Western Conception of the Self 'Peculiar' within the Context of the World Cultures?" *Ethos* 21 (2): 107–53.

Stack, Steven. 1987. "Celebrities and Suicide: A Taxonomy and Analysis." *American Sociological Review* 52 (3): 401–12.

Steglich, Christian, Tom A. B. Snijders, and Michael Pearson. 2009. "Dynamic Networks and Behavior: Separating Selection from Influence." *Sociological Methodology* 40 (1): 329–93.

Stephan, K. H., and G. E. Stephan. 1973. "Religion and the Survival of Utopian Communities." *Journal for the Scientific Study of Religion* 12 (1): 89–100.

Sterelny, Kim. 2012. *The Evolved Apprentice: How Evolution Made Humans Unique*. Boston: MIT Press.

Stoinsky, Tara S.., Joanna L. Wrate, Nicky Ure, and Andrew Whiten. 2001. "Imitative Learning by Captive Western Lowland Gorillas (*Gorilla Gorilla*) in a Simulated Food-Processing Task." *Journal of Comparative Psychology* 115: 272–81.

Strimling, P., M. Enquist, and K. Eriksson. 2009. "Repeated Learning Makes Cultural Evolution Unique." *Proceedings of the National Academy of Sciences* 106 (33): 13870–74.

Sunstein, Cass, and Richard Thaler. 2008. *Nudge: Improving Decisions about Health, Wealth, and Happiness*. New Haven, Conn.: Yale University Press.

Sutton-Smith, Brian. 1959. *The Games of New Zealand Children*. Berkeley, Calif.: University of California Press.

———. 1961. "Sixty Years of Historical Change in the Game Preferences of American Children." *Journal of American Folklore* 74 (291): 17–46.

Symons, Donald. 1992. "On the Use and Misuse of Darwinism in the Study of Human Behavior." In *The Adapted Mind: Evolutionary Psychology and the Generation of Culture*, edited by J. Barkow, J. Tooby, and L. Cosmides, 137–63. New York: Oxford University Press.

Tarde, Gabriel. 1893 (1993). *La logique sociale*. Paris: Les empêcheurs de penser en rond.
_____. 1897 (2000). "Contre Durkheim à propos de son *Suicide*." In *Le suicide un siècle après Durkheim*, edited by M. Berlandi and M. Cherkaoui, 219–55. Paris: Presses Universitaires de France.
_____.1895 (1903). *The Laws of Imitation*. Translated by E. C. Parsons. New York: Henry Holt & Co.
Tehrani, Jamshid, and Mark Collard. 2002. "Investigating Cultural Evolution through Biological Phylogenetic Analyses of Turkmen Textiles." *Journal of Anthropological Archeology* 21: 443–63.
Tehrani, Jamshid, and Felix Riede. 2008. "Towards an Archeology of Pedagogy: Learning, Teaching and the Generation of Material Culture Traditions." *World Archeology* 40 (3): 316–31.
Tennie, Claudio, Josep Call, and Michael Tomasello. 2009. "Ratcheting up the Ratchet: On the Evolution of Cumulative Culture." *Philosophical Transactions of the Royal Society B* 364 (1528): 2405–15.
Thierry, Bernard. 1994. "Social Transmission, Tradition and Culture in Primates: From the Epiphenomenon to the Phenomenon." *Techniques et Culture* 23 (24): 91–119.
_____. 1997. "De la relation entre le développement des facultés d'attribution et les prémices de l'évolution culturelle chez les primates." In *Les neurosciences et la philosophie de l'action*, edited by J.-L. Petit, 243–58. Paris: Jean Vrin.
Thiesse, Anne-Marie. 2001. *La création des identités nationales: Europe, XVIIIe-XXe Siècle*. Paris: Le Seuil.
Thomas, Rosalind. 1990. *Oral Tradition and Written Record in Classical Athens*. Cambridge, England: Cambridge University Press.
Tomasello, Michael. 1999. *The Cultural Origins of Human Cognition*. Cambridge: Harvard University Press.
_____. 2008. *The Origins of Human Communication*. Boston: MIT Press.
_____. 2009. "Cultural Transmission: A View from Chimpanzees and Human Infants." In *Cultural Transmission: Psychological, Developmental and Methodological Aspects.*, edited by U. Schönpflug, 33–47. New York: Oxford University Press.
Tomasello, Michael, and Josep Call. 1997. *Primate Cognition*. New York: Oxford University Press.
Tomasello, Michael, Brian Hare, Hagen Lehmann, and Josep Call. 2007. "Reliance on Head versus Eyes in the Gaze Following of Great Apes and Human Infants: The Cooperative Eye Hypothesis." *Journal of Human Evolution* 52 (3): 314–20.
Tomasello, Michael, Ann C. Kruger, and Hilary H. Ratner. 1993. "Cultural Learning." *Behavioral and Brain Sciences* 16: 495–552.
Tooby, John, and Leda Cosmides. 1992. "The Psychological Foundations of Culture." In *The Adapted Mind: Evolutionary Psychology and the Generation of Culture*, edited by J. Barkow, J. Tooby, and L. Cosmides, 19–136. New York: Oxford University Press.

Trainer, Jill M. 1983. "Changes in Song Dialect Distribution and Microgeographic Variation in Song of White-Crowned Sparrows (*Zonotrichia Leucophrys Nuttali*)." *The Auk* 100: 568–82.

Trevor-Roper, Hugh. 1983. "The Invention of Tradition: The Highland Tradition of Scotland." In *The Invention of Tradition*, edited by E. Hobsbawm and T. Ranger, 15–42. Cambridge, England: Cambridge University Press.

Trudgill, Peter. 2011. *Sociolinguistic Typology: Social Determinants of Linguistic Complexity*. Oxford; New York: Oxford University Press.

Turner, Stephen. 1994. *The Social Theory of Practices: Tradition, Tacit Knowledge, and Presuppositions*. Chicago: University of Chicago Press.

Tylor, Edward Burnett. 1871. *Primitive Culture: Researches into the Development of Mythology, Philosophy, Religion, Art, and Custom*. Vol. I. London: Routledge, Thoemmess Press.

UNESCO. 1945. *Constitution of the United Nations Educational, Scientific and Cultural Organization*.

———. 2001. *UNESCO Universal Declaration on Cultural Diversity*.

Van Baaren, Rick B., Rob B. Holland, Kerry Kawakami, and Ad van Knippen. 2004. "Mimicry and Prosocial Behavior." *Psychological Science* 15 (1): 71–74.

VanderWeele, Tyler J. 2011. "Sensitivity Analysis for Contagion Effects in Social Networks." *Sociological Methods & Research* 40 (2): 240–55.

Van Gennep, Arnold. 1935. *Le folklore de la Flandre et du Hainaut français (Vol. 5: Département du Nord)*. Saint Pierre de Salernes: Gérard Montfort.

———. 1937 (1999). "Continuité et discontinuité du folklore." In *Manuel de folklore français*, vol. 4, 2926–47. Paris: Robert Laffont.

Van Schaik, Carel P., Marc Ancrenaz, Gwendolin Borgen, Birute Galdikas, Cheryl Knott, Ian Singleton, Akira Suzuki, Sri Suci Utami, and Michelle Merrill. 2003. "Orangutan Cultures and the Evolution of Material Cultures." *Science* 299 (102): 102–105.

Van Schaik, C. P., and G. R. Pradhan. 2003. "A Model for Tool-Use Traditions in Primates: Implications for the Coevolution of Culture and Cognition." *Journal of Human Evolution* 44: 645–64.

Vansina, Jan. 1985. *Oral Tradition as History*. London: James Curry.

Virányi, Zsófia, and Friederike Range. 2009. "How Does Ostensive Communication Influence Social Learning in Dogs?" *Journal of Veterinary Behavior: Clinical Applications and Research* 4 (2): 43–108.

Visalberghi, Elisabetta, and Dorothy Fragaszy. 2002. "'Do Monkeys Ape?' Ten Years after." In *Imitation in Animals and Artefacts*, edited by K. Dautenhahn and C. Nehani, 473–99. Boston: MIT Press.

Voelkl, Bernard, and Ludwig Huber. 2007. "Imitation as Faithful Copying of a Novel Technique in Marmoset Monkeys." *PLoS ONE* 2 (7): e611.

Vygotsky, Lev. 2012 (1933). *Thought and Language*. Edited and translated by A. Kozulin. Boston: MIT Press.

Ward, T. H. G. 1949. "An Experiment on Serial Reproduction with Special Reference to the Changes in the Design of Early Coin Types." *British Journal of Psychology* 39: 142–47.

Warner, Robert R. 1988. "Traditionality of Mating-Site Preferences in a Coral Reef Fish." *Nature* 335: 719–21.

Weick, Karl E., and David P. Gilfillan. 1971. "Fate of Arbitrary Traditions in a Laboratory Microculture." *Journal of Personality and Social Psychology* 17 (2): 179–91.

Weisner, Thomas. 1996. "The 5 to 7 Transition as an Ecocultural Project." In *The Five to Seven Year Shift: The Age of Reason and Responsibility*, edited by A. J. Sameroff and M. M. Haith, 295–326. Chicago: The University of Chicago Press.

Weisner, Thomas, and Ronald Gallimore. 1977. "My Brother's Keeper: Child and Sibling Caretaking." *Current Anthropology* 18 (2): 169–90.

West, Stuart, Ashleigh Griffin, and Andy Gardner. 2007a. "Evolutionary Explanations for Cooperation." *Current Biology* 17: R661–72.

West, S. A., A. S. Griffin, and A. Gardner. 2007b. "Social Semantics: Altruism, Cooperation, Mutualism, Strong Reciprocity and Group Selection." *Journal of Evolutionary Biology* 20: 415–32.

West, Stuart A., Claire El Mouden, and Andy Gardner. 2011. "Sixteen Common Misconceptions about the Evolution of Cooperation in Humans." *Evolution and Human Behavior* 32 (4): 231–62.

Whitehouse, Harvey. 2000. *Arguments and Icons: Divergent Modes of Religiosity*. New York: Oxford University Press.

Whiten, Andrew, Jane Goodall, William C. McGrew, Toshisada Nishida, Walter Reynolds, Y. Sugiyama, C. E. G. Tutin, Richard Wrangham, and Christopher Boesch. 1999. "Culture in Chimpanzees." *Nature* 399: 682–85.

Whiten, Andrew, Victoria Horner, and Sarah Marshall-Pescini. 2003. "Cultural Panthropology." *Evolutionary Anthropology* 12: 92–105.

Whiten, Andrew, and Alex Mesoudi. 2009. "Establishing an Experimental Science of Culture: Animal Social Diffusion Experiments." *Philosophical Transactions of the Royal Society B*, 363: 3477–88.

Wilkinson, Anna, Karin Kuenstner, and Ludwig Huber. 2010. "Social Learning in a Non-Social Reptile (*Geochelone Carbonaria*)." *Biology Letters* 11 (2): 614–16.

Wilson, David Sloane. 2002. *Darwin's Cathedral*. Chicago: The University of Chicago Press.

Winking, Jeffrey, and Nicholas Mizer. 2013. "Natural-Field Dictator Game Shows No Altruistic Giving." *Evolution and Human Behavior* 34 (4): 288–93.

Wood, David, Jerome S. Bruner, and Gail Ross. 1976. "The Role of Tutoring in Problem Solving." *Journal of Child Psychology and Psychiatry* 17 (2): 89–100.

Wray, Alison, and George W. Grace. 2007. "The Consequences of Talking to Strangers: Evolutionary Corollaries of Socio-Cultural Influences on Linguistic Form." *Lingua* 117: 543–78.

Xu, Jing, and Thomas L. Griffiths. 2010. "A Rational Analysis of the Effects of Memory Biases on Serial Reproduction." *Cognitive Psychology* 60 (2): 107–26.

Yates, Frances Amelia. 1974. *The Art of Memory*. Chicago: The University of Chicago Press.

Yip, Paul, K. Fu, K. Yang, B. Ip, C. Chan, E. Chen, D. Lee, F. Law, and K. Hawton. 2006. "The Effects of a Celebrity Suicide on Suicide Rates in Hong Kong." *Journal of Affective Disorders* 93 (1): 242–52.

Yoffie, Leah R. C. 1947. "Three Generations of Children's Singing Games in Saint Louis." *Journal of American Folklore* 60 (235): 1–51.

Zipf, George Kingsley. 1935. *The Psycho-Biology of Language*. Cambridge, Mass.: Cambridge University Press.

Zohar, Ada H., and Levia Felz. 2001. "Ritualistic Behavior in Young Children." *Journal of Abnormal Child Psychology* 29 (2): 1–21.

Zucker, Lynne G. 1977. "The Role of Institutionalization in Cultural Persistence." *American Sociological Review* 42 (5): 726–43.

INDEX

Abu-Lughod, L., 14, 17
accessibility, 104–5, 136–40, 145–6, 154, 168, 174–5
Alexander, J., 198
Allen, J., 112
Allport, G. W., 126, 150
Amos, C., 91
animal traditions, 54, 58, 213
  birds, 229
  black-capped chickadees, 142–3
  British blue tits, 51, 57, 62, 69
  deer, 243
  dolphins, 51
  domestic dogs, 72
  great apes, 66, 234
    chimpanzees, 51, 57, 59–60, 72, 142, 216, 219–21, 229, 231–2, 240
    gorillas, 59
    orangutans, 231–2
    Tai forest chimpanzees, 63
  insects, 243
  lions, 94
  macaques, 35, 59
  marmosets, 59
  meerkats, 243
  rats, 59
  red-footed tortoises, 62
  starlings, 65
  tropical fishes, 51
  vervet monkeys, 64
Aral, S., 23, 114
Arendt, H., 210
Ariès, Ph., 189–91
Aristotle, 84
Asch, S., 100–1, 106
Atran, S., 18, 26, 75, 111, 147
attraction, 136, 140–1, 144–7, 168, 210–11, 217–18
  cognitive and motivational, 148–53
  local and general, 148–9, 155–6, 158–62
  psychological factors of, 155
Aunger, R., 36, 181
authority, 40–1
Axsom, D., 101

Baaren, R. B. van, 50
Baillargeon, R., 66
Bakeman, R., 82–3
Baker, M. C., 142, 229
Baller, R. D., 24
Bandura, A., 100
Bangerter, A., 126
Baron, J. N., 112–13
Baron, R., 101, 106

Barry, H., 182
Barth, F., 18–9, 46, 134
Bartlett, F., 124–7, 150
Basalla, G., 222
Baucomont, J., 200, 203
Baum, W., 127
Bell, A. V., 18
Bentley, R. A., 140, 143–4
Berger, J., 135, 143
Berliner, D., 45
Bicchieri, C., 108–9
Bikhchandani, S., 108–10
Birch, L. L., 249
Blackmore, S., 36, 47
Bloch, M. (anthropologist), 68, 138
Bloch, M. (historian), 171
Boas, F., 44
Boesch, C., 51, 63, 234
Boesch-Akerman, H., 51
Bolton, H. C., 188, 203
Bourdieu, P., 81
Bowles, S., 33, 102
Boyd, R., 33, 35, 42, 47, 58–9, 84, 87–92, 95, 97–8, 102, 148, 176, 220, 223, 229, 239, 241
Boyer, P., 15, 26–7, 38–41, 147, 153, 157–8, 161
Boyette, A., 182
Brumann, C., 14, 17
Brunton, R., 17
Bryan, J., 102–3
Burguière, A., 175
Buttelmann, D., 69, 72
Bybee, J., 132

Caldwell, C., 127, 225
Call, J., 63, 220
Carassa, A., 67
Caro, T. M., 61, 63–4, 230
Cavalli-Sforza, L-L., 89, 176, 180–1
Chapais, B., 243
Chartier, R., 145

children
　"the age of reason", 77
　baby learning, 83
　Dogon, 183, 189
　of Fiji, 17
　!Kung, 183
　Kwoma, 183
　peer culture, 180, 185–94, 196–7, 200–201, 207–8, 210–11, 253, 257, 265–6
children's rhymes, 127, 199
　Am stram gram, 205
　Eenie meenie miny moe, 188, 193, 195, 200–1, 205
　Enge-benge, stupe-stenge, 205
　Little fatty doctor..., 186
　mots sauvages, 188, 206
　Onery, twoery, tickery..., 201, 204, 210
　Santa femina goda, 200, 204
　skipping rhymes, 193, 198
　Three gray greedy geese, 196
　Tinker, tailor..., 188
Chomsky, N., 26, 182
Christakis, N., 87, 104, 110, 112–14
Chudacoff, H. P., 190, 193
Claidière, N., 129
Clark, G., 222
Clauset, A., 141
Close Encounters of the Third Kind, 70
clusters method, 24–5, 110, 112–13
Clutton-Brock, T., 243
cognition, 20, 231
　cognitive biases, 148, 151, 244–5
　cognitive capacities, 211, 236, 238, 240, 245, 248
　　to communicate, 61
　cognitive cost, 92–3
　cognitive science, 150, 182
　cognitive style, 32
　detecting agency, 157–8, 161
　face recognition, 249

mind-reading, 66–8, 241
social cognition, 239
cohort, 170, 186
Coleman, J. S., 118
collaborative learning, 69
collective conscience, 14–15, 149
collective memory, 154
common environment problem, 112–14
communication, 20, 67–70, 73, 252
non-verbal, 81–2
ostensive, 54, 60–1, 63–6, 69, 71–2, 74–7, 79–80, 82–5, 214, 217–18, 230–1, 241, 243–6
ostensive cues, 72, 231
competition of practices, 123
Comte, A., 171–4, 247
conformity, 87–93, 100–1, 104–7, 119, 202, 204
anti-conformity, 123
conservation, 40–1, 127, 214, 223, 228, 252
conditions, 218–19, 233–5
conservatism, 40, 172–3, 201–2, 210, 215, 221
contagion, 23–4, 112–13
Conway, L. G., 101, 122
cooperation, 33–4, 67, 97, 252
among non-kin, 243
animal, 94
altruism, 88, 93–4, 98, 102–3
cooperative learning, 231–2, 241–2
docility hypothesis, 87, 94–6, 98, 100
Corsaro, W. A., 184, 194, 202
Cosmides, L., 31
Coultas, J. C., 102
Cournot, A. A., 171
Crisp, Q., 252
Csibra, G., 60–1, 63, 66, 72–4, 79, 231, 243–5
cultural complexity, 225
cultural consensus theory, 18
cultural differences, 32–3, 35, 37, 102

cultural epidemiology, 26–7, 47, 114, 124, 147–9, 155
cultural group selection, 33, 95, 97
cultural integration, 41–2
culture
cognitive approach to, 149
coherence of, 17
definition of, 12, 36, 216, 224
distributive views of, 13, 19–20
elementary unit of, 43
embodiment of, 81
evolution *of* and *towards*, 214
piecemeal approaches to, 19
quantitative view of, 21, 52
social life and, 216
transmitted and evoked, 31, 33, 36
cumulative culture, 35, 52, 58–9, 211, 214–15, 220, 222, 224, 226–8
accumulation threshold, 236
"ratchet effect", 235–6

Danchin, É., 62, 65
Dana, J., 102
D'Andrade, R., 18
Dawkins, R., 43, 123
De Vienne, E., 178
De Vries, J., 266
De Waal, F., 232
deference, 87–93, 104–5, 115, 119
Déléage, P., 178
demography, 97, 138, 170–1, 228
demographic scarcity, 159, 177–9
depopulation, 229
Dennett, D. C., 43, 47, 123
Descombes, V., 49
Deutscher, G., 164
diffusion, 21, 23, 237–8
inequalities of, 160
multi-scale methods, 167
of names, 115, 135, 140–1, 143
statistical approach to, 161
of tetracycline antibiotics, 118

diffusion chains, 36, 42, 168, 186–7
  imaginary, 39
  sequential vs. linear, 124–9, 131, 135, 139, 150
  synthetic, 125
  types of, 138–9, 163–4
Dijksterhuis, A., 102
distribution, 23, 36–7, 134
Doris, J., 32–4
Driscoll, C., 119, 241
dual inheritance theory, 87–92, 95, 97–9, 105, 119
Dunbar, R., 126, 178, 243
Duncan, C. J., 249
Durkheim, É., 14–5, 24, 30, 46, 62, 111, 115, 154, 173, 184

E.T. the Extra-Terrestrial, 70, 72
Ebbinghaus, H., 133, 153
Efferson, C., 102
Elias, N., 156, 162
Ellis, Sh., 182
Enquist, M., 133, 154
Erasmus, 156, 158–60
Eriksson, K., 132, 154
evolutionary theory, 93, 99, 241
  Evolutionism, 189–92
  food preferences, 249–50
  gene–culture coevolution, 96
  gradualism, 221–3
experimental cultural market, 106
experimental economics, 33–4, 95, 102
extreme accumulation hypothesis, 234–6, 242, 245–7

Farroni, T., 231
Fehr, E., 95
Feldman, M., 89, 176
Ferrari, P. F., 59
Fessler, D. M. T., 157
Ficken, M. S., 142–3

fidelity, 69, 73, 121–2, 124, 129, 132–4, 136, 207, 252
  faithful imitation, 54–5, 57, 85
Fine, G. A., 192, 201
Fisher, J., 51
Fiske, A. P., 62, 77, 79–80
Flop Problem, 53, 86, 120–2, 209, 211, 217
Franks, B., 67

Galef, B. G., 51, 57
Gambetta, D., 90, 177
games, 185, 188–9, 259–60, 262–3
  The bear and its watcher, 196
  Chinese Whispers, 124, 126, 131
  coordination of, 202
  cootie-lore, 194, 204
  cross-generational, 191, 255, 257–66
  Gargantua, 190, 195, 197–9, 209–10, 253–8, 261, 264–6
  marble games around Neuchâtel, 193
  medieval, 196, 253
  toy-making, 193
  yo-yo, 16, 191–2, 253
Gayon, J., 214
Geertz, C., 48, 241
Gelman, S. A., 244
generations, 169–71, 174–6, 186, 211, 265–6
Gergely, Gy., 60–1, 66, 71–3, 231, 243–5
Gigerenzer, G., 91–2
Gintis, H., 33, 87, 95, 98, 102
Gladwell, M., 104, 152
Glassie, H., 16, 37, 135
Goldgar, A., 109
Goodall, J., 142
Goody, J., 138
Gosselin, G., 38
Gray, R., 221
Greenfield, P., 83
Griaule, M., 189, 202

Grice, P., 60–1, 82
Griffiths, T. L., 128, 151
Guglielmino, C. R., 239
Gurven, M., 102
Guzmán, A., 98

Hahn, M. W., 140, 143
Haidt, J., 18
Halbwachs, M., 154
Hall, K. R. L., 126
Hanawalt, B. A., 190
Harris, J. R., 182, 192
Harrison, L. E., 20
Hawkes, K., 230
Hawks, J., 179
Hawton, K., 113
Heath, Ch., 157
Heck, J. O., 209
Henrich, J., 87–91, 98, 102, 105, 119, 229, 235, 241
Henrich, N., 88, 91, 105
Herder, J. G., 2–3, 5, 7, 16, 85–6, 98–9, 217, 238, 251
heuristics, 92–4, 119
Hewlett, B., 83, 180–1
Heyes, C., 54, 56, 59, 67
Higham, T. M., 126
Hill, K., 119
Hirschfeld, L., 147, 194
Hobsbawm, E., 38, 41
Hocart, A., 17
Holden, C., 96
Homo erectus, 240, 242
homogeneity and heterogeneity, 13–14, 20, 44, 199–200, 208–9
homophily, 25, 112–14
Hood, B. M., 231
Hoppitt, W., 82–3, 112
Hrdy, S. B., 94, 182, 229, 231, 242–3
Hugo, V., 170
human exceptionality, 213, 215, 221, 226, 228

human public domain, 76, 228, 232–3, 236, 246, 251
Human Relations Area Files, 40, 182
Hume, D., 38, 161–2, 172–3, 175, 210
Hunt, G., 221
Huntington, S. P., 20

imitation, 30, 69–71, 73–4, 79–80, 82–3, 85, 120
  compulsive, 54, 57, 87–8, 93, 98, 100, 104–5, 111, 114
  fashion-imitation and habit-imitation, 37, 134–5
  flexible, 93, 99–103, 107–8, 111
  "rational", 71–3
  "true", 55–9, 69, 71
imitation hypothesis, 53, 86, 120, 187, 201, 215, 226, 236, 239
informational cascades, 108–10
intentions and intentionality, 55, 60, 66, 69, 71–3
invention, 35, 215, 228, 233–4
  diffusion of innovations, 105, 117
  reinvention, 52, 126, 128, 133

Jablonka, E., 222
Jacobs, R. C., 127–8
Jakobson, R., 205
James, C., 146
Jones, E. L., 20

Kalish, M., 128
Kaplan, H., 229, 242
Karsenti, B., 123
Kashima, Y., 126, 129
Katz, E., 118
Keesing, R., 157, 159, 178
Király, I., 72
Klein, D. B., 110
Kline, M., 229
Kobayashi, H., 231

Köhler, W., 147
Konner, M., 77, 181, 183
Kramer, K. L., 182
Kroch, A. S., 115
Kroeber, A., 19, 25–6, 44
Krutzen, M., 51
Kummer, H., 142
Kuran, T., 109–10
Kurke, L. E., 126

Labov, W., 115–17
Laland, K., 20, 47, 58, 96
Lamba, Sh., 102
Lancy, D. F., 62, 77–8, 178, 181–3
Langmuir, E., 190
language, 26, 61, 66, 85–6
   accents, 116
   complexity and learnability, 164–6
   dissemination of, 166–7
   historical linguistics, 131
   learning, 132
   Old English, 27–9
   phonological changes, 115
   sociolinguistics, 115
   sound symbolism, 147
   survival, 132
   Swahili, 167
   word frequency, 132
Le Roy Ladurie, E., 199
Leach, E., 44
Levinson, S., 60
Lieberson, S., 115–16, 135, 143
Lightfoot, D., 27–9
Lillard, A., 67
Lord, A. B., 127
Lost World, The, 188
Lowie, R. H., 44, 178
Lupyan, G., 166–7
Lyman, R. L., 19, 43–4
Lyons, D. E., 103
Lyons, R., 112–14

MacDonald, K., 83, 181
McElreath, R., 102, 241
Machery, E., 32
Machiavelli, N., 170
MacIntyre, A., 38
Mackay, C., 104, 109
Mackie, D. M., 101
McKone, E., 249
"madness of crowds", 104, 110–11
Mameli, M., 99
Mannheim, K., 170
Marino, L., 122
Mauss, M., 15, 38, 81
Mead, M., 15, 64, 182
Mehl, J-M., 196, 255–7, 266
Meltzoff, A., 56, 71–2
memes, 43, 47
memorability, 152–4, 201, 204–7, 211
Mentré, F., 170–1, 175, 247
Mercader, J., 51, 234
Mergen, B., 198
Merton, R. K., 116, 118
Mesoudi, A., 47, 110, 125–6
Milgram, S., 102
Mill, J. S., 247–8
Mithen, S., 223
Miyamoto, Y., 33
Moll, H., 67
Mollenhorst, G., 187
Moore, R., 66
Moretti, F., 143–5
Morris, B., 17

Nadel, J., 72
Needham, J., 179
Nettle, D., 102, 166
Newell, W. A., 185, 192, 201, 203
Nichols, Sh., 156, 158, 162
Nisbett, R. E., 20, 32–3
Nora, P., 171
Norenzayan, A., 153
Northway, M. L., 126

Ohmagari, K., 80–1, 180
Opie, I., 185–8, 190, 192–203, 207
opinion leaders, 117–18
Origgi, G., 243
Orme, N., 196
Ormerod, P., 142
Ostler, N., 132

Pagel, M., 132, 142
Parlebas, P., 196
Pedagogy theory, 73, 243–5
peoples
    the Aché, 118
    the Aka, 181
    Asian and Western, 32–3
    of Bali, 64
    Burmese, 68
    the Cree, 80–1
    the Efe, 182
    the Fang, 26
    of Fiji, 46, 88
    the Hill Pandarams, 17
    Inuit, 31
    Kachin, 44
    the Kpelle, 78–9
    !Kung, 82–3, 181, 183
    the Kwaio, 157–9, 175, 177, 218
    Lamarela, 33–6
    Lepcha, 183
    Machiguenga, 33–4
    Manchu, 146–8, 160–2
    Mayan, 182
    of Melanesia, 229, 235
    the Ok, 18
    Papua New Guinea, 133–4
    Pashtuns, 46
    of Rovere, 116, 118
    of Southern America, 18
    of Tasmania, 235
    the Tsimane', 102, 118
    of Vanatinai Island, 183
Petroski, H., 26

Petty, R. E., 101
Phillips, D. P., 113
philosophy, 32, 38, 60, 68, 170, 175
Piaget, J., 173, 193
Pitt Rivers, A. H. L-F., 222
Plato, 147, 170, 210
Pollock, L., 190
Pouillon, J., 38
Powell, A., 178, 228
prestige, 89, 115–9
proliferation, 125–6, 129–33, 135–6,
    139, 145–6, 180, 207
    selection for, 208
Proust, M., 1, 130–1
psychology, 32, 74, 83, 99, 120, 147
    cross-cultural, 20
    of memory, 133, 205–6
    of persuasion, 101
    social, 124
    of social influence, 104

Quinn, N., 68

Rabelais, F., 190–1, 195, 197–8, 209–10,
    253–7, 261, 264, 266
Radcliffe-Brown, A. R., 44
Range, F., 72
Read, D., 229, 235
Reali, F., 151
Reber, R., 151
receptive powers, 252
reconstruction, 26, 30, 57, 77, 79, 81–2,
    125, 180, 225, 240
redundancy and repetition, 125–6,
    129–34, 136, 145–6, 153, 205
Reed, J. S., 16
relevance, 72–3, 244
religion
    adalo, 157–9
    American Christians, 18, 181
    Chaldean Christians of Chicago, 105
    Christianity and charity, 96–7

religion (*continued*)
   Christianity and the Roman world, 117
   Hare Krishna, 31
   kava ceremony, 188
   Scottish Protestantism, 38
   Theravada Buddhism, 68
reputation systems, 119
Reyes-Garcia, V., 118
Rhine, R. J., 101
Richerson, P. J., 35, 42, 47, 58–9, 84, 87–92, 95, 97–8, 148, 176, 220, 223, 239, 241
Rivers, W. H. R., 229
Rogers, A. R., 100, 241
Rogers, E., 105, 115, 117–18
Rogoff, B., 77, 182
Rouxel, J., 227
Rozin, P., 156
Rubin, D., 127, 133, 152, 188, 193, 199–201, 205–6
Rubin, R., 205
Rushton, J. P., 103

Saki (H. H. Munro), 252
Salganik, M. J., 106–7, 111
salience, 29, 35, 56, 103, 105
Sampson, G., 164
Samuelson, S., 194
scaffolded learning, 63, 67
Schaik, C. P. van, 231
Schönpflug, U., 121
Severi, C., 138
Shadoks, Les, 227–8
Shennan, S., 178, 180, 228
Sherry, D. F., 51, 57
Shils, E., 38
Shweder, R. A., 15
Simmel, G., 175
Simon, H., 87, 91, 94–6, 141
Slobin, D., 147
Small, M., 141

Sober, E., 96
sociability, 228, 231–2, 236, 242–3, 251–2
social influence, 102, 120
   generalist influentials, 118–19
   majority bias, 90
   Michael Jordan's underwear, 90–2
   and personal knowledge, 99–101, 103, 106, 108
social learning, 60, 68, 74, 91–2, 99
   asocial learning, 100
   faculty, 54
   types of, 55
social networks, 113–14, 118, 137–8, 232
social norms, 156–9, 162, 178
Southgate, V., 72
Sperber, D., 19, 26, 47, 55, 60, 75, 82, 129, 147, 149, 152, 243, 249
Spier, L., 44
Spiro, M., 68
stability, 41, 52, 127–9, 131–5, 141, 143, 223
Stack, S., 113
Steglich, C., 23, 112
Stephan, K. H., 142
Sterelny, K., 239
Stoinsky, T. S., 59
Strimling, P., 154, 177
success, 135–6, 147, 149–50, 217
   of books, 143–5
   of children's games, 206–8
   inequalities of, 141–2
suicide, 23–4, 30, 90–2, 111, 113
Sunstein, C., 104
Sutton-Smith, B., 201
Symons, D., 250

Tarde, G., 3, 13, 21–2, 24, 30, 37, 46–7, 53–4, 57, 86, 104–5, 111, 115–18, 120, 122–3, 133–5, 183–4, 224, 247

teaching, 61, 63, 73–4, 79–80, 82
  "assisted development", 229–31
  institutionalized, 75
  instructing, 77–8, 81
  "molding", 64–5
  punishment, 77
Tehrani, J., 25, 239
Tennie, C., 220
Thierry, B., 60, 221, 234
Thiesse, A-M., 39
"three degrees" hypothesis, 87, 114
Thomas, R., 199
time dispersion, 174
Tomasello, M., 35, 54–9, 61, 69, 74, 84, 220, 223, 232, 239
Tooby, J., 31
traditionalism, 40–1, 135, 203–4, 207, 211
traditions
  as representations, 47–9
  classical definitions of, 38
  the common theory of, 39–40
  continuity of, 39–40
  definition of, 37
  disappearance of, 28
  extreme, 214–15, 218–19, 233–6
  failed, 227
  laboratory, 128, 137
  origins and sources of, 193–5, 203
Trainer, J. M., 234
transmission
  in animals, 217
  chains, 21
  child-to-child, 192, 194
  continuum of, 31, 82
  vs. diffusion, 12–13, 176
  the existence of, 50
  indirect, 76, 84
  inertia of, 123–4, 130, 144, 233
  involuntary, 62, 65
  mechanisms, 84, 123–4, 129
  non-ostensive voluntary, 63–5, 230

non-verbal, 79
numerosity of, 51
obstacles to, 178–9
oral, 138, 153
parental involvement, 83–4, 230
quantity of episodes of, 131–3, 162, 180
of religious rituals, 133
rumor, 150
scarcity, 179
sexual division of, 178
vertical and horizontal, 169, 176–7, 179–80, 184, 207, 211, 265
wholesale, 98
transmission chain experiments, 127–9, 131
Trevor-Roper, H., 39
Trudgill, P., 165–6
Turner, S., 38
two actions method, 56–7, 129
Tylor, E. B., 13, 25, 37, 43, 185, 187–91, 196

UNESCO, 215

Van Gennep, A., 40–1, 185, 188, 192, 200, 204, 206
VanderWeele, T. J., 113
Vansina, J., 199
Virányi, Zs., 72
virus metaphor, 123–4
Visalberghi, E., 57
Voelkl, B., 59
Vygotsky, L., 63, 74

War of the Ghosts, The, 124, 126–7
Ward, T. H. G., 126
Warner, R. R., 51
Wear-and-Tear Problem, 53, 55, 69, 85–6, 120–2, 125, 129, 187, 199, 207, 209–11, 217
Weick, K. E., 126–127
Weisner, T., 182–3

300 • Index

West, S. A., 243
Whitehouse, H., 133
Whiten, A., 47, 59, 125–6, 219, 221
Wilkinson, A., 62
Wilson, D. (linguist), 60, 82
Wilson, D. S. (biologist), 96–7
Winking, J., 102
Wood, D., 63
Wray, A., 165

Xu, J., 151

Yates, F. A., 138
Yip, P., 113
Yoffie, L. R. C., 198

Zipf, G. K., 140
Zohar, A. H., 208
Zucker, L. G., 127–8

[handwritten notes:]

Take a broad category
make it specific enuf to be
  solved
Solve w/o loosing its generality

Biology — Energy / the Sun (disappeared
w/ dis ap of fossil fuel) — enlightenment thker
[Thos Hobbes] — need a king or God — to manage
[Mandeville] — vice a good thy — snglld alot of
[Hume] — RSN slave / the passions — synonomes /
mind [way human bgs think]
[Adam Smith] — patron saint / capitalism
  [psychologist not an Economist] — not just
given vice — invented sympathy — can't undstd the
pain of another unless you place yourself on
the rock
sympathy / compassion — intimate w/ each Or
h. bgs are self-organizing
design something w/o a designer
closely knit society + w/o social K will
not work — — greedy — inter action
human bg — —